"To realize more of the promise of the Civil Rights Movement, massive racial and ethnic wealth gaps must be narrowed. Deeply problematic, unstable, and widespread heirs' property ownership has plagued Black and Brown communities for decades. This book should be the go-to book for those interested in helping disadvantaged heirs' property owners significantly improve their ability to maintain and further build upon the wealth, culture, and history associated with their property as well as for those committed to helping make our property system less racialized and more just."

—**Derrick Johnson**, President and CEO, NAACP

"Heirs' property has long represented highly unstable and problematic second-class property ownership, which has contributed to exacerbating the racial wealth gap. This book not only analyzes and describes this little known and poorly understood problem, but provides a road map to ameliorating it. Utilizing the very successful model state property statute the book highlights, a statute principally drafted by Professor Thomas Mitchell, scholars and advocates can help heirs' property owners across the country maintain their family property and generational wealth. For those interested in real social change, this is a necessary volume!"

—**Melvin L. Oliver**, President, Pitzer College and Co-author, *Black Wealth/White Wealth: A New Perspective on Racial Inequality*

"This treatise on heirs' property is groundbreaking. This is the most significant analysis of how African Americans lost property and thereby lost one of the key pillars for generational wealth in America. I recommend this text to lawyers, pastors, activists, real estate agents, and civil rights organizations. It is a text that provides a framework for presenting a case for reparations."

—**Rev. Dr. Janette C. Wilson**, Esq., Senior Advisor, RainbowPUSH; National Executive Director, PUSH Excel; and Pastor, Maple Park United Methodist Church

"This book concisely describes the social injustice background of forced heirs' property sales and the remedial Uniform Partition of Heirs Property Act, and thoroughly sets out remedies, replete with examples and models. It should be on the bookshelf of every real estate and property law professor and every common ownership/wills and trust lawyer."

—**David Callies**, FAICP, Kudo Chair in Law, emeritus, the University of Hawai'i and Past Chair, ABA Section of State and Local Government Law

"Appleseed centers have witnessed far too many families lose their inherited heirs' property, including land and homes, to unjust development deals and forced sale actions. This book is an invaluable resource for advocates fighting the structural racism that has led to grievous wealth disparities in our communities."

—**Benet Magnuson**, Executive Director, Appleseed Network

"Sadly, I know too many families, including my own, who are still wrestling with the question: 'What do we do with this land?' This book is necessary for families who need to have what is often a difficult, sensitive, and emotional conversation with each other if they are ever going to use their land to build generational wealth and offer financial stability for themselves and their children yet unborn."

—**Juan R. Thomas**, Chair-elect, ABA Civil Rights & Social Justice Section, 2021–2022 and Council Member, ABA State and Local Government Law Section, 2018–2021

"This badly-needed book is not another treatise on property law, but a recognition of the challenge facing families whose property may be lost due to internal disagreements. It provides a path to resolution of heir contests and addresses the issue of unknown heirs; narrates how these issues arise; and makes recommendations grounded in history and law. Important reading for trustees and historians, as well as lawyers."

—**Adriane Dudley**, Past Chair, ABA State and Local Government Law Section; Delegate, ABA House of Delegates; and Partner, Dudley Rich LLP, U.S. Virgin Islands

AMERICAN BAR ASSOCIATION
State and Local
Government Law Section

Heirs' Property and the Uniform Partition of Heirs Property Act

Challenges, Solutions, and Historic Reform

THOMAS W. MITCHELL AND ERICA LEVINE POWERS, EDITORS

Foreword by Reginald M. Turner, President, American Bar Association

Cover design by Elmarie Jara/ABA Design

Printed in the United States of America.

26 25 24 23 5 4 3 2

Library of Congress Cataloging-in-Publication Data

Names: Mitchell, Thomas W, editor. | Powers, Erica Levine, editor. | American Bar Association. Section of State and Local Government Law, sponsoring body.

Title: Heirs' property and the Uniform Partition of Heirs Property Act : challenges, solutions, and historic reform / Thomas W Mitchell, Erica Levine Powers.

Description: Chicago, Illinois : American Bar Association, [2022] | Includes bibliographical references and index. | Summary: "This book explores the history and basics of the Uniform Partition of Heirs Property Act (UPHPA), adopted in 19 jurisdictions so far in every region of the country and introduced in at least seven more in 2021 alone, and the ongoing efforts to prevent the loss of family land and homes across generations"--Provided by publisher.

Identifiers: LCCN 2022006140 (print) | LCCN 2022006141 (ebook) | ISBN 9781639051205 (paperback) | ISBN 9781639051212 (epub)

Subjects: LCSH: National Conference of Commissioners on Uniform State Law. Partition of Heirs Property Act. | Partition of decedents' estates--United States--States. | LCGFT: Uniform laws.

Classification: LCC KF779.P37 H45 2022 (print) | LCC KF779.P37 (ebook) | DDC 346.7305/2--dc23/eng/20220308

LC record available at https://lccn.loc.gov/2022006140

LC ebook record available at https://lccn.loc.gov/2022006141

Dedicated to my wife and colleague, Lisa Alexander, and my daughter, Kira, who sustain me with their love and joyfulness and who each shine brightly in their own distinctive ways

And to my mother, Dr. Anita Mitchell, a courageous person who has sacrificed a lot for her convictions while serving many, and who instilled in me a love of the ocean and of adventure

And to the memory of my father, Dr. Claude Wilson Mitchell, a real trailblazer who overcame many challenges, who taught me to fight for justice, and who possessed the common touch and true humility
T.W.M.

Dedicated to Neville and Llew, for their love and support, and in memory of my parents.
E.L.P.

Contents

PART III Proactive Planning by Heirs and Lawyers

About the Editors

Thomas W. Mitchell is a professor at Boston College Law School, where he is the holder of the Robert F. Drinan, S.J. Endowed Chair and the director of an initiative that addresses land and housing challenges disadvantaged families and communities face. Prior to joining Boston College, he served on the faculty of Texas A&M University School of Law and the University of Wisconsin Law School as a full professor with a chair in law. He is a national expert on property issues facing disadvantaged families and communities and has published leading scholarly works addressing these matters.

Professor Mitchell has done extensive law reform and policy work, most prominently serving as the principal drafter of a widely adopted uniform real property act named the Uniform Partition of Heirs Property Act (UPHPA) that is designed to substantially enhance the ability of disadvantaged families to maintain ownership of their property and their generational wealth. States with a majority of the US population have enacted the UPHPA into law. In 2021, the Uniform Law Commission accepted another proposal Professor Mitchell developed to address a different tenancy-in-common ownership problem, and this likely will result in another uniform act being promulgated. He also has helped to develop federal policy proposals, working with some in Congress and others in the United States Department of Agriculture, to help disadvantaged farmers and property owners.

In 2020, he was named one of twenty-one recipients of the MacArthur Fellowship in recognition of the substantial impact his overall professional work has had in assisting disadvantaged farmers and property owners, people who are disproportionately but not exclusively African American and other people of color. He is the only lawyer in his MacArthur Fellowship class. In 2021, he was awarded the Howard University Alumni Award for Distinguished Postgraduate Achievement, an award that Thurgood Marshall and Vice President Kamala Harris, among other Howard luminaries, also have received. In 2021 as well, *The Journal of Black Innovation* named Professor Mitchell as one of the 50 Most Important African Americans in Infrastructure to recognize that his work protecting property rights for people of color helps create a more just and equitable infrastructure system. He is a previous recipient of the Elizabeth Hurlock Beckman award, a national award he received for the substantial work he has done mentoring law students who have then worked as lawyers to advance social justice.

Professor Mitchell is a graduate of Amherst College, the Howard University School of Law, and the University of Wisconsin Law School, where he received an LLM (master of laws) and served as a William H. Hastie Fellow.

Erica Levine Powers is a mediator and transactional/regulatory land use lawyer in Albany, New York, who recently served as senior zoning and land use attorney in the City of Atlanta Law Department. She is admitted in Massachusetts, Maryland, and New York. She is the immediate past chair of the ABA Section of State & Local Government Law. A cum laude graduate of Harvard College in Modern European History and Literature, she holds JD and LLM (Taxation) degrees from Boston University School of Law. Initially counsel to the Massachusetts Commissioner of Banks and then a corporate transactional lawyer at Gaston Snow & Ely Bartlett in Boston, she served as counsel to the Deputy Mayor/Collector Treasurer of the City of Boston and as general counsel to the Massachusetts Department of Food & Agriculture. She has been a visiting professor of planning (sabbatical coverage) at Cornell University, Iowa State University, the University of Iowa, and Massey University in New Zealand. She is an affiliated scholar in the Department of Geography & Planning at the University at Albany (SUNY), where she served as an adjunct faculty member in land use and environmental planning from 2009 through 2013 and developed a graduate seminar on hydraulic fracturing. She is the lead editor and a contributing author of *Beyond the Fracking Wars* (ABA/SLG, 2013), acclaimed for its scope and objectivity.

About the Contributors

David J. Dietrich graduated from Whitman College with a BA degree with honors in 1979. He served in the Peace Corps in Abidjan, Ivory Coast, 1979 to 1980. He attended the University of Montana College of Law and graduated with a Juris Doctor (JD) in 1984.

Mr. Dietrich is a fellow of the American College of Trust and Estate Counsel (ACTEC) and a past chair (2016 to 2017) of the Real Property, Trust and Estate Law Section of the American Bar Association (ABA). In the early 2000s, he co-chaired Property Preservation Task Force formed by the ABA's Real Property, Trust and Estate Law Section, which contributed to the Uniform Law Commission's adoption of the Uniform Partition of Heirs Property Act, now law in nineteen states and the US Virgin Islands. Mr. Dietrich is currently on the University of Montana Tax Institute Advisory Board and is vice chair of Humanities Montana. In the early 2000s, he served for six years on the board of directors of the Montana Land Reliance, a private land trust in Montana, protecting more than one million acres.

Mr. Dietrich has a diverse real estate (ranching and agricultural) and estate planning background, living in south central Montana, Billings, the largest and most diverse city in the Northern Great Plains, west of Minnesota. His firm, Dietrich & Associates, P.C., has provided real estate tax and estate planning services to the region for more than 30 years involving both complex and simple wills, trusts, and real estate transactions, including conservation easements, individual business organizations, real estate litigation, will contests, and probate litigation.

His publications include *Conservation Easements: Tax and Real Estate Planning for Landowners and Advisors,* published by the ABA in 2011; "Selected Post-Mortem Estate Tax Elections for the Small Business Owner"; "Pleasing Mother Earth and the IRS: Using Conservation Easements to Save Open Space, Income and Estate Taxes," presented at the Heckerling Institute for Estate Planning for the University of Miami in January 2003; and other tax and real estate–related programs for the ABA and State Bar of Montana. He was the principal lobbyist in the 2021 Montana legislature for the Uniform Law Commission's (ULC's) Uniform Directed Trust Act and has lobbied, in past legislative sessions, for the ULC and the State Bar of Montana, for the Uniform Partition of Heirs Property Act, the Uniform Power of Appointment Act, and the Uniform Access to Digital Assets Act.

He and his family enjoy living in the Big Sky Country; he is an avid skier, outdoorsman, hunter, fly fisherman, and photographer.

W. Andrew Gowder, Jr. is a founder and partner in the law firm Austen & Gowder, LLC. His 35-year practice is focused on land use, property, land conservation, historic preservation, state and local government law, benefit and nonprofit corporate formation, governance, and counsel. His practice includes both representing leading environmental and preservation groups in litigation and providing counsel and strategic advice to nonprofit organizations, local governments, and responsible landowners and developers to assist them in doing their good work and achieving their missions.

He is an editor and writer of books and articles on topics relating to sustainable development, the greening of local government, the financing of public infrastructure, the ownership of property, the land use entitlement process, heir's property, and protection of the environment and historic preservation, and he teaches and lectures frequently on those topics.

Mr. Gowder has long been active in the American Bar Association, serving in many leadership roles, including as chair of the ABA Section of State and Local Government Law. He has also been involved in leadership in the Urban Land Institute at the national, regional, and local levels, serving for more than 10 years on the Executive Committee of the Sustainable Development Council (three years as its chair), currently as chair of the Carolinas Rethinking Southern Cities Regional Initiative Council and formerly as chair of the ULI South Carolina District Council, where he continues to serve on its Governance Committee and its Diversity, Equity and Inclusion Committee.

His practice and professional work have led him to achieve the professional designation of CRE (Counselor of Real Estate), an AV-Preeminent Rating from Martindale-Hubbell, the highest available rating for lawyers in that system, and he has for many years been named Best Lawyer in America in Land Use.

He earned his JD, cum laude, in 1986 from Wake Forest University School of Law, and his BA, summa cum laude, in 1983 from Wofford College, where he was Phi Beta Kappa.

Mavis Gragg is a self-described "death and dirt" attorney and conservation professional with nearly two decades of experience in real estate, conflict resolution, estate planning, and probate. An heirs' property owner herself, Ms. Gragg's mission is to empower families to maintain and optimize ownership of real estate for intergenerational wealth resiliency and growth. Drawing from her personal and legal experience, she founded the Gragg Law Firm, PLLC, in which she assisted her clients in estate planning, estate administration, and heirs' property matters. This experience led her to explore innovative strategies and tools that aid problem solving and growth opportunities for family real estate ownership. In her role at the American Forest Foundation, she serves as the director of the Sustainable Forestry and African American Land Retention Project—a program that supports African American family forest owners throughout the southeastern United States. She also founded HeirShares, which is building groundbreaking technology to facilitate affordable solutions for family real estate ownership, including confirming ownership. Ms. Gragg was honored to be appointed to the North Carolina Parks and Recreation Authority in 2019 and later as chair by Governor Roy Cooper. The Authority is the state board charged with allocating funds for state parks capital projects, repairs, and renovations of facilities, and land acquisition and to local governments for parks, public beach access, and improvements in state parks. She is also a current member and past board chair of a local land trust, Triangle Land Conservancy. She is passionate about education and art. She and her sister founded Black Women Drone and the Gragg Family Fund, which supports minority students in attending college and with travel abroad. She also serves on the North Carolina Museum of Art Foundation Board and is cofounder of Pop Box Gallery, a zero commission, pop-up art gallery. A native of Black Mountain, North Carolina, Ms. Gragg is an alumna of the University of North Carolina at Chapel Hill (BA, Industrial Relations) and Pepperdine University School of Law (Juris Doctor and Master of Dispute Resolution). She would like to express her sincere gratitude to Leila Hatem (Duke University School of Law, '21) for their assistance with research for her book chapter and her family and friends for their support.

K. Scott Kohanowski directs the Homeowner Stability and LGBT Advocacy Projects at the City Bar Justice Center (CBJC), a nonprofit civil legal services provider affiliated with the New York City Bar Association. With a team of just over thirty professionals who provide high-quality, free civil legal services benefiting more than 24,000 New Yorkers in need each year across twelve practice areas, CBJC mobilizes law firms, corporate legal departments, and other legal institutions to provide pro bono legal services and thereby bridge the access to justice gap; educates the public on pertinent legal issues; fosters strategic community relationships; and impacts public policy. He has worked at CBJC since 2010 training attorneys, supervising cases placed with pro bono and staff attorneys, providing direct legal services to distressed homeowners, and engaging in law reform to preserve housing and communities. His areas of expertise include foreclosure defense, heirs' property and community stabilization, and real property antifraud advocacy, with an acute focus on racial equity and social justice across all communities. He is a 1996 graduate of the University of Minnesota with a BA in Portuguese and Spanish, summa cum laude, and a 2001 graduate of NYU School of Law. Mr. Kohanowski worked at Morrison and Foerster LLP in real estate finance prior to transitioning to the public interest realm. He serves on the New York City Bar Association's Mortgage Foreclosure Task Force and Condo/Coop Committee, the New York City Deed Theft Task Force, and the New York City Non-Profit Legal Services Foreclosure Prevention Task, and formerly served on the City Bar's Housing and Urban Development and LGBT Rights Committees. He is co-chair of the ABA State and Local Government Law Section subcommittee on Heirs Property, a member of the New York State Bar Association and the National Consumer Law Center, and is a former executive board member of the LGBT Bar Association of Greater New York. He and his husband split their time between Brooklyn and the Catskills in New York.

Karama Neal, PhD, is an heirs' property landowner and was the founder of Heirs of Arkansas, a statewide grassroots organization created to promote passage of the Uniform Partition of Heirs Property Act. Her 2015 TEDx talk focused on this successful effort for which she was later awarded the 2020 Advancing Equity Award from the Clinton School of Public Service. In 2021, she was appointed administrator of the Rural Business-Cooperative Service at the US Department of Agriculture (USDA) Rural Development. The views expressed in this chapter do not necessarily represent the views of the USDA or the United States. Prior to joining USDA, she served as president of Southern Bancorp Community Partners, a nonprofit community development loan fund and financial development organization promoting economic mobility in rural Arkansas and Mississippi. She has published and spoken often about heirs' property, family economic security, and other topics. A graduate of Swarthmore College, she holds a PhD in genetics from Emory University and an

MA in bioethics from Loyola University Chicago. She also completed executive education in impact investing at the University of Oxford Saïd School of Business. She lives in Little Rock and is grateful to Anisha Phillips, JD, for legal research and to Judge Olly Neal (ret.) for an early review of the manuscript.

Benjamin Orzeske is chief counsel at the Uniform Law Commission (ULC). He supervises a staff of legislative attorneys who work to enact uniform laws in all fifty United States, the District of Columbia, Puerto Rico, and the US Virgin Islands. In addition to the Uniform Partition of Heirs Property Act, Mr. Orzeske personally provides legislative support for the Uniform Commercial Code and for uniform laws in the areas of real property, trusts and estates, investment management, and elder law. He also serves as the ULC's internal legal counsel.

Mr. Orzeske is a graduate of the University of Illinois and the DePaul University College of Law. He is a member of the American Bar Association Section of Real Property, Trust and Estate Law, where he serves on the Section Council, and also a member of the ABA Business Law Section. He is a past chair of the Chicago Bar Association's Legislative Committee. He also serves as the ULC's staff liaison to the Joint Editorial Boards for Uniform Real Property Acts and Uniform Trust and Estate Acts.

John Pollock is an attorney who has worked on heirs' property issues in a pro bono capacity for nearly 15 years. He is the founder and coordinator of the Heirs Property Retention Coalition (HPRC), which has worked since its inception in 2006 to develop and advance the UPHPA. His day job is serving as the coordinator for the National Coalition for a Civil Right to Counsel, which works to advance the right to counsel for indigent litigants in civil cases involving basic human needs. He graduated from Northeastern University School of Law in 2005, and lives in Montgomery, Alabama.

Steven Stapleton is chair of the ABA's State and Local Government Law Section and is a lawyer with Clark Hill PLC in Grand Rapids. He represents clients and provides crisis communication in various areas of commercial litigation, particularly labor and employment matters, including the enforcement of noncompete agreements, business ownership disputes, and a variety of specialized contentious claims, including sports-related sexual abuse litigation.

Mr. Stapleton advises senior management teams for employers across the country. He assists clients on corporate governance and restructuring, rule and policy drafting, contract review, and employment-related issues. He has established a niche representing sports-related entities and governing bodies and is deeply familiar with the obligations those organizations face under various state and federal laws. He serves as outside general counsel to the Michigan Amateur Hockey Association and is a member of the USA Hockey Legal Council. Steve serves as special counsel to the Arizona Amateur Hockey Association, Connecticut Hockey Conference, Texas Amateur Hockey Association, Utah Amateur Hockey Association, C2 Attack Volleyball Club, and RipFest Diving and advises many other governing bodies, conferences, leagues, teams, administrators, and coaches. He represents coaches and university athletic department personnel in National Collegiate Athletics Association–related investigations.

He counsels educational and sport-related organizations and helps clients implement and monitor comprehensive player safety and background screening and safe sport programs and, with Clark Hill Sports Industry Team members, conducts sensitive investigations related to allegations of sexual abuse and harassment. He counsels clients in the context of amateur/collegiate competition and represents the sports client in actions seeking to impose discipline or other sanctions related to athletic competition.

Jennie L. Stephens has served as the chief leader of the Center for Heirs' Property Preservation (the CHPP) since its inception in 2005. At the CHPP, she is responsible for overall strategic planning and resource development. She has worked for more than 25 years in the nonprofit field in such positions as fiscal director at a community action agency, sponsored programs director at a historically black college, and senior program director at Coastal Community Foundation. She also has several years of experience in consulting as a program reviewer, strategic plan facilitator, and grants writer. More recently, she had the pleasure of being a speaker at TedXCharleston with a talk titled, "Heirs Discover Money Does Grow on Trees" (https://youtu.be/TMeaii8csFY) and has been selected to be a 2018 BALLE Fellow, a member of 25 brilliant leaders who are building healthy and equitable rural economies across the United States and Canada

In celebration of the Center's 15th Anniversary—and the 35th anniversary of the Aspen Institute Community Strategies Group, which helped spark the Center's start-up—she spoke and presented at the national virtual symposium, "All Land Is Not Creating Equal: Unleashing Family and Community Wealth through Land Ownership." And in March of 2021, she was featured in the BET documentary series "Disrupt and Dismantle" with Soledad O'Brien.

Ms. Stephens received a bachelor's degree in Business Administration from the College of Charleston, a master's degree in Public Administration from the University of Charleston/University of South Carolina, and earned a PhD in Organizational Leadership from Regent University in Virginia Beach, Virginia.

Her passion in life is to help people help themselves.

Reginald Turner is president of the American Bar Association, the world's largest voluntary association of lawyers, judges, and other legal professionals. A lawyer with Clark Hill in Detroit, Mr. Turner is an accomplished litigator, government affairs advocate, and strategic advisor.

Mr. Turner is past president of the National Bar Association and the State Bar of Michigan. He served as chair of the ABA Commission on Racial and Ethnic Diversity in the Profession and the ABA Commission on the Lawyer's Role in Assuring Every Child a Quality Education. In the ABA House of Delegates, he served as the state delegate for Michigan and as chair of the Rules & Calendar Committee, the Committee on Issues of Concern to the Profession, and the Committee on Credentials and Admissions. He is a past chair of the Fellows of the American Bar Foundation.

Among his numerous presidential, gubernatorial, mayoral, and county executive appointments, Mr. Turner served as a White House Fellow and as an aide to Housing and Urban Development Secretary Henry Cisneros during the Clinton administration and represented Detroit Mayor Dennis Archer on the Detroit Board of Education from 2000 to 2003. In 2003, Governor Jennifer Granholm appointed him to the Michigan State Board of Education, and he won a statewide election for a full term in 2006.

Mr. Turner earned his bachelor's degree at Wayne State University and law degree at the University of Michigan Law School.

Joshua F. Walden was born in Mt. Airey, North Carolina, and has lived in South Carolina since 1979. He grew up in Chapin, South Carolina, approximately 20 miles outside of Columbia. He received a bachelor's degree in Psychology from the University of South Carolina in 1996. Mr. Walden earned his Juris Doctorate from the University of South Carolina School of Law and was admitted to the South Carolina Bar in 2000.

Mr. Walden is a member of the South Carolina and Charleston Bar Associations and has practiced primarily in the fields of real property and estate planning/probate law. He has served as a guardian ad litem for cases in the family court for the South Carolina Department of Social Services and South Carolina Department of Juvenile Justice and is a South Carolina Board Certified Civil Court Mediator. Mr. Walden joined the Center for Heirs' Property Preservation in Charleston, South Carolina, in September 2009, as the supervising attorney. He currently practices law and serves as the Center's chief operating officer.

Heather K. Way is a clinical professor at The University of Texas School of Law, where she co-directs the Entrepreneurship and Community Development Clinic. An expert in affordable housing and community development, Professor Way's work focuses on advancing housing justice, opening paths to economic opportunity, and fostering equitable and inclusive communities.

As a policy innovator, Professor Way's work has contributed to numerous high-impact legal reforms at the state and local levels, including, most recently, laws to facilitate the creation of community land trusts and broaden heirs' property owners' access to property tax relief programs. Professor Way is the cofounder of the Uprooted Project, which provides resources and strategies for addressing displacement in gentrifying neighborhoods in Texas.

Professor Way is a frequent commentator in the media and the author of numerous articles and reports on a wide variety of housing and community development topics. She is also the author of *Real Property for the Real World*, a book of hands-on case studies for law students in property law courses.

After receiving her law degree from The University of Texas School of Law in 1996, Professor Way clerked for the Honorable William Wayne Justice in the Eastern District of Texas. She began her legal career as a Skadden Fellow representing tenants and community groups at Legal Aid of Central Texas in Austin. Following her fellowship, she cofounded and directed Texas Community Building with Attorney Resources (Texas C-BAR), a statewide pro bono program for community organizations at Texas RioGrande Legal Aid.

Foreword

It is my great pleasure to introduce *Heirs' Property and the Uniform Partition of Heirs Property Act: Challenges, Solutions, and Historic Reform,* published by the American Bar Association's Section of State & Local Government Law. It explores the history and basics of the Uniform Partition of Heirs Property Act (UPHPA), adopted in twenty jurisdictions so far in every region of the country and introduced in at least seven more in 2021 alone, and the ongoing efforts to prevent the loss of family land and homes across generations.

Heirs' property affects people of every economic status, race, ethnicity, age, and gender, in every part of the United States, but African Americans and other people of color have been disproportionally affected by fractionalization of ownership among widely dispersed heirs and significant loss of personal, family, and economic legacy.

Heirs' property first came to the attention of the ABA as a result of the 2001 Associated Press articles entitled "Torn from the Land." This award-winning three-part series, written by Todd Lewan and Dolores Barclay, chronicled African American land loss, and the concluding article in the series focused on predatory partition actions. To seek ways to address the heirs' property problems the AP article brought to light, the Section of Real Property, Trust and Estate Law (RPTE) formed the Property Preservation Task Force in 2002 with David Dietrich, one of the chapter authors and later the RPTE section chair, as co-chair.

David Dietrich invited Professor Thomas W. Mitchell, the lead editor of this book, to join the Property Preservation Task Force and contribute his substantial expertise. In 2006, the Property Preservation Task Force submitted a proposal to the Uniform Law Commission (ULC), requesting the Uniform Law Commission to establish a drafting committee to develop a model state statute (a "uniform act") to address partition law abuse. The ULC accepted the proposal in early 2007 and formed a drafting committee soon thereafter.

Professor Mitchell served as the reporter (the person vested with principal authority for drafting a uniform act) for the ULC's drafting committee for the Uniform Partition of Heirs Property Act. The ULC promulgated the UPHPA in 2010, and the ABA approved it for consideration by the states in 2011. Professor Mitchell is extremely distinguished for his heirs' property scholarship and advocacy. The MacArthur Foundation named Professor Mitchell a MacArthur Fellow (commonly known as the MacArthur Genius Grant) in 2020 for his heirs' property advocacy and scholarship, making him one of only twenty-one people awarded the MacArthur Fellow in 2020 and the only lawyer in the group. Howard University awarded Professor Mitchell its Alumni Award for Distinguished

Postgraduate Achievement in 2021 for his property law work on behalf of disadvantaged communities, an award that Thurgood Marshall and Vice President Kamala Harris, among other Howard University luminaries, also have received.

Many chapter authors, starting with Professor Mitchell, have been involved in the drafting, adoption, and implementation of the UPHPA and in related drafting now taking place at the Uniform Law Commission and state level. In addition, a group of chapter authors and editors have participated in the ABA's "Preserving Family Real Estate, Generational Wealth, and Heritage: A Virtual National Institute on Heirs' Property" on August 25 and 26, 2021, chaired by Erica Levine Powers, the immediate past chair of the Section of State & Local Government Law and the coeditor of this book. These programs will be available on demand through the ABA Section of State & Local Government Law.

This book is an extremely important contribution to ABA goals of economic justice, civil rights, and the rule of law. It reaches multiple audiences and should be widely read. I am proud that the Section of State & Local Government Law is issuing it when my colleague, Steven F. Stapleton, is section chair, and am thrilled that it is coming out during my year as ABA president. My thanks to all who have made this valuable book possible.

Reginald M. Turner
President, American Bar Association

Introduction

Heirs' property constitutes a very common legal form of family property ownership within the African American community as well as within other socioeconomically disadvantaged communities. It is a problematic form of ownership that mostly arises when someone dies without having made a will or other type of estate plan. Until recently, the very existence of this type of common real property ownership was hardly known at all, with limited exceptions. However, during the past decade or so, there has been a dramatic and unexpected uptick in interest in a range of heirs' property matters, among academics and other researchers, those in the media, elected officials and other policy makers, those in the for-profit business sector as well as those in the nonprofit sector, and philanthropic organizations. As a result of this development, many people are now cautiously optimistic that meaningful progress can be made on a range of issues that have negatively impacted heirs' property owners for decades, issues that many believed would never be addressed.

There are a number of severe problems associated with heirs' property ownership. These problems include but are not limited to the following: (1) the ownership represents the most unstable, insecure form of common ownership of real property in the United States, largely though not exclusively due to a property law known as partition law; (2) those who own heirs' property often find themselves legally trapped in such ownership without the ability to come to any agreement with their fellow common owners on how to use the property or how to upgrade their ownership to a different and much more rational ownership structure; (3) a substantial percentage of heirs' property owners lack clear title to their property, which prevents these owners from being able to build and preserve wealth because they are ineligible for many commercial loans and a vast number of governmental programs at the local, county, state, and federal levels; and (4) heirs' property ownership is often hard to sustain due to the heirs' inability to participate in important local and state property tax relief programs or to get notice about certain procedures governments take to recoup delinquent property tax payments. In many places, heirs' property ownership also has been a contributing factor to exacerbating neighborhood blight and public safety problems, including gun violence.

Unfortunately, because the rules governing heirs' property ownership are very suboptimal and are counterintuitive in some important ways, many families experience tremendous problems with their heirs' property ownership. Sadly, many of these families have ended up losing their heirs' property involuntarily in various ways, along with the real estate wealth associated with their ownership. Losing this generational wealth often has proved devastating to those heirs' property owners who have been affected.

It would not be surprising if those directly affected—in the aggregate—have lost tens of billions of dollars in wealth, if not more. For African American, Latino, and some other families of color that own heirs' property, their heirs' property ownership typically represents their single greatest economic asset. When these families lose their heirs' property in transactions that result in the families receiving compensation significantly below market value, as is typical, yawning racial and ethnic wealth gaps are exacerbated. In addition to these negative wealth impacts, families that have lost their heirs' property often have experienced a substantial decline in their quality of housing, a loss of a significant part of their family's heritage, and a deterioration of their physical and mental health, among other serious economic and noneconomic negative impacts.

I. TAKING HEIRS' PROPERTY OUT OF THE SHADOWS: GENERATING PUBLIC CONSCIOUSNESS AND DEVELOPING LAW REFORM PROPOSALS TO ADDRESS CERTAIN HEIRS' PROPERTY ISSUES

In the past few years, heirs' property has gone from being an obscure property issue outside of the communities in which such ownership long has been most prevalent and very problematic to one that has become a hot topic among a growing number of important stakeholders. During the 2020 presidential campaign, Senator Elizabeth Warren made addressing heirs' property issues a cornerstone of her plan to address discrimination against farmers and landowners of color. In the general election, now President Joseph Biden made a commitment to address heirs' property issues and closely analogous common property issues that have harmed African American, Latino, and Native American communities, among others.

In the past year, major business organizations such as the Business Roundtable, the National Association of REALTORS®, and the American Land Title Association have made a commitment to use their substantial influence to support legal reforms to assist heirs' property owners. There also has been an outpouring of media stories by influential local, state, and national media organizations during the past few years—including a number that have won major media awards—that have highlighted certain serious heirs' property problems. All of these positive developments have been very welcome. These developments also have helped generate new thinking about the ability of property law to evolve to address serious injustices, as it pertains to heirs' property issues and otherwise. This much needed rethinking is overdue but very welcome because prior to these developments, there had been a longstanding consensus opinion among many lawyers and law professors that nothing could be done to address the substantial legal issues heirs' property owners have faced. This consensus opinion was predicated in part upon the belief that heirs' property owners simply lacked sufficient political and economic power to persuade elected officials and other policy makers to address their concerns.

The initial impetus for certain key stakeholders to learn more about, and to seek to address, long-ignored problems that have bedeviled heirs' property owners for generations has been certain catastrophic racial incidents. Often, high-profile media coverage of these incidents has helped reveal to many Americans who were not very cognizant of these matters that there are serious, continuing racial injustices in our society. Some, though not all, of these incidents have specifically negatively impacted African American farmers and property owners, though tragedies such as the murder of George Floyd have spawned a more general commitment to addressing racial injustices no matter what they may be.

Fortunately, a 2001, award-winning investigative report about Black land loss in the South, by two Associated Press reporters, served as the catalyst for what has turned out to be the historic reform of partition law, the property law that has been used by many to force the sales of many parcels of heirs' property. These sales have proven to be ruinous for an untold number of families and disadvantaged communities. This book includes several chapters that focus to one degree or another on different aspects of this groundbreaking legal reform measure, which is known as the Uniform Partition of Heirs Property Act (UPHPA). All of our authors for these chapters have been deeply involved in this work, several for more than twenty years.

Chapter 1 details the historic background of partition law abuse, particularly as it relates to African American property loss, describes the history of the development of this remarkable policy reform, and outlines key provisions of the UPHPA. Chapter 2 provides an overview of the Uniform Law Commission and the process of enactment of the UPHPA in nineteen states and the United States Virgin Islands so far, including a list of lessons learned. Chapters 4 and 5 highlight the role of grassroots organizations in recognizing the need for this reform, and in participating in important ways in the drafting of the UPHPA as well as in efforts to enact it into law in a number of states. Because the UPHPA will be considered in several more states over the course of the next few years, these lessons and experiences are extremely useful for those working for enactment.

Although partition law abuse first became widely known as a result of the AP reporting on how problematic partition sales have been a major source of Black land loss, it turns out that the problem African American families have had for decades with their heirs' properties in the rural South actually represented the canary in the coalmine in many ways. Though mostly overlooked until very recently, a very large number of families from many different racial and ethnic groups own heirs' property that is located in every region of the United States, and many of these families have experienced substantial problems with their ownership. The more universal nature of heirs' property ownership helps explain why the UPHPA has been enacted into law thus far in several states in every region of the country, states that in the aggregate contain a majority of the US population. Although families from many racial and ethnic groups have experienced problems with heirs' property, it is important to note that African American heirs' property owners in certain places appear to have been targeted by predatory real estate speculators and developers in a more intensive way than has been the case with some other heirs' property owners.

Further, heirs' property is not a purely rural phenomenon implicating agricultural land alone. To this end, many disadvantaged African American families and others own heirs' properties in cities and other metropolitan places throughout this country. For example, chapter 3 describes the modification of the UPHPA when introduced in New York to address predatory partition actions by developers who had purchased small heirs' property shares from heirs in gentrifying urban neighborhoods, including many neighborhoods throughout New York City. Equally important for both planning and policy reform is chapter 8, which sets out the adverse impact of state laws that deny property tax relief, particularly the homestead exemption, to heirs' property owners, with especially harmful consequences in many gentrifying urban areas and the further undermining of African American and Latino housing stability. This chapter also describes a relatively new statute in Texas that addresses this homestead exemption problem, a statute that has the potential to serve as a model for other jurisdictions that might be interested in making heirs' property ownership more sustainable by addressing this problem.

II. AVOIDING HEIRS' PROPERTY OWNERSHIP: STRUCTURING FAMILY REAL PROPERTY OWNERSHIP IN MORE RATIONAL AND SUSTAINABLE WAYS

The rules that govern heirs' property ownership—rules more generally known as the tenancy-in-common default rules—make this form of common real property ownership a form that sophisticated real estate, estate planning, and business lawyers strongly dissuade their clients from having. Families with sufficient resources often hire attorneys to help them structure the ownership of their family's real estate holdings in ways that ensure its stability over time and that allocate the rights and responsibilities various people have in connection with the properties—including, for example, how property taxes are to be paid—in a sensible and rational way. These lawyers advise their clients to structure their family property ownership using limited liability companies, trusts, or tenancy-in-common agreements, for example, so these families can avoid many of the downsides of the rules that govern heirs' property ownership.

Unfortunately, however, lawyers sometimes create heirs' property by drafting simple wills that replicate the default heirs' property rules that a state mandates in those instances when heirs' property is formed due to the failure of someone to make a will or other estate plan. Chapter 7 includes an analysis of probate procedures under the Uniform Probate Code (UPC) and the intersection of the UPHPA and the UPC, which can work to an heir's advantage under the UPHPA.

Three chapters pay particular attention to the need for planning. Chapter 5 includes a description of the work of the Center for Heirs' Property Preservation in Charleston, South Carolina, which provides free legal services to economically disadvantaged heirs' property owners, including a will drafting clinic and the opportunity to develop and steward the growth of the land, including forestry. Chapter 6, written by an heirs' property heir, focuses on strategic planning for the long-term use and development of the land, of which estate planning is one part. This chapter eloquently makes the case for heirs to go to private lawyers and for private lawyers to engage in this work, with a particular focus on African American lawyers and law students. Chapter 7 provides details of the various business entities and other alternative ownership forms that can be used to avoid or get out of the default tenancy-in-common rules that govern heirs' property ownership, with the advantages and disadvantages of each, and a list of resources for lawyers engaging in this practice.

Although there are many severe outstanding problems with heirs' property ownership that still need to be addressed, the current period represents a golden age of sorts for those who have worked for decades to address many vexing heirs' property issues. For a very long time, heirs' property issues in the aggregate represented a major societal problem that flew under the radar though these issues were hiding in plain sight. Commendably, a number of people in different sectors labored in the shadows and did what they could do with very limited tools and resources to address various heirs' property issues, whether by trying to help individual families one by one or by trying to lay the groundwork for more systemic change that hopefully might happen at some later time in history.

During the past decade or so, there has been exponential growth in interest in addressing many heirs' property matters, and those interested represent an impressive range of stakeholders. Despite the undeniable positive and unexpected trend in increased awareness of various heirs' property issues and some substantial tangible successes in addressing some of these issues, most Americans still know little about heirs' property. Fewer still know anything about the many legal issues heirs' property owners face that greatly imperil both the ability of these families to build and maintain generational wealth and preserve their family heritage and the ability of the communities with which many heirs' property owners have been strongly associated to preserve their history and culture. Sadly and to their great detriment, many of the people who lack critical knowledge about the laws governing heirs' property ownership are heirs' property owners themselves.

Those who have contributed to the publication of this book hope it will increase the general awareness of heirs' property issues in the United States. The book was designed in part to be a resource to help families who own heirs' property address some of the legal issues associated with their ownership that have confounded them up until now. On a more systemic level, the book offers elected officials and other policy makers who might be open to addressing important heirs' property matters with helpful resources to facilitate their work.

In the end, we hope that the significant progress that has been made to date to address important heirs' property issues will generate additional law and policy solutions and other helpful initiatives designed to transform in fundamental ways how disadvantaged families own property. A major goal of this work is to replace what often has been second-class, troublesome heirs' property ownership governed by problematic default rules, with much more stable and rational ownership that will help unlock many benefits and opportunities often associated with property ownership that have been out of the reach of many disadvantaged families. Addressing critical heirs' property issues at the family level at an appropriate scale in turn could help transform in important ways the many struggling neighborhoods and communities in which heirs' property is often concentrated.

Thomas W. Mitchell
and Erica Levine Powers

PART I

Heirs' Property Partition Reform

1

The Uniform Partition of Heirs Property Act: Advancing Social and Racial Justice Through Historic Property Law Reform

—Thomas W. Mitchell

I. INTRODUCTION

As indicated in the introduction to this volume, one of the major problems with heirs' property ownership is that it represents the most insecure form of common real property ownership in this country. For the past 150 years or so, predatory real estate speculators, developers, lawyers, and some others have preyed upon African American, Latino, and some other heirs' property owners by using an archaic property law known as partition law to force the sale of an untold number of their properties. The vast number of properties that families and communities have lost in partition actions have included numerous agricultural properties, single-family homes, and even, in some instances, properties that were comprised of tens of thousands of acres of land with vast open spaces.[1] The properties in almost every case were sold for prices well below market value, oftentimes for fire-sale prices.

[1] *See, e.g.*, Thomas W. Mitchell, *Reforming Property Law to Address Devastating Land Loss*, 66 Ala. L. Rev. 1, 31–36 (2014). As indicated, African American families and others have lost a large number of their single-family homes in urban and other areas either as a direct result of partition actions or as a result of how those that acquired many of these homes were able to use partition law to coerce disadvantaged families under duress into selling their homes "voluntarily" for below-market prices. *See, e.g.*, Lydia Hu, *Going, Going, Gone: New Tactic by Real Estate Investors Forcing New Yorkers from Their Homes*, Spectrum News NY1 (Mar. 9, 2019, 7:00 AM), https://www.ny1.com/nyc/all-boroughs/news/2019/03/19/going--going--gone--new-tactic-by-real-estate-investors-forcing-some-new-yorkers-from-their-homes-ny1-investigation/.

In referencing widespread, unjust forced sales of African American–owned heirs' property, John Pollock coined the phrase that this legal injustice is "the worst problem almost no one's heard of." Some others have adopted this phrase to describe the problem.[2] In addition to losing ownership of their property, these families and communities have lost much more, resulting in devastating multigenerational harm. The good news is that there has been an incredibly dramatic uptick in interest in heirs' property matters in the past several years, among academics, those in the media, elected officials and other policy makers, and many in the general public.

This chapter addresses a number of matters. First, it addresses the range of communities that have experienced significant problems with heirs' property ownership and how low will-making rates have contributed to the problem. Second, it provides an overview of key legal features of heirs' property ownership, as well as a description of partition law abuse. The chapter then addresses the development and key features of the Uniform Partition of Heirs Property Act (UPHPA), the most comprehensive and substantial reform of partition law in this country since major changes were made to partition law in states throughout the country in the early to mid-1800s.[3] Finally, the chapter addresses the impact the UPHPA has had in changing partition law and in providing tangible, long-hoped-for relief for heirs' property owners throughout the United States.

II. HEIRS' PROPERTY OWNERSHIP IS WIDESPREAD, ESPECIALLY AMONG AFRICAN AMERICANS AND SOME OTHER COMMUNITIES OF COLOR

Heirs' property is owned by a surprisingly diverse set of families in terms of the race and ethnicity and even socioeconomic background of the owners.[4] In addition to African American heirs' property owners, there are many white American, Latino, Native Hawaiian, and even some Native American heirs' property owners.[5] Further, heirs' property is located in every region of the country. Although many heirs' property owners are low-income individuals, a sizable number are middle class, and there even are some who are wealthy.

Although there are heirs' property owners from every racial and ethnic group, due in part to the overall high percentage of Americans who fail to make a will or other estate plan, heirs' property ownership disproportionately impacts disadvantaged communities, including most prominently the African American community. One major reason African Americans have a high incidence of heirs' property ownership is that there is a massive racial will-making gap in this country. This gap is little known, even among estate planning attorneys.

---

[2] Anna S. Persky, *In the Cross-Heirs,* A.B.A. J. (May 2, 2009, 4:40 AM), http://www.abajournal.com/magazine/article/in_the_cross-heirs/.

[3] *See* Unif. Partition of Heirs Prop. Act (Unif. L. Comm'n 2010), available at https://www.uniformlaws.org/viewdocument/final-act-with-comments-62?CommunityKey=50724584-e808-4255-bc5d-8ea4e588371d&tab=librarydocuments.

[4] *See, e.g.*, Mitchell, *supra* note 1, at 31–36.

[5] It is important to note, however, that far more individual Native Americans own what is called individual trust property that in some important ways is similar to heirs' property but in other ways, including how partition law works, is quite different. Many people are not aware of these differences, which unfortunately results in these people improperly conflating heirs' property with individual Indian trust property. *See, e.g.*, Jessica A. Shoemaker, *No Sticks in My Bundle: Rethinking The Indian Land Tenure Problem*, 63 U. Kan. L. Rev. 383, 441–43 (2015).

TABLE 1.1 Racial and Ethnic Disparities in Will-Making

	Respondent Has a Will	Respondent Has a Will, By Education Level		
		No High School	High School	College and Above
	Percent			
All respondents	56.93	47.13	58.92	65.71
White	64.23	56.76	65.26	72.04
Black	23.68	20.15	22.89	32.34
Other	27.24	20.79	34.54	38.63
Non-Hispanic	60.66	54.26	61.06	68.09
Hispanic	19.38	14.57	28.30	31.67

Note: Data presented is from two separate tables in the unpublished working paper by Francesconi, Pollak, and Tobasso.[9]

One recent study revealed that 64 percent of white Americans have a will, but only 24 percent of African Americans have a will.[6] Not surprisingly, within every racial or ethnic group, those with more education make wills at a higher rate than those with less education.[7] In the study, the least educated white Americans (those without a high school degree) had a will-making rate of 57 percent, which was 15 percentage points below the will-making rating for the most educated white Americans (see Table 1.1). Somewhat disturbingly in comparison, the most educated African Americans (those with a college degree and other professional or graduate degrees, if any) had a will-making rate of just 32 percent. Though this rate was 12 percentage points above the will-making rate for the least educated among African Americans, it also was 25 percentage points below the will-making rate for the least educated white Americans.[8]

Some have claimed that the lack of access to affordable legal services and a distrust of the legal system have contributed to such low estate planning rates within the African American community.[10] Others have suggested that legal and other barriers that prevented families from being able to make

[6] Thomas W. Mitchell, *Historic Partition Law Reform: A Game Changer for Heirs' Property Owners, in* Heirs' Property and Land Fractionation: Fostering Stable Ownership to Prevent Land Loss and Abandonment 67–68 (Cassandra Johnson Gaither, Ann Carpenter, Tracy Lloyd McCurty, and Sara Toering eds., 2019). The Hispanic will-making rate was very similar to the African American will-making rate. *Id.*

[7] *Id.* at 69.

[8] *Id.* This study also revealed that the Hispanic-white will-making gap was nearly identical to the Black-white will-making gap.

[9] Marco Francesconi, Robert A. Pollak, and Domenico Tabasso, Unequal Bequests (Nat'l Bureau of Econ. Research, Working Paper No. 21692, 2015) (data can be found in the online appendix to the published manuscript and in an unpublished table on file with author).

[10] *See, e.g.*, Will Breland, *Acres of Distrust: Heirs Property, the Law's Role in Sowing Suspicion Among Americans and How Lawyers Can Help Curb Black Land Loss*, 28 Georgetown J. Pov. L. & Pol'y 377, 393–95, 402–403 (2021); e-mail from Susan N. Gary, Professor Emerita, Univ. of Ore. Sch. of Law, to Thomas W. Mitchell, Professor, Texas A&M Univ. Sch. of Law (July 28, 2021, 13:43 CST) (on file with author).

wills in past generations gradually ripened into a social norm of not making a will or estate plan even when some earlier barriers were removed or at least lowered. However, others have pointed out that among African Americans, will-making rates were higher in past generations according to some research, even during the period of Jim Crow, than they are today. More research could shed much-needed light on the causes of this phenomenon, but no matter the reason, such low rates of will making explain in part why heirs' property ownership is particularly prevalent among African Americans. To this end, one groundbreaking study in 1984 estimated that 41 percent of Black-owned land in the South at the time was heirs' property.[11]

It is critically important to highlight that African American heirs' property owners as a whole lack adequate access to African American attorneys who can help them resolve their heirs' property issues. Overall, African Americans are severely underrepresented in the legal profession. Although African Americans constitute more than 14 percent of the US population according to the 2020 census,[12] only 5 percent of lawyers in the United States in 2020 were African American, a percentage that did not improve upon the 2010 percentage.[13] Further, among African American lawyers, there is a severe underrepresentation of lawyers who practice in transactional areas most relevant to assisting African American heirs' property owners, including in the areas of real estate law, business law, estate planning law, and tax law. For example, in the entire state of Oregon, there are only five African American attorneys who practice in the area of estate planning and administration in any significant way, according to one African American estate planning attorney who works there for a leading nonprofit organization.[14]

Owing to the lack of estate planning, many families own heirs' property that becomes more problematic from one generation to another. In these families, heirs' property initially was created in most instances when the property was transferred by intestate succession because there was no will or estate plan. Making matters worse, after heirs' property is initially created, the individual, fractional interests in the property often are then transferred by intestate succession. This pattern often repeats itself across several generations.

As a result, heirs' property ownership groups tend to have significantly more common owners than other tenancy-in-common ownership groups. It is not uncommon for heirs' property to be owned by 25, 50, 100, 200, or even more common owners. These owners are often dispersed across the country. The ownership group often includes people who do not realize they own a fractional interest in the property, people who have never visited the property, and people who do not know the other cotenants who are members of their extended family and are more connected to the property. This type of ownership is sometimes called fractionated heirs' property.[15]

---

[11] *See* Emergency Land Fund, The Impact of Heir Property on Black Rural Land Tenure in the Southeastern Region of the United States 64, 475 (1984).

[12] Nicholas Jones et al., *2020 Census Illuminates Racial and Ethnic Composition of the Country*, United States Census Bureau (August 12, 2021), https://www.census.gov/library/stories/2021/08/improved-race-ethnicity-measures-reveal-united-states-population-much-more-multiracial.html.

[13] Laura Bagby, *ABA Profile of the Legal Profession: Diversity and Well-Being*, 2 Civility (August 13, 2020), https://www.2civility.org/aba-profile-of-the-legal-profession-diversity-and-well-being/.

[14] E-mail from Ekua A. Hackman, Fellow Attorney, The Commons Law Center, to Thomas W. Mitchell, Professor, Texas A&M Univ. Sch. of Law (Sept. 3, 2021, 17:53 CST) (on file with author).

[15] *See* Thomas W. Mitchell, *From Reconstruction to Deconstruction: Undermining Black Landownership, Political Independence, and Community Through Partition Sales of Tenancies in Common*, 95 Nw. U. L. Rev. 505, 508 (2001).

III. LEGAL OVERVIEW OF HEIRS' PROPERTY OWNERSHIP AND PARTITION LAW

To appreciate why heirs' property owners are so susceptible to losing their property involuntarily, one needs to know something about the general characteristics of tenancy-in-common ownership, under what attorneys refer to as the default rules. These default rules come into play when a tenancy in common arises as a result of intestate succession. In addition to understanding these default rules in general, one needs to understand how partition law works. Partition law governs how a tenant in common can exit a tenancy in common when the common owners cannot come to agreement about how a cotenant can exit the common ownership group.

A. General Overview of Heirs' Property Ownership

Heirs' property ownership is a subset of the most prevalent form of common real property ownership in the United States, tenancy-in-common ownership.[16] This type of ownership often is referred to as "undivided ownership," which means that each of the individual members of the common ownership group—known as a tenant in common or cotenant—owns a fractional interest in the entirety of the property instead of having exclusive rights to any specific part of the property.[17] Each cotenant also is legally responsible for paying its proportional share of the costs of maintaining ownership of the entire property, including the property taxes, insurance, and other such expenses.[18]

Such ownership is analogous to owning shares in a corporation, given that a shareholder owns a fractional interest in the corporation but does not have any specific claim to exclusive ownership of any particular corporate asset. Any tenant in common has a unilateral right to transfer his or her fractional ownership interest (or any subset of such interest) to another person, company, or entity, during his or her life. In addition, a cotenant's fractional interest can be transferred upon the cotenant's death to others either pursuant to a will or other estate plan or under the laws of intestate succession.[19] For family-owned tenancies in common, any outsider who acquires the fractional interest of any family member has the exact same rights and responsibilities in connection with the property that any family member who has an interest in the property possesses.[20]

Heirs' property ownership is a more common phenomenon than most people realize, in part because the weight of the evidence suggests that at least half of American adults fail to make wills or other estate plans.[21] In every state in the United States, if someone who owns real property dies without a will or other type of estate plan, his or her property will be transferred according to state laws known as intestacy laws. In almost every instance, if a decedent who dies owning real property

[16] *See* Mitchell, *supra* note 6, at 67; U.S. Department of Agriculture Forest Service, Southern Research Station, General Technical Report.

[17] *See* Mitchell, *supra* note 6, at 67.

[18] E. H. Schopler, *Contribution, Subrogation, and Similar Rights, as Between Cotenants, Where One Pays the Other's Share of Sum Owing on Mortgage or Other Lien*, 48 A.L.R.2d 1305 (stating that a "cotenant, or tenant in common, is obliged to contribute his or her pro rata share toward expenses such as property taxes, encumbrances on the land, and necessary insurance").

[19] 4 Thompson on Real Property, Thomas Editions § 32.02 (David A. Thomas ed.).

[20] *Cf.* Georgia Appleseed, Heir Property in Georgia, 14 (2d ed. 2010); Deeds.com, *Adding Someone to Your Real Estate Deed? Know the Risks* (Feb. 19, 2019) ("A deed that conveys an interest in your real estate ownership ('adds someone on') has the legal effect of giving that additional person the same bundle of rights to which you are entitled").

[21] *See* Mitchell, *supra* note 6, at 67.

is survived by at least two family members who qualify as heirs under the applicable state intestacy laws, the state intestacy laws will mandate that those qualifying heirs will become owners of the property under the tenancy-in-common form of ownership.[22] Sometimes, heirs may assume their ownership interests subject to rights a creditor of the decedent family member may have, which obviously can pose some difficulties for the heirs.

Having a will does not necessarily prevent the formation of heirs' property, although many people, including many attorneys, think otherwise. Sometimes an attorney who drafts a simple will can "create" heirs' property, perhaps without fully understanding the potential negative consequences of doing so, for example, by leaving a house to "all my children." They can do so by drafting the will in a way that unwittingly replicates or closely approximates the outcome if there had been no will and the property in question was transferred by intestate succession.[23]

Many if not most people who own heirs' property—including, perhaps surprisingly, some attorneys who have little or no expertise in transactional areas of law such as real estate, wills, trusts, and estates, and business organizations—also are not aware that there are many legal ways to structure or restructure family ownership of real property in a proactive way. These alternatives include but are not limited to establishing a limited liability company, some type of trust, and a so-called tenancy-in-common agreement. These options each have certain benefits and disadvantages. However, any knowledgeable lawyer who helps their clients form common real property arrangements would strongly advise their clients never to own property in common with others under a tenancy in common governed by the rules a state mandates under state intestacy laws—in short, under the heirs' property form of ownership.[24]

B. Insecure Ownership

Transactional lawyers, including real estate, business, and estate planning lawyers, know that heirs' property ownership represents the most unstable form of common real property ownership in the United States. They also know that partition sales almost never yield market value prices, but instead can be financially ruinous.[25] Partition law is a main factor, though not the only one, that makes heirs' property ownership very unstable. The application of partition law can result in a family very suddenly and unexpectedly losing their property involuntarily, for example when a third-party purchaser of one relative's small, fractional interest seeks partition. In contrast to the suddenness of a partition sale, there are other factors that often can make heirs' property ownership gradually more unstable over time, such as the inability of many heirs' property owners to access property tax relief programs as discussed in chapter 8.

---

[22] *See* 86 C.J.S. Tenancy in Common § 11; 2 American Law of Property § 6.5 (A. James Casner ed., 1952).

[23] *See* Ga. Heirs Prop. L. Ctr., *About Heirs Property*, https://www.gaheirsproperty.org/heirs-property.

[24] *See, e.g.*, Thomas W. Mitchell, Stephen Malpezzi, & Richard K. Green, *Forced Sale Risk: Class, Race, and The "Double Discount*," 37 Fla. St. U. L. Rev. 589, 615–17 (2010).

[25] *Id.*

1. *General Background of Partition Law*

Partition law governs how any individual cotenant who no longer wants to own property with others under a tenancy in common can exit the ownership structure if the owners as a whole cannot work out the terms of exit in a consensual way.[26] Any cotenant, including either a family member or non-family-member cotenant, may file a lawsuit known as a partition action irrespective of the size of the fractional interest such a cotenant owns or when such a cotenant acquired its interest.[27] For example, a real estate speculator targeting property an African American family has owned in rural Georgia dating back to 1870 can acquire the two percent fractional interest of a distant second cousin living in Pittsburgh, Pennsylvania, and then turn right around and file a partition action the same day it acquired its small interest.[28] In that lawsuit, the speculator can request the court to resolve the partition action by ordering a forced sale of the property—known as a partition sale—even if all of the other cotenants whose interests can be traced back to their ancestor's acquisition of the property in 1870 want to maintain ownership of the property.

Theoretically, in resolving a partition action, a court can order a range of remedies. However, the two dominant remedies courts consider are what's referred to as a partition in kind (sometimes partition by division) and partition by sale.[29] Although in an overwhelming number of states and other jurisdictions, the law indicates that the physical division of the property ostensibly is the preferred remedy, for partition actions that are not governed by the UPHPA, the ostensible preference for a physical division is very weak. This reality has resulted in partition by sale becoming the de facto preference in many states.[30] Although most state partition statutes indicate that a court should order partition in kind unless "great prejudice" would result from such a remedy, almost no state statute defines "great prejudice."[31]

Many state court judges have filled the definitional vacuum by developing and applying a narrow test to determine whether great prejudice would result. This test limits courts to analyzing whether a partition sale would theoretically be more economically advantageous to the cotenants as a whole because there are economies of scale making the property more economically valuable if maintained as a whole than if it were to be divided.[32] Courts that apply this so-called economics-only test to resolve a partition action do not factor in the importance the property may have to the family because of its family heritage value, its cultural value, its historical value, or any other noneconomic values.[33] Even the economic analysis is very narrow. It is limited to considering whether there are theoretical economies of scale in ordering the entire property sold. For example, no consideration is given to the economic contributions various cotenants have made to maintaining ownership of the property or the negative economic impact a sale could have on the ability of a cotenant who occupied the property to secure quality alternative housing in the general vicinity after the forced sale.

---

[26] *See* Mitchell, *supra* note 6, at 68.

[27] *See* Mitchell, *supra* note 1, at 10.

[28] *Id.*

[29] *Id.* at 11–18.

[30] *See* Mitchell, *supra* note 15, at 513–15.

[31] *See* Mitchell, *supra* note 1, at 12.

[32] *Id.*

[33] *Id.*

2. *Heirs' Property Owners Particularly Susceptible to Ruinous Coercive Sales*

Many families that own heirs' property are particularly susceptible to losing their property as a result of a partition action initiated by a real estate developer or speculator due to four factors. First, these families tend to be "property rich and cash poor," meaning that besides their heirs' property, they are otherwise low-income or low-wealth.[34] Second, these families have a lack of access to affordable legal services.[35] Third, these families have low rates of will-making or estate planning.[36] Fourth, the properties implicated are located in areas in which the real estate values tend to be rapidly increasing.[37] This can implicate rural properties, such as farm properties located near an urban area experiencing sprawl, or urban properties, such as single-family homes in neighborhoods undergoing rapid gentrification.

Further, another factor that has contributed to many court-ordered or otherwise coerced sales of heirs' property is that many heirs' property owners have believed in certain erroneous myths that have given these owners a false sense of security about their ownership.[38] These include the myth that heirs' property cannot be sold under any circumstances or that it cannot be sold unless all of the common owners consent to a sale.[39] A related myth is that the property cannot be sold if the property owners keep up with all of their financial obligations in connection with the property, including paying the property taxes, any mortgage obligations, property insurance payments, and so on.[40] There are also myths that perpetuate incorrect beliefs that certain heirs or cotenants have superior rights to the properties in question because, for example, they occupy the properties while fellow cotenants are not in possession or because they pay all or more of the property taxes than their fellow cotenants.[41]

Although all of these myths are completely false, at least two factors help explain how they took hold. First, the actual rules governing heirs' property ownership are extremely counterintuitive.[42] Second, a substantial percentage of heirs' property owners are low-income and lack access to affordable legal services.[43]

Prior to the promulgation of the UPHPA and in jurisdictions that have not enacted the UPHPA into law, many heirs' property owners only have learned how the general partition law actually works after it was too late for them to do anything to save their property. Sometimes they discovered how

[34] *See, e.g.*, Greg Barlow, *Defying Great Odds—Mitigating Property Loss Through Historic Partition Law Reform in the U.S.*, Law & Society Ass'n (Aug. 26, 2020), https://lawandsociety.site-ym.com/news/523353/Defying-Great-Odds--Mitigating-Property-Loss-Through-Historic-Partition-Law-Reform-in-the-U.S..htm.

[35] *Id.*

[36] *Id.*

[37] *Id.*

[38] *See* Mitchell, *supra* note 15, at 521; *See also*, Ga. Heirs Prop. L. Ctr., *Heirs Property Myths and Facts*, https://www.gaheirsproperty.org/myths-facts-about-heirs-property (detailing several myths certain heirs' property owners incorrectly believe).

[39] *See* Mitchell, *supra* note 15, at 521 (citing a study that revealed that 75 percent of heirs' property owners incorrectly believed that their property only could be sold if all of the cotenants consented to a sale).

[40] *See* Mitchell, *supra* note 1, at 30.

[41] *Cf.* Ga. Heirs Prop. L. Ctr., *Heirs Property Myths and Facts*, https://www.gaheirsproperty.org/myths-facts-about-heirs-property.

[42] *See* Mitchell, *supra* note 1, at 12.

[43] *Id.*

the general partition law works only after one of their common owners petitioned a court for a forced sale of the property.[44] In other instances, a cotenant who sought to coerce his fellow cotenants to sell their interests to him explained to his other cotenants how the general partition law actually works and the utter futility they would experience if they would seek to preserve their ownership if a partition action were to be filed.[45] This type of activity has resulted in many de facto coercive sales—sales that may well be more numerous than actual court-ordered partition sales—and it gives the false impression that these sales were voluntary sales.

Worse still, heirs' property owners rarely receive any economic benefit as a result of a partition sale, for predictable reasons, and often end up financially ruined by such a sale,[46] because the economics-only test is deeply flawed. This is the case because judges who use the test often incorrectly compare the fair market value of the entire property against the combined market value of the parcels that would result from a division. These judges usually order the property sold if their analysis suggests the property as a whole has so-called economies of scale.[47] The problem with this analysis is that under the general partition laws—but not under the UPHPA—the entire property is sold under a forced-sale procedure that will yield forced-sale value and often fire-sale value.[48] As Justice Scalia succinctly stated, "market value, as it is commonly understood, has no applicability in the forced-sale context; it is the very antithesis of forced sale-value."[49]

Therefore, when courts order partition sales, disadvantaged families rarely realize the mythical economic benefits the courts posit will flow from these sales. As mentioned previously, many heirs' property owners are "property rich and cash poor." This often results in the winning bidder—often a third-party speculator or developer that bought out the fractional interest of a family member—making a low-ball bid that represents an economically disastrous fire-sale price well below even a forced-sale price.[50]

In addition, some families have claimed that the notice procedure for a partition sale is so poor that family members who could have contributed financially to helping a family make a more competitive bid did not contribute because they were not given adequate notice of the sale.[51] To this end, in adjudicating partition actions, courts often authorize notice by publication in a local newspaper, sometimes a local newspaper that only exists to publish online notices. Such notice often results in cotenants who were not personally served lacking the basic knowledge that a partition action had been filed. Some out-of-state cotenants even have claimed that courts have authorized notice by

---

[44] *Id.*

[45] *Cf.* Hu, *supra* note 1.

[46] Todd Lewan & Dolores Barclay, *Quirk in the Law Strips Blacks of Land*, TENNESSEAN, Dec. 11, 2001, at 8A (noting that the forced partition sales the reporters documented mostly yielded below-market value, bargain prices, which resulted in the families being stripped of a significant amount of their real estate wealth).

[47] *See* Mitchell, Malpezzi, & Green, *supra* note 24, at 610–14.

[48] *Id.* at 603–606.

[49] BFP v. Resolution Trust Corp., 511 U.S. 531, 537 (1994).

[50] Mitchell, *supra* note 1, at 31.

[51] *See* Louisiana Appleseed, *Louisiana Appleseed's Heirs' Property Panel, June 2021*, YOUTUBE (July 1, 2021), https://www.youtube.com/watch?v=j68zYYp6Ni4.

publication in cases in which the plaintiffs did not personally serve the out-of-state cotenants even though the plaintiffs knew their addresses or otherwise knew how to locate them.[52]

In sum, partition sales have had a devastating social and economic impact on many disadvantaged communities. Economically, it is important to note the massive racial and ethnic wealth gaps in this country. According to one study, the typical Black family has only 13 percent of the wealth of the typical white family and the typical Hispanic family has just 19 percent of the wealth of the typical white family.[53] Partition sales have been a leading cause of property loss within the African American community, and this asset depletion certainly has contributed to the massive Black-white racial wealth gap that exists in our country.[54] Given that partition sales usually yield prices well below market value and often fire-sale prices, Black and Latino families and communities likely have lost tens of billions of dollars in wealth (and perhaps more) as a result of losing their heirs' property due to partition law abuse.[55]

Families and communities that have lost their heirs' property also have endured incalculable harm to their heritage, culture, and history.[56] For example, few Americans know that in 1950, Hilton Head Island in South Carolina had a population that was 90 percent African American, a population that largely consisted of people of Gullah-Geechee descent. Many of these families owned land on the island. Beginning in the 1950s, white real estate speculators did everything they could do to acquire as much land on the island as possible, including by filing a large number of partition actions against African American heirs' property owners. Sadly, the African American population on the island now stands at just six percent[57] and African Americans now own fewer than 1,000 acres on the island.[58] As a result, the incredibly important history of African Americans in general and

---

52 These claims cannot be dismissed out of hand and should be investigated given that they raise serious concerns about potential fundamental due process violations. In Georgia, for example, regarding cotenants who reside out of state, a "court may order service by publication as in its judgment is right in each case." GA. CODE ANN., § 44-6-162. This means that the court has substantial discretion to permit the petitioner to only provide information about the partition suit in a local Georgia newspaper even though an out-of-state cotenant rarely would find out about the partition suit by such publication. *See* Caitlin Henderson, Note, *Heirs Property in Georgia: Common Issues, Current State of the Law, and Further Solutions*, 55 GA. L. REV. 875, 889 (2021). Some even have claimed that because the standards courts use to determine whether notice by publication may be appropriate are very poorly elaborated, notice by publication has been permitted even with respect to cotenants who live in the same town where the land in question is located. Rishi Batra, *Improving the Uniform Partition of Heirs Property Act*, 24 GEO. MASON L. REV. 743, 753 (2017). Batra suggests that courts should not have permitted notice by publication in these cases because the defendant cotenants in these cases were cotenants the plaintiff easily should have been able to locate and sometimes were cotenants the plaintiff in fact knew. *Id.*

53 Neil Bhutta et al., *Disparities in Wealth by Race and Ethnicity in the 2019 Survey of Consumer Finances*, https://www.federalreserve.gov/econres/notes/feds-notes/disparities-in-wealth-by-race-and-ethnicity-in-the-2019-survey-of-consumer-finances-20200928.htm, Sept. 28, 2020.

54 *See* Mitchell, *supra* note 15, at 511.

55 To this end, the fourteen partition cases that resulted in the forced sale of African American family-owned properties that the Associated Press featured resulted in those African American families alone losing millions of dollars in real estate wealth. *See* Lewan & Barclay, *supra* note 46. Latinos also have lost a substantial amount of generational wealth as a result of partition law abuse. *See, e.g.*, Mitchell, *supra* note 1, at 35–36.

56 *See, e.g.*, Nisha Bhakta, *A Clash Between Culture and Law: A Comparative Look at the Conflict Between Quiet Title Actions in Hawaii, the Kuleana Act of 1850, and the Displacement of Indigenous People*, 49 CAL. W. INT'L L.J. 137, 139–140, 161 (2018); David Slade & Angie Jackson, *SC Land Slipping Away From Families Amid Fragile Claims and Explosive Growth*, POST AND COURIER (Dec. 5, 2018); Tenisha Waldo & Jill Coley, *Fighting a Losing Battle*, POST AND COURIER (Aug. 5, 2007).

57 World Population Review, https://worldpopulationreview.com/us-cities/hilton-head-island-sc-population.

58 Leah Douglas, *African Americans Have Lost Untold Acres of Land Over the Last Century*, THE NATION, June 26, 2017.

Gullah-Geechee people, in particular on Hilton Head Island, is in real danger of being completely erased from the consciousness of the public at large.[59]

In addition, many who have been displaced because of the involuntary loss of their heirs' property have experienced a dramatic decline in the quality of their housing, with some even ending up homeless.[60] Others have gone from being relatively economically independent to experiencing significant downward economic mobility.[61] Furthermore, according to some, families that have lost their heirs' property also may experience a diminished ability to participate in the civic and political lives of their communities.[62]

Still others have experienced a significant decline in their physical wellbeing and mental health as a result of involuntarily losing their heirs' property.[63] More generally, many African Americans (and others) have experienced severe health challenges that emanated from their losing property rights due to discrimination, including many Black farmers.[64] These negative health impacts are not a new phenomenon. In fact, for generations, African Americans have experienced substantial health problems that have been linked to their loss of property rights, including the African American couple who lost their very successful beachfront resort in Manhattan Beach, California, about 100 years ago as a result of the city engaging in blatant eminent domain abuse in 1924. After losing their "Bruce's Beach" resort after Manhattan Beach condemned it based on the false pretext that the city needed it to build a park when in fact the city's real goal was to rid Manhattan Beach of some of the small number of African American property owners in the city at that time, Willa and Charles Bruce were forced to take jobs as cooks in someone else's restaurant in South Los Angeles. In addition to the tremendous social and economic losses the couple experienced, Willa ended up having a mental breakdown due to the severe emotional, social, and economic stress she experienced, and both Willa and Charles died prematurely within eight years of the unjust eminent domain taking.[65]

---

[59] Carol Motsinger & David J. Gross, *His Ancestors Fought for Their freedom in the Civil War. Now, He Fights to Preserve What They Left Him*, Greenville News (July 20, 2021), https://www.greenvilleonline.com/story/news/local/south-carolina/2021/07/20/hilton-head-island-south-carolina-fight-past-future-complicated-alex-brown-tourism-travel/7058921002/.

[60] *See, e.g.*, Hu, *supra* note 1.

[61] African Americans often have experienced downward economic mobility when they have lost their property involuntarily. *See, e.g.*, Michael Scott Moore, *California's Novel Attempt at Land Reparations*, The New Yorker, May 27, 2021, available at https://www.newyorker.com/news/us-journal/californias-novel-attempt-at-land-reparations (noting that a Black couple that had their beachfront property in Manhattan Beach, California, unjustly taken by eminent domain went from operating a very successful resort business to taking on menial jobs as cooks prior to their premature deaths).

[62] *See* Mitchell, *supra* note 15, at 535–41.

[63] *See, e.g.*, VICE News, *How Property Law Is Used to Appropriate Black Land*, YouTube (Aug. 11, 2020), https://www.youtube.com/watch?v=ls3P_FicO7I (demonstrating, among other things, how a devastating partition sale of more than 400 acres of land in Louisiana that an African American family named the Lewis family had owned since the late 1800s resulted in deep psychological pain to many members of the Lewis family, perhaps especially to the family's matriarch, who had to relocate to Washington, D.C. to live with one of her family members).

[64] *See, e.g.*, Shalini Chatlani, *Black Louisiana Farmers' Land Leases Are Vanishing. Some Say Racist Policies Are to Blame*, WWNO – New Orleans Pub. Radio (Oct. 19, 2021), https://www.wwno.org/news/2021-10-19/black-louisiana-farmers-land-leases-are-vanishing-some-say-racist-policies-are-to-blame (noting how certain Black farmers in Louisiana who believed they were victims of discrimination died prematurely due to the stress of losing their property rights and how others contemplated suicide or experienced other severe mental health challenges).

[65] *See* Moore, *supra* note 61.

IV. HISTORIC PROPERTY LAW REFORM

A. Background

At the turn of this century, there was near consensus among law professors and practicing lawyers familiar with partition law that this archaic law simply could not be changed in any substantial way to benefit disadvantaged heirs' property owners. Some of the resistance was simply based on the reputation property law has of being an area of law that has been particularly resistant to change and where inertia and tradition often carry the day. In commenting on the pace of change in property law, one Ohio state appellate judge stated that there is a "slow evolution of property law, which is somewhat comparable to geologic change."[66] Partition law squarely fits this paradigm, since prior to the UPHPA, partition law in many states had remained essentially unchanged for more than 100 years.

Some skeptics also could point out that there was empirical data suggesting that partition law reform to benefit disadvantaged heirs' property owners would be incredibly difficult if not impossible to achieve. In fact, in several southern states, certain civil rights and grassroots organizations and their supporters had attempted to reform partition law starting in the 1970s and carrying through the 2000s. All of these attempts to reform partition law in any substantial way failed in each instance, though some of these groups were able to get a very small number of states to reform their partition laws in some very limited ways.[67] A narrative developed among many that framed calls for partition law reform as just a racial justice measure that simply, if sadly, would forever be doomed to fail, based on an assumption that African Americans would forever lack sufficient economic and political power to be able to persuade important stakeholders to change an unjust law.

It was critically important to counter this well-entrenched, but incorrectly narrow, narrative during the drafting of the UPHPA. In my role as reporter (principal drafter) for the UPHPA, I went to great lengths to make the Uniform Law Commission (ULC) aware that there are heirs' property owners from families of many different races and ethnicities although a disproportionate number of heirs' property owners are African American.[68] I also emphasized that, despite the fact that nearly all of the academic publications and media articles about heirs' property framed it as a purely rural phenomenon, it is not a purely place-based issue. Although there are many who own heirs' property in rural America, there also are a large number of parcels of heirs property in cities such as Atlanta, New Orleans, New York, and Oakland, to name just a few.[69] To one degree or another, heirs' property owners as a whole, irrespective of their race and ethnicity or where the properties are located, have experienced severe problems with their ownership, including problems with partition law.

---

[66] Bebout v. Peffers, No. 86-CA-02, 1986 WL 9303 (Ohio Ct. App. Aug. 18, 1986) (J. Miligan, concurring at *8).

[67] Mitchell, *supra* note 1, at 36–38.

[68] *See* UNIF. PARTITION OF HEIRS PROP. ACT at Prefatory Note, at 5–6.

[69] *See, e.g.*, Frank S. Alexander, *Louisiana Land Reform in the Storms' Aftermath*, 53 LOY. L.R. 727, 732 (2007); David Pendered, *Georgia's Estimated $34-plus Billion in Heirs Property Could Ease Wealth, Housing Gap*, SAPORTA REPORT (Dec. 2, 2019), https://saportareport.com/georgias-estimated-34-plus-billion-in-heirs-property-could-ease-wealth-housing-gap/columnists/david/; *Report on Legislation by the Commercial Law and Uniform State Laws Committee, the Housing and Urban Development Committee, and the Pro Bono and Legal Services Committee: The Uniform Partition of Heirs Property Act* 2, NEW YORK CITY BAR (June 2019), https://www.nycbar.org/member-and-career-services/committees/reports-listing/reports/detail/support-for-the-uniform-partition-of-heirs-property-act; Carey L. Biron, *Will Power: Could Property Inheritance Help Close U.S. 'Wealth Gap'?*, THOMPSON REUTERS FOUNDATION (Nov. 12, 2019), https://www.reuters.com/article/usa-homes-inheritance/feature-will-power-could-property-inheritance-help-close-u-s-wealth-gap-idUKL8N27F50B.

B. Analysis of the Uniform Partition of Heirs Property Act

The UPHPA constitutes the most sweeping change to partition law since the early to mid-1800s when partition law was reformed in states throughout the country to permit courts to order partition by sale for the first time, if only under extraordinary circumstances.[70] The UPHPA features a logical hierarchy of remedies designed to maximize the property rights for the common owners as a whole. This stands in stark contrast to the reality of many general partition laws in states throughout the country. These laws often prove to be of great benefit to the one cotenant or small subset of cotenants that seek a forced sale but ruinous to the other cotenants. Although the UPHPA represents fundamental reform of partition law, it was crafted in a very thoughtful way to balance a number of objectives and to maintain a number of core features of tenancy-in-common ownership and the general partition law.

The UPHPA's enhanced property rights protections help families that own heirs' property secure their ownership where possible and maintain their real-estate wealth even if the court decides that ordering a partition sale is the most equitable remedy. Some of the protections draw directly from legal mechanisms lawyers for wealthy families often use to protect their clients' family-owned property.[71] The enhanced protections include increased notice requirements. To this end, the UPHPA requires that a plaintiff in a partition action who seeks to serve some cotenants only by publishing information about the lawsuit in a newspaper (printed or online), must post a conspicuous sign on the property with relevant information about the partition action, if a court determines that the property may constitute heirs' property.[72]

In addition, under the UPHPA, a court must determine the value of the property, and the default mechanism under the act is for the court to appoint an impartial, licensed real estate appraiser to determine the fair market value of the property.[73] Further, pursuant to the UPHPA, courts that appoint so-called commissioners, "partitioners," or referees—people courts appoint to help the courts resolve a partition action in ways that can differ depending upon the jurisdiction—must appoint impartial people.[74] This provision addresses the fact that in some states, courts sometimes appoint the lawyer for the party that seeks the forced sale to be a commissioner, at least in terms of handling how the property will be sold, which is manifestly unjust. A number of other important UPHPA protections are addressed in detail later in the chapter.

Although the UPHPA, as promulgated by the ULC, does change partition law in a very substantial way, it is important to make clear what it does not do. It does not impact partition law of properties other than tenancy-in-common property that meets the UPHPA's definition of "heirs property." The UPHPA does not override written agreements cotenants enter into that address how to partition their property. The act does not prevent cotenants from transferring their interests to anyone else, whether by sale, gift, will, intestacy, or otherwise. The act does not prevent any cotenant

[70] Gillian K. Bearns, *Real Property - Giulietti v. Giulietti - Partition by Private Sale Absent Specific Statutory Authority*, 26 W. New Eng. L. Rev. 125, 142 (2004).

[71] *See* Unif. Partition of Heirs Prop. Act at Prefatory Note, at 3.

[72] *Id.* § 4(b).

[73] *Id.* § 6(a), (d).

[74] *Id.* § 5.

from filing a partition action or for petitioning a court for partition by sale in a partition action. Further, the UPHPA does not prevent a court from ordering any of the remedies courts normally order in partition actions, including partition by sale.

This section of the chapter reviews a number of key provisions of the UPHPA.

1. The Scope of the UPHPA

The committee that drafted the UPHPA decided for pragmatic reasons to limit the scope of the UPHPA to family-owned tenancies in common that were not subject to a private, written agreement governing the partition of the property. In part, this decision was made because all of the troubling partition law cases the ULC, the drafting committee, and the grassroots organizations that helped draft the UPHPA knew about involved family-owned tenancies in common for which there was no written agreement governing partition. In addition, the committee was concerned that expanding the scope of the act to include tenancy-in-common properties that were not family owned potentially could generate strong opposition from certain quarters that would severely threaten the efforts to enact the UPHPA into law in many states and other jurisdictions.

All of those who participated in the drafting of the UPHPA agreed with the decision to limit the applicability of the UPHPA to family-owned tenancies in common. At the same time, some of these people (including me) also believed that the core features of the UPHPA would represent a significant improvement in partition law no matter whether a tenancy-in-common property was family owned or not. In recent years, some states have expressed interest in expanding the UPHPA, including interest in having it become those states' general partition law so that it would apply to partition actions involving all tenancy-in-common properties. In 2020, Virginia became the first state to reform its partition law to make nearly all of the provisions of the UPHPA the state's general partition law.[75] New York expanded the "standard UPHPA" to add several protections, as is discussed in chapter 3.

To determine whether a tenancy-in-common property qualifies as heirs' property, two affirmative criteria must be established. First, at least one of the cotenants must have acquired title from a relative.[76] However, there is no requirement that such a relative has to have acquired title from an older relative. This means, for example, that this requirement would be satisfied if a younger sibling transferred his fractional ownership interest to an older sibling in an intragenerational transfer instead of an intergenerational transfer. Further, despite the fact that the act uses the terms "heirs property," none of the cotenants need to have acquired their interests by intestate succession from a relative who failed to make a will or other estate plan. Therefore, the acquisition from a relative requirement can be satisfied in numerous ways. For example, it can be satisfied if a cotenant received their fractional interest by way of a gift from another family member, bought their fractional interest from a family member, acquired their fractional interest by way of a quit claim deed from a family member, received their interest by way of a family member's will or other estate plan, or acquired their interest by intestacy.

---

[75] Va. Code Ann. § 8.01-81 et seq.

[76] Unif. Partition of Heirs Prop. Act § 2(5)(B).

Second, there has to be some indicia of significant family ownership. Such significant family ownership is established if any of the following tests are satisfied:

1. 20 percent or more of the interests are held by cotenants who are relatives.
2. 20 percent or more of the interests are held by an individual who acquired title from a relative, whether living or deceased.
3. 20 percent or more of the cotenants are relatives.[77]

2. *Courts Are Required to Determine Whether Tenancy-in-Common Property in Every Partition Action Qualifies as Heirs' Property under the UPHPA*

The UPHPA requires courts to play a somewhat more active role than courts often (but not always) play in a lawsuit between private parties. As background, it is important to note that in jurisdictions that have enacted it into law in its original form, the UPHPA constitutes a specific statute that coexists with the more general partition statute. Even so, the UPHPA in these jurisdictions requires courts to determine whether the property that is at issue in any partition action constitutes heirs' property as defined under the UPHPA. If it is determined to be heirs' property, the UPHPA automatically will be the governing law for the partition action. Courts are required to make such a determination and then to apply the UPHPA if the property constitutes heirs' property whether or not any party notifies the court that the UPHPA may apply.

The incredible significance of this requirement is hard to overstate, though it might be lost upon those who are not experienced litigation attorneys. The parties in litigation often are responsible for identifying for the court the legal authority that supports their claims, though there are exceptions to this requirement. In many instances, a party's failure to identify such legal authority can result in a waiver of an argument or a claim the party makes that is premised upon such authority.[78]

The drafters of the UPHPA wisely argued that, for the UPHPA to be effective, the court should determine whether the UPHPA should apply and to do so the court first needed to determine whether the property in question in any particular partition action is heirs' property. The drafting committee pointed out that many if not most heirs' property owners would be unlikely to know about the existence of the UPHPA. Hardly any in the subset of these owners who would represent themselves pro se would know to invoke the UPHPA so that they could benefit from its enhanced private property protections. Even some of the lawyers retained by those who seek to maintain their heirs' property might not be familiar with the UPHPA. In contrast, third parties such as real estate developers and speculators almost always have the ability to hire experienced lawyers. However, these lawyers would have no incentive to make the court aware of the UPHPA because their clients would have a much

---

[77] *Id.* § 2(5)(C)(i)-(iii).

[78] *See, e.g.*, Bel-Ray Co. v. Chemrite (Pty) Ltd., 181 F.3d 435, 440-41 (3d Cir. 1999) (holding that pursuant to the Federal Rules of Civil Procedure, a court may hold that a party waived a potential conflicts of law issue if that party failed to notify the court of the potential applicability of the law of a foreign country); Chisolm v. Mapp, 347 So.2d 697 (Fla. Dist. Ct. App. 1977) (failure of party to assert specific statute at trial results in waiver of party's claim that the statute should have barred the trial court's admission of certain testimony). Sometimes, specific court rules expressly address this issue of waiver. *See, e.g.*, PA R BRADFORD CTY CT RCP Rule 210 ("Briefs shall contain the particular theories, statutes, rules of court, or cases upon which the litigant relies. The failure to specifically cite a statute, rule of court, or case shall be deemed to be a waiver of any claim that said authority is applicable.").

greater chance of acquiring properties in partition actions for a price significantly below market value under the general partition law as opposed to under the UPHPA.

3. *Three Pillars of the UPHPA*

For those partition cases for which the UPHPA ends up being the governing law, there are three main pillars of the UPHPA that offer heirs' property owners substantially enhanced private property protections than they otherwise would have under the general partition law. These provisions are designed to bolster the ability of families that own heirs' property to maintain ownership of their property and to preserve their real estate wealth. First, cotenants that want to maintain ownership of the property have a right to buy out the fractional interests of any cotenant that requested a court to order a forced sale of the property.[79] Second, the UPHPA fortifies the weak preference most states have for a physical division of tenancy-in-common property instead of a forced sale.[80] Third, for those cases for which the partition by sale is the most equitable remedy, the drafters of the UPHPA developed a novel sales procedure that is far more likely to help a family maintain a substantial amount of its generational, real estate wealth.[81]

a. The Buyout Procedure

The buyout procedure is an example of how carefully the drafters of the UPHPA balanced various interests and considerations and drew upon a very diverse set of legal sources. The drafters noted that those who petition courts in partition actions for a forced sale of properties implicitly at least signal that they are comfortable with exchanging their fractional interests for a monetary payment. In seeking a forced sale, for example, these type of cotenants obviously have no guarantee that they would be the winning bidder at a partition sale. In drafting the UPHPA's buyout procedure, the UPHPA's drafters considered how wealthy owners of common real properties structure their ownership. As a result of this consideration, the UPHPA's buyout provision is analogous to how the exit of an individual owner is handled for those who own real property under a trust or a privately negotiated tenancy-in-common agreement, for example, as chapter 7 makes clear.

A cotenant that is bought out will likely receive somewhat more in compensation under the UPHPA's buyout procedure than they would receive if they tried to sell their fractional interest on the open market due to some discounts that often apply to cotenants who sell their fractional interests on the market.[82] The sales price for the buyout is determined by multiplying the court-determined value of the property—its appraised fair market value price in almost every case—by the fractional interest of the cotenant that is subject to being bought out. Therefore, if the court determined that the property in question was valued at $1 million and the cotenant that petitioned the court for partition by sale owns a three percent interest, then the buyout price would be $30,000.

The buyout procedure can help families retain their family-owned property for two reasons. First, if the buyout procedure is invoked and the cotenants given the right to buy out a cotenant that

---

[79] UNIF. PARTITION OF HEIRS PROP. ACT § 7.

[80] *Id.* §§ 8 & 9.

[81] *Id.* § 10.

[82] Mitchell, *supra* note 1, at 52.

requested a forced sale proceed to do so, the family as a whole can retain ownership of the property. Just as importantly, the buyout mechanism can have a prophylactic impact in stemming the filing of partition actions by those who might otherwise seek to use partition law to acquire family-owned properties against the will of many heirs' property owners.[83] To this end, many speculators and others likely will be less inclined to file partition actions with the goal of acquiring heirs' property for a bargain price because the UPHPA could result in having those cotenants being bought out themselves. Further, whatever distribution they might receive from the buyout effectively would be reduced by the attorney's fees and other transaction costs they would incur in litigating a partition action.

The buyout provision also enables a court to order a second buyout of the fractional interests of cotenants that do not participate in the partition action by filing required pleadings, which in legal terms mean they do not appear in the action.[84] One of the parties must make a motion requesting the court to order this buyout and the court has discretion to grant or to deny the motion. This feature of the buyout provision was designed to help address a different problem with heirs' property ownership: the problem families face with highly fractionated ownership that can make it incredibly difficult to manage heirs' property.[85]

It is important to note, however, that the UPHPA's drafting committee gave courts the authority to grant or deny a party's motion for this second buyout because the committee recognized there are a range of reasons heirs' property owners might not appear in a partition action. There are heirs' property owners who do not appear because they are completely inactive owners, including some who do not fulfill their obligations to pay their share of their family's common property expenses, for example. Helping the active cotenants consolidate their ownership in such cases can have many positive benefits. However, there are others who do not appear for understandable reasons, including because they do not receive adequate notice of the partition action or because they cannot afford to hire an attorney and are not able to represent themselves pro se.[86]

b. Reinforcing the Preference for Partition in Kind

The UPHPA's fortification of the preference for partition in kind realigns partition law with the values that undergirded it during an earlier period in history. In this earlier period, a forced sale of someone's property was viewed more universally as a radical remedy that should be ordered sparingly, only when equity clearly justifies it.[87] Therefore, the UPHPA helps close the gap between what in theory was the preferred remedy in a partition action with what had become the de facto preference for partition by sale in many states. As a result, the UPHPA's test almost assuredly will result in courts ordering partition in kind more frequently than they have done for the past several decades under the general partition laws.

The UPHPA recalibrates the preference for partition in kind by explicitly rejecting the so-called economics-only test and replacing it with a totality of the circumstances test that requires a court

[83] *See* Mitchell, *supra* note 6, at 73.

[84] Unif. Partition of Heirs Prop. Act § 7(g)(h).

[85] *Id.* § 7 cmt. 4.

[86] *Id.*

[87] *Cf.* Andre v. Tobon, 209 Wis.2d 602, 1997 WL 88128 *1 (Ct. App. Wisc. 1997).

to consider a number of both economic and noneconomic or human values.[88] Even the economic factors are expanded beyond considering whether the property has economies of scale making it potentially more valuable if maintained as a whole. For example, the UPHPA enables courts to consider whether some of the cotenants have paid more and others less than their apportioned, pro rata share of the expenses needed to be paid to maintain ownership of the property.

In addition to these economic factors, the courts are required to consider whether there has been longstanding ownership among any cotenants, which can be evidence of family heritage value, for example, or whether it has other special values such as cultural or historic value. The court also must consider whether the remedy it may order might result in any cotenant having to cease engaging in their lawful use of the property, for commercial or residential use, and the degree of economic or noneconomic harm such a cotenant would experience from having to discontinue that use. For example, a court would have to consider whether an indigent heir who was occupying the property as her primary residence might experience a serious reduction in her quality of housing if she would be forced to leave the property as a result of a partition sale.[89]

c. The Open-Market Sales Procedure

The third and final main pillar of the UPHPA is the open-market sales procedure.[90] This sales procedure is a completely innovative way of handling a partition sale; it is designed to mimic the way in which a sale of real estate between a willing seller and a willing buyer transpires. My initial inspiration for recommending this innovative sales procedure to the drafting committee came from Scotland. In 1972, the highest court in Scotland reformed the Scottish partition law to permit courts that order partition by sale to order a sale nearly identical to the UPHPA's open-market sale instead of restricting courts to ordering an auction sale. The Scottish high court made this reform in part because it had discovered that the Scottish auctions used to sell properties ordered by the courts to be sold in partition actions typically yielded below-market prices. As indicated previously, auction sales used under the general partition laws in the United States also typically yield below-market prices.

The open-market sales procedure works in the following way. A court appoints a licensed real estate broker to list the property in question for its court-determined value, which in almost every case will be the property's appraised, fair market value. The appointed broker is required to use commercially reasonable practices in marketing the property, which in most cases would mean marketing the property in a way that is nearly identical to how the broker would market properties in that broker's normal inventory. The broker does not have an artificial deadline to arrange for a sale of the property, which allows for the property to be exposed to the marketplace for an adequate period of time. Further, bidders under an open-market sale are permitted to make bids that are contingent

---

[88] Unif. Partition of Heirs Prop. Act § 9. *See also* Mitchell, *supra* note 1, at 55–56.

[89] In New York City, a trial court recently appeared to consider the claim made by an heir who was a longtime owner-occupier of a single-family home in Queens that a partition sale would likely result in her having to move into a homeless shelter. Even though the court noted that New York's UPHPA did not apply to that case because the case was filed before the UPHPA became effective and that the law does not apply retroactively, the court did state that the UPHPA expresses the general will of the legislature to disallow the use of partition law in ways that can have devastating impacts upon heirs' property owners. *Cf.* 3333 98 Group Corp. v. Oakes (Sup. Ct. NY 2021).

[90] Unif. Partition of Heirs Prop. Act § 10.

upon their being able to secure financing at a somewhat later time, just as happens in so-called willing seller–willing buyer market transactions.

The open-market sales procedure is completely different from the judicial sale or sheriff's sales at the courthouse that all states use as the primary means of conducting a partition sale. The judicial or sheriff's sale typically uses the procedures for a type of forced sale known as an execution sale, which has none of the features economists require for a sale to be considered a fair approximation of an asset's market value. Unsurprisingly, consistent with what economic theory would predict, the typical partition sale yields a price well below market value. Even though many courts incorrectly have believed that partition sales typically yield fair market value prices, other courts have been quite cognizant that a partition sale, as a type of forced sale, normally yields a below-market, forced-sale price and often prices amounting "to only 50% or less of the appraised or arm's length value."[91] In contrast, the UPHPA's open-market sales procedure has almost all of the features that economists require for a sale to be considered a fair approximation of an asset's market value.

V. THE UPHPA'S REMARKABLE SUCCESS

A. The UPHPA Is One of the Most Adopted Uniform Real Property Acts Ever

At the time the UPHPA was promulgated in 2010, most people familiar with it thought the UPHPA would garner fewer than five enactments, and many believed it woud be a complete failure with not a single enactment. Skepticism about the UPHPA's success was based on two factors. First, the ULC historically has had substantial difficulty securing enactments for its uniform real property acts. The median number of enactments for this subset of uniform acts is one and the average is about five.[92] Second, some people thought the prospects for the UPHPA were particularly bleak, not only because it is a uniform real property act but also because it is an act that promotes racial justice. Some thought its racial justice aspect was noble in theory but would prove to be fatal in fact to enactment efforts in many states, including but not limited to the southern states.

Instead, at this time, the UPHPA has been enacted into law in nineteen states and one U.S. territory: from California to New York, from Montana to Florida, from Illinois to Texas, from New Mexico to Virginia, as well as Hawaii and the United States Virgin Islands.[93] Although many skeptics claimed there was no chance any southern state would enact the UPHPA into law, the South in fact is far and away leading the way, with eight enactments. Overall, the UPHPA now ranks as one of the five or six most successful uniform real property acts the Uniform Law Commission ever has produced out of the forty-five or so uniform real property acts it has promulgated since its establishment in 1892. Given the significant number of large states that have enacted it into law already, including California, Florida, Georgia, Illinois, New York, and Texas, it is now the law in states and jurisdictions with a clear majority of the US population. It is also very likely that the UPHPA will become law in a majority of the states within the next few years.

---

[91] *See* Smith v. Rusmisell, 517 S.E.2d 494, 498 (W. Va. 1999) (quoting Koay v. Koay, 359 S.E.2d 113, 116 (W. Va. 1987)).

[92] *See* Mitchell, *supra* note 6, at 76.

[93] *See* https://www.uniformlaws.org/committees/community-home?CommunityKey=50724584-e808-4255-bc5d-8ea4e588371d.

B. Substantial Real-World Positive Impact

More important than the number of enactments, based on reports from many states assessing the effectiveness of the UPHPA, the act is working very well and as intended. It is helping many families maintain ownership and control of their property. The UPHPA is also helping families preserve their generational wealth in different ways.

Here are some selected examples of how the UPHPA has helped certain families with their heirs' property problems. In Georgia and South Carolina, the UPHPA has led to a significant reduction in the number of abusive partition actions filed by real estate developers, speculators, and others, according to several lawyers in those states. In New York City, the UPHPA is helping African American heirs' property owners maintain ownership and possession of their properties as well as the wealth associated with this property ownership. Some of these owners are longstanding owner-occupiers of single-family homes in rapidly gentrifying neighborhoods who have been targeted by real estate speculators that successfully forced other heirs out of their homes by using partition law prior to New York's enactment of its version of the UPHPA in 2019. In Texas, a property that was sold using the UPHPA's open-market sales procedure yielded a sales price of $2.5 million in a partition action in which all of the lawyers agreed that the property would have sold for no more than $1 million if the auction sales procedures provided for under the general partition law had been used instead. Though seemingly a dramatic result, the result in this case in fact is completely consistent with what real estate economics theory would predict would be the impact of the UPHPA's open-market sales procedure replacing the auction sale procedure.

In Montana, the UPHPA has helped stabilize the ownership of certain ranch properties that were in danger of being targeted for a partition sale. In 2017 in Hawaii, Mark Zuckerberg dismissed eight lawsuits he had filed seeking the forced sale of certain kuleana lands (Native Hawaiian-owned heirs' property parcels with a unique history) located within the interior boundaries of his then 700-acre estate on the island of Kauai. He dismissed the lawsuits in part because of the extremely bad media coverage he had received, including some media outlets that prominently noted that Zuckerberg had filed his lawsuits two days before the UPHPA was to become law in 2017 in an effort to prevent the kuleana landowners from being able to avail themselves of the UPHPA's enhanced protections.[94] In all the jurisdictions that have enacted the UPHPA into law, farmers and ranchers who own heirs' property are eligible for expanded or priority access to a number of important programs administered by the United States Department of Agriculture but farmers and ranchers who own heirs' property in states that have not enacted the UPHPA into law who are not entitled to such expanded or priority access.

VI. CONCLUSION

For decades, heirs' property owners suffered one tragic loss after another, which resulted in disadvantaged families losing a massive number of properties, whether urban, suburban, or rural ones. This loss resulted in a massive depletion of generational wealth and it has had a devastating impact on many families and communities given that their heirs' property often had constituted their most substantial asset. Such loss also had a devastating impact on the history, culture, and heritage of

[94] *See, e.g.*, Duane Shimogawa, *New Hawaii Law Likely Influenced Timing of Kauai Lawsuits by Facebook's Zuckerberg*, Pacific Business News, Jan. 20, 2017.

many families and communities, including African American, Latino, Native Hawaiian, and poor white families and communities, as well as some Native American families and communities. Although the problem of partition law abuse had been hiding in plain sight for generations, elected officials and other policy makers mostly ignored the plight of heirs' property owners and were unwilling to reform partition law to make it more just.

Partly as a result of the unexpected success of the Uniform Partition of Heirs Property Act, heirs' property issues have become much more well known among many Americans and even many others outside of this country. Although the UPHPA cannot help families that already have lost their heirs' property get their property back, it is providing much-needed relief to the many families in every region of this country that still own heirs' property, whether in rural or metropolitan areas. Families that own heirs' property in jurisdictions that have enacted the UPHPA into law are experiencing much more stable ownership. This enhanced stability is giving many of these families "breathing room": to make plans, for example, to reorganize their ownership into an alternative legal ownership structure to make it more stable and functional; to make much needed estate plans; and to use their properties in much more valuable ways, whether economically, environmentally, culturally, or otherwise. Beyond reforming an arcane and archaic area of property law long viewed as being immune to reform, it also is giving hope to others that other deep-rooted injustices considered nearly impossible to change in fact can be addressed, especially when a diverse set of stakeholders work arm in arm to bring about such change.

2

Enactment: The Transition from Uniform Act to State Law

—Benjamin Orzeske

I. INTRODUCTION

The Uniform Law Commission's (ULC's) drafting process is designed to produce high-quality legislation. A new uniform act such as the Uniform Partition of Heirs Property Act (UPHPA) is likely to be more modern, more comprehensive, and more thoroughly vetted than existing state statutes on the same subject. However, it is not law until it is enacted by state legislatures.

The UPHPA represents an attempt to reform an area of the law that dates from sixteenth-century Britain. It was a challenge to overcome the accumulated inertia of the past five hundred years and the deeply held views of many real estate lawyers that partition law simply did not need reforming, despite strong evidence of how the existing law unjustly deprived heirs of their property. Nevertheless, over the past ten years, the UPHPA has been adopted in nineteen states and the United States Virgin Islands. In the next few years, we should reach a tipping point when the UPHPA will be the majority doctrine, instead of what some had considered a radical new property law regime.

This chapter begins with a general overview of the enactment process. It continues with a review of the enactment activity in a few representative states and an analysis of how momentum for enacting the UPHPA built over time and across geography.

II. THE GENERAL PROCESS OF ENACTING UNIFORM LAWS

Enacting legislation requires a team. First, there must be enough local advocates who care about an issue to get the attention of their legislators. Then someone must draft a bill that will accomplish the desired objectives without causing unintended consequences. You have to identify potential allies and opponents and build a coalition of supporters strong enough to overcome any potential opposition.

And you must find a legislator willing to sponsor the bill and work to convince that sponsor's colleagues to vote in its favor at each step of the legislative process. In most states, that means at least one committee hearing and one floor vote in each chamber before a bill is passed and transmitted to the governor for final approval.

Uniform laws have a few baked-in advantages that can simplify the process. The ULC has a longstanding reputation for producing quality legislation, and uniform acts are predrafted for easy adaptation into bill form, complete with legislative notes to guide the bill drafter when alternatives are available and when citations to existing law are necessary. The ULC's legislative staff will also prepare an enactment kit for each uniform act that includes a summary, talking points, a fact sheet, and endorsements from any supporting organizations. These materials are vital for explaining the act to legislators, many of whom are not lawyers and nearly all of whom operate under serious time constraints. Ideally, uniform law commissioners in each state will be familiar with the issue and predisposed to support enactment, potentially forming part of the coalition in support.

In most states, ULC commissioners have an annual legislative agenda. The ULC constitution states that each commissioner has a duty "to seek introduction and enactment of Uniform Acts promulgated by the Conference that are appropriate for their State."[1] The commissioners meet periodically to decide which uniform laws are appropriate and work with legislators to introduce a few bills in each legislative session.

But not all introductions of uniform acts are initiated by commissioners. Legislators, state bar associations, industry lobbyists, or concerned citizens might also work to enact uniform laws. The reporter and observers who served on the drafting committee will have invested significant time and effort in creating the law and will often advocate to see their work put into effect.

III. ORGANIZING LOCAL STAKEHOLDERS

A. Heirs' Property Advocates

In 2002, the American Bar Association's Section of Real Property, Trust and Estate Law (RPTE) formed the Property Preservation Task Force, co-chaired by real estate attorneys David Dietrich from Montana and Julius J. Zschau from Florida. The task force studied the problem and then invited Professor Thomas Mitchell to become a member, which he did. Mitchell's research into land loss and partition law abuse helped the task force crystallize the issues and identify potential avenues for reform. Ultimately, the task force submitted a proposal to the ULC suggesting a new uniform state law to govern the partition of heirs' property.

Heirs' property was a novel issue for the ULC. Consequently, the UPHPA initially had no organized, experienced group of supporters to tout its benefits to state legislators across the country. Contrast this situation with, for example, an update to the Uniform Commercial Code, which generally attracts lobbying support from state bankers' associations and local economic development groups, or with uniform acts designed to prevent exploitation of seniors, which are promoted by AARP's state offices and other consumer advocates. There were no experienced lobbyists ready to promote the interests of heirs property owners in state capitols.

---

[1] Uniform Law Commission Constitution § 6.1, available at https://www.uniformlaws.org/aboutulc/constitution.

There was, however, a dedicated group of local and regional nonprofit organizations with experience helping heirs' property owners preserve their rights, mostly concentrated in southern states where exploitation of heirs was most prevalent. Primarily due to the organizing work of public interest attorney John Pollock, advocates from those organizations banded together to form a new national group called the Heirs' Property Retention Coalition (HPRC). Many of the organizations appointed representatives to the UPHPA drafting committee, where some participated in a vital way in creating the UPHPA, and in the process developed a detailed understanding of how the act worked to prevent land loss. For more information about the role that the HPRC played in developing the UPHPA, see chapter 4.

After the UPHPA was approved at the ULC's annual meeting in 2010, Professor Mitchell and the coalition turned their focus to helping get the new uniform act enacted into law. Though they had no experience in running a multistate legislative campaign, the HPRC began working to identify potential supporters and organize them into state-based coalitions. The group held monthly conference calls with Professor Mitchell and the ULC legislative counsel to strategize and develop enactment plans for each targeted state.

B. Neutralizing Opposition

As critical as it is to organize support, it is arguably even more important to diffuse any opposition. The legislative process requires a bill to progress through multiple steps before it becomes a law. In a typical state, these steps include introduction, committee assignment, one or more committee hearings in the first house, a floor vote in the first house, committee hearings in the second house, a floor vote in the second house, possible reconciliation if any amendments passed in either house, and finally, approval or veto by the governor. While successful navigation of *every* step is necessary for enactment, an opponent can prevent advancement at *any single stage* of the process and effectively kill the legislation.

Neutralizing the opposition begins at the drafting stage when controversial issues should be discussed openly with potential opponents and, when possible, a consensus reached. The UPHPA drafters knew that influential lobbyists representing the real estate industry and the real property bar could scuttle efforts at law reform if the legislation would negatively impact their interests. As a result, the UHPHA was thoughtfully drafted so that it could hopefully garner support from the real estate industry, or at minimum encourage neutrality while still protecting heirs' property owners from exploitation.

Many provisions of the UPHPA reflect this thought process. First, the act narrowly defines "heirs' property" to exclude many of those who own tenancy-in-common property from its scope while including the vast majority of family-owned tenancy-in-common properties.[2] Almost all tenancies in common involving unrelated parties can be partitioned under an enacting state's preexisting law.[3] The UPHPA primarily protects those potentially vulnerable cotenants who received their interests in

---

[2] Unif. Partition of Heirs Prop. Act § 2(5) (Unif. L. Comm'n 2010).

[3] Interestingly, in 2020 the State Bar of Virginia successfully argued to expand the scope of that state's UPHPA legislation to cover *all* partition actions, rather than only those involving heirs' property. This indicates that the UPHPA's reforms of the partition process are also beneficial in other contexts, should states have the political will to apply them more broadly. *See* Va. Code Ann. §§ 8.01-81 to 8.01-93 (West, Westlaw through 2021 Reg. Sess.).

the land passively, through inheritance, and may not fully understand the ramifications of the default rules governing legal partition.[4]

Furthermore, tenants in common remain free under the UPHPA to transfer their individual interests voluntarily. Many of the potential concerns from the real estate industry were alleviated because the UPHPA does not prevent transfers of property between a willing buyer and a willing seller who negotiate a mutually agreeable price.

The UPHPA was also drafted to ensure each selling cotenant receives maximum value in a buyout. Under the act, the value of any cotenant's interest in the property is not discounted either due to the inherent instability of tenancy-in-common property and the concomitant concern that a forced sale would yield a below-market price because individual cotenants lack control; or due to a clouded title that sometimes prevents easy management or alienability of heirs' property. Instead, the court first determines the market value of the entire property *based on sole ownership of the fee-simple estate.*[5] The value of each cotenant's interest is then determined by multiplying the fractional share of ownership by the appraised value of the entire tract, thus ensuring fair compensation in any court-supervised buyout.

Finally, the UPHPA also was drafted to preserve the traditional right of a cotenant to request a partition, regardless of how the cotenant's property interest was acquired. Stated differently, both cotenant heirs of a previous owner and cotenants who purchased the fractional interest of a family member have the same right to request partition when joint management is untenable. Once a court determines that the property subject to a partition action qualifies as heirs' property, both heirs and non-heir cotenants stand to benefit from the enhanced legal protections the UPHPA provides. Instead of treating family members differently from others, the UPHPA protects *all* cotenants from forced sales based on the *remedies* they may seek in a partition action.

IV. ENACTING THE UPHPA IN THE STATES

A. Initial Obstacles

Following the lengthy drafting process, the UPHPA was approved at the ULC's annual meeting in the summer of 2010. But the new act was not immediately embraced in most states. In general, uniform real property acts have been slower to gain widespread enactment than uniform acts in other areas of the law.[6] There are a few reasons. Local interests such as realtors and real estate attorneys tend to oppose any additional real estate regulation, so introducing real property legislation carries some political risk. There is also a perception among some state legislators that uniformity of law is less essential with respect to the law of real property, compared to say, commercial law or civil procedure, because most transactions and legal disputes over real property do not involve parties in multiple

[4] The protection is necessary because partition law is counterintuitive to most non-attorneys. Most people are surprised to learn that *owners* can be ordered by a court to sell their property. It goes against the common understanding of the rights of ownership.

[5] Unif. Partition of Heirs Prop. Act § 6(d).

[6] *See, e.g.*, Unif. Condominium Act (amended 1980) (Unif. L. Comm'n 1977) (which has been enacted in fourteen states); Unif. Real Prop. Transfer on Death Act (Unif. L. Comm'n 2009)(which has been enacted in nineteen states); Unif. Com. Real Est. Receivership Act (Unif. L. Comm'n 2015) (which has been enacted in eleven states); Unif. Nonjudicial Foreclosure Act (Unif. L. Comm'n 2002) (which has not been adopted anywhere).

states. The ULC viewed the UPHPA as an exception because cotenant heirs often reside in various states, and the issue affects family property owners in every state.

Enacting the UPHPA is also challenging because it addresses an archaic area of the law that tends to impact disadvantaged families. For the most part, these families lack any significant wealth, and hence tend to lack political influence. Families often have little understanding about potential legal consequences because partition law can be very counterintuitive. Unfortunately, the way many heirs first learn about partition law is by being named as a defendant in a partition action and forced to defend their interests in court. Relatedly, many of these families also do not understand how the UPHPA can help to solve their problems. Therefore, the issue has not been a priority for most legislators because there have not been many individual constituents asking them to sponsor UPHPA legislation, though that is beginning to change as the UPHPA becomes more widely recognized as a viable reform.

Until a few years ago, the issue of partition abuse by real estate speculators who take advantage of heirs did not receive much attention in the media. Even though the tactic of using forced partition sales to acquire land for below-market prices has been practiced in the United States since the mid-1800s, there was almost no research on systemic land loss that revealed the widespread scope of the problem. Combined, these factors help explain why elected officials were unaware of the ways in which partition law could be used to dispossess many families of their property and wealth.

Thankfully, the issue of land loss through abusive partition actions is now receiving more attention. Professor Mitchell's two decades of scholarly research and publications and his extensive outreach work have led to more reporting on the issue in recent years, which in turn led to more public consciousness and demands for reform.[7] As awareness of the problem grew, so did demand for the UPHPA. As the chart below illustrates, a few successes in the early years created momentum that led to increased legislative activity and expanding acceptance of the UPHPA's reforms. Along the way, UPHPA proponents learned valuable lessons and used their increasing experience to become more effective advocates.

Year[8]	**UPHPA Bills Introduced**	**Enactments**
2011	3 – NV, OR, USVI	1 - NV
2012	2 – GA, SC	1 - GA
2013	5 – CT, DC, HI, MT, SC	1 - MT

[7] *See, e.g.*, Lizzie Presser, *Their Family Bought Land One Generation After Slavery. The Reels Brothers Spent Eight Years in Jail for Refusing to Leave It*, ProPublica (Jul. 15, 2019), https://features.propublica.org/black-land-loss/heirs-property-rights-why-black-families-lose-land-south; Michelle Chen, *Black Lands Matter: The Movement to Transform Heirs' Property Laws*, The Nation (Sep. 25, 2019), https://www.thenation.com/article/archive/heirs-property-reform/; Lidya Hu, *Going, Going, Gone: New Tactic by Real Estate Investors Forcing Some New Yorkers from Their Homes*, Spectrum News/NY1 (Mar. 19, 2019), https://www.ny1.com/nyc/all-boroughs/news/2019/03/19/going--going--gone--new-tactic-by-real-estate-investors-forcing-some-new-yorkers-from-their-homes-ny1-investigation.

[8] Most state legislative sessions begin in January, but ending dates vary widely. While a minority of state legislatures work throughout the year, most sessions end in late spring or early summer. The Uniform Law Commission tracks legislative data using a calendar that runs from October 1 through September 30. Therefore, the bills shown to be introduced in the 2011 legislative year were actually introduced between October 1, 2010 and September 30, 2011. Subsequent years on the chart follow the same calendar.

Year	UPHPA Bills Introduced	Enactments
2014	5 – AL, CT, DC, HI, SC	1 – AL
2015	4 – AR, CT, HI, SC	2 – AR, CT
2016	4 – HI, MS, SC, WV	2 – HI, SC
2017	5 – DC, MO, MS, NM, TX	2 – NM, TX
2018	7 – DC, IA, KS, MS, TN, WV, USVI	1 – IA
2019	15 – DC, FL, IL, IN, KS, MA, MO, MS, NE, NJ, NY, OK, VA, WV, USVI	4 – IL, MO, NY, USVI
2020	11 – DC, FL, IN, MA, MS, NE, NJ, NY, OK, VA, WV	3 – FL, MS, VA
2021	7 – CA, DC, KY, IN, MA, NC, NJ, UT	1 – CA
2022	9 – DC, KY, MD, MS, NJ, OK, TN, UT (through April 4)	1 – UT – as of April 4

B. Early Enactments: 2011 to 2014

The UPHPA was approved by the ULC in July 2010, at which point most state legislative sessions had ended for the year. The first three UPHPA bills were introduced in early 2011 but only the bill introduced in Nevada became law. Three introductions for a new uniform act are not a lot, but the modest number was also unsurprising.

As a general rule, most state legislators would rather not be the first to sponsor a bill to adopt a new uniform act on an unfamiliar subject. It is politically safer to let a legislator in another state introduce the act and then monitor its progress to determine whether any powerful interest opposes the bill, or whether any issues arise that necessitate amendments to the uniform language. Once a few states have successfully adopted a new uniform act, legislators are more comfortable that no hidden surprises of this sort will arise.

Immediately after the UPHPA's approval in July 2010, the ULC staff began to create an enactment kit. The contents of the kit are important to the success of a uniform act. The fact sheet, summary, or talking points contained in the enactment kit may be the only things many legislators read on the subject. Therefore, the kit materials are designed to be clear, succinct, and persuasive.

Two Nevada uniform law commissioners were instrumental in passing the UPHPA. Commissioner Terry Care was the chair of the ULC's Legislative Council, the body of commissioners that oversees the national effort to enact uniform laws. In that capacity, he had studied the UPHPA and was familiar with its purpose. Commissioner Care was also a well-known and respected former Nevada state senator with a long history of being able to secure introductions of uniform acts. Commissioner Richard Segerblom served in the Nevada Assembly in 2011 and signed on as the primary sponsor of the UPHPA bill.

Commissioner Care took the lead and testified in favor of the bill at the committee hearings of both houses. He had a clear and persuasive story to tell, relating the history of his own family's ranch and the emotional attachment that tied his family members to the land. He described the problems the legislation would solve. He diffused potential objections by addressing them before the questions were even asked. The Nevada commissioners' careful preparation and strong testimony combined with the lack of any opposition resulted in the UPHPA's first enactment. The governor signed the UPHPA into law on May 20, 2011.[9]

In 2012, the UPHPA was introduced in Georgia and South Carolina—two states with a history of exploitative partition sales. Although there were HPRC members in each state who were eager to have their states enact the UPHPA into law, only in Georgia did the UPHPA become law.[10] The success in Georgia resulted from the fact that a very well-organized and coordinated coalition of grassroots and "grasstop" organizations, mostly consisting of people from Georgia but with some national representatives as well, mapped out and executed a very smart plan to secure enactment.

In 2013, the UPHPA was introduced in five jurisdictions. The adoptions in Nevada and Georgia proved that the uniform act was viable, and advocates could point to those successes when seeking sponsors for a UPHPA bill. For the third straight year, only one UPHPA bill was enacted into law, this time in Montana.

Montana's UPHPA enactment was spearheaded by a local citizen whose family owned a ranch. After a dispute between cotenants threatened the family's continued ownership, one of the family members asked her representative in the Montana Senate, Kendall Van Dyk, to sponsor a bill that would alter the law governing tenancies in common.

Senator Van Dyk listened and wanted to help his constituent. The senator's staff and the constituent decided to investigate what other states had done regarding this issue, and that led to their discovery of the UPHPA. Senator Van Dyk introduced a bill to enact the Montana Uniform Partition of Heirs Property Act in January 2013.

ULC staff then began lining up potential supporters. Senator Van Dyk's constituent was prepared to testify in favor of the bill, but other local supporters were hard to find. Fortunately, one local real estate attorney knew all about partition actions and the UPHPA. David Dietrich from Billings, Montana, had co-chaired the Property Preservation Task Force for the American Bar Association's RPTE Section to develop legal strategies to assist heirs' property owners. In fact, Mr. Dietrich spearheaded the early efforts to convince the ULC to draft a uniform law governing the partition of heirs' property. He understood that the UPHPA would improve upon Montana's current partition law and would benefit all owners of heirs' property in the state. Just as importantly, Mr. Dietrich understood Montana politics.

As discussed in chapter 7, Mr. Dietrich helped develop a winning strategy by emphasizing the UPHPA's protection of individual property rights. Mr. Dietrich argued that Montana heirs' property owners would benefit from the UPHPA because of the act's requirement for an independent appraisal of the property and its open-market sale provisions that substantially increase the likelihood of cotenants receiving proceeds commensurate with the fair market value of their property. He stressed how the act works to preserve family-owned real estate by removing the real estate speculator's profit incentive without infringing on any cotenant's right to sell his or her share of the property.

---

[9] A.B. 244, 76th Leg., 26th Spec. Sess., 2011 Nev. Stat. 309.

[10] H.B. 744, 151st Gen. Assemb., Reg. Sess., 2012 Ga. Laws 97.

The argument appealed to both Republican and Democratic members of the legislature. The UPHPA passed the Montana Senate unanimously and passed the House with only one dissenting vote. Montana became the third state to enact the UPHPA when the governor signed the bill on April 22, 2013.[11]

In 2014 the UPHPA was introduced in Alabama, and reintroduced in four other states. For the fourth consecutive year, only one of the bills was signed into law, and it was the newest introduction, in Alabama. Alabama is one of a handful of states with a governmental agency tasked to review statutory law and make recommendations for revision to the legislature.[12] The Alabama Law Institute (ALI) was created by the Alabama Legislature in 1967 for that purpose.

In the states that have law revision agencies, a committee composed of volunteer lawyers and agency staff will often study new uniform acts and make a recommendation to the legislature as to the act's relevance, how it relates to current state law, and its appropriateness for the particular state. If utilized, this process can, on the one hand, create an extra hurdle before a uniform act can be adopted into law. On the other hand, a favorable recommendation from the state law revision commission on a proposed uniform law usually means the legislation will be enacted without controversy or much debate. Consequently, ALI approval is crucial for enacting uniform legislation in Alabama.

ULC Commissioner Robert McCurley was ALI director from 1975 to 2012 and began serving as a uniform law commissioner in 1993. By coincidence, in 2007 McCurley was also appointed by the ULC president to chair the newly formed committee to draft a "Uniform Tenancy-in-Common Partition Act" (later to be renamed the UPHPA). Commissioner McCurley presided over the UPHPA drafting committee meetings for three years as the committee debated the various provisions of the uniform act. Naturally, he strongly supported enactment of the resulting UPHPA in his home state.

After the UPHPA was approved by the ULC in 2010, the ALI began to study the new uniform act for possible adoption in Alabama. The ALI committee concluded its review in 2013 and recommended adoption of the UPHPA by the legislature. Largely as a result of the ALI's favorable recommendation, a UPHPA bill was introduced in the Alabama Senate. The bill passed both houses of the legislature with no opposition and became the fourth enactment of the UPHPA when Governor Bentley signed the legislation in April 2014.[13]

To review, in the first four years following its approval by the ULC, the UPHPA was enacted in only one state each year: Nevada, Georgia, Montana, and Alabama in that order. The act was starting to gain attention from legislators in other states. Fortunately, there were no evident problems with the law in the adopting states and some early indications that the law was working as intended to reduce the number of forced partition sales and help families retain their real estate.

---

[11] S.B. 207, 63rd Leg., Reg. Sess., 2013 Mont. Laws 913.

[12] Other similar state agencies include the California Law Revision Commission, the Louisiana State Law Institute, the New Jersey Law Revision Commission, the New York Law Revision Commission, and the Oregon Law Commission. These bodies, often affiliated with an in-state law school, provide legal research and technical expertise for complex or highly specialized legislation. They also ensure that proposed legislation will not conflict with any existing laws and recommend conforming updates to a state's statutory code.

[13] S.B. 162, 2014 Leg., Reg. Sess., 2014 Ala. Laws 1080.

C. Building Momentum: 2015 to 2018

In 2015, UPHPA legislation was introduced in Arkansas for the first time and reintroduced in three other states. For the first time since the act's approval in 2010, multiple states adopted a UPHPA law in 2015 when the Arkansas and Connecticut bills crossed the finish line. Although the Arkansas bill passed in the year it was first introduced, one person in particular had been laying the groundwork for enactment since at least 2013. Dr. Karama Neal is a geneticist and bioethicist who serves in the US Department of Agriculture promoting rural development. The work Dr. Neal did in Arkansas, together with the efforts of certain Arkansas uniform law commissioners and the lobbyist for the Arkansas Bar Association, is detailed in chapter 4 of this book, which she coauthored with John Pollock. These efforts proved successful, and Governor Asa Hutchinson signed the legislation in February 2015, making Arkansas the fifth state to adopt the UPHPA.[14]

Meanwhile, another multi-year effort was about to bear fruit. Connecticut's delegation of uniform law commissioners had worked with the Connecticut Bar Association to introduce a UPHPA bill beginning in 2013. Although there was no serious opposition, the issue was obscure, and the bill was not prioritized in a busy legislative session. The following year, the Connecticut UPHPA bill received a hearing and was passed by the house, but the session ended with the bill still awaiting consideration in the senate. Finally, in 2015 the UPHPA legislation passed both houses of the Connecticut General Assembly and was signed by Governor Malloy in July.[15]

In 2016, UPHPA legislation was reintroduced in Hawaii and South Carolina, and introduced for the first time in Mississippi and West Virginia. The former two states had attempted to adopt the UPHPA in each of the previous three legislative sessions without success—but that was about to change. The obstacles to enactment in Hawaii and South Carolina were similar, and arose from an unanticipated source. Court administrators in both states objected to the UPHPA because they said it imposed additional burdens on their office without any additional appropriation of state funds.

At a surface level, this argument has some appeal. Compared to a partition action under existing laws, actions under the UPHPA required some additional procedures. However, when one digs deeper, it is far from clear that the UPHPA creates more burdens for court administrators taking into account partition actions in the aggregate. In the states where the UPHPA had already been adopted, evidence showed that the overall number of partition actions declined after enactment, which could offset some of the anticipated additional administrative costs for each case by reducing the overall number of partition cases the court had to hear. Regardless of whether the administrators' concerns over their workload were justified, their representatives in both Hawaii and South Carolina were successful in blocking passage of the UPHPA in the three previous legislative sessions. Political realities required a change in tactics.

After consulting with the ULC and the UPHPA's reporter, Professor Mitchell, the Hawaii bill sponsor's legislative staff began to negotiate with the state court administrators. Most of the extra duties identified by the administrators involved sending notice of various events to the parties to a partition action. The solution was to shift the noticing duty from the court administrators to a "special master," a person appointed by the court to "fulfill the notice requirements pursuant to this

[14] H.B. 1245, 90th Gen. Assemb., Reg. Sess., 2015 Ark. Acts 434.

[15] S.B. 900, 2015 Leg., Reg Sess., 2015 Conn. Acts 1033 (Reg. Sess.).

chapter" that would otherwise fall to the office of court administration.[16] The statute specifies that "[t]he costs of the services of the special master and the expenses of the notices shall be paid by the cotenants at the conclusion of the partition action; provided that the court may in its discretion order the payment of costs and expenses from the estate of the deceased, the proceeds of the partition by sale, the cotenants, or a combination thereof."[17] With that relatively minor change in allocation of the noticing responsibilities, the court administrators dropped their opposition and Hawaii adopted the UPHPA in July 2016.[18]

Meanwhile in South Carolina, political pressures favoring passage of the UPHPA were building. The story of the South Carolina adoption, including the bill's tribute to Senator Clementa C. Pinckney, who was murdered along with eight of his parishioners in the Mother Emmanuel AME Church in Charleston, where Senator Pinckney served as a senior pastor, is told in chapter 4. The 2016 version of the bill included amendments similar to those in the Hawaii bill, shifting some responsibilities away from the office of court administration. With the administrators' concerns satisfied, the tribute bill was quickly passed and signed into law by Governor Haley in April 2016, bringing the total number of UPHPA states to eight. The South Carolina act, an act that appears to be providing vital assistance to heirs' property owners based on feedback from a number of sources in the state, serves as an enduring legacy to Reverend Pinckney.[19]

In 2017, four more states and the District of Columbia introduced UPHPA bills, two of which were enacted. The UPHPA passed in New Mexico without controversy.[20] The process was more difficult in Texas, where the State Bar of Texas's Real Estate, Probate & Trust Law (REPTL) Section initially seemed as if it might oppose the UPHPA based on an incorrect understanding of its effects. After Professor Mitchell met with the leadership of the real property bar to review the legislation in detail, REPTL decided against opposing the UPHPA and took a neutral position instead. It also helped that the House sponsor was a Republican from rural Texas and that the Senate sponsor was a Democrat from Dallas. An African American family from rural Texas provided compelling testimony at the hearing, as did Professor Mitchell. In the end, the UPHPA bills were passed unanimously in both chambers of the legislature and Governor Abbott signed the UPHPA into law.[21]

In 2018, a then-record seven jurisdictions considered the UPHPA. Only the Iowa bill was signed into law.[22] Its passage was significant, however, because Iowa had a relatively new partition statute that explicitly made court-ordered partition *sale* the preferred remedy. It was one of the very few states that did not have a statutory preference for partition in kind. That statute led to an Iowa Supreme Court case in which the court affirmed a trial court decision ordering a partition sale of a nearly 500-acre farm owned by a brother and sister as tenants in common against the wishes of the sister, who was operating the farm without her brother's involvement. The Iowa decision set off a

---

[16] Haw. Rev. Stat. Ann. § 668A-6 (West 2017).

[17] *Id.*

[18] S.B. 2408, 28th Leg., Reg. Sess., 2016 Haw. Sess. Laws 829.

[19] H.3325, 121st Gen. Assemb., Reg. Sess., 2016 S. C. Acts 1261.

[20] H.B. 181, 52nd Leg., 2017 N.M. Laws 395.

[21] S.B. 499, 85th Leg., Reg. Sess., 2017 Tex. Gen. Laws 572.

[22] S.F. 2175, 87th Gen. Assemb., Reg. Sess., 2018 Iowa Acts 268.

firestorm of anger among the Iowa farming community, which unexpectedly created an opening for consideration of the UPHPA, referred to as the "Save the Family Farm Act" by its supporters.

A new objection to the UPHPA was raised in Kansas and West Virginia. Representatives from the oil and gas industry opposed the UPHPA in those states because oil producers sometimes use partition actions to force a sale of land when some cotenants oppose exploration or production. They correctly determined that the UPHPA could prevent them from acquiring development rights in some cases.

Once the issues were revealed, the ULC legislative staff, in consultation with Professor Mitchell, attempted to negotiate with representatives of the Kansas and West Virginia oil producers. They drafted a set of proposed amendments that would carve out an exception from the UPHPA for severed mineral estates. In theory, the UPHPA rules would govern partition of the surface estate, but more lenient partition rules would apply to mineral estates. Though no satisfactory compromise has yet been achieved, attempts to pass bills are expected to continue in both states.

To sum up, after only four states adopted the UPHPA in the first four years following its approval, seven states adopted the act in the next four years, bringing the total number of enactments to eleven by 2018. Proponents of the UPHPA were able to overcome actual or threatened opposition from state bar associations and court administrators in some states, learning along the way which arguments were most convincing and could apply in other states. We also learned about the interaction of partition law with oil and gas law, and began to strategize about overcoming industry objections.

D. The Dam Bursts: 2019 to the Present

The Agriculture Improvement Act of 2018, which President Trump signed into law that December, contains certain provisions that specifically reference the UPHPA and provide states with additional incentives for enactment. The following year, fifteen jurisdictions introduced bills to enact the UPHPA. Some of these were directly attributable to the new federal law. Advocates for farmers drove the main legislative effort in Illinois, Nebraska, and Mississippi. However, other bills were either previously in the works or compelled by events other than the federal legislation. The 2019 New York legislation,[23] discussed in chapter 3, is particularly important because it made clear that partition abuse affecting heirs' property owners is not simply a rural phenomenon, as many heirs' property advocates had assumed, but it is also an issue faced by disadvantaged heirs' property owners in metropolitan areas.

Ultimately, four of the fifteen UPHPA bills were enacted in 2019: Illinois, Missouri, New York, and the US Virgin Islands. The first two enactments, both in states with significant farm economies, were influenced to various degrees by the 2018 Farm Bill. In Illinois, the Illinois Farm Bureau championed the effort to get the UPHPA enacted into law.[24] In Missouri, the sponsor officially renamed the UPHPA the "Save the Family Farm Act," following the lead of Iowa supporters, and the Missouri Farm Bureau testified in favor of the bill. The branding proved effective when the bill passed both houses of the legislature with strong support and was signed into law later that same month.[25] It also helped that the primary sponsor was a state senator from the majority Republican caucus.

[23] S. 4865-A, 242nd Leg., Reg. Sess., 2019 N.Y. Sess. Laws 1579 (McKinney).

[24] H.B. 3677, 101st Gen. Assemb., Reg. Sess. (Ill. 2019).

[25] S.B. 83, 100th Gen. Assemb., 1st Reg. Sess., 2019 Mo. Laws 586.

The enactment experience in the US Virgin Islands reinforced the need to build a ground game to support efforts to get a bill enacted into law in any particular jurisdiction. In contrast to the failed effort to pass the UPHPA in 2011, the 2018 bill was reintroduced as part of a legislative package with three other uniform property acts.[26] The package was viewed in part as a needed reform of the territory's property law and there was strong local support for the package. AARP's Virgin Islands chapter strongly supported the package and Professor Mitchell was able to secure important local support for the UPHPA from some leading local nonprofit organizations and government officials.

In 2020, there were eleven UPHPA bills introduced, three of which were enacted. The Florida[27] and Virginia[28] enactments are discussed in detail in chapter 4. In Mississippi, the act had been introduced four times previously but had failed each time. Although many families in Mississippi own heirs' property, and though there had been some local support for the UPHPA prior to 2020, enactment prospects for the UPHPA were poor until the Mississippi Farm Bureau lent its lobbying resources to the cause because of the incentives contained in the 2018 federal Farm Bill. The farm bureau's robust support as the primary champion made the UPHPA a bipartisan bill that was quickly passed and signed into law.[29]

2021 was not quite as successful, in part because many legislatures held abbreviated sessions due to the COVID pandemic. The UPHPA was introduced in seven states plus the District of Columbia, but only the California bill was enacted. In making an exception to its longstanding policy against endorsing state legislation, including uniform acts, the American Land Title Association endorsed the UPHPA in January 2021. The California Association of REALTORS® took the lead in promoting the UPHPA in the California legislature and the Massachusetts REALTORS, Maryland REALTORS, and North Carolina REALTORS endorsed UPHPA bills in their respective states.

At the time this book went to publication, 2022 was off to a roaring start with UPHPA bills introduced in eight states and the District of Columbia.

V. CONCLUSION: ENACTMENT LESSONS LEARNED

The enactment history for the UPHPA shows a steady progression of increasing success. When the act was first approved, its reforms to the partition process were perceived by many as novel—even radical—and untested. But as the problem of predatory partition sales received more attention, more state legislators saw the UPHPA as a potential solution and were willing to consider its enactment.

This is not to say that the increasing acceptance of the UPHPA happened organically. The various organizations that comprised the Heirs' Property Retention Coalition, the Uniform Law Commission, law reform advocates, Professor Mitchell, environmental activists, antipoverty activists, and the many owners of inherited property continuously beat the drum for reform. Professor Mitchell's decades of research into land loss also gave all of those advocating for the UPHPA the ammunition necessary to make their case. His willingness to share his expertise through media interviews, with many state and federal elected officials and other policy makers, with many advocacy and trade associations, and at

---

[26] B. 32-0327, 32nd Leg., Reg. Sess. (V.I. 2018) (included the UNIFORM CUSTODIAL TRUST ACT, THE UNIFORM DISCLAIMER OF PROPERTY INTERESTS ACT, THE UNIFORM REAL PROPERTY TRANSFER ON DEATH ACT, and the UNIFORM PARTITION OF HEIRS PROPERTY ACT).

[27] C.S.C.S.S.B. 580, 26th Leg., Reg. Sess., 2020 Fla. Laws 538.

[28] H.B. 1605, 2020 Gen. Assemb., Reg. Sess. (Va. 2020).

[29] S.B. 2553, 2020 Leg., Reg. Sess. (Miss. 2020).

legislative hearings as the national expert on partition reform has been essential in raising the profile of this issue generally and of the UPHPA in particular. The twenty hard-won enactments are largely due to the tireless advocacy of the people who cared enough to fight for them.

Our work to enact the UPHPA in every state continues. We hope future advocates for the UPHPA can benefit from the lessons learned over the past ten years, which we now attempt to list:

1. **Law reform is a multi-year process.** Don't be discouraged if a bill fails to pass the first time. As shown by the experience in Hawaii, Mississippi, and South Carolina, persistence pays off in the long run.
2. **Build a coalition of mainly in-state stakeholders.** Lawmakers serve the needs of their constituents. Where matters of state law are concerned, it is vital to have motivated in-state advocates for any particular law reform measure.
3. **Do not reinvent the wheel.** Seek to learn from successful enactment efforts in other states and consider consulting or working with out-of-state national experts to access their expertise and duplicate their results.
4. **Know your audience.** All of the following arguments in support of the UPHPA are 100 percent true: The UPHPA advances racial justice. The UPHPA protects individual property rights by preventing court-ordered sales. The UPHPA helps families who own property in both rural and urban environments. Enactment of the UPHPA will provide farmers and ranchers who own heirs' property with improved access to many vital US Department of Agriculture programs. Frame your arguments to appeal to those who wield the political power in a given state.
5. **Support can come from many sources.** Depending on the state, advocates for the UPHPA have included but have not been limited to environmental groups, farm bureaus, public interest law firms, the overall state bar, the real property bar, the trust and estate bar, civil rights activists, state uniform law commissioners, community development and fair housing organizations, realtors, law professors and university-based extension personnel, organizations that advocate for senior citizens, deed recorders, and individual heirs from all walks of life. Some might call them strange bedfellows, but all of them have helped get the UPHPA adopted into law.
6. **Talk to your opponents.** Identify their concerns and look for common ground. Try to find a way to resolve their issues without undermining your own goals.
7. **Be flexible.** Every state is different. Court procedures vary widely. Keep the main goals of your legislation in mind at all times but be ready to adapt your bill as needed to accommodate local customs.

It is difficult to measure the impact of this historic legislation, in part because a major effect of its enactment is to discourage the filing of abusive partition actions, and one cannot count the number of cases that are *not* filed. Suffice to say that many thousands of heirs' property owners now benefit from the UPHPA's enhanced protection of their property interests. The amount of family wealth retained because of the UPHPA will also be difficult to measure, but its effects will be felt by the future generations who will not be born into poverty, who will not have to support their parents and grandparents financially, and who will grow up realizing all the financial and other benefits of owning their real estate.

3

Taking the Uniform Partition of Heirs Property Act (UPHPA) out of the Rural Context and Strengthening It: The New York Experience and a Framework for UPHPA Advocacy

—K. Scott Kohanowski

I. INTRODUCTION: TARGETING OF HEIRS' PROPERTY

Mr. Wilson called the City Bar Justice Center's (CBJC's) civil legal hotline in 2015 because his childhood home that he continued to occupy had been targeted by speculators.[1] Mr. Wilson was 71 years old, lived alone, and was estranged from his siblings, but he was deeply enmeshed in his lifelong community in Jackson Heights, a neighborhood in Queens, New York, that has experienced rapid gentrification in recent years. As an elderly, openly gay, African American man, his neighbors and local church were the extended family that substituted for the problematic relationship Mr. Wilson had with his brothers—both of whom resided out of state and lived with medical conditions that strained their finances.

Mr. Wilson's parents had attempted to structure the ownership of the family home so that their children would always have a safe and secure place to live. While still living, his parents recorded

[1] Pseudonyms are used to protect privacy but the underlying narrative and facts are true.

a deed that transferred the family home to their three sons to hold as joint tenants with right of survivorship. The understanding was that any child could live in the home, and when that child passed, their interest would merge into the survivors' interests. Such an arrangement, however, is dependent on the continuing good faith of each of the joint owners. A defining feature of joint tenancy with right of survivorship is that any co-owner can convert the joint tenancy to tenancy in common, and transfer or encumber their individual interest.

The speculators had been canvassing Mr. Wilson's neighborhood for investment opportunities because property values in Jackson Heights had increased considerably in the decades prior. They learned that Mr. Wilson had a strained relationship with his brothers and trouble keeping up with property expenses. They located the brothers and purchased their fractional interests for an amount significantly below market value. The brothers were an easy target because of their poor health, financial situation, and antagonistic relationship with Mr. Wilson. The speculators then approached Mr. Wilson and offered to purchase his remaining interest for approximately 25 percent of its true value. They threatened to bring a costly partition action—a lawsuit forcing the sale or division of the family property—if he refused their offer.

Gentrification had reached Mr. Wilson's neighborhood like it had in other predominantly minority parts of the city such as Harlem in Manhattan and Bedford-Stuyvesant in Brooklyn. New York City continued to experience a housing shortage that drove up prices throughout the city, especially in areas that had been artificially suppressed in the past. Historically Black neighborhoods had been subject to redlining and other discriminatory real estate practices that restricted market forces and concentrated poverty.[2] When redlining was a common practice, redlined homes were regularly underappraised and could not be purchased with conventional financing. Such a home valued at $30,000 in the 1960s could now be worth a million dollars or multiples thereof. Although the Fair Housing Act (Title VIII of the Civil Rights Act of 1968) barred the more obvious forms of discriminatory practices, many homes in these stately neighborhoods are a legacy of such practices, and the effects are still being felt.

Mr. Wilson's home, like many others in previously redlined areas, was unmortgaged because his and other African American families were largely locked out of federal lending programs. Other owners of these redlined homes were subject to nontraditional lending practices, often predatory in nature. Additionally, the original owners often could not afford or otherwise access quality estate planning services to ensure the smooth transfer of real property to subsequent generations. A common result in these situations is that a home with significant equity—sometimes in the millions—is owned by the heirs of the original title holder, either by operation of law or some inartful arrangement. Many of these homes are still occupied by one or more of the heirs and are ripe for speculation by investors taking advantage of old, intrafamily animosities; nonoccupant heirs who are unaware of the value of their interest or who are simply disinterested; and a lack of access to affordable, quality legal counsel, and limited financial means.

Mr. Wilson's case was referred to me because I direct the Homeowner Stability and LGBT Advocacy projects at the CBJC, and there are scant services available for these nuanced legal issues, especially those that involve inheritance rights. The CBJC, in addition to operating the largest free

[2] *See A 'Forgotten History' of How the U.S. Government Segregated America* (NPR broadcast May 3, 2017, 12:47 PM), https://www.npr.org/2017/05/03/526655831/a-forgotten-history-of-how-the-u-s-government-segregated-america.

civil legal services hotline in New York City, runs a dozen pro bono projects designed to bridge the justice gap by leveraging the resources of the private bar to address unmet legal needs of the underserved.[3] Our homeowner stability work is primarily focused on foreclosure defense and resolution of title issues that may threaten the housing of city residents; we are also focused on deceptive and fraudulent business practices that can result in the displacement of low-income homeowners. I had never seen a case like Mr. Wilson's and was shocked to learn that existing partition law could be artfully employed to strip equity from a family property, rendering lifelong occupants homeless and cut off from their close-knit communities.

II. THE INEQUITIES OF TRADITIONAL PARTITION LAW

Partition law in New York was largely a common law legacy of feudal estates in old England and is very rigid in its process. Any fractional owner had an absolute right to a partition of jointly held property.[4] The preexisting partition law of many states, including New York,[5] contains an express stated preference for partition in kind; but in practice, partition by sale is readily granted. Partition in kind generally is more appropriate for large, undeveloped parcels outside of urban areas. For example, if two siblings inherit a 100-acre farm, a court can easily divide the 100 acres into two parts and allocate a 50-acre parcel to each sibling with minimal damage to the property value. Partition in kind, however, is largely impossible when the value of the real property is the improvement on the land, such as a Harlem brownstone worth many millions of dollars or a parcel that is too small to divide. A court cannot easily divide a home or small parcel into two parts and allocate a portion to each heir without drastically diminishing the value of the real property. The home must therefore be partitioned by judicial sale so that each sibling can recover their share of the net monetary value of the home. As we know from the foreclosure context, forced judicial sale results in a transfer of the property at a significant discount compared with property sold at an arm's length, brokered sale outside of the judicial process.[6]

While partition is an action in equity, the court is limited in its review of the equities and is focused on which party has benefited from the use of the property.[7] The traditional analysis is not whether the court should permit a partition of the home—which is an absolute right—but how to allocate the proceeds if the home is partitioned by sale. This prevalent view of the law heavily disfavors any heir occupant because they have often been living in the home for decades, if not their whole life. Anyone who has lived elsewhere for some or all of that time, including the purchaser of that individual's interest, receives a substantial economic benefit for their lack of use and enjoyment, as explained below—even in those instances when such a cotenant chose not to use or otherwise enjoy the home. Comparable rental values in New York City, which are some of the highest in the

[3] *See* City Bar Justice Center, https://www.citybarjusticecenter.org/ (last visited Mar. 2, 2021).

[4] It excluded tenancy by the entirety because of the protected status of property acquired jointly during a marriage.

[5] N.Y. Real Prop. Acts. Law § 901 (Consol.).

[6] *See* Thomas W. Mitchell, Stephen Malpezzi & Richard K. Green, *Forced Sale Risk: Class, Race, and the "Double Discount,"* 37 Fla. St. U. L. Rev. 589, 603–06 (2010).

[7] *See* Bentley v. Dox, 785 N.Y.S.2d 253, 254 (2004) (quoting Grossman v. Baker, 583 N.Y.S.2d (1992)) ("[T]he right to partition is . . . absolute in the absence of countervailing conditions . . . [and therefore] such issues as the interests of the parties and whether partition may be had without great prejudice should first be determined.").

nation, may be deducted from the occupants' share of the proceeds for the period that they had use of the home to the exclusion of other parties. This prevailing analysis of partition law often results in the heir occupants not only being displaced from their childhood homes but also receiving a drastically reduced share of already diminished sale proceeds. This minimizes and fails to recognize the extent of caretaking and upkeep that the occupants have had to sustain over decades—including preventing the problems associated with abandoned and vacant properties, such as vandalism, neglect, and other waste of the property.

Mr. Wilson did not have the resources on his own to mount a legal defense against a well-funded speculator, and he was exhausted and demoralized from the aggressive investor tactics. We assisted Mr. Wilson in negotiating a transfer of his remaining one-third tenancy-in-common interest for more than he was initially offered, but for far less than he would have received if the property had been sold in a brokered, arm's-length transaction. Mr. Wilson used the funds to relocate to a rental apartment in a different area of the city so he could move on with his life. Even if he had mounted a defense, it is unlikely that he would have received more proceeds following the forced judicial sale because of his lifelong use and occupancy and the depressed value obtained at a forced judicial sale. The speculator, on the other hand, obtained a high-valued property in a rapidly gentrifying part of the city for approximately $400,000. The home sold the following year to another investor for $950,000 and now two years later, has a market value estimated at approximately $1,200,000. The speculator succeeded in stripping at least $500,000 of accumulated equity from the family home, and the sole remaining heir occupant is now living in a modest apartment experiencing difficulties maintaining his monthly rental expenses.

III. CONTINUING EFFECTS OF HISTORIC RACIST HOUSING POLICY

The foreclosure crisis—which hit its peak in 2010 when banks seized more than 1 million homes and the number of foreclosure filings reached a record 2.9 million[8]—has had a lasting impact on low-income Americans. While wealthy Americans were able to recover from the Great Recession by 2013, many poor families have still not been able to recover economically from the crisis that began more than a decade ago.[9] Recovery has been particularly difficult for Black families, who were targeted by subprime mortgage lenders during the crisis and who saw their wealth continue to decline as white families stabilized in the years following the crisis,[10] contributing to a further decrease in homeownership.[11] Black and Brown communities have also been disproportionately impacted by

[8] Corbett B. Daly, *Home Foreclosures in 2010 Top 1 Million for First Time*, Reuters (Jan. 13, 2011, 12:21 AM), https://www.reuters.com/article/us-usa-housing-foreclosures/home-foreclosures-in-2010-top-1-million-for-firsttime-idUSTRE70C0YD20110113.

[9] "The average household income of the bottom 20 percent of Americans fell $571 between 2006 and 2016, according to Census data, while for the top 20 percent of Americans it grew by $13,749." Alana Semuels, *The Never-Ending Foreclosure*, The Atlantic (Dec. 1, 2017), https://www.theatlantic.com/business/archive/2017/12/the-neverending-foreclosure/547181/.

[10] Tracy Jan, *White Families Have Nearly 10 Times the Net Worth of Black Families. And the Gap Is Growing*, Wash. Post (Sept. 28, 2017, 7:00 AM), https://www.washingtonpost.com/news/wonk/wp/2017/09/28/black-and-hispanic-families-are-making-more-money-but-they-still-lag-far-behind-whites/.

[11] Troy McMullen, *The "Heartbreaking" Decrease in Black Homeownership*, Wash. Post (Feb. 28, 2019), https://www.washingtonpost.com/news/business/wp/2019/02/28/feature/the-heartbreaking-decrease-in-black-homeownership/.

the COVID-19 pandemic.[12] While Black families have made some economic gains in recent years, research shows that the racial wealth gap is growing, rather than shrinking.[13] Meanwhile, property values in rapidly gentrifying urban areas such as New York City have increased exponentially, leaving many homeowners in these communities asset rich and income poor.[14] Low- to moderate-income homeowners find themselves in a precarious position because housing expenses such as property taxes, utilities, and insurance rates have outpaced income growth.[15]

About a year after we assisted Mr. Wilson, an elderly African American woman from another part of Queens reached out to the CBJC's Planning and Estates Law Project. Ms. Jones had lived in her home since she was five months old, when her mother moved them into the house that her grandmother and aunts had purchased together in 1946. She lived in the upstairs of the house, taking care of her disabled veteran cousin, while two other cousins lived on the first floor. Ms. Jones initially reached out to the CBJC for assistance petitioning for letters of administration for the estate of her mother who had passed intestate. We learned during the course of that assistance that her family home was being targeted by the same speculator who had successfully targeted Mr. Wilson.

When Ms. Jones's grandmother passed away in 1961, title was transferred to her four children, who all lived in the home. The most recent deed of record remained in the name of Ms. Jones's mother, aunts, and uncle—all of whom had since passed intestate with multiple heirs dispersed widely. The speculator had initially approached Ms. Jones to purchase her fractional intestate interest and she declined. He then located the nonoccupant heirs, purchased their shares for an amount significantly below market value, and commenced a partition action naming Ms. Jones as defendant. Ms. Jones's sole source of income is social security retirement, and the speculator was counting on her lack of financial resources and access to quality legal counsel to realize a significant profit on his investment. The speculator also employed aggressive and threatening tactics in an attempt to intimidate Ms. Jones into leaving her home, including changing the locks on common areas of the house that restricted access to necessary mechanical equipment and electric boxes.

New York City, like many urban areas, is home to a high-priced real estate market, rapid gentrification, an aging population, and residents who lack access to financial and legal assistance. These factors create an environment ripe for opportunistic and outright deceptive real estate practices. New York has a robust network of legal service organizations providing assistance to stabilize homeownership. These services are primarily residential mortgage foreclosure defense but include deed theft and

[12] *See* Amara Omeokwe, *Coronavirus Pandemic Threatens to Widen Racial Homeownership Gap*, Wall St. J. (Sept. 20, 2020, 11:00 AM), https://www.wsj.com/articles/coronavirus-pandemic-threatens-to-widen-racial-homeownership-gap-11600614000.

[13] *See Neil Bhutta, et al., Disparities in Wealth by Race and Ethnicity in the 2019 Survey of Consumer Finances,* Federal Reserve Board (Sept. 28, 2020), https://www.federalreserve.gov/econres/notes/feds-notes/disparities-in-wealth-by-race-and-ethnicity-in-the-2019-survey-of-consumer-finances-20200928.htm.

[14] *Asset Rich and Cash Poor in Bed-Stuy*, Ctr. N.Y.C. Neighborhoods (Apr. 13, 2015), https://cnycn.org/asset-rich-and-cash-poor-in-bed-stuy/.

[15] In fact, low-income households face the greatest burden in the gap between property tax growth and income growth. From 2005–2016, New York residential property tax has grown at an average rate of 6.4 percent annually, while incomes have grown only by about 2 percent annually. For households making less than $50,000 annually, property tax rates have grown by 98 percent during this time period, while median incomes have declined. These numbers take into account tax credits and other programs designed to reduce property tax burdens on seniors and low-income households. Steven Giachetti & Preston Niblack, *Growing Unfairness: The Rising Burden of Property Taxes on Low-Income Households*, N.Y.C. Comptroller Scott M. Stringer 1, 1–3 (Sept. 2018), https://comptroller.nyc.gov/wp-content/uploads/documents/Property_Taxes_in_New_York_City.pdf.

other forms of predatory and deceptive business practices. Our network of legal service providers and housing counselors are vigilant in trying to identify new forms of predatory real estate activity as they arise, especially within communities of color and the aging.

This newly identified speculative scheme appeared especially insidious because it employed old family grievances; an understandable lack of knowledge in how counterintuitive property law functions; and a facially legitimate legal process that can strip hundreds of thousands, and even millions, of dollars of accumulated intergenerational wealth—while displacing heir occupants from their homes and communities. There was no way of knowing how prevalent this sort of activity is because the New York court system did not track partition cases.[16] It is also unlikely that there is any reported case law, as these matters either settle before a request for judicial intervention is made, or defendants default in appearing because they are unrepresented and unable to navigate a complicated legal process pro se. There is no right to counsel in most civil legal matters and certainly not in partition actions, even when the end result is homelessness of very vulnerable individuals.

IV. A MODEL FOR ADVOCACY AND LAW REFORM

The CBJC recognized the similarities in the investment schemes we were seeing in Black-held heirs property in New York City and an almost identical predatory practice by developers targeting historically Black-held lands in the rural South.[17] The identification of the use of partition law in rural areas to divest families of intergenerational wealth held in real property resulted in the Uniform Law Commission promulgating the Uniform Partition of Heirs Property Act (UPHPA)[18] to mitigate its rigid application. Among the primary issues addressed by the drafters of the UPHPA were (1) problematic partition sales of large tracts of farmland and undeveloped property and (2) perceived disregard by the courts of the factors favoring partition in kind over a partition by sale. While these particular issues are not urban heirs' property issues, the unmodified UPHPA provides a valuable framework to address some of the more inequitable features of existing partition law—whether in the rural or urban context—such as inadequate notice of the action,[19] fair valuation of the property,[20] cotenant buyout,[21] guidance on balancing the equities when partitioning in kind,[22] and an alternative

---

[16] New York trial courts require a Request for Judicial Intervention (RJI) to be completed to assign the case to a judge. The RJI form included a series of boxes to check in order for the case to be assigned to the correct part. There was no box to check for a partition action; it instead required the party completing the RJI to write in the type of action. This information was not trackable—unlike other types of real property cases like residential mortgage foreclosures. A modified form of RJI was introduced effective February 1, 2022.

[17] Kate McGuire, of the CBJC's Planning and Estates Law Project, identified the connection between predatory partition activity in the Gullah Islands of South Carolina and what was happening to the homes occupied by callers to the CBJC's legal helplines.

[18] Nat'l Conf. of Comm'rs. on Unif. St. Laws, Uniform Partition of Heirs Property Act (2010), https://www.uniformlaws.org/HigherLogic/System/DownloadDocumentFile.ashx?DocumentFileKey=2df84a2e-2ad1-1735-2caf-e3536111a141&forceDialog=0 [hereinafter UPHPA].

[19] *Id.* at § 4 (service; notice by posting).

[20] *Id.* at § 6 (determination of value).

[21] *Id.* at § 7 (cotenant buyout).

[22] *Id.* at § 9 (considerations for partition in kind).

to the judicial auction process that better maximizes the sale price if partition by sale is unavoidable.[23] The UPHPA, however, provides little opportunity for unrepresented parties to appear meaningfully in the judicial process; there is no priority or right of first refusal for heirs that occupy the property, no balancing of the equities when determining respective shares or proceeds if partition by sale occurs, and no explicit inclusion of the terms and manner by which the outside investor acquires its interest in the property when balancing the equities. In a perfect world, low-income heir occupants would also have a right to counsel to protect their right to safe, stable, and affordable housing.

Seeking judicial redress or putting in a powerful defense are only some of the tools in an advocate's belt. Litigation can be costly, lengthy, and unpredictable. Whether a favorable settlement or even judgment can be obtained is often dependent on the respective leverage and resources of the parties. Leverage can be obtained by ensuring that the client is well-represented so that the matter can be determined on the merits. The media can also be an effective tool to gain leverage by bringing the matter to the attention of the public, elected officials, other advocates, and the decision makers within an agency or corporate or financial institution, to protect its public image when other forms of escalation fail. Working with the media has the additional benefit of educating the public on new predatory schemes so they can recognize when they are being targeted and learn how to obtain legal assistance.

Ms. Jones was prepared for the long haul on the partition lawsuit brought against her. She was particularly aggrieved by the aggressive nature of the speculators and their brazen attempt to purchase her interest at a significant discount; the speculators believed that she would not know how to defend or advocate for herself. Given the novel nature of the investment scheme, we initially reached out to a local news outlet with wide regional reach and a reputation for investigative journalism involving social justice issues. Investigative reporter Lydia Hu picked up the story and prepared a two-part series that looped over several days, garnering significant attention by the public, local politicians, practitioners, and academics interested in heirs'[24] property issues. The piece explained in layman's terms the nature of this predatory real estate scheme; the existing law that the investors used as a sword to strip wealth from family homes and displace heirs; and the UPHPA, which was designed to address the harsher consequences of existing partition law. She also interviewed Professor Thomas Mitchell of Texas A&M Law School, the principal drafter of the UPHPA and recognized national expert on partition law.

The response to the media coverage was swift and effective. Senator Brad Hoylman and Assembly Member Jeffrey Dinowitz immediately introduced the UPHPA to the New York State Legislature in response to the media coverage. Professor Mitchell and Alan Kolod, chair of the Commercial Law and Uniform State Laws Committee of the New York City Bar Association, reached out to me to coordinate efforts to promote the passage of the UPHPA. We were also able to place Ms. Jones's case for full representation with pro bono counsel at a top-tier, private law firm, thus ensuring that

---

[23] *Id.* at § 10 (open-market sale, sealed bids, or auction). An open market practice—instead of a judicial auction with minimal notice, no right of inspection, and no marketing—builds on the experience in bankruptcy of conducting sales professionally to maximize value with extensive advertising, opportunities for due diligence, and inspection rights.

[24] *See* Lydia Hu, *Going, Going, Gone: New Tactic by Real Estate Investors Forcing Some New Yorkers from Their Homes*, Spectrum News (Mar. 19, 2019, 7:00 AM), https://www.ny1.com/nyc/all-boroughs/news/2019/03/19/going--going--gone--new-tactic-by-real-estate-investors-forcing-some-new-yorkers-from-their-homes-ny1-investigation.

she would have quality legal representation. Sophisticated legal counsel does indeed level the playing field and can effectively distill the underlying issues so that they can be determined on their merits and significantly increase bargaining power.

V. MODIFYING THE UPHPA TO BETTER ADDRESS URBAN HEIRS' PROPERTY

The legislative response was almost too swift, as there were several modifications we wanted to make to the standard UPHPA to make it significantly more useful for all heirs' property owners in New York, such as changes that would better address the specific issues encountered in the urban context. The uniform law, for example, facially excludes Ms. Jones because the definition of heirs' property requires 20 percent or more of the interests to still be held by an heir or some combination of heirs.[25] The investor, or investors, only needed to acquire 80 percent or more of the purported interests to circumvent application of the UPHPA. While Ms. Jones could make out tenancy-in-common adverse possession and constructive trust claims to overcome that threshold,[26] other similarly situated heir occupants may not have such claims or know to plead them. We also wanted to include an alternative dispute resolution (ADR) process, preference for heir occupant buyout, and explicit authority for courts to consider the methods and terms of the investor acquisition of the fractional shares of the property when considering the equities.

Thomas Mitchell, Alan Kolod, and I then prepared a version to address these concerns while maintaining the parts that had particular applicability to rural properties. The latter was important to secure buy-in from legislators representing the large swaths of upstate New York that contain large tracts of farm and undeveloped land. It was also important not to so drastically alter the uniform law that it would no longer be supported by the Uniform Law Commission. Farmers and ranchers who own heirs' property and who are located in states that have adopted the UPHPA are entitled to greater access to certain United States Department of Agriculture (USDA) programs and benefits as compared to otherwise similarly situated farmers and ranchers who are located in states that have not adopted the UPHPA.[27] These expanded benefits include greater access to lending; disaster relief; conservation programs; and a low-interest loan program designed to assist owners of heirs' property to clear title to their property, stabilize their ownership, and facilitate estate planning.

Existing residential mortgage foreclosure procedures in New York provided the framework to adopt an ADR process under the UPHPA. In response to the 2008 foreclosure crisis, New York legislated protections for homeowner defendants, primarily embodied in New York Civil Practice Laws and Rules Section 3408 (NY CPLR 3408). New York has long been a judicial foreclosure state requiring residential mortgage foreclosures to pass through the judicial process. We learned early in the

[25] *See* UPHPA, *supra* note 18, at § 2(5).

[26] Ms. Jones inherited half of her mother's quarter share in the home through the New York laws of intestacy. Her mother, however, had exclusive control over one of the two units in the home for a period of more than twenty years. The other family members made no contributions to the upkeep of the home and allowed Ms. Jones to occupy the home undisturbed; and as such, they held their interests in constructive trust for the benefit of Ms. Jones.

[27] Thomas W. Mitchell, *Historic Partition Law Reform: A Game Changer for Heirs' Property Owners*, *in* HEIRS' PROPERTY AND LAND FRACTIONATION: FOSTERING STABLE OWNERSHIP TO PREVENT LAND LOSS AND ABANDONMENT 65, 78–81 (Cassandra Johnson Gaither, Ann Carpenter, Tracy Lloyd McCurty, & Sara Toering eds., 2019), https://www.srs.fs.usda.gov/pubs/gtr/gtr_srs244.pdf.

crisis, however, that most defendants were unable to obtain counsel and protect their homes even if they had significant defenses and counterclaims. These defenses and claims often arose from the origination of the loans and involved predatory and subprime lending practices and assignment of the loans to the secondary market. A series of legislative enactments provided homeowner defendants with significant protections—most significantly, a court-monitored settlement conference process to bring the parties together to engage in good-faith negotiations to avoid the unnecessary foreclosure of the home. During these conferences, all motions are held in abeyance, a court-appointed referee oversees the negotiations, pro se defendants are given an opportunity to locate counsel to help them navigate a complicated procedural landscape, and the parties can argue their respective claims and defenses in reaching a settlement.

New York subsequently revised NY CPLR 3408 to give defendants a second opportunity to plead their defenses and claims. If a foreclosure defendant failed to answer within the standard timeframes required under the NY CPLR, they would now have an additional 30 days following the initial settlement conference to do so. It had become apparent that most pro se defendants did not understand how to answer a summons and complaint within the very strict timeframe under the NY CPLR.[28] They were defaulting at exceedingly high rates, inadvertently losing critical defenses, such as whether the plaintiff had standing to bring the action by proving it owned the underlying mortgage debt. Pro se defendants, however, were responding to simple notices that they must appear at the courthouse at a specific time and date to attend the settlement conferences. The appearance at a settlement conference is typically the first time the defendants interact with the courts during the course of the lawsuit and the first opportunity to empower the defendants to save their homes from unnecessary foreclosure. The legislative fix not only allowed the defendants a second opportunity to answer the complaint, but it required the court to advise the defendant of their extended right to answer. It was also another opportunity to inform pro se defendants of the availability of free legal services to assist in doing so. This legislative fix furthers the initial purpose of the foreclosure prevention legislation to avoid unnecessary foreclosures by resulting in a greater number of cases being determined on their merits versus default.

There are many parallels between defendants in residential foreclosure matters before the enactment of NY CPLR 3408 and the types of defendants we were seeing in these predatory partition actions. Most of the defendants had low to moderate income, had limited access to quality legal counsel, and were attempting to navigate a complex legal process while unrepresented. As a direct result of these factors, many had defenses and counterclaims that were not raised, resulting in the lawsuits being determined on default. Communities of color are disproportionately impacted by foreclosure and this predatory activity. There are clear reasons why public policy must address the issue of stable housing. Mediating the positions and differences of opposing parties in these kinds of cases would result in greater justice and confidence in the system, alleviate the burden placed on the courts from unnecessary litigation, and allow defendants to meaningfully participate in the judicial process to protect a significant asset and their rights.

A primary goal in modifying the UPHPA for New York was to give defendants some right to mediation or other ADR. New York courts and much of the real property litigation bar were already

---

[28] *See* Lynn Armentrout, *Foreclosed Homeowners Foreclosed from Telling Their Stories*, N.Y.L.J. (Mar. 16, 2016, 12:00 AM), https://bit.ly/2WKLtKT.

familiar with the CPLR 3408 settlement conference process, as it had been implemented and practiced in all counties throughout New York State for a full decade. It therefore made sense to promote an ADR procedure in the partition context that would not be a heavy lift for the courts and practitioners and would not require reinventing the wheel. If we modified CPLR 3408 to apply to partition actions and incorporated it into the model UPHPA, the New York Office of Court Administration could simply add this category of partition actions onto their existing foreclosure settlement conference docket. We also suspected that the number of these partition cases was very few in comparison to foreclosure cases, so it would minimize the burden on an already overwhelmed court system.

In addition to the substantial ADR provision, our modified UPHPA (1) expanded the definition of heirs' property to include properties that were occupied by an heir who had any ownership interest, instead of a 20 percent or greater threshold; (2) gave buyout priority first to heir occupants, then nonoccupying heirs, and last to any nonfamily cotenants, provided that none of these cotenants requested partition by sale; (3) explicitly provided for the courts to consider the method and terms by which the third-party investor acquired its fractional interest in the property when considering the equities; and (4) provided for a second broker to list the property if the first failed to locate a buyer. We also eliminated some extraneous language inapplicable to New York.

The incorporation of an heir occupant's right of first refusal to buy the property is an imperfect solution. But it acknowledges that the heir occupant has a superior right because it is their home, and it recognizes the intrinsic value of connection to a historic family property. Many low- and moderate-income homeowners do not have ready access to the capital required to purchase the fractional interests of another party. When determining the value of the other interests, however, the court would now be empowered to discount the value of the third-party investor's interest if they acquired that interest at a discount from its true market value. The investor is then unable to capitalize on the deceptive or otherwise aggressive tactics employed to divest the interest from other family members. There may also be creative ways for the heir to access the necessary capital to purchase the other fractional interests, such as grants or guaranteed loans.[29]

VI. THE ROLE OF A BAR ASSOCIATION IN LAW REFORM

We now had a significantly improved piece of legislation that addressed the issues we had encountered with our clients and their urban homes. The next step was to lobby for its enactment. The CBJC is affiliated with the New York City Bar Association (City Bar), a 25,000-member professional organization that is housed in the same building in midtown Manhattan. Through reports, amicus briefs, testimony, statements, and letters drafted by members of its approximately 150 committees, the City Bar comments and advocates on public policy and legislation coordinated through its policy department.

In this case, three City Bar committees—Commercial Law and Uniform State Laws, Housing and Urban Development, and Pro Bono and Legal Services—reviewed our proposed modified law and prepared a report supporting and recommending its adoption to make it work more effectively in New York City and other urban areas, while retaining its important protections applicable

[29] New York has previously had some funds available through its mortgage assistance and similar programs, and certain homeowners may qualify for a home equity conversion mortgage loan.

to rural areas.[30] The City Bar's policy department, staffed by Maria Cilenti and Elizabeth Kocienda, played a key role in communicating the position of the City Bar to key actors in the New York Legislature and to the governor, coordinating the report, engaging with state legislators to introduce the modifications to the bill, monitoring its passage through both houses of the New York State Legislature, and then arranging for a detailed explanatory letter to the governor.[31] Governor Cuomo signed the New York version of the UPHPA[32] on December 6, 2019, less than a year from the date that the CBJC became aware of Ms. Jones's partition case—an incredibly fast period of time from identifying a justice gap and legislating a fix.

VII. CONCLUSION

New York has now had more than a year to process its version of the UPHPA since its enactment. During most of that time, the courts have had limited operations due to the COVID pandemic, and there has been no real opportunity to fully understand the practical effects of the law on the New York State court system.[33] The CBJC and our network of legal service providers, however, have seen a considerable uptick in the number of heirs' property owners seeking legal services to help them respond to pending and new partition lawsuits and to address underlying issues around heirs' property that make them susceptible to predation—such as settling title and resolving property tax and other liens. Heir occupants have also now been successful in locating pro bono counsel, either through legal services corporations or private placement with volunteer attorneys, now that there are more effective tools to help the heirs remain in their homes.[34] Two recent decisions illustrate how the NY UPHPA has already enhanced the ability of targeted heirs to protect their interests.[35]

A confluence of factors—continued state support of quality legal services to stabilize homeownership; an existing model law from the Uniform Law Commission; a robust local investigative media; a participatory local bar association, coupled with its policy and lobbying prowess; and a sympathetic legislative and executive branch—resulted in the speedy enactment of complex, protective legislation after the issue was initially identified. While it is still too early to know the full effect of the NY UPHPA on predatory partition activity in New York City, it is likely that the law has

---

[30] *See* Report on Legislation by the Commercial Law and Uniform State Laws Committee, the Housing and Urban Development Committee and the Pro Bono and Legal Services Committee, N.Y.C. Bar Ass'n (June 12, 2019), https://www.nycbar.org/member-and-career-services/committees/reports-listing/reports/detail/support-for-the-uniform-partition-of-heirs-property-act.

[31] *See* Letter to the Governor, Andrew Cuomo, N.Y.C. Bar Ass'n Statement of Support for N.Y. Unif. Partition Heirs Prop. Act (Aug. 22, 2019), http://documents.nycbar.org/files/UPHPA_Cuomo_FINAL_8.22.19.pdf.

[32] Uniform Partition of Heirs Property Act, N.Y. Real Prop. Acts. Law § 993 (Consol. 2019).

[33] Full implementation of the NY UPHPA requires a modification of the Uniform Court Rules and the form of Request for Judicial Intervention (RJI). The modified RJI will allow for the tracking of partition cases as they are filed and will ensure that the courts know to schedule the requisite settlement conference.

[34] Since the enactment of the NY UPHPA, I have placed several more matters similar to Ms. Jones with law firms that handle pro bono cases, and I favorably settled one case that commenced immediately after the law was enacted. I am aware of many more partition cases that my legal services colleagues have taken on for full representation.

[35] *See* Kings Heritage Corp. v. Evans, No. 511400/2019, 2020 NYLJ LEXIS 1592 (N.Y. Sup. Ct. Sept. 18, 2020); Short Form Order, 3333 98 Corp. v. Oakes, No. 718544/2018 (N.Y. Sup. Ct. Queens Cnty. filed Mar. 11, 2021), NYSCEF Doc. No. 155. Both cases were commenced prior to the enactment of the NY UPHPA, which is not retroactive, but the court took notice of the new law and the practices it is meant to address when considering the equities.

greatly disincentivized the practice by significantly reducing the ability of investors to quickly realize a windfall by stripping the equity of families accumulated over generations and held in these family homes. It is certain, however, that the NY UPHPA has already contributed to the preservation of family homes and wealth and has moderated the effects of gentrification—especially in historically African American neighborhoods. The NY UPHPA and the advocacy behind its development and passage into law can now be effective models to protect vulnerable heirs' property owners from similar predatory activity in other states with large urban areas.

PART II

The Role of Nonprofit Organizations

4

The Uniform Partition of Heirs Property Act: Grassroots Advocacy and Action

—John Pollock and Karama Neal

I. THE ALLURE OF PARTITION REFORM FOR HEIRS' PROPERTY ADVOCACY ORGANIZATIONS

The Uniform Partition of Heirs Property Act (UPHPA) has seen particularly broad enactment compared to many other uniform acts, particularly uniform real property acts, in part because of the robust involvement of grassroots organizations. Then-Uniform Law Commission (ULC) president Martha Walters mentioned that the ULC had not previously seen such involvement, and it likely occurred for many reasons.

First, the UPHPA targets a *significant* part of the land retention process. The UPHPA can help prevent a forced sale of family-owned property, providing families an opportunity to clear property title, implement land and property management plans, and stabilize the future of their property.

Second, the UPHPA addresses an *egregious* problem. Partition sales have fundamentally undermined property and wealth retention and accumulation in disproportionate ways within the African American community and other low-wealth communities where land is often the only asset. Heirs' property owners who have been subjected to inequitable forced sales often have received pennies on the dollar for their interest in their property, including sometimes being required to pay a portion of the fees of the attorney for the person seeking the sale. But beyond the economics, existing law has refused to recognize the ancestral, historical, and sentimental value that land frequently holds for low-income families. Additionally, few low-income landowners have access to counsel to resist a partition sale, whereas all those seeking sale are represented. Through changes to the sale process and court's calculus of whether to divide or sell property, as well as through its broad applicability without owners having to know to invoke it, the UPHPA is responsive to these concerns.

Third, the UPHPA targets a *malleable* aspect of state property laws. While still challenging, changing the partition sale process is less complex and fraught than changing the intestacy laws that cause so much heirs' property to be created in the first place.[1] Fourth, the UPHPA facilitates *proactive movement* by families seeking to both retain and improve the economic, community, and sentimental value of their property, including families that had experienced barriers that kept them from addressing their family-property issues. While trying to identify and connect with all owners, families may inadvertently cause some owners (particularly those who were unaware they were part owners of the property) to want to sell their individual interest and so put the family's collective property ownership at risk. Certain features of the UPHPA, like the right of those who oppose a partition sale to purchase the interests of any owners seeking a sale, protects families in their effort to clear title before a partition or other title action forces the issue.

A. The Uniform Law Commission Submission and Drafting Process

1. *Identifying, Developing, and Submitting a Proposal to the Uniform Law Commission*

Civil rights organizations addressing land-loss issues have known full well about partition sale abuses for a long time and, as a result, some reform preceded the UPHPA. For instance, South Carolina enacted a buyout option in 2006,[2] the same year that grassroots advocates began to work together to help shape what became the UPHPA. However, there had been no systemic reform of partition laws in any states prior to the UPHPA.

In 2006, John Pollock, an attorney with the Southern Poverty Law Center (SPLC), compiled a fifty-state survey of partition laws in response to the SPLC's interest in reforming Alabama's partition law. His survey revealed that although some state laws had good elements, none had a desirable model, suggesting the need for both nationwide reform and model language. After drafting a model law drawn from the best elements from state laws, Pollock contacted Professor Thomas Mitchell, one of the few people in the country to have written about partition reform and to have developed concrete ideas for legal reform. Mitchell informed Pollock that the American Bar Association's Property Preservation Task Force (PPTF), on which he served, coincidentally had begun working in 2005 on a proposal requesting the ULC to draft a uniform partition act.

It was clear that both proposals would benefit from the support of individuals and organizations with significant experience in this area. To this end, Mitchell provided Pollock with referrals to several heirs' property organizations in the southeast, and Pollock discovered a few more organizations and individuals. Although some had worked in this space for decades, there had been little collaboration between them, but they were all very familiar with the scourge of partition sales. Upon

---

[1] *See, e.g.*, *Escheat: The State's Effort to Seize Property*, L. Offs. of Stimmel, Stimmel & Roeser, https://www.stimmel-law.com/en/articles/escheat-states-effort-seize-property#:~:text=Escheat%20is%20a%20legal%20term,it%20under%20the%20intestate%20laws (last visited Dec. 23, 2020) ("States are often aggressive in enforcing their rights to escheat since such laws are considered as a source of revenue for the states both in terms of ownership and as later sale to third parties who will eventually pay property taxes since it enables a property into active use which can otherwise be dormant.").

[2] S.C. Code Ann. § 15-61-25.

reviewing Pollock's draft, they saw the benefit of collaborating on such a proposal to the ULC, as well as working together outside the ULC process to improve services and information provided to heirs' property owners. They thus decided to form the Heirs' Property Retention Coalition (HPRC),[3] and started holding monthly meetings that included modifying the draft.

Once formed, the HPRC chose to submit its draft (which included both specific statutory language drawn from actual laws identified in Pollock's research and justifications for each provision) to the PPTF for that entity's consideration, reasoning that any ultimate proposal to the ULC would be better received coming from the American Bar Association (ABA), especially given that the ULC was originally formed by the ABA, rather than from advocacy groups unknown to the ULC. The PPTF and HPRC collaborated closely to modify and streamline the HPRC proposal and to include the modified version as part of the PPTF's overall proposal to the ULC requesting the ULC to create a uniform partition act drafting committee. Ultimately, the ULC accepted the PPTF proposal in February 2007.

2. *The Uniform Law Commission Drafting Process*

Due to fear over the involvement of industry groups listed as observers or rumored to be working behind the scenes,[4] the HPRC obtained a grant from the Southern Poverty Law Center to enable three of its members to be physically present at all four of the drafting sessions, which were held at costly venues all over the country.[5] This in-person presence proved essential. By being present, HPRC observers were able to more actively and effectively engage in the back-and-forth, "read the room" as to where the committee was going and what action needed to be taken, and engage informally with individual committee members during the break. While the ULC did provide a conference line for one of the sessions, it proved difficult for HPRC members to effectively participate on the phone.

Additionally, the HPRC learned the "reporter" drafting role is critical, as the reporter puts together proposed language and research for the committee to review and sets the tone for the meetings. Recognizing this, the HPRC urged the PPTF to be among the voices calling for the ULC to select Mitchell for the reporter role. As a reporter, Mitchell's deep knowledge of land loss and partition (particularly its impact on African American communities) and his passion were unsurprisingly essential for success.

---

[3] The HPRC membership list is at http://hprc.southerncoalition.org/.

[4] The National Association of Realtors® (NAR), American College of Real Estate Lawyers (ACREL), and American Bankers Association had representatives on the expected observers list, although only ACREL visibly participated, and it was very supportive of the UPHPA. Additionally, the HPRC had heard that the American College of Mortgage Attorneys (ACMA) and International Council of Shopping Centers (ICSC) intended to work back channels.

[5] HPRC members who wanted to participate in the drafting process could not afford the travel and lodging expenses themselves, so the SPLC grant was key. HPRC's attending members were HPRC coordinator John Pollock; Carolyn-Gaines Varner, an attorney with Legal Services Alabama, with more than 30 years of experience in heirs property; and Craig Baab, an attorney for Alabama Appleseed. HPRC also worked with the Lawyers' Committee for Civil Rights to secure corporate lawyer Greg Peterson's involvement, but he was able to pay his own way. It bears mentioning that partly as a result of the positive experience the ULC had with the HPRC's participation, the ULC apparently has some grant money available to help groups unable to otherwise attend, though the ULC currently is redesigning this grant program and has not yet made any information about it publicly available.

3. *The Uniform Law Commission Drafting Experience*

ULC drafting committees are made up of a certain number of voting members plus liaisons from the ABA. Some voting members may not attend all of the meetings, and with the UPHPA, the absence of certain people at a meeting sometimes had a significant impact on the course of the discussion. While observers do not vote, they are able to participate fully and robustly in the drafting session debates. Most of the UPHPA drafting committee's voting members had no exposure to heirs' property and partition issues and had not encountered low-income landowners. Recognizing this gap in their knowledge, they responded graciously by giving much credence and weight to the HPRC observers' experience with partition sales and heirs' property in general.

The experience of HPRC observers was critical for another reason beyond the voting members' unfamiliarity: it stood in for more traditional empirical data. One of the historical obstacles to both heirs' property and partition reform has been the lack of data demonstrating the extent of the problem. Partition cases are typically blended among the other probate records, making them difficult to identify, and they are often brought in rural areas where court records often are still kept in paper form, making extensive study extremely difficult. Moreover, orders for partition sale are very rarely appealed since so few low-income landowners have access to counsel, and state lower court decisions (unlike state appellate court decisions) are not reported for the most part. This makes it exceptionally difficult to establish the scope of the problem. Even the exact scope of heirs' property ownership, while understood to be significant, is largely unknown, although attempts have been made to measure it.[6]

Although data limitations prevented the HPRC from providing much empirical data that addressed the number of partition actions, case dispositions, and the demographics of the parties,[7] HPRC observers had much more information about partition actions than most others who participated in the drafting of the UPHPA, including all of those who opposed partition reform and who lacked any empirical data supporting the status quo. Some HPRC observers had direct experience with partition cases (in particular, Carolyn Gaines-Varner had been handling them for 30 years), while others had either prepped with other HPRC members possessing such experience or had spoken to many heirs' property owners that had gone through the process. This enabled the HPRC observers to talk persuasively about how partition law actually impacts heirs' property owners on the ground. For example, relating the fact that virtually no low-income landowners have counsel helped convince the drafting committee to require judges to determine in every partition case whether the property is heirs' property and the UPHPA applies, rather than requiring landowners to have to both assert their property is heirs' property and that the UPHPA should govern the action.

The drafting committee's receptivity to the advocates' on-the-ground experience had its limits. Early in the drafting process, committee members frequently referred to the theoretical harm

---

[6] *See, e.g.*, Ga. Appleseed, Unlocking Heir Property Ownership: Assessing the Impact on Low and Mid-Income Georgians and Their Communities (2013); Janice Dyer et al., *A "Disadvantaged Class": Ownership Characteristics and Partition Sales of Heir Property in a Black Belt County*, 24(2) S. Rural Soc. 192 (2009).

[7] North Carolina has some of the best available data. *See, e.g.*, Janice Dyer, *Statutory Impacts of Heir Property: An Examination of Appellate and Macon County Court Cases* (2008). The HPRC also had access to unpublished court data on partition sales in North Carolina.

the UPHPA could have on commercial property as a justification to narrow or weaken the act. In response, the HPRC worked with the Lawyers' Committee for Civil Rights Under Law to recruit Greg Peterson, a corporate attorney from DLA Piper with extensive commercial real estate experience, to provide a credible response. Time and time again, Greg was able to refute such claims of theoretical harm based on his extensive real estate experience, and the drafting committee came to respect and defer to his perspective on many of these issues.

That said, while observers have an active voice in the debate, they do not vote, so ULC observers must develop priorities. The HPRC set its overarching priorities as: (1) broad applicability of the act, given the vast breadth of heirs' property among low-income landowners and farmers; and (2) recognition in the act that land ownership is often not fungible due to the many different types of value (historical, sentimental, familial, etc.) associated with such ownership. As to the first goal, some drafting committee members and the ULC's executive director argued the ULC's decision to create a drafting committee was predicated on having the UPHPA only apply to "poor black sharecroppers" holding multigenerational farm property. The ULC leadership claimed that having a broader scope might require delaying the process in order to return to the Joint Editorial Board for Uniform Real Property Acts, a body that vets proposals requesting the ULC to form committees to draft uniform real property acts, for approval of a broader mandate.[8] In the end, the HPRC observers and Professor Mitchell crafted an elaborate definition of "heirs property" that was very broad while still satisfying the drafting committee.[9]

For the second goal, altering the way judges weigh whether to divide or sell property was critical. Historically, most state court judges have ordered a sale in every case in which they believe that the land will be more valuable sold than divided.[10] Besides the fact that this economic conclusion is almost always erroneous,[11] such an approach ignores the fact that for many families, the economic value is secondary, tertiary, or nowhere on the list. Rather, the value is the connection to their family's history, the property's roots in a particular community, the property's historical value, and other noneconomic factors. For this reason, HPRC observers fought hard for (1) the balancing test provisions in the UPHPA, which includes noneconomic factors alongside the economic ones; and (2) the buyout option, as it empowers owners to retain their interest in the land to which they have a substantial connection rather than receive compensation that cannot make them whole.

The HPRC advocated for other reforms that were important but not among its two most important priorities, including an important reform the HPRC ultimately was not able to have incorporated in the final act. The HPRC advocated that owners objecting to a forced sale should not have a portion of the petitioner's attorney's fees taken out of their monetary distributions from

---

[8] Both the HPRC and the drafting committee agreed the UPHPA should not apply where all the owners signed an agreement to be governed by different partition rules, but that was not enough of a limitation.

[9] It was also critical (and fortuitous) that then-ULC president Martha Walters joined one of the drafting sessions to advocate strongly for broader applicability. This helped to reverse the drafting committee's earlier decision to adopt a very narrow definition of heirs' property that would have resulted in very few families being covered by the UPHPA.

[10] *See, e.g.*, Ashley v. Baker, 867 P.2d 792, 796 (Ak. 1994).

[11] *See* Thomas Mitchell, *Forced Sale Risk: Class, Race, and the "Double Discount,"* 37 Fla. St. U. L. Rev. 589 (2010) (finding that forced sales often sell for well below market value). This is unsurprising given that auction sales utilize none of the practices (such as thorough marketing and the use of a realtor) that would increase the chances of a higher sales price.

the sale, a disturbing practice most states permit under the so-called "common benefit" exception to the American Rule on attorney's fees under which each party is normally responsible for their own attorney's fees. Having to pay a portion of the attorney's fees of the party who petitioned the court for a sale reduces the already deficient payout heirs' property owners receive from a sale they never wanted,[12] making a mockery of the notion that these heirs property owners benefited from the partition sale.

However, instead of the HPRC's moderate proposal, the voting members initially decided to adopt instead the pure American Rule on attorney's fees, which would prevent any attorney's fee award in a partition action. The HPRC observers greatly feared this would affect the UPHPA's enactability by increasing state bar opposition, but did not push back due to their prioritization of the fights around scope and the equitable balancing test governing whether property is divided or sold. However, at the final drafting session, the ULC leadership and several voting members of the drafting committee unexpectedly claimed that the proposed attorney's fee reform would negatively impact the ability to enact the UPHPA into law and the drafting committee then decided to eliminate any attorney fee reform rather than returning to the HPRC's modest limitation. At that stage, it would have been strategically unwise for the HPRC to resist.

II. STATE-LEVEL GRASSROOTS ADOPTION EFFORTS

Once the UPHPA was finished, the focus quickly turned to enactment, to build on the momentum. The HPRC met monthly with a ULC legal counsel staffer and Professor Mitchell to identify promising jurisdictions, increase the UPHPA's profile among the commissioners, and identify what steps the HPRC members would take in each state. The HPRC obtained support letters (included in the UPHPA Enactment Kit distributed by the ULC)[13] from key national organizations such as the NAACP, National Black Caucus of State Legislators,[14] National Bar Association (NBA), and Appleseed. Other key endorsements that happened outside the HPRC's purview came from two sections of the ABA and ACREL, as well as the Council of State Governments, which listed the UPHPA as one of their pieces of "suggested state legislation." All of this laid the groundwork for state-level activity.

Just as grassroots efforts with the ULC contributed to the development of the UPHPA, in several states, grassroots groups led or substantially contributed to passage of the UPHPA through multisector coalitions, the members of which were directly connected to or informed by families who own and manage heirs' property. Here, we review successful efforts to pass the UPHPA by drawing upon

[12] Given that properties typically sell for well below market value at auction, dispossessed owners rarely if ever benefit economically, and then their already-deficient payout is further diminished by having a portion of the petitioner's attorney fees taken out.

[13] The Enactment Kit is at https://www.uniformlaws.org/viewdocument/enactment-kit-34?CommunityKey=50724584-e808-4255-bc5d-8ea4e588371d&tab=librarydocuments (last visited Nov. 11, 2020).

[14] Thomas Mitchell had a lengthy conversation with staff of the National Black Caucus of State Legislators and helped them draft their letter of support. Email from Thomas W. Mitchell to Karama Neal (April 8, 2021) (on file with author).

some parts of the enactment efforts in Georgia, Arkansas, South Carolina, Florida, and Virginia to identify best practices at each stage of the campaigns.[15]

A. Existing Infrastructure Supporting Advocacy

In the southern states, several heirs' property service organizations were created during the past several decades to assist families with legal issues, land management, and other issues. Many of these groups became part of the HPRC. There is also a general familiarity in the South with heirs' property (or "heir property" as it is referenced in many places), particularly among African American populations in the region. This section provides some illustrative examples of some of the good organizational and other forms of infrastructure that was in place in certain southern states to support efforts to enact the UPHPA into law.

Some of this infrastructure consisted of organizations across the South that first learned about and worked on heirs' property as a result of Hurricane Katrina in 2005.[16] Many families who evacuated New Orleans and the Gulf Coast sought assistance in getting federal and other aid to repair or rebuild their properties damaged by the storm but found that their properties' status as heirs' property prevented them from receiving assistance.[17] Organizations such as Georgia Appleseed, South Carolina Appleseed, and Alabama Appleseed soon recognized the surprisingly broad scope of the problem.[18] As a result, the three Appleseed entities mentioned became members of the HPRC and worked on introduction and passage of the UPHPA.[19]

Georgia Appleseed recognized the need for a nonprofit legal services organization singularly devoted to heirs' property.[20,21] To that end, it initiated a research study in 2009 to understand the prevalence and economic value of heirs' property in the state. Four years of research was published in 2013, but much of the data and preliminary results was available in time to support UPHPA advocacy efforts.[22] This data, based on a detailed analysis of property tax records in select representative counties in the state, was extrapolated to predict "tens of thousands of heirs' property parcels with a

---

[15] A current list of UPHPA passages is at https://www.uniformlaws.org/committees/community-home?CommunityKey=50724584-e808-4255-bc5d-8ea4e588371d. The states discussed herein passed the UPHPA in 2011 (Georgia), 2015 (Arkansas), 2016 (South Carolina), and 2020 (Virginia and Florida).

[16] La. Appleseed, Protect Your Property: Heir Property in Louisiana (2011), https://www.appleseednetwork.org/uploads/1/2/4/6/124678621/protect-your-property.pdf.

[17] *See, e.g.*, Robert Kluckow, The Impact of Heir Property on Post-Katrina Housing Recovery in New Orleans (Dec. 2014) (MA Thesis, Colorado State University) (DOI: 10.13140/RG.2.2.13565.97767); John Ydstie, *No Title? No Easy Access to Post-Katrina Aid*, (NPR, April 28, 2008), https://www.npr.org/templates/story/story.php?storyId=90005954.

[18] Interview by Karama Neal with Craig Baab, Alabama Appleseed (Sept. 2020).

[19] Interview by Karama Neal with Sue Berkowitz, SC Appleseed (Sept. 2020).

[20] Ga. Appleseed, https://gaappleseed.org/ (last visited Mar. 4, 2021).

[21] Interview by Karama Neal with Sharon Hill, formerly of Georgia Appleseed (Sept. 2020).

[22] *See* Ga. Appleseed, Unlocking Heir Property Ownership: Assessing the Impact on Low and Mid Income Georgians and Their Communities (2013). https://gaappleseed.org/media/docs/unlocking-heir-property.pdf.

value of hundreds of millions of dollars" in Georgia.[23] This economic research helped build support for legislative reform among Georgia legislators.[24]

In South Carolina,[25] the late Senator Clementa Pinckney[26] sponsored 2006 legislation[27] that gave family members opposing a partition sale the right to buy out the interests of the owner(s) seeking sale. This provision is somewhat similar conceptually to that which was ultimately included in the UPHPA. In addition to this policy foundation, the Center for Heirs' Property Preservation,[28] founded in 2002 as a direct service legal organization, created legal familiarity and support for heirs' property issues, particularly in the coastal region of the state.

B. Coalition Building

Legislative success is never due to a single individual. The focus states each took unique paths to developing broad coalitions, some of which were more formal than others, to support their UPHPA passage efforts. The coalition building that took shape in Arkansas and Virginia provides helpful illustrative examples of the effective coalition building that has been done.

In Arkansas,[29] beginning in 2013, Karama Neal started a statewide grassroots advocacy organization, Heirs of Arkansas, focused solely on passage of the UPHPA.[30] Neal connected with other heirs' property owners through radio broadcasts, podcasts, and social media, at family reunions, community and municipal organizations, and through an organizational newsletter.[31] This activity framed the issue as important to the preservation of family land and farms without focusing on race and created a community of people and organizations that were informed about and invested in UPHPA passage.[32] This approach was informed by what she learned from HPRC members about efforts in other states. This informal coalition allowed her to solicit and receive UPHPA endorsement from the Harold Flowers Law Society, an affiliate of the National Bar Association. Given this activity, Heirs of Arkansas attracted the attention of two of the state's uniform law commissioners, Elisa White and Lynn Foster, the latter of whom was a property law professor. Drawing upon the

---

[23] *Id.*

[24] Interview by Karama Neal with Crystal Baker, formerly of Georgia Appleseed (Sept. 2020).

[25] Unless otherwise noted, information on the South Carolina passage effort is from interviews conducted by Neal with Jennie Stephens and Joshua Walden of the Center for Heirs' Property Preservation and Sue Berkowitz, formerly of South Carolina Appleseed, September 2020.

[26] A full record of Senator Pinckney's property rights and other legislation is at https://www.scstatehouse.gov/member.php?code=1479545277 (last visited Nov. 11, 2020).

[27] Senator Pinckney was one of two primary sponsors of what became Act 302 of 2006, "An act to amend Chapter 61, Title 15, Code of Laws of South Carolina, 1976, by adding Section 15-61-25, relating to partitions, so as to give one or more of the joint tenant or tenants in common the right of first refusal to purchase the subject property before its judicial partition."

[28] Ctr. for Heirs Prop. Preservation, https://www.heirsproperty.org/ (last visited Mar. 4, 2021).

[29] Unless otherwise noted, information on the Arkansas passage effort is from Calvin King of the Arkansas Land and Farm Development Corporation and Neal. The former was interviewed by the latter in Sept. 2020.

[30] Heirs of Ark., https://heirsofarkansas.wordpress.com/ (last visited Mar. 4, 2021).

[31] Heirs of Arkansas newsletters and other information are at https://heirsofarkansas.wordpress.com/ (last visited Nov. 11, 2020).

[32] *See, e.g.*, Karama Neal, *Preserving Family Farms in Arkansas*, Ark. Democrat Gazette (Aug. 4, 2019), https://www.arkansasonline.com/news/2019/aug/04/preserving-family-farms-in-arkansas-201/ written to defend the Arkansas law from repeal efforts.

momentum of the family-based advocacy and Foster's experience in the field, the two uniform law commissioners successfully petitioned the Arkansas Bar Association to add the UPHPA to their 2015 legislative agenda.

Virginia's effort benefited from having an existing effective coalition at the core of the heirs' property coalition. In Virginia, the Black Family Land Trust (BFLT), a conservation land trust that has worked since 2004 to preserve and improve the economic viability of African American–owned land—including heirs' property—was a member of the Virginia's United Land Trusts (VaULT). BFLT executive director, Ebonie Alexander, talked with Mitchell in 2018, who asked her about the potential to organize a coalition to advocate for passage of the UPHPA in Virginia. Subsequently, at the suggestion of the BFLT,[33] VaULT, with more than a dozen regional land trust members, supported the UPHPA and joined with the Virginia League of Conservation Voters and others to formally work toward passage. Some of the VaULT members had paid lobbyists and were willing to have them facilitate the passage effort. This coalition framed the issue as one of access to legal services, without focusing on race,[34] and worked with a legislator to get the UPHPA introduced in 2019. That effort failed in committee, but VaULT executive director Ellen Shepard noted that that failure was "for the best."[35]

Starting in July 2019, the coalition started meeting regularly to develop a master strategy for UPHPA passage. For the rest of the year, coalition members worked diligently[36] as they researched the prevalence and location of heirs' property in the state, crafted a new message centered on using the Farm Bill provisions to return federal funds back to Virginia, identified legislative sponsors, and studied the potential impact of the UPHPA in Virginia. Chris Nolen, a state uniform law commissioner, helped address the concerns of the Virginia Bar Association, which had publicly opposed the UPHPA after it was first introduced in 2019.[37] The regular collective work of this multisector coalition positioned them well for the 2020 legislative session.

C. The Legislative Process

Successful engagement with state legislatures requires knowledge of the political environment and may take several tries. The grassroots groups in the state coalitions each worked with someone experienced in their statehouse, whether a formal lobbyist or not.

Until the Arkansas Bar Association got engaged, Neal had been intentionally vocal about the efforts to pass the UPHPA. However, the Arkansas Bar's lobbyist, Jack McNulty, recommended a quiet approach, correctly recognizing that with the support of the state's largest bar association, the legislators were likely to see the UPHPA as a technical legal issue and quickly pass it based on the bar's recommendation. While McNulty navigated the legislature, Neal continued to participate in HPRC calls to keep them and the ULC updated and to be prepared for any challenges. House Bill

---

[33] Interview by Karama Neal with Ebonie Alexander, BFLT (Mar. 2021).

[34] *Id.* and interview by Karama Neal with Nancy Hyde, VaULT (Mar. 2021).

[35] Interview by Karama Neal with Ellen Shepard, VaULT (Mar. 2021).

[36] Neal, *supra* note 33.

[37] Neal, *supra* note 35.

1245 of 2015 was introduced on February 3, 2015, and became Act 107 of 2015[38] on February 18, 2015, with no dissenting votes.[39]

The coalition in South Carolina also took a quiet approach to UPHPA passage. The coalition members were very engaged in the process. Sue Berkowitz of SC Appleseed and Mitchell were in regular contact, and Mitchell eventually testified in the state legislature. With only two weeks left in the 2015 session,[40] Mitchell intervened to save the House of Representatives bill after it was declared dead because the Judiciary Committee chair "put a hold" on the bill after there was a unanimous vote in support of the bill by a subcommittee of the House Judiciary Committee, a vote that normally would have signaled likely approval by the entire Judiciary Committee.[41] The hold was released after Mitchell contacted the South Carolina Bar president as part of Mitchell's "Hail Mary" attempt to keep the bill alive.[42] The bar president agreed to try to help and then contacted an influential attorney who secured a weekend meeting with the House Judiciary chair, who ultimately agreed to release his hold.[43] With only ten days left in the session, the bill was first approved by the Judiciary Committee and then was ultimately passed by the House of Representatives in the last thirty minutes of the session.[44]

There was some potentially significant opposition in the Senate the next year and two Republican senators expressed some concerns about the UPHPA. Berkowitz compiled a list of the concerns[45] and in response, Mitchell drafted a detailed memorandum addressing each, which was disseminated to all the members of the South Carolina Senate Judiciary Committee.[46] The memorandum sufficiently addressed one of the senator's concerns but the other one, Senator Paul Thurmond (son of Strom Thurmond) continued to try to defeat the UPHPA bill.[47] Given Thurmond's opposition, there was still some concern about broader opposition. Given the 2015 murder of Senator Clementa Pickney,[48] who had championed earlier property rights legislation, the UPHPA bill in South Carolina was renamed in his honor toward the end of the South Carolina Senate's consideration of the UPHPA bill—in part to dampen any opposition to it[49]—and final discussions and passage proceeded swiftly.[50]

---

[38] Act 107 of 2015 is at https://www.arkleg.state.ar.us/Acts/FTPDocument?path=%2FACTS%2F2015%2FPublic%2F&file=107.pdf&ddBienniumSession=2015%2F2015R (last visited Nov. 11, 2020).

[39] *HB 1245 Bill Information*, Ark. State Legislature, https://www.arkleg.state.ar.us/Bills/Detail?id=HB1245&ddBienniumSession=2015%2F2015R (last visited Apr. 10, 2021).

[40] Email from Thomas W. Mitchell to Karama Neal (Feb. 25, 2021) (on file with author).

[41] Email from Thomas W. Mitchell to Karama Neal (April 8, 2021) (on file with author).

[42] *Id.*

[43] *Id.*

[44] *Id.*

[45] Mitchell, *supra* note 40.

[46] Mitchell, *supra* note 41.

[47] *Id.*

[48] *See*, Emanuel Nine Mem'l, https://emanuelnine.org/ (last visited Nov. 11, 2020) for additional information about the murder of Rev. Clementa Pinckney, pastor of Emanuel AME Church, and eight of his parishioners on June 17, 2015.

[49] Mitchell, *supra* note 41.

[50] *See 2015-2016 Bill 3325: Uniform Partition of Heirs Property Act*, S.C. Gen. Assembly, https://www.scstatehouse.gov/sess121_2015-2016/bills/3325.htm (last visited Nov. 11, 2020).

In the end, Paul Thurmond was the only senator to vote against the bill,[51] although his opposition predated the murder of his colleague, Senator Pickney.

After one failed attempt in 2019, the Virginia coalition regrouped to refine their approach. All the members that had lobbyists put the UPHPA on their legislative agendas.[52] They approached an urban Democrat in the House of Delegates and a rural Republican in the Senate who became lead sponsors of the bill.[53] The Virginia Secretary of Agriculture and Forestry testified in the legislature in support of the UPHPA.[54] Throughout this process, VaULT provided logistical and communications support.[55]

The Boyd-Graves Conference of the Virginia Bar Association, which attempts to reach consensus on ways to improve civil laws (in contrast to criminal laws) in Virginia, wanted to study the UPHPA in a comprehensive way because it would represent such a major reform of Virginia partition law if enacted into law. After thoroughly studying the UPHPA, the Boyd-Graves committee decided that the three basic pillars of the UPHPA would improve Virginia partition law, but the committee wanted to modify the UPHPA language in some limited ways to make it more consistent with Virginia's priorities. Mitchell and Orzeske worked closely with the Boyd-Graves committee throughout the review process, including by working with the committee to draft language that would still meet ULC and Farm Bill standards so that Virginia could qualify for the benefits of the Farm Bill.[56] Not only did the Boyd-Graves Conference end up supporting the UPHPA with some minor changes, it in fact successfully advocated that Virginia's version of the UPHPA should cover all partition actions involving any tenancy-in common property and not just family-owned tenancy-in-common property that meets the UPHPA's definition of heirs' property.[57]

The final bill passed both chambers unanimously[58] and the governor later held a ceremonial signing ceremony[59] on the family land of Ralph Sampson.[60] Sampson is a famous, former Virginia

---

[51] *See Senate Journal 3/8/2016*, South Carolina General Assembly, https://www.scstatehouse.gov/sess121_2015-2016/sj16/20160308.htm#p13 (last visited Nov. 11, 2020) for the voting record for the Clementa C. Pinckney Uniform Partition of Heirs' Property Act.

[52] Neal, *supra* note 33.

[53] Neal, *supra* note 34.

[54] Bettina Ring, *Keeping Land Intact, in Farm and Forestland, and in the Family*, Richmond Times-Dispatch, (Jul. 17, 2020), https://richmond.com/opinion/columnists/bettina-ring-column-keeping-land-intact-in-farm-and-forestland-and-in-the-family/article_5d7b2348-98c7-515b-9957-8cff37abe111.html. Virginia interviewees noted that it was highly unusual for a secretary to testify in the legislature.

[55] *Id.*

[56] Mitchell, *supra* note 41.

[57] Neal, *supra* note 34.

[58] Neal, *supra* note 33.

[59] Jennifer L. McClellan & Parker C. Agelasto, *Keeping Land in the Family*, Richmond Free Press (July 23, 2020), http://richmondfreepress.com/news/2020/jul/23/keeping-land-family-sen-jennifer-l-mcclellan-and-p/.

[60] Ian Munro, *Northam Signs Heirship Bill on McGaheysville Farm*, Daily News Record (July 20, 2020), https://www.dnronline.com/news/northam-signs-heirship-bill-on-mcgaheysville-farm/article_e618e41e-4b91-579d-9055-3f707ba566f1.html.

and professional basketball player[61] and his family owns an historic, African American farm that is heirs' property. He attended the signing ceremony and was one of the featured speakers.[62]

The Florida coalition included an attorney, Jami Coleman, who had worked on heirs' property cases for many years.[63] She was involved in the real property section of the state bar and reached out to a state senator who became the lead sponsor in the Florida Senate in the 2020 session.[64] Defenders of Wildlife coordinated with the sponsors throughout the session and invited several representatives of environmental, housing, and social justice organizations who testified in support of the bills before each committee.[65] Prior to the Senate hearing, Mitchell, on behalf of the ULC, held extensive negotiations with the Florida Bar's Real Property, Probate and Trust Law Section (RPPTL) leaders as the RPPTL initially had vigorously opposed the UPHPA.[66] Ultimately, RPPTL changed its position and took a neutral position in part because there were some members of the RPPTL leadership who strongly supported the UPHPA and because several legislators very much wanted Florida to qualify for the Farm Bill benefits.[67]

There was excellent testimony given in support of the UPHPA House and Senate bills. Among other local advocates, Jami Coleman and the lobbyist for Defenders of Wildlife testified in favor of the UPHPA and Coleman also gave media interviews speaking from experience on the need for UPHPA passage.[68] The national representatives who testified in support of the UPHPA bills were Orzeske, who testified at a House Judiciary Committee hearing, and Mitchell, who provided expert testimony at the Senate Judiciary Committee hearing.[69] In the end, the UPHPA passed both chambers unanimously and was enacted into law on June 20, 2020.[70]

Overall, the coalitions paid close attention to the political environment in their states and in addition to working with lobbyists or related professionals, leaned on Orzeske and Mitchell for additional support. All these contributions were needed for success.

D. Lessons Learned

Given the variety of people, professions, communities, and interest groups that have long been concerned with heirs' property, and the general sentimental appeal of family home and land, the UPHPA remains well positioned for successful grassroots efforts. Given the perception when the UPHPA was

[61] *Ralph Sampson's Biography*, The History Makers, https://www.thehistorymakers.org/biography/ralph-sampson-41 (last visited Apr. 10, 2021).

[62] McClellan & Agelasto, *supra* note 59.

[63] Interview by Karama Neal with Kent Wimmer, Defenders of Wildlife (Mar. 2021).

[64] *Id.*

[65] *Id.*

[66] Mitchell, *supra* note 41.

[67] *Id.*

[68] Mitchell, *supra* note 41.

[69] *Id.*

[70] Neal, *supra* note 63; Kent Wimmer, *Defenders Helps Florida Pass a Uniform Partition of Heirs Property Act*, Defenders of Wildlife (June 27, 2020), https://defenders.org/blog/2020/06/defenders-helps-florida-pass-uniform-partition-of-heirs-property-act.

being drafted that significant partition reform stood little chance of success, there are several lessons that can be applied to the UPHPA or other advocacy efforts:

- *Assess the foundation*—Grassroots efforts in several states were successful because they identified and built upon a previously existing foundation of support. The foundation need not be policy based to support a new policy effort; the foundation may be based in practice, research, education, or other areas.
- *Build a broad coalition*—Whether it was the HPRC in terms of its involvement in creating the UPHPA or many of the coalitions that formed to advocate for the UPHPA in different jurisdictions, many were successful in part because they had a healthy variety of members. The members represented many different sectors and consisted of people from diverse backgrounds, including with regard to race and ethnicity. Each member could speak about the UPHPA from their own perspective and could seek to tap their own network in support of the shared goal. These could include education, lobbying, communications, research, and other resources.
- *Tell the story*—Advocates should be prepared to make their case for passage using both qualitative and quantitative approaches, if possible. However, if quality data is not available in a particular state, which unfortunately is often the case, advocates should seek to use stories from heirs' property owners in their state and should consider referencing data from another state that has similar, relevant characteristics.
- *Tailor the message*—Advocates feel passionately about heirs' property for a variety of reasons, but not all those reasons will resonate with legislators, potential partners, and others. For example, potential decision makers may be inclined to support the UPHPA because it enhances private property rights; others may support it because it promotes racial justice; while others may support it because it enables heirs' property owners in certain states to have broader access to US Department of Agriculture programs. It is critical that advocates understand what will attract people to their cause and what will repel them.
- *Attend to operations*—Successful coalitions need not only a shared mission but also the means to facilitate routine operations. These can include scheduling meetings so members stay engaged, taking and distributing meeting minutes so members stay informed, printing information brochures to solicit new members, and the like. Passion alone, however, is generally insufficient.
- *Recruit strategic allies*—Much of the grassroots work described herein was successful in part because the coalitions sought out well-established, well-connected people who were in positions to influence powerful stakeholders. While these more well-connected allies may not have initiated the advocacy effort, once aligned with the grassroots efforts, they can use both their influence (e.g., public endorsement) and their resources (e.g., paid lobbyist) in support of the effort. Successful efforts often benefit from both bottom-up and top-down approaches.
- *Be tenacious*—It is not unusual for it to take several legislative sessions for a bill to pass. In Mississippi, for example, the UPHPA failed to pass in the first four legislative sessions in which UPHPA bills were introduced; however, the UPHPA was passed overwhelmingly the fifth time around. If an early attempt is unsuccessful, advocates can learn from that process to improve the likelihood of passage later.

- *Don't stop*—Legislative change addressing one particular legal issue is a critical step but it is rarely, if ever, the last step needed. Often, additional legal reform is needed to address different but related problems. Further, engaged coalitions can expand their focus to include issues such as access to legal services and access to capital, two of the issues that often plague heirs' property owners. In building upon initial success, it can be helpful to learn from work done in other states.

The sustained involvement of a variety of stakeholders has contributed significantly to the passage of the UPHPA and of progressive property rights work. While the ULC only approves at most five new acts per year (very few of which have to do with civil rights or racial justice), there are other bodies creating model legislation and the ongoing efforts related to the UPHPA can serve as a guide for others as they pursue progressive legislative policy change.

5

Working with Heirs' Property Families: The Center for Heirs' Property Preservation and The Georgia Heirs Property Law Center

—Jennie L. Stephens, Joshua F. Walden, and W. Andrew Gowder, Jr.

The proverb that states "it takes a village to raise a child" is appropriate when applied to the creation of two legal service organizations in the American South to address the prevention and resolution of the issue of heirs' property. These organizations are the Center for Heirs' Property Preservation located in South Carolina and The Georgia Heirs Property Law Center, Inc.[1] While both organizations address the negative impacts of heirs' property, each state's unique laws and needs resulted in complementary but different organizations.

Section I of this chapter outlines the events leading to the creation of these public interest organizations, their mission, and services. Section II serves as a case study of the Center for Heirs' Property Preservation.

---

[1] The authors would like to thank Skipper StipeMaas for her contributions of background information on the Georgia Heirs Property Law Center.

I. ORIGINS OF TWO HEIRS' PROPERTY PUBLIC INTEREST ORGANIZATIONS

A. The Center for Heirs' Property Preservation: Development and Mission

The impetus for the creation of the Center for Heirs' Property Preservation (CHPP) was the voices of rural residents, farmers, and African Americans in coastal South Carolina. In 1996, the Trident Community Foundation, then located in an urban area, now known as Coastal Community Foundation of South Carolina, the Foundation) received a Ford Foundation grant to address economic development issues in rural communities.

To learn about the rural economic development issues in the communities surrounding it, the Foundation staff convened focus groups. At almost every meeting, Foundation staff would hear, "I own land, but . . ." The phrase that completed that sentence directed their attention to the issue of heirs' property, a form of communal land ownership created through intestacy that restricts the economic advantage in owning land.

Heirs' property was an anomaly to the Foundation's staff. Therefore, an advisory committee of attorneys, judges, and nonprofit organizations was created to develop and implement a pilot project conducted by the local Urban League.[2] The project report[3] was utilized to (1) examine the extent of the issue of heirs' property on one of the Sea Islands—Wadmalaw Island, South Carolina, near Charleston; (2) develop a working model that would explore the obstacles in resolving heirs' property; (3) create internships for second- and third-year law students to work on cases involving heirs' property; and (4) create volunteer opportunities for attorneys in the region to assist lower-income persons with title resolution.

The conclusions reached after conducting this pilot project were that (1) legal education must be provided, because of the extreme myths concerning heirs' property ownership that were circulating in the community; (2) outreach to community leaders, the faith community, pro bono attorneys, and governmental tax offices must be conducted to ensure that the education reached those who were most affected by the issue; and (3) emphasis should be placed on prevention (i.e., "staunch the bloodflow of land loss[4]") through conducting wills clinics at which wills, powers of attorney, and other legal documents could be drafted. During this pilot, retired Charleston County, South Carolina, Master in Equity, Judge Louis B. Condon, a member of the Heirs' Property Advisory Committee, stressed that the indicator of success for the pilot should not be the number of cases resolved, but the amount of educational information distributed that would provoke the people to take action to resolve their title issues.[5]

The Foundation, in partnership with the South Carolina Bar Foundation, conducted a second pilot project from 2002 to 2004 in which a full-time attorney and paralegal were hired to conduct the prescribed legal education outreach seminars and deliver legal services to heirs' property owners

[2] Peter Plastrik, *An Heirs' Property Collaborative Initiative for Coastal South Carolina*, Coastal Community Foundation of South Carolina Archives.

[3] Toya Hampton, J. Morgan Kearse, Shirley Washington, & Loretta Mouzon, *From the River to the Road: A Ten-Week Pilot Project*, Coastal Community Foundation of South Carolina Archives (1998).

[4] *Id.* at 3.

[5] Shirley Washington, Loretta Mouzon, & Richard Hendry, *From the River to the Road: Phase II – Pilot Project*, Coastal Community Foundation of South Carolina Archives (1999).

who met the project's criteria. The project was a success; however, it needed a home. Consequently, the advisory committee recommended the creation of a permanent institution that would adopt and perfect the strategies used in the demonstration projects. Hence, the Center for Heirs' Property Preservation (CHPP) was created in 2005 to prevent the loss of heirs' property in four counties in coastal South Carolina.

The advisory committee that created the CHPP opted not to spend resources to determine the amount of heirs' property, but to provide the much-needed and missing delivery of direct legal services for this issue. In 2009, the CHPP partnered with The Conservation Fund and students from the Charleston School of Law to determine the amount of heirs' property in its seven-county service area. The research revealed that there were at least 47,000 acres, of which 50 percent was contained in three of the seven counties.

Since its inception, the CHPP has grown to serve twenty-two of the forty-six counties in the state and has changed its mission statement to protecting heirs' property and promoting the sustainable use of land to provide increased economic benefit to historically underserved families through legal and forestry education and services.

B. The Georgia Heirs Property Law Center: Development and Mission

The Georgia Heirs Property Law Center, Inc. (GHPLC), founded in 2015, grew out of the legal community's deepening understanding that heirs' property was the hidden story behind blight and generational poverty throughout both rural and urban Georgia, finding that Georgia's heirs' property was statewide, affected every demographic and socioeconomic level, and hampered the community stabilization efforts of local governments and nonprofits, as well as the economic wellbeing of families.

In 2001, as the CHPP was taking shape, in various parts of the South groups of grassroots leaders, legal practitioners, and scholars began meeting to find systemic ways to address heirs' property and its devastating consequences for families and communities in their states.[6] The origins and development of the Uniform Partition of Heirs Property Act (UPHPA), including the role of the Heirs Property Retention Coalition (HPRC) are discussed in chapters 1, 2, 4, and 7 of this book.

Hurricane Katrina highlighted the problems that heirs' property caused tenants in common in recovering from national disasters. In the wake of Katrina, many families in Louisiana sought federal disaster assistance or payment for insurance claims but were denied because they could not document clear title to their property—properties on which generations of their families lived. In response, the Appleseed Network created a collaborative project with several of its centers to study how Hurricane Katrina evacuees were impacted by the issue of heirs' property.

There were obvious similarities between Georgia and Louisiana heirs' property owners. Georgia Appleseed began its heirs' property project in 2008 under the guidance of the Georgia Appleseed Young Professionals Council (YPC), in concert with its sister Alabama Appleseed organization, which

[6] Gabriel Kuris, *A Huge Problem in Plain Sight: Untangling Heirs' Property Rights in the American South, 2001–2017*, Innovations for Successful Societies (2018), http://successfulsocieties.princeton.edu/.

conducted tax database research to quantify the amount of land owned as heirs' property, and its sister South Carolina Appleseed organization, which was a partner in the creation of the CHPP.[7]

In addition to the YPC, a full-time law school fellow was engaged to develop a plan for the heirs' property project utilizing pro bono attorneys. This plan consisted of the development of a user-friendly manual for heirs' property owners, titled "Heir Property in Georgia"; conducting an educational seminar titled "Heir Property in Georgia: How to Preserve Your Family's Land," which was conducted by attorneys in partnership with community groups; and researching the tax database to determine the extent of the heirs' property issue in Georgia.[8]

The tax database research revealed that hundreds of millions of dollars' worth of tax-appraised property across Georgia was probable heirs' property, essentially "frozen equity."[9] Documenting the statewide prevalence of heirs' property coincided with the Uniform Law Commission's 2010 promulgation of the UPHPA, which offered several due process protections for disadvantaged landowners. In 2012, Georgia was the first southern state to enact the UPHPA, serving as the model for other southern states.

The critical infusion of public attention and pro bono research galvanized support for an independent legal services agency dedicated to heirs' property prevention, remediation, and education in Georgia. The GHPLC launched as an independent 501(c)3 in 2015 with the mission of increasing generational wealth, economic value, and community stability by securing and preserving the property rights of low- and moderate-income Georgians. Between 2015 and 2020, the GHPLC has closed 457 matters: 171 title clearing matters, 102 title audits, and 184 estate planning matters. The GHPLC has completed 318 community outreach and education programs reaching 12,595 individuals. The GHPLC's founding executive director, Skipper StipeMaas, herself an heirs' property owner, and staff work collaboratively throughout the state, with targeted outreach in Atlanta and South Georgia.

1. The GHPLC's Service Delivery Model

As the GHPLC has built its practice, it has incorporated different sectors impacted by heirs' property, such as banking, real estate, probate and superior courts, agriculture and forestry, local government, university research and extension, environmental groups, state agencies, and housing nonprofits.

The GHPLC mitigates the negative impacts of heirs' property by working with families, municipalities, and nonprofits:

1. Remediating "tangled title"[10] by assisting clients in determining goals for their land, identifying the ownership interest of all heirs, facilitating title searches and surveys, and resolving titles through negotiated agreements, probate, and litigation

---

[7] GA. APPLESEED, UNLOCKING HEIR PROPERTY OWNERSHIP: ASSESSING THE IMPACT ON LOW AND MID-INCOME GEORGIANS AND THEIR COMMUNITIES (2013), https://gaappleseed.org/media/docs/unlocking-heir-property.pdf.

[8] *Seeds of Justice,* SEPT. 2009 ISSUE (Ga. Appleseed, Atlanta, GA), https://gaappleseed.org/media/docs/newsletter_2009-09.pdf.

[9] *Seeds of Justice,* 2012 ISSUE (Ga. Appleseed, Atlanta, GA), https://gaappleseed.org/media/docs/newsletter_2011-12.pdf; *see supra* note 7.

[10] Cassandra J. Gaither, Ann Carpenter, Tracy Lloyd McCurty, & Sara Toering, eds., *Heirs' Property and Land Fractionation: Fostering Stable Ownership to Prevent Land Loss and Abandonment,* U.S. DEPARTMENT OF AGRICULTURE FOREST SERVICE, SOUTHERN RESEARCH STATION (2019) at 98.

2. Preventing heirs' property by drafting simple wills and more complicated estate plans
3. Providing asset education to help property owners steward and enhance the value of their property
4. Providing educational programs to heighten awareness of and increase access to public and private sector programs for land management, home improvement, or disaster relief
5. Increasing a deeper awareness and understanding of heirs' property by providing research, education, and planning to government agencies and their employees, elected officials, attorneys, judges, and nonprofit and neighborhood leaders

II. CASE STUDY: THE CHPP'S SERVICE DELIVERY MODEL

The CHPP utilizes a three-bucket strategy to accomplish its mission, as follows:

1. Prevention—that is, preventing the loss and growth of heirs' property by conducting free wills clinics to draft simple wills, conducting education seminars on heirs' property and sustainable forestry, and probating estates within the ten years required by South Carolina law
2. Resolution—that is, resolving title issues by providing direct legal services and mediation needed for families to obtain clear title to their land
3. Land utilization—that is, promoting the sustainable use of the land to benefit landowners economically by providing forestry education and access to technical assistance, resources, and programs to help families develop and implement long-term forest management plans on their land to increase the value of and income from their land

The foundation of the CHPP's service delivery model is education.

A. Prevention: Combating the Growth of Heirs' Property

When one thinks of the "heirs' property problem" one usually envisions property passed down through multiple generations by intestate inheritance resulting in a hundred or more tenancy-in-common owners. The CHPP has always taken the approach that if it can provide communities and families with early education and access to a trusted legal resource, it can prevent such a scenario and keep families from the quagmire of multigenerational heirs' property. Preventing the problem is as important as, and preferable to, fixing the problem.

1. Attorneys Earning Trust

To provide true context for the CHPP's legal work with landowners, it is important to understand that the baseline for our attorneys' successes in the communities we serve begins with earning the trust of the community.[11] Not only must the organization achieve a level of trust and acceptance, but the CHPP's attorneys individually must develop the same quality of relationships with those who serve as the gatekeepers for their respective communities. The number of years spent by CHPP attorneys earning the trust of local pastors, grassroots organizations, gatekeepers, families, and individual heirs is the key reason the CHPP is recognized as a trusted legal resource. Furthermore, maintaining that

[11] Joshua Walden, *The Process of Serving Heirs' Property Clients*, U.S. ENDOWMENT FOR FORESTRY AND COMMUNITIES (2015).

trust is a continuous process of attorneys nurturing and reaffirming the CHPP's commitment by way of every interaction.

2. *Free Community Wills Clinics*

Free wills clinics have always been a staple of the CHPP's services. While providing access to a trusted attorney, the CHPP is supplying the most basic and necessary tool for families to avoid the heirs' property problem and reaching individuals who might not otherwise be able to afford an attorney. The importance of these clinics cannot be overstated. In addition to the benefit listed above, they provide the local bar and law schools the opportunity to volunteer. These partnerships prove beneficial for all involved and serve as a key component to outreach, education, and garnering community trust.

3. *Estate Administration (Probate)*

Drafting wills and educating the public to the necessity of estate planning and legally resolving someone's estate is only part of the process when tackling the prevention of multigenerational heirs' property. Ultimately, to preserve or restore clear title, family members must be able to access a trusted, affordable attorney to properly administer the estate, whether testate or intestate.

An interesting development over time is that the CHPP has experienced a steady increase in the number of applicants who need estate administration for a loved one. After 15 years of service, the CHPP is seeing many of the wills drafted by its staff years ago brought back by the appointed personal representative as a new applicant. This speaks volumes about the education/outreach and wills clinic components of the CHPP's work, and has occurred to such an extent that the majority of clients are probate administration cases who are also provided associated estate planning, post-resolution.

B. Resolution: Hurdles in the Process

The CHPP does not handle partition sale actions and will only file a quiet title and/or partition-in-kind action if the CHPP has 100 percent confirmed heir agreement. While the available legal mechanisms and resulting strategies available to an attorney dealing with multigenerational heirs' property will be determined by that lawyer's state law and version of the UPHPA where applicable, a few consistent and universal problems associated with these types of cases deserve mention. In the end, the goal for the client is to proceed in a way that makes the land least vulnerable to a forced partition sale. To accomplish this goal, the following challenges must be met.

1. *The Family Tree and Genealogy*

Building the family tree in multigenerational cases is one of the most difficult and time-consuming aspects of the work. While the client and heirs are often responsible for communicating with other family members in the information-gathering process, the attorney needs to shape and guide the process in such a way as to keep the family as organized as possible and on track.[12] In a hypothetical case where the client is charged with completing a family tree that begins with the original decedent owner acquiring land in 1905, dying intestate in 1930, leaving a spouse and eleven children (who have all since died intestate), with each child leaving at least eight children (some of whom have also passed intestate), the client and heirs can become overwhelmed at the prospect of "eating the elephant."

---

[12] *Id.*

To assist the client, CHPP attorneys draft the first version of the family tree, and the client and heirs will work from the initial template. The process of identifying those key heirs who will assist in the process and be responsible for their "branch" of the family tree is imperative and will increase the likelihood for success. In the above example, securing at least one heir representative for each of the eleven heir lines would be ideal. Furthermore, while maintaining a master family tree, the attorney should create subtrees, particular to a specific branch, from which each heir representative can work and provide new information to the attorney, along with associated documentation such as birth and death certificates, obituaries, family bibles, family reunion programs, and so on. This helps focus the effort of each heir/branch representative without the constant reminder of the true scope of the family tree as a whole. As information is provided, it is also important for the attorney to provide updated trees to those obtaining the information, as these serve to provide evidence of progress and motivation to continue the work.

It is also important to make the client and heir line representatives aware of any community resources that might assist in the process, such as local historical genealogy societies, libraries, churches, funeral homes, probate court records, register of deeds records, or services such as ancestry.com. Often, clients are unaware of available resources, and providing a referral list will prove extremely helpful to the family.

The task of completing the family tree and securing the associated confirming documentation usually requires coordinating with the client and heirs from numerous states, and can involve family members working together who may have had almost no contact over the years, or who have long-standing disagreements over the land or other familial matters not tied to the land. The successful completion of the family tree is intrinsically connected to the "family agreement" aspect of the work, as the collection of the information can be delayed or stopped because of long-standing conflicts or disagreements that crop up during the process.

2. *Family Agreement and the Role of Mediation*

As difficult as the family tree process can be, family disagreement may be the biggest hurdle CHPP clients face in multigenerational cases. Unlike the family tree challenge, where the likelihood of success can sometimes be predicted based on the sheer number of folks involved, "agreement" often has nothing to do with the size of the heir group. While dealing with fewer heirs can make the communication aspect easier, quicker, and more cost effective, it certainly does not guarantee "agreement" success.[13] Therefore, obtaining confirmation of full heir agreement among a large group of heirs often proves even more difficult, due to the added layer of the logistical challenges of communication with a very large group. The sources of disagreement and tension can vary greatly and can manifest themselves in ways that result in complete gridlock.

The following are some of the conflicts and family dynamics that are common among clients:

- Heirs who pay taxes vs. heirs who do not pay taxes
- Heirs who live on the land vs. heirs did not know they were heirs until someone contacted them
- Heirs whose family stayed on the land vs. heirs whose family left and have never lived on the land

[13] *Id.*

- Heirs who consider only blood heirs as rightful owners vs. heirs who have inherited by way of marriage
- Older vs. younger heirs
- Discrepancy in formal education among heirs across the board, and the myths and assumptions they have about each other that cause division and distrust
- Heirs who are contributing to cover associated costs vs. heirs who will not, or cannot, contribute to costs
- Heirs who want to keep the land vs. heirs who want to sell; heirs who want to develop vs. heirs who want to live on the land; heirs who want to farm/timber vs. heirs who want everyone to leave it the way it is

Family mediation has always played a significant role in the CHPP's success. These types of issues are expected. CHPP attorneys are trained to deal with family discord and the legal department has developed tools to navigate this inevitable hurdle. Being certified as a family court mediator or simply being trained in general family mediation is truly an asset for any attorney dealing with this aspect of the process. The ability and willingness to patiently guide a family through points of contention is a necessary component to the CHPP's work and sets the CHPP apart from many other legal-aid organizations.

Under the CHPP model, the likelihood of successfully resolving a case that involves multiple generational heirs' property is often contingent on a family's willingness to compromise and participate in mediation over a long period of time. CHPP attorneys must contend with the inevitable ebb and flow of family dynamics and the understandable frustration heirs feel when they work over a period of years in an attempt to reach full agreement.

Two cases, one successfully resolved and one closed due to an inability to move forward because of disagreement among the heirs, evidence the difficulty of the process. The basic facts, and number of heirs involved, were very similar yet the outcomes were vastly different.

a. Case No. 1 (37 Heirs with 26.4 Rural Acres)

The CHPP was approached in 2012 by a great-granddaughter of the decedent owner, who died intestate in the 1920s. Over the course of time, and years of intestate inheritance, the subject property was inherited by thirty-seven heirs in varying degrees of interest. At the time of application for CHPP services, there were three lines of inheritance through three siblings, all being deceased. One heir owned a full one-third interest while the remaining two-thirds interests were held by the remaining thirty-six heirs, who made up the other two lines of inheritance. Three of the thirty-six lived on the property and wanted to have their parcels "cut-off" for purposes of sole ownership.

They had also received numerous unsolicited letters from developers who wanted to buy their land. These communications caused much distress among the family, as the heir who owned one-third interest (who lived in Philadelphia) had expressed, on numerous occasions, a desire that the property be sold and the proceeds divided among the heirs. The remaining thirty-six heirs were spread across South Carolina, North Carolina, Georgia, Washington, Philadelphia, and New York, which made consistent and timely communication difficult.

Over the next three years, the CHPP attorney worked with the client and the family to develop the family tree, collect evidence as to familial history, and reach an agreement on how to divide the land. After multiple meetings and mediation sessions, twenty-six heirs indicated they did not want their interests and desired to transfer their ownership to some of their respective siblings who expressed a desire to remain a part of the tenancy-in-common group and eventually live on the property.

The willingness of the twenty-six was contingent on their respective siblings being able to have a portion allocated to them as a separate parcel with no co-ownership with the other heirs. Additionally, the one-third owner refused to participate in the family meetings and mediation sessions over the course of the first year and a half (other than saying via letters to the CHPP attorney that he was only interested in discussing the process once the other heirs had a check to buy out his interest). Certain heirs also wavered when the time came to actually commit to transferring their interests, which caused delays in moving forward with the agreement.

As is almost always the case, the issue of paying the taxes and the costs associated with the process (surveys, recording fees, filing fees, etc.) and the inability or refusal of some heirs to contribute to costs was a point of contention throughout. Eventually, the group collectively agreed on a physical division of the property into three parcels and a partition survey was performed. The one-third owner agreed to take a back parcel which had roughly eight acres of dense yellow pine, which was further incentive as it was the only portion of the property with sellable timber.

Upon completion of the survey, one "taking" heir changed his mind and indicated he wanted a small parcel only to himself and not as part of his sibling group. This required revisiting and confirming an alteration to the original agreement with all thirty-seven heirs and an eventual second modified survey cutting a small 1-acre parcel out of the eight acres designated for his sibling group.

Due to the instability of the "agreement" at times and the fact that three heirs actually lived on the land with their families, the CHPP attorney decided that accomplishing the agreed-upon partition should be settled prior to filing with the court so as to avoid any possibility of disagreement that might lead to a forced partition sale. During the last year, the attorney sent quitclaim deeds to all transferring heirs, across six states, which eventually resulted in the CHPP being able to cull the number of owners down to the agreed-upon eleven taking heirs.

The case was closed in 2015 with an agreed-upon partition dividing the property into four parcels in accord with the final agreement. The execution and recording of quitclaim deeds to bring about the agreed-upon partition resulted in four parcels being owned by eleven heirs. The successful quiet title action was filed in 2015, after the recording of the survey and all associated deeds, and resolved title to all four parcels.

b. Case No. 2 (58 Heirs with 74.9 Rural Acres)

The CHPP was approached originally in 2016 by the grandson of the original decedent owner, who died intestate in 1944. Over the course of time, and years of intestate inheritance, the subject property was inherited by fifty-eight heirs in varying degrees of interest. At the time of application for CHPP services, there were seven lines of inheritance through seven siblings, six of whom were deceased. Nine of the fifty-eight heirs lived on the property and wanted to have the property divided equally among the seven inheriting lines. The heirs were spread over the states of South Carolina, Georgia, New York, and Texas.

From 2016 through 2020, CHPP worked with the client and the family in hopes of reaching an agreement. The CHPP attorney and heirs constructed the family tree and collected the appropriate supporting evidence and had a title search performed in anticipation of having a survey completed. During the process, multiple family meetings and mediation sessions were held, which sometimes involved relatively mild conflicts over the issues of patriarchal control of the property, heirs who lived on the property vs. those who did not, the payment of taxes, and revenues associated with an existing hunting lease.

At the beginning of 2020, almost all of the points of contention seemed resolved, and the family was to meet with the CHPP attorney to discuss the title search and the next steps associated with having a survey completed. The survey meeting devolved into a very confrontational situation because of one group of heirs' assertions that another heir's birth was the result of an adulterous relationship by her mother, thereby removing her as an heir. For two months after the family meeting, the CHPP attorney attempted to facilitate a resolution to the divide but all attempts proved futile—many heirs were so discouraged, they simply refused to participate any longer.

C. Metrics of Success

Since 2005, the CHPP has provided 2,787 persons with free, one-hour "Advice and Counsel" (A&C) sessions, with 608 of these persons becoming clients to receive direct legal services to resolve title issues. From 2018 to 2020, the average annual tax-assessed value of the land on which A&C was provided was $30 million. A total of 280 titles have been cleared on family land with a total tax-assessed value of $16.5 million. A total of 1,168 simple wills have been drafted at free, community wills clinics since 2009. These combined strategies are designed to help these landowners gain economic empowerment to be in control of their own assets.

III. THE CHPP MAKING THE LAND WORK FOR THE PEOPLE

In 2008, the CHPP underwent a strategic planning process that led the organization to incorporate land utilization services into its toolkit, specifically education to create awareness of how heirs' property owners can make their wooded or rural acreage wealth-building assets. These educational workshops were called HP 102 Seminars: Making Your Land Work for You. This planning process was in response to several funders asking the organization what was the next step for landowners once they had resolved their title issues.

The CHPP continued to conduct these educational seminars until it learned of the Sustainable Forestry and African American Land Retention Program (SFALR), which was created by the U.S. Endowment for Forestry and Communities (the Endowment) in response to the loss of land among African Americans and their lack of representation in the forest industry in the South. The South, called the "Nation's wood basket,"[14] is home to millions of acres of forest land owned by non-industrial private landowners. However, many African Americans who own forest land were not

---

[14] U.S. Forest Service Southern Research Station, *Compass: Perspectives and Tools to Benefit Southern Forest Resources from the Southern Research Station* (2010), https://www.srs.fs.usda.gov/compasslive/compasspdfs/compass17.pdf.

aware of the available resources and, therefore, could not access them to make their land productive and earn income.

The forest industry in South Carolina contributes $21 billon to the state's economy. SFALR's purpose was to use sustainable forestry as a tool to "aid in stabilizing African American land ownership across generations and enhance family wealth by increasing income and land asset value."[15] Although the focus of this program was sustainable forestry, the Endowment recognized that heirs' property played a major role in the loss of land among African Americans and increased the likelihood that forests would be lost to development.

A. Sustainable Forestry

The CHPP, along with its partners, successfully obtained a grant from The Endowment and began its Sustainable Forestry Program (SFP) in June 2013 to address the need to restore and conserve forested acres and increase their value and productivity for African American landowners by providing education, technical assistance, forest management resources, and access to markets. Together, the US Department of Agriculture (USDA)—through the National Resources Conservation Service (NRCS), the Farm Service Agency (FSA), and the Forest Service—along with the South Carolina Forestry Commission, local land trusts and industrial forest corporations, and the CHPP created a comprehensive system of landowner support to expand and increase the practice of sustainable forestry and decrease the underutilization and loss of land.

The CHPP's Sustainable Forestry Program helped build a bridge of trust between African American landowners and USDA, which made it easier for these landowners to submit applications for financial assistance for their prescribed forestry practices to NRCS cost-share programs. In addition, the state FSA personnel used a similar procedure to that used in getting funds to landowners from the tobacco settlement, to help heirs' property owners obtain a farm tract number (i.e., a social security number for the land), which is a requirement for accessing NRCS cost-share programs.

The CHPP recognized that forestry program participants who owned heirs' property, while receiving some benefit, would remain "locked-out" of the majority of possibilities until their title issues were resolved. Therefore, direct legal services remained a necessary component to the holistic approach to resolving heirs' property to allow a family to fully utilize its property.

When the SFP was added to the CHPP's toolbox of services, the number of persons receiving advice and counsel doubled. The potential income from operating forestry enterprises was the "carrot" to motivate individuals to have difficult conversations with their families to resolve the title issues to their land. Heirs' property owners of forested land with merchantable timber were instructed not to cut the timber since they did not have a "clear" title. Additionally, the CHPP also recognized that addressing land utilization for African American landowners who currently have clear title would play an important role in preventing the creation of heirs' property and, therefore, decrease the likelihood of African American land loss.

The CHPP built upon its track record of successfully handling issues of land tenure, heirs' property, and estate planning and expanded its services to low-income African American landowners by

---

[15] U.S. Endowment for Forestry and Communities, *Request for Proposals: Sustainable Forestry and African American Land Retention* (2012).

providing them with business development and management assistance and making them aware of the appropriate sustainable forestry techniques. Pairing an on-staff forester with staff attorneys via traditional outreach methods allowed the CHPP to engage and educate landowners on sustainable forestry and the benefits and possibilities thereof.

Once a landowner became a forestry program participant, staff foresters became "connectors" between landowners, service providers, and the appropriate governmental agencies. As participants navigated the processes associated with true land management and the usually unfamiliar and sometimes complex steps associated with cost-share programs available to historically underserved landowners through the USDA, staff foresters continued to play a significant role in providing direct on-the-ground technical assistance and continuing education workshops on business management, financing, and market access.

B. Traditional Agriculture

The CHPP's land utilization work initially focused on sustainable forestry, but not all family land lends itself to forestry taking account of topography, and historical and ongoing best-use considerations. As a result, the CHPP has begun to initiate training and hire new land utilization staff who also have a background in land management practices involving traditional crop agriculture.

C. Conservation Easements

The CHPP's expansion into the land utilization/forestry aspect of its work naturally resulted in more historically African American rural land being fully utilized by families and protected. Since these working landscapes were of larger acreage, landowners were exposed to the concept of conservation easements and associated opportunities through governmental and private sources. As landowners were being educated on these possibilities, the "conservation world" began to take notice of African American landowners whose ancestors had been practicing "conservation" for generations. As these landowners are provided the legal services to clear title to their land and engage in sustainable forestry or traditional agriculture as a means of creating generational wealth, large rural tracts are less likely to end up as big box stores or gated communities. In turn, urban sprawl is slowed, and the health of the regional ecosystem is preserved.

D. Housing Repairs and Natural Disasters

Clear title and land utilization is not just about heirs' property families who own significant rural acreage. One of the most common reasons for an applicant to apply for direct legal services revolves around the need for home repairs. Utilizing the equity in a home for the purpose of expansion or needed repairs is something many take for granted but is unavailable in an heirs' property situation. Very often, such a need is precipitated by a major weather event resulting in significant damage to the family home. Absent clear title, a family can have an extremely difficult time accessing local, state, and federal funding associated with disaster relief. Thus, many families are displaced with no recourse or immediately available avenue of assistance. Long after the hurricane has passed, and the television crews have departed, these families are generally forgotten, and many remain displaced for years after or live in homes that are unsafe as a result of the extensive damage.

The CHPP has always worked with state and county agencies, as a referral for homeowners, and local nongovernmental organizations to offer title clearing services to homeowners who find themselves in such a predicament.

IV. CONCLUSION

The CHPP has been assisting families with resolving heirs' property for 16 years and helping historically underserved landowners create sustainable forestry enterprises for eight of those years. During this time, the CHPP has received numerous calls from families owning land in other states who need title resolution assistance, private attorneys working with these families, and other nonprofits that would like to provide similar services to its constituents. Most recently, the issue of heirs' property has risen to become a national priority due to the enactment of the Uniform Partition of Heirs Property Act (UPHPA) in many states, its inclusion in the 2018 Farm Bill, and media coverage.

Though enactment of enabling legislation is crucial, ultimately heirs' property owners will need direct legal services to resolve their specific ownership issues by obtaining clear marketable title or consolidating ownership into a "manageable" number of heirs, or transfer into an agreed-upon legal entity. Also, there will be a need to prevent the growth of heirs' property by conducting educational seminars and drafting wills and estate plans. Low- to moderate-income families do not have the resources to engage private attorneys. Pro bono attorneys have a limited amount of time that they can provide for "free." Hence, there remains the need for both public interest organizations like the CHPP and GHPLC and public/private partnerships to be created to address the issue of heirs' property in local jurisdictions across the United States and for donors to financially support these entities. Truly, it will take a village of advocates to address this complex legal, family, community, environmental, and economic problem.

PART III

Proactive Planning by Heirs and Lawyers

6

Practically Speaking: Strategies to Prevent and Resolve Heirs' Property Legal Issues

—Mavis Gragg

I. PROLOGUE: AN HEIR'S PERSONAL PERSPECTIVE ON ESTATE PLANNING

In 2012 my siblings and I, and our cousin, became heirs' property owners when our parents and our cousins were killed in a car crash. We inherited several pieces of real estate, including our childhood home, grandmother's and great-grandmother's homes, that were part of our family's American Dream, acquired over a nearly 100-year period by our hardworking, low-wage-earning African American family in the rural Appalachian Mountains of North Carolina. In an instant, we became heirs' property owners, tenants in common saddled with complex challenges we have had to navigate over the past decade.

Like most American families, my parents placed a high value on inheritance for maintaining ownership of our family's real estate. They took great pride in the fact that they and our ancestors had built wealth that could be shared from one generation to the next through the inheritance. They, along with my grandparents and great-grandparents, worked hard to build and own homes so that we and future generations of our family could enjoy and benefit from the real estate assets. And like most Americans, their plan was simple—they believed that when they (my parents) died, my siblings and I would automatically inherit, under the law, the family real estate, care for it, and then the next generation of family members would inherit the property, care for it, and pass it on to the next generation, and so on. My parents, despite my urging, and in spite of the fact that I am a lawyer, did not have succession plans or estate plans in place. In fact, they had told me, "You'll take care of it," when I begged them to plan.

My parents believed that the laws related to inheritance, known as intestacy, supported their vision for the family real estate and other assets. Many families retain ownership of their family real estate by operation of the set of state laws that apply (intestate succession) when people die owning assets and there is no will to inform who inherits their assets. Typically, real estate inherited from a deceased person through intestate succession goes to the people whom the deceased want to receive the property after they die—their immediate family. Even individuals who have wills plan for their real estate to be inherited by their next of kin, which often is multiple people. Those jointly inheriting real estate, whether through a will or intestate succession, automatically inherit as tenants in common[1].

Because of this, many people erroneously assume that intestacy—the absence of a will—works well for family real estate. It does not work well for heirs' property tenants in common, and it disproportionately impacts disadvantaged communities, including most prominently the African American community. In chapter 1, Professor Mitchell refers to the phenomenon of a massive racial will-making gap in this country as it affects African Americans, citing studies relating to lack of access to affordable legal services and a distrust of the legal system, and noting the severe underrepresentation of African American lawyers who practice in transactional areas most relevant to assisting African American heirs' property owners.

Maintaining ownership of family real estate as heirs' property creates many challenges, including the risk of loss. Determined to help other families avoid the type of pain and loss my siblings and I experienced, I started a law practice in which I helped numerous families resolve heirs' property issues and do succession planning to optimize their family's intergenerational wealth. I also did significant outreach and education in which I heard numerous horror stories about challenges heirs' property owners were experiencing or had experienced.

I was particularly interested in helping families who are land rich and cash poor and families from communities that have experienced tremendous loss of real estate owned as heirs' property. Time and time again I encountered families who value real estate as a significant asset for intergenerational wealth. Many of them maintained or tried to maintain ownership through inheritance, either by intestate succession or through wills. Most of the heirs' property owners were struggling with legal and financial issues such as not having clear title—legal proof of current ownership—because they had retained ownership over generations through intestacy. Clear title refers to ownership of the property being clear of any claims and encumbrances, with all owners identified and confirmed.

Co-owner conflict and threat of loss through partition actions, as described in chapters 1, 3, and 5, were among other challenges. Partition actions are lawsuits in which a co-owner seeks a court-ordered physical division of real estate or, if physical division is not possible, the sale of the property. Physical partition necessarily decreases the overall value of the intergenerational asset, whereas forced sales often yield a dollar amount significantly less than the fair market value of the real estate once all fees and expenses related to the sale have been paid.

Over time it became clear that some strategies that individuals, including attorneys working on heirs' property matters, use to prevent or resolve heirs' property issues do not sustain family property

[1] Although it is possible to explicitly state in a will a specific type of ownership other than tenants in common, most people with wills do not make that specification and, thus, the heirs inherit as tenants in common by operation of law.

over multiple generations. I also honed in on other strategies that not only prevent or resolve heirs' property issues, but also optimize ownership of real estate as an intergenerational asset.

II. DEVELOPING AN ENTITY-CENTERED STRATEGY: PREPARATION, DEVELOPMENT, AND AVOIDANCE OF "SIMPLE" SOLUTIONS THAT CAN CAUSE COMPLEX ISSUES

In this chapter, drawing on my personal and professional experiences with heirs' property, I discuss the various strategies to address issues with heirs' property. We'll first look at an entity-centered strategy that can be used as an approach to prevent or resolve heirs' property issues, including alternatives. This is followed by a discussion of how to prepare for developing a strategy, and how to avoid simple solutions that can cause complex issues. It is my hope that in reading this chapter, readers will commit to building and implementing comprehensive succession plans for family real estate and be equipped with foundational knowledge to pursue this planning. I also hope this will serve as a reference for lawyers working in this complex area of law practice and as an inspiration to other lawyers and law students to work on heirs' property matters.

A. A Note About Intergenerational Wealth

Before we look closely at how to plan for multiple generations of family-owned real estate, it's important to discuss the term "intergenerational wealth" in connection with family-owned real estate. Intergenerational wealth refers to assets that are passed down from generation to generation within a family. Accumulation and transfer of wealth between generations allows the family to use their wealth over time to support each generation. When it comes to real estate ownership, the advantages are more than financial. Family-owned real estate can provide multiple generations with housing, income, recreation, and stewardship of natural resources. Families that are part of groups that have experienced and continue to experience adversity due to systemic racism or systemic poverty are better able to combat those systemic issues when they have intergenerational wealth. Family-owned real estate, when well managed, can help families thrive, and it greatly enhances the resiliency a family has in the face of change. And these effects extend to the communities, food systems, industry, and beyond.

B. Entity-Centered Strategy for Preventing and Resolving Heirs' Property Issues

Aside from intestate succession (inheritance by law), estate plans, specifically wills, are considered the primary strategy for intergenerational ownership of real estate and other assets. Estate planning is the process of anticipating and arranging, during a person's life, for the management and disposal of that person's estate, in the event the person becomes incapacitated and when they die. Although estate plans play a role in planning to avoid heirs' property and to remedy issues with heirs' property, it's important to have the mindset of succession planning, with estate plans being a tool in a broader succession plan. The same is true for deeds, which are discussed more thoroughly later in this chapter. Succession planning is strategic. It's also expansive in that it is addresses more than ownership transfers.

Succession planning, most often considered in the context of business, is strategizing to ensure continuity when change occurs, particularly when there is significant change in the people involved, such as when someone leaves their role, becomes incapacitated, or dies. When it comes to family real estate, succession planning focuses, not only on the transition of ownership, but also on the succession of management of the real estate, and how the property is used. The primary benefit of succession planning is that a good succession plan ensures smooth transitions despite any significant changes.

Entity-centered succession plans in which the property is owned and managed by an entity provide the greatest opportunity for strategically managing family real estate over multiple generations. In chapter 7, David Dietrich provides a thorough analysis of the various entity types that should be considered in any planning strategy. He includes an entity chart that compares various characteristics of the entity types, including management, liability, and some taxation, and model forms of a tenancy-in-common agreement (TIC), a trust, and a limited liability corporation (LLC).

In this chapter, we look closely at trusts and limited liability companies, as well as other tools that complement an entity-centered estate plan or which are more manageable by families even if they do not achieve optimal sustainability.

1. Trusts

Trusts are one option you must consider in developing a comprehensive strategy that addresses management, decision making, and use and enjoyment of real estate for the family for multiple generations. Trusts are created by a settlor(s) who transfers legal title of assets to a fiduciary, the trustee(s), to manage the assets on behalf of the beneficiaries of the trust. There are three distinct roles that are often held by the same individual or individuals: "settlors," "co-trustees," and "beneficiaries."

For example, a couple with children and grandchildren, desiring for their family home to stay in the family for generations to come, could use a trust to achieve this goal. An attorney would draft the trust document for the couple in which they would be the "settlors." The couple would also appoint themselves as the "co-trustees" responsible for managing the trust asset—the family home. Management of the home would not likely look much different from how they manage the property as individual owners while the couple is alive and of capacity. The main difference would be that transactions related to the home would be conducted in the name of the trustee(s) of the trust rather than the couple as individuals. They would also nominate themselves as the beneficiaries of the trust. A beneficiary of a trust is the person or persons whom the trust is meant to benefit. The trustee has a fiduciary duty to the beneficiaries to manage the trust's assets as outlined in the trust agreement and for the benefit of the beneficiaries.

Two key factors of the trust lend themselves to smooth transition when there is change. In the trust document, successor trustees would be identified. You can even define a process for appointing successor trustees and give the beneficiaries decision-making power over appointment of successor trustees. You can also name successor beneficiaries of the trust, and drafting of the trust document provides flexibility to develop a succession of beneficiaries that supports the overall goals of the family's use of the property. Additionally, the trust document can outline decision-making power beyond succession, such as conditions for use of the property, management of income generated by the property, and more.

Developing a trust requires working with an attorney experienced in drafting trusts for the purposes of intergenerational family ownership. This is because there are various factors to consider, such as the type of trust. There are categories of trusts and a trust can fit into multiple categories of trusts. A trust can be created during the life of the settlor, known as an *inter vivos* trust. A trust can be created through a will, referred to as a testamentary trust. The death of the testator triggers creation of the testamentary trust, with the terms of the trust being defined in the will. Trusts can also be revocable or irrevocable. A revocable trust can be changed or terminated whereas, with certain exceptions detailed in chapter 7, an irrevocable trust cannot be changed. It is even possible to create a condition in which a revocable trust becomes irrevocable, such as the death of the settlor.

For many people trusts are viewed as a legal tool for the wealthy or as too complex to merit use for their own planning. However, there are numerous benefits to using trusts if you desire for real estate to remain "in the family" for multiple generations and, especially, if you want to avoid creating heirs' property with the attendant risk of loss of the real estate. With the trust being the sole owner of the real estate, the statutory framework for ownership by tenants in common or joint tenants with rights of survivorship is not a factor. The settlor(s) determine decision-making authority for the trustee and beneficiaries. Succession of roles can be predetermined in the trust document, creating a clear understanding of who manages the trust assets and who benefits from them. Yet another benefit is that individuals' creditors cannot make claims on the trust property since the individuals do not own the trust property.

Some states offer statutory provisions that deepen the value of using trusts for intergenerational family land management with family trust companies. The family trust company is an entity organized to serve as a trustee of the family's trusts.[2] The family trust corporation is attractive to families seeking privacy,[3] flexibility,[4] and limited liability[5] when managing their wealth. However, generally, trust companies are expensive to manage and are thus used by the wealthy[6] since they require working with attorneys with tax, banking, and trust expertise, accountants, and financial professionals to manage the company.[7]

2. *Limited Liability Companies and Other Business Entities*

There are various types of business entities that can be considered for a succession plan aimed at preventing or resolving heirs' property issues. Each entity carries unique benefits and drawbacks. They also vary in complexity, legal requirements, and taxation. Among the business entities, I believe limited liability companies (LLCs), discussed in chapter 7, are most practical for management of heirs' property, subject to a well-drafted operating agreement as discussed below.[8]

---

[2] Iris J. Goodwin, *How the Rich Stay Rich: Using a Family Trust Company to Secure a Family Fortune*, 40 Seton Hall L. Rev. 467, 473 (2010).

[3] Brian M. Malec & Scott A. Bowman, *Florida Family Trust Companies: Tax and Nontax Considerations*, 89 Fla. Bar J. 42 (2015).

[4] *See* Goodwin, *supra* note 2, at 481 (noting families wish to bypass a big bank's red tape when making investment decisions).

[5] *Id.* at 477 (noting a private trust company offers protection to the family because the corporate veil must be pierced to hold an individual family member liable).

[6] Malec & Bowman, *supra* note 3.

[7] *Id.*

[8] In my experience they are relatively easy to manage and they provide liability protection.

The role-players in an LLC are the members (owners) and manager(s). Members own the LLC, which owns the subject real estate. They have some decision-making authority—typically major decisions such as changes in membership or transfer of assets owned by the LLC. Within the membership of the LLC you can have various classes of members, each with unique authority, responsibility, and distribution of income.

The manager is tasked with the day-to-day responsibility of managing the LLC and its assets. Members (owners) of the LLC can hold both roles as member managers. You can also have a manager who holds no ownership interest in the LLC. It is important to distinguish the type of authority and responsibilities a manager has and educate the members about the manager's authority and responsibilities.

Creating an LLC is fairly straightforward as it requires completion of paperwork required by the state where the LLC is being formed and filing that paperwork with the prescribed fee with the Secretary of State's office. Typically, LLCs and other business entities are required to make annual filings with the Secretary of State. Failure to do so can result in the entity being dissolved by the state. Therefore, families using LLCs for their succession plan, should be very careful to ensure the entity registration remains up to date. If the entity is terminated, the ownership might revert back to the owners who contributed their shares to the entity, but that is not clear-cut and depends on the operating agreement and numerous conditions; see chapter 7 for a description of the legal issues.

Equally important is using and maintaining an operating agreement for the LLC. Many families overlook this important document when using an LLC to manage their real estate, because this document is not required to form an LLC with the state. However, the usefulness of the LLC is born out of the operating agreement. The document outlines the business's financial and functional decisions, including rules, regulations, and provisions. In it the family can plan for succession of ownership and management in a way that meets their vision for the property. Failure to have a customized operating agreement for the LLC can render your succession planning effort ineffective. In addition, failure to have any operating agreement results in reliance on the generic requirements of state law, which completely misses the benefit of having a plan for the specific family and real estate. All members (owners) of the LLC should understand very clearly how the operating agreement functions, what it obligates them to, and any power differences between owners.[9] For example, some families using LLCs for ownership and management of their family real estate experience internal conflict due to different needs and expectations. Other issues can arise, such as member shares being diluted, which results in their ownership and authority being decreased. Chapter 7 explores some of these issues in depth.

3. *Additional Tools for Succession Planning*

A succession plan could use multiple entities within the strategy. For example, the real estate could be owned by a trust that leases the property to a family-owned LLC established for a farming operation. Another similar example, aimed at generating liquidity for intergenerational wealth, could be creating a trust for young children, transferring real estate into the trust, and leasing that real estate to yourself. The cash paid for the rent is paid to the trust and becomes a trust asset for the benefit of the

[9] In my practice, I would provide an FAQs document as a way to clearly communicate important details expressed in the operating agreement.

children now or when they reach a designated age. If a business entity is used for succession planning for family land, it is imperative to ensure that the estate plans of the person(s) owning the business entity are addressed in the entity governance documents and their estate planning documents.

a. Wills

As stated above, aside from inheritance through intestate succession, estate plans, specifically wills, are a primary strategy families use to plan for intergenerational real estate ownership.[10] However, wills do not support ownership and management transitions beyond the next generation of owners. Wills are personal to the individual executing the will, that is, individuals with wills can only control so far from the grave. Still, wills are important and should be included in the overall succession plan strategy, as they empower testators to choose an executor to settle their affairs and choose heirs for their assets, including any real estate asset.[11]

Wills are very useful for planning for intergenerational family real estate ownership when they are done well and are tailored to the principal's individual circumstances and goals. A will used as part of a comprehensive succession plan could, for example, facilitate transfers of property acquired later into the trust or other entity when the principal dies. In this scenario, a landowner, while alive, establishes a trust and transfers his or her real estate into that trust. At the same time, the testator also executes a will providing that all real estate owned by the landowner is bequeathed to the trust they have established. When the landowner later passes away, if they have not transferred the property they own personally to the trust, the will provides for that to happen.

Unfortunately, wills can also create heirs' property and often do, especially in families with step-children and multiple remarriages.[12] For example, leaving a residence to "all my children" creates a tenancy in common, with all of the attendant heirs' property problems.

b. Power of Attorney Documents

A power of attorney is a legal document used during the life of the principal to authorize someone (the agent) to act on their behalf while they are alive. The agent's authority extinguishes upon the death of the principal, unless it is revoked. The agent holds a fiduciary duty to the principal and their power is limited by the power of attorney document and the relevant laws.[13]

While most people who have power of attorney documents provide their agent with general authority, that is, authority to make all of the same types of decisions they can make, it is possible to

---

[10] Traditional estate plans include advanced healthcare directives, powers of attorney, and wills. They can also include a trust. Most estate plans, though, are will centered.

[11] If a deceased person owns an interest in a company, the company governing documents may limit certain actions prescribed by the will. For example, the operating agreement for a family LLC owning real estate may exclude nonblood family members from becoming owners of the LLC.

[12] A Florida study sought to analyze the ways in which state intestacy laws affect twenty-first-century decedents, analyzing hundreds of wills of decedents domiciled in Florida. Researchers examined two Florida counties, Alachua and Ecambia, and found that many single-family wills fell in line with the intestacy default rules, while almost all wills for families with stepchildren and multiple remarriages deviated from the default rules. Those on subsequent marriages were more likely to (1) use trusts, (2) disinherit a spouse, and (3) spread their estate between a surviving spouse and children. Danaya C. Wright & Beth Sterner, *Honoring Probable Intent in Intestacy: An Empirical Assessment of the Default Rules and the Modern Family*, 42 ACTEC L.J. 341, 344–45 (2017). https://scholarship.law.ufl.edu/cgi/viewcontent.cgi?article=1829&context=facultypub.

[13] Unfortunately, clients cannot assume that agents will always act within the scope of their fiduciary duty.

limit the powers for a specific type of decision or for a specific transaction, such as transferring real estate or signing a contract related to the real estate. Individuals and families managing real estate should consider the usefulness of power of attorney documents in their succession plan. They could help streamline to manage a big transaction related to the family real estate. For example, family members sharing ownership of a home that they lease to third-party tenants could each appoint one specific family member as their agent for the purposes of managing the rental property. The scope of the document would be limited to the specific property and the leasing of that property.

Deep consideration should be given before appointing someone as an agent in a power of attorney. Most form or template powers of attorney give full authority to the agent, so great care should be given when using power of attorney documents. It is prudent to work with an attorney to draft a power of attorney tailored to your specific needs rather than relying on simple power of attorney documents.

Despite their usefulness, it's easy to rely on powers of attorney in a way that leads to problems. Power of attorney agents often use their authority to transfer real estate on behalf of the principal for the purpose of making advance gifts to future heirs. A common scenario for this is when a principal needs to qualify for financial support for government benefits such as disability or long-term care. An agent will transfer real estate to the principal's children, seeking to decrease the principal's total net worth in order to qualify for government benefits.

Agents acting under authority of a power of attorney document should also be cautious not to breach their fiduciary duties. They should be particularly careful not to create heirs' property when it comes to transferring real estate on behalf of the principal. One scenario is the agent transferring the property to multiple anticipated heirs as tenants in common, either intentionally or unintentionally. This creates the same legal issues associated with heirs' property except the principal/property owner is still living.

Even transferring the property to multiple people as joint tenants with rights of survivorship (as discussed below) is not failproof if the goal is multigenerationally owned real estate. With this approach you only ensure that the number of owners does not expand beyond the grantees in the deed. However, the control over the intergenerational planning stops when the last joint tenant owner dies, unless that owner implements a succession plan that effectively avoids creating multiple owners while continuing succession of ownership in the family.

Given that an agent acting under the authority of a power of attorney document can effectively create heirs' property, an agent should be cautious in making any transfers of real estate, and consult an attorney to advise on the optimal plan and what is within their rights as an agent. To comply with their duties as a fiduciary and to avoid any self-dealing, they should also avoid actions that the principal would not normally make or that change the estate plan of the principal in a significant way.

Most important, your family real estate strategy should not center around a power of attorney document and the agent, because it's quite possible that the principal's goals may not be met fully or at all.

c. Deeds

Deeds are also important tools that are almost always used in implementing a plan for the family real estate. A deed is a legal instrument used to convey or confirm an interest in property. In it the property owner (grantor) expresses that they are transferring an interest to the new owner (grantee).

The text of the deed includes a legal description of the property; the grantor owner signs the deed, usually before a notary public, and then it is recorded in the county where the property is located to put the public on notice of the transfer. Thoughtfulness and clarity on using deeds is important to ensure their effectiveness in planning for intergenerational family land ownership without creating or exacerbating the challenges and risks associated with heirs' property.

Deeds are widely viewed as effective tools to prevent or resolve heirs' property issues without incurring the costs of succession planning or even the costs of the estate administration process. However, using deeds as a succession planning strategy comes with great risks, including creating heirs' property.

I. Warranties Provided by Deeds

Deeds are often categorized by the type of title warranty provided by the grantor or by the type of interest the deed creates in the grantee. When planning for succession of family land, one should consider both the type of warranty and the type of interest created by the deed. A general warranty deed is a deed in which the grantor pledges to warrant that they own the property free and clear of all claims related to the entire ownership history of the property. A special warranty deed has exceptions to what the grantor warrants- typically limited to the period that the grantor owned the property interest. Unlike the others, in a quitclaim deed the grantor makes no warrants that they own the property free and clear of all claims.

Among the three types of warranty deeds, quitclaim deeds are the most popular among people seeking to manage intergenerational ownership of family land. Many view the quitclaim deed as an easy solution. They are "easy" in so far as they do not require the grantor to convey clear title, which requires hiring an attorney to perform a title search and render an opinion that the title is clear. In relying on a quitclaim deed, any grantee should be aware that they have no assurances that they received an interest free of claims and they should know the grantor is not obligated to defend any claims should they come up.

II. Types of Interests Conveyed in Deeds

Another category of deeds is defined by the type(s) of interest(s) the deed conveys. Common types of interests include tenants in common and joint tenants with rights of survivorship (JTWROS). Tenants-in-common interests are typically inherent in a deed transferring ownership to two or more individuals when the deed does not explicitly provide for rights of survivorship.

There are also life estate deeds, transfer on death deeds (TODDs), and lady bird deeds. Life estate deeds provide for the property to be transferred to a grantee(s) with another grantee having lifetime rights for the property. This is commonly used by parents seeking to bypass the need for a will or succession plan by giving their children ownership presently and retaining lifetime rights for themselves.

When it comes to planning for intergenerational ownership, there are multiple drawbacks of life estate deeds and deeds creating JTWROS. One factor that could undermine the usefulness of a life estate deed is the possibility of remaindermen beneficiaries dying before the life tenant, creating unexpected owners of the property. Typically, life estate deeds used for succession planning create tenants-in-common remaindermen owners (same as heirs' property). The share of a remainderman beneficiary who predeceases the life tenant will go to their heirs, creating the same challenges as heirs' property.

I spoke to a family in which the mother transferred multiple properties to her three children and held a life estate in the properties. Her goal was to avoid probate and qualify for long-term care assistance. She later was diagnosed with dementia and had no power of attorney documents. Two of her children died intestate, survived by minor children and spouses. To add to the conundrum, all of the parcels were in a high-demand real estate market. Rather than serving as intergenerational wealth the property was gridlocked in a myriad of legal issues that could have been prevented with a more comprehensive plan. The ease of drafting both types of deeds is offset by the fact that neither option offers prescribed, long term, multigenerational family ownership. In addition, neither option will ensure that title will remain clear, since the owners succeeding the grantees named in either type of deed are not identifiable without further documentation or planning.

As with heirs' property, the co-owners have to make decisions about the property unanimously, which can lead to inaction and conflict. There are also tax implications created by both options. The transfer of interest in each type of deed triggers a gift tax. Families will seek to minimize this in a JTWROS deed by transferring a very small percentage, such as one percent, to the children, with the parent retaining a 99 percent share.

An additional tax implication is that the step-up in basis for tax purposes is lost. Using the same parent-child scenario, the parent bought a home in 2000 for $140,000. When his or her child inherited the home after her parent's death, the home was worth $250,000. When the child sold the home, her tax basis was $250,000. She paid taxes on the difference between the selling price and her stepped-up basis of $250,000. If the parent had transferred the property to the child as JTWROS prior to his or her death, the child wouldn't get the step-up in basis and would have to pay taxes on the difference between the selling price and the value on the date of transfer from the parent to him- or herself and the child, that is, there would be a higher tax liability than if the property was inherited by the child. An additional and equally significant drawback to these options is that the property also becomes subject to the creditors of the remaindermen beneficiaries—for example, the child—or JTWROS.

A third scenario for planning with deeds is simply transferring the property entirely to the anticipated heirs. Again, the parent to child(ren) scenario is most common. This option carries the same drawbacks as the life estate deed and JTWROS.

Some of the drawbacks of the aforementioned deed options may not be an issue for individuals in states that recognize transfer on death deeds (TODDs). TODDs do not create a current interest in property for the beneficiaries.[14] Therefore, the owner retains full power over the property and the property transfers outside the probate process.[15] Beneficiary deed, revocable transfer on death (TOD) deed, nontestamentary transfer, deed upon death, enhanced life estate deed, power of sale deed, Italian deed, and lady bird deed are commonly used terms to refer to a TODD.[16] In a TODD,

[14] Stephanie Emrick, *Transfer on Death Deeds: It Is Time to Establish the Rules of the Game*, 70 FLA. L. REV. 469, 474 (2018).

[15] *Id.* at 470.

[16] *Id.* at 479.

the beneficiary's interest in the property only becomes possessory upon the death of the grantor[17] and thus, the grantor maintains certain rights, including the right to mortgage the property.[18] The owner also retains the right to revoke or amend the beneficiary designation.[19] To do so, the grantor can record a new transfer on death deed, which will automatically supersede the previous deed.[20]

d. Tenancy-in-Common Agreements

Tenancy-in-common agreements (TICs) are yet another tool that can be considered for the succession plan. These are contracts between tenant-in-common owners, such as heirs' property owners and they are discussed in greater detail in chapter 7. TICs offer a good alternative when, for example, the costs of implementing and sustaining an entity are unaffordable or the complexity of managing an entity under the applicable laws and governance documents will be too difficult for the family. TICs also present an option to better manage and retain a property while resolving other issues, before the property ownership can be transferred to an entity.[21] As with the other tools, an attorney should be engaged to help think through the key elements and function of the TIC.

4. Succession Planning for Existing Heirs' Property

If the subject property is currently owned as heirs' property there are additional considerations for succession planning. Transferring ownership shares into an entity can be part of a strategy to offset the risk of loss in a partition action. For succession planning, thought has to be given to which family members will benefit from the property owned in the trust. Typically, heirs' property owners consist of a mixture of blood and nonblood relatives, most of whom are spouses but can also include adoptees. Will they continue to benefit from the property? Should they? Buyouts will also be likely and maybe even necessary to secure ownership under a single entity. In addition to buyouts of nonblood owners, it's quite likely that some current owners do not want to continue having a relationship with the property.

If the subject heirs' property is or is likely to become subject to a partition action, the attorney and client must consider transferring ownership shares to an entity as a strategy to avoid loss. This particular scenario underscores the need for a thorough intake process and clarity on the financial capacity of the client and the capabilities of the attorney.

I was consulted by a family with a farm they had owned for nearly 100 years. The farm was about 90 acres and there were approximately seventy owners with varied interest shares in the property. A commercial farm bought a couple of owners' shares and pursued a partition sale action. An ideal strategy for this family would be to transfer enough of the ownership interests in the property to make a physical partition (partition in kind) possible, since the court must first consider partition in kind and can only order a partition sale if the property cannot be physically divided equitably proportional to each owner's share. Unfortunately for this family, they were up against a very impressive

[17] *See id.* at 474 (highlighting that the beneficiary has no interest in the property during the lifetime of the grantor owner).

[18] *Id.* at 478.

[19] *Id.* at 474.

[20] *Id.* at 478–79.

[21] One scenario where a TIC could be useful could be when a family with heirs' property owners is seeking a temporary solution while they work on resolving conflicts or choice of entity questions.

petition that made it easy for the county clerk presiding over the proceeding to determine the property could not be physically divided because of how many interests there were, the various sizes of the ownership interests, and how, with those factors combined, the property could not be divided equitably. If, for example, the largest shareholders and a group of others transferred their shares to a single owner, preferably an entity, the county clerk could have physically divided the property.

In states that have adopted the Uniform Partition of Heirs Property Act, this strategy is even more powerful because one of the early procedural steps is buyouts of the interests of the petitioning owner. Empowered by this legislation and a sufficiently combined interest entity owner, the family would have likely succeeded in keeping most if not all of their farm. This family's property was in North Carolina, where the Uniform Partition of Heirs Property Act has been introduced but not yet enacted.

5. *Confirming Owners of Heirs' Property and Resolving Other Issues: The Roles of Heirs and their Attorneys; the Family Tree and the Succession Plan; Managing Expectations*

When an entity-centered strategy or even a strategy using a TIC agreement is the goal for heirs' property owners, implementation of such a strategy most often is preceded by resolving other issues first, in order to proceed with implementing the strategy. As we learned in other chapters of this book, heirs' property owners own the real estate as tenants in common. The law requires that all decisions effecting the entire property by made by unanimous agreement of the owners. This can include a range of decisions as simple as giving a license to hunt on the property, to leasing the real estate, to using the property as collateral for a loan, or even transferring ownership of the entire property.

For any of the decisions to be legally effective, all owners must agree. This requires, then, that all current owners have been legally confirmed, that is, a title search must be completed and a legal opinion rendered of who the current owners are. If the property is heirs' property and there is no clear title, that is, the owners have not been confirmed by an attorney, the steps to implementation of the succession plan begin with the family tree, followed by confirmation of owners, owner decision making, and then, finally, implementation of the succession plan strategy.

The family tree should begin with the family members listed in the last deed showing full ownership (100 percent) of the property being held by the family. This is often the original deed in which the property came into the family. From that starting point, all family members, to the youngest generation, should be added to the family tree. The tree should include all possible family members, including children not born of marriage, adopted and "adopted" children, and even spouses, including disliked spouses. Information about the date and location of death for deceased family members should be listed, along with the names and information for their immediate family members. If an estate was administered for any deceased family member(s) that information should be included too. For every living person, the tree should inform of their marital status. The marital status of living family members is important to ensure that spouses are identified and sign any deeds transferring interests in land. This is because they have a future right to an interest in that share.

Building a family tree for confirming heirs' property owners can most affordably and effectively be done by the family members, rather than an attorney[22]. Attorneys play an important role, however, in that they use the family tree to trace the ownership using the relevant laws, deeds, and estate

[22] My company, HeirShares, is building an application for that purpose. The tree builder can be used by families, attorneys and others to more affordably and efficiently build a family tree to be used by attorneys to confirm ownership.

documents (including probated wills). Landowners can save a lot of money if they provide a full family tree as described, along with any supporting documentation such as death certificates for all deceased family members, wills, trust documents, marriage certificates and divorce decrees, adoption records, and paternity records.

With the property owners confirmed, the third step is to seek agreement by the owners on a succession plan. The owners could facilitate their own discussion. However, a neutral third party, perhaps an attorney but perhaps a mediator or trained facilitator, could facilitate the discussion, to ensure all owners participate in the discussion and make a decision. The family can decide who will continue being connected to the property and negotiate buyouts of interests. They should also consider and choose the strategy they will implement to maintain the property.

While the four steps to implementing a succession plan for heirs' property are pretty straightforward, special consideration should be given to financing the costs of the effort and managing expectations. Legal fees can be affordable, especially if the landowner client and attorney agree to a payment structure that is feasible for the client. It is possible to borrow money to pay legal fees and purchase co-owner shares. The 2018 Farm Bill provided for an heirs' property lending program for resolving heirs' property matters, and there are other similar programs.[23]

However, due diligence should be performed to ensure the plan of action is feasible. There are numerous factors, including family conflict, the size of the family tree, economic viability of the property, and the value of the client's share. When possible, I would try to estimate the value of my client's share early on, in order to counsel them on the strategy. One client had a share worth less than $3,000.00. It didn't make sense to proceed because the family was high conflict and the legal expenses alone would have exceeded $3,000.00 by a lot.

It's also helpful to manage expectations by having a good understanding of what is possible and what is not possible. Some, maybe many, heirs' property matters cannot be resolved without great expense and emotional pain. Sometimes an entity-centered succession plan is not feasible due to the costs, complexity, or family discord. It makes sense, then, to prepare as best as possible before diving into the work.

6. *Preparing to Do Planning to Avoid or Resolve Heirs' Property Issues*

Given the complexity of heirs' property matters and of succession planning, there are steps landowners and attorneys can take to prepare for planning. Landowners can be best prepared to develop and implement a strategy for their family real estate if they have a clear goal(s) for the real estate, a budget for the work to be done, an attorney who can adequately and will ethically advise on heirs' property prevention or resolution, and the necessary documentation and information about the property and the family. A baseline goal for family real estate is to retain ownership of the property for the benefit of the family for multiple generations. Additional goals often center around how the property is used and how it is managed.[24]

[23] The US Department of Agriculture (USDA) Heirs Property Lending program provides for the USDA secretary to loan money to qualified institutions—money that is then loaned to heirs' property owners for clearing title, succession planning, dispute resolution, appraisals, surveys, and more. As of the date of this writing, the program was in the lender identification stage.

[24] Some attorneys also rely heavily on will-centered estate plans to avoid heirs' property. Wills do not prevent heirs' property. Also, many attorneys, especially those who do not commonly work with heirs' property owners, will counsel clients with heirs property to pursue partition actions, which often result in the forced sale of the property.

Having a budget before starting to plan or resolve is also important since the costs could be a barrier to completion. The costs for planning for intergenerational family real estate typically start at the low thousands, but can be higher depending on the complexity and whether any ongoing legal services are needed. Likewise, the costs for resolving heirs' property disputes start typically in the low thousands and can range greatly. Therefore, it is important to know how much money is available and the degree of tolerance to spend thousands of dollars.

Knowing the goal(s) for the property and the budget, the next step is identifying an attorney. It's important to work with an attorney to develop and implement your strategy, and the attorney should have experience working with families, real estate law, estate law, and business law. Knowledge of tax laws is important, and attorneys can collaborate with tax attorneys and accountants to ensure the clients are adequately advised regarding taxes.

Qualities to look for, in addition to subject matter experience, are willingness and ability to serve as a counselor, advocate, and problem solver; flexibility in developing the scope of work and in payment structure for the work; and a personal value for real estate as an intergenerational family wealth asset. The bottom line is, the ideal attorney is skilled and knowledgeable and values real estate as a source of intergenerational wealth. We're not unicorns, but that is a unique mix of capabilities that merit spending time identifying attorneys who meet those criteria.

Equally important to being prepared is the information and documents necessary for planning and for resolving issues. Key information needed includes, of course, the property address, the ownership history, current use of the property (how and by whom), and family dynamics. Supporting documents specific to the property include deeds, tax records, and a map related to the property. Other important documents are related to the family and include vital records such as death and birth certificates, wills of any living or deceased owner, and other records of the family members, such as a family tree.

Attorneys can be best prepared to assist with family land matters by understanding their own capacity to handle family land matters and the ethical considerations (e.g., identifying who the client should be). Capacity considerations for attorneys include skills and experience, workload, fee and payment structure flexibility, and other service providers who can aid the work, such as foresters, accountants, and real estate professionals. For fee and payment structure, I was able to expand my capacity to work on heirs' property matters by accepting smaller payments over a longer period. This required me and the client to agree on how this affected the work planning, and for me to balance matters with quicker turnaround vs. longer turnaround.

The attorney should also prescreen any matter by conducting a consultation or intake with the aim of determining what the issue is and the potential work and costs involved. The attorney's main objective in the initial meeting should be to understand the potential client's goals for the property and the current circumstances related to the property. They should also assess whether the potential client's goals can realistically be achieved, and what is likely to be required to achieve this goal.

I found it very beneficial to provide the potential client with the opportunity to share freely about the history of the property, their connection to it, family members, and interpersonal relationship dynamics while actively listening. It may be tempting to have a directive conversation with the potential client for efficiency. However, allowing them to tell the story, so to speak, serves to help deescalate high emotions and to draw out information that might not be elicited by directive conversation.

Once the attorney and client agree to work together, the engagement letter must carefully spell out who the client is and who isn't the client, the scope of work and what work is not included, and the fee and payment structure.

The following chart captures the key preparations that should be made by landowners and attorneys.

Landowners	Attorneys
• Goal for the real estate • Budget amount • Attorney • Property documents and Family Information	• Capacity to do the work • Prescreen of the matter • Scope of work and Engagement letter

Ultimately, lawyers serve vital succession planning functions that cannot be replicated by do-it-yourself (DIY) efforts. Access to trustworthy, high quality legal services is key to building and implementing a strategy. Depending on the circumstances you may need an attorney well versed in estate, real estate, and business law. If you need to clear title, you will need an attorney in the state where the property is located. Finding a good fit can be challenging. Attorneys in urban areas often have higher fees, but they are often more plentiful, offering a variety of firms to choose from.

Attorneys in rural areas are often in small practices that cover a wide range of practice areas. However, they may not have expertise as it relates to succession planning for family real estate. While it's possible to find a rural attorney with the needed skills and experience, it's critical to vet them and ensure they serve with the client's best interests in mind. Unfortunately, many heirs' property owners have worked with unscrupulous attorneys, often in the rural setting. Therefore, it may be necessary to reach far to get the legal services you need.

All of these factors impact building a strategy. Considering these factors in relation to your own circumstances and goals before launching in strategy building will help you be more intentional in your strategy building.

7. *Simple-Seeming Solutions That Lead to Complex Problems*

a. Avoid the Do-It-Yourself Approach

Let's face it. Identifying, affording, and working with an attorney can be very challenging. Many users are drawn to the DIY approach because of the perception that attorney fees are not affordable or that the value of their assets is too low or the nature of their circumstances too simple to merit hiring an attorney. The DIY approach to estate planning is very tempting, but it should be avoided.[25] Users ought to beware; the autogenerated document can create incorrect or unintended transfers,[26]

[25] *Do It Yourself Estate Planning*, ABA Task Force, https://www.americanbar.org/groups/real_property_trust_estate/resources/estate_planning/diy_estate_planning/ (last visited July 28, 2020). DIY estate planning software generates wills and other estate planning documents, documents typically otherwise prepared by a trust and estates attorney. There are numerous providers of DIY wills including Lawdepot.com, LawyerAhead, RocketLawyer, Nolo, Corporate Filing Solutions Made Easy, BusinessRocket.net, We The People, and Standard Legal. Of these, LegalZoom is the most widely advertised, with more than 500,000 clients.

[26] *See* Deborah L. Jacobs, *The Case Against Do-It-Yourself Wills*, Forbes (Sept. 7, 2010), https://www.forbes.com/2010/09/07/do-it-yourself-will-mishaps-personal-finances-estate-lawyers-overcharge.html#5e31885c375c (noting that the DIY will lacked a residuary clause and subsequently devised $400,000 of stock to the son the drafter intended to disinherit).

disastrous tax consequences,[27] and may be unenforceable if not properly drafted and executed.[28] This holds true with planning for intergenerational ownership of family land.

Practitioners have identified numerous issues with these services, notably that DIY wills often do not capture the testator's intent. User errors associated with DIY online tools further undermine drafter intent.[29] Moreover, the software itself can facilitate user error. For example, LegalZoom allows users to insert whatever language they wish in the directives, emboldening users to add clauses that may contradict the rest of the will.[30] Like LegalZoom, RocketLawyer allows users to edit the completed will.[31] And when there are errors or omissions in a will, the state intestacy laws still apply.[32]

While many DIY software users are drawn to the affordability and ease of use presented by DIY estate planning software, DIY providers may not be able to provide services to meet complex client needs.[33] Without the assistance of a seasoned practitioner, a testator may draft and execute a will with adverse tax consequences.[34] Laymen users of DIY software do not realize that their software package may fail to provide critical estate planning documents and, absent any legal training, users would not know to request these documents.[35]

Online providers tend to lure users into a false sense of security[36] but offer little protection, with some providers even requiring waivers that eliminate any recourse should there be an error in the produced documents. There's also precedent for courts declining to accept documents that do not meet the legal requirements, as *In re Will of Ferree*.[37] Practitioners are not certain that DIY estate planning tools serve their purported goal: broadening access to estate planning.[38] Explanations attributing greater access to estate planning to DIY tools ignore inequities in access to technology,

---

[27] ABA Task Force, *supra* note 25 (stressing the importance of careful estate planning to maximize tax savings); *see also* Lindzey Schindler, *Skirting the Ethical Line: The Quandary of Online Legal Forms*, 16 Chap. L. Rev. 185, 193–94 (2012) (concluding that the LegalZoom's estate plan would cost the user hundreds of thousands in taxes).

[28] In re Estate of Chastain, 401 S.W.3d 612 (Tenn. 2012) (declaring the will unenforceable because it did not satisfy the formalities); In re Will of Ferree, 848 A.2d 81 (N.J. Ch. 2003), *aff'd*, 848 A.2d 1 (N.J. Super. Ct. App. Div. 2004).

[29] One testator did not fill in the name of the loved one where the DIY software prompted "insert name here." Ultimately, the user left $200,000 to "insert name here." *Id.*

[30] *Legal DIY Websites Are No Match for a Pro*, Consumer Reports Magazine (Sept. 2012), https://www.consumerreports.org/cro/magazine/2012/09/legal-diy-websites-are-no-match-for-a-pro/index.htm.

[31] *Id.*

[32] Jacobs, *supra* note 26.

[33] ABA Task Force, *supra* note 25.

[34] With online tools and kits, the risk is: "you don't know what you don't know." Legal practitioner David Hiersekorn used LegalZoom to create his own will and assessed the tax consequences. The software put his and his wife's retirement accounts into a trust and named the trust as a beneficiary of the retirement accounts (which is not incorrect but could create adverse tax consequences if botched). Additionally, and contrary to the drafter's intent, the trust effectively disinherited Hiersekorn's son from a previous marriage if Hiersekorn were to die before his wife. Ultimately, Hiersekorn concluded that his LegalZoom will would cost him "tens of thousands in probate fees and potentially hundreds of thousands in taxes." Lindzey Schindler, *Skirting the Ethical Line: The Quandary of Online Legal Forms*, 16 Chap. L. Rev. 185, 193–94 (2012).

[35] Marguerite C. Lorenz, *The Problems with Do-It-Yourself Online Will*, Forbes (Mar. 29, 2020), https://www.forbes.com/sites/nextavenue/2019/03/29/the-problems-with-do-it-yourself-online-wills/#57c31d6b22b8.

[36] *Id.*

[37] In re Will of Ferree, 848 A.2d 81 (N.J. Super. Ct. Ch. Div. 2003), *aff'd*, 848 A.2d 1 (N.J. Super. Ct. App. Div. 2004).

[38] *See* Emily S. Taylor Poppe, *The Future is Bright Complicated: AI, Apps & Access to Justice*, 72 Okla. L. Rev. 185, 201–02 (2019) ("Yet we should be realistic about the extent to which technology will actually address unmet legal needs, particularly among those who are unlikely to benefit from technological interventions.").

overestimate the role of cost in individuals' decisions to defer to intestacy, and fail to account for the popular conception that estate planning is a lawyer's domain.[39]

b. Rely on Attorneys and Best Practices

There are best practices that support planning for family land ownership and management. This holds true for real estate meant to provide a source of intergenerational wealth and home. Careful considerations should be given to ensuring that the plan developed avoids rather than creates heirs' property. Likewise, lawyers advising clients on planning strategies for family land should know their own capacity and utilize resources, including other attorneys, to ensure they meet the needs and goals of the client. Attorneys should also not try to dictate or apply a cookie cutter approach to advising clients seeking a comprehensive succession plan. And they should not try to reduce their own responsibility or exposure to malpractice claims in a way that results in the client getting less than what they need in a strategy.

8. *Strategies and Resources to Maintain and Steward Family Real Estate*

This book, including this chapter, focuses primarily on the legal and policy aspects of heirs' property and family-owned real estate. However, it is important to take care with the financial management and growth of the property, as well as any natural resources associated with the property. Doing so, I believe, will incentivize owners to do succession planning and to address any legal issues. It's possible even to leverage income-producing opportunities to financially support succession planning and resolving legal issues. Thoughtful management of the financial aspect of real estate and any natural resources related to the property will also help maintain and grow the economic value of family real estate and, thus, increase the intergenerational wealth. Let's take a look at financial liabilities and strategies to manage them; using and managing multiple dwellings and improvements on family property; physical damage, hazards and hazard insurance, and the impact of clear title on government programs; stewardship of natural resources on the property; and income opportunities with real estate.[40]

a. Financial Liabilities

All real estate has some financial liability attached to it. Property taxes are the most likely. Whether heirs' property or not, property owners should always stay informed about the tax authority with jurisdiction over your property, when property tax appraisals occur, the current tax rate, and tax relief programs the tax payer or property can qualify for.[41] Tax relief programs can greatly reduce the annual tax payment property owners own. So, they are worth learning about.

---

[39] *Id.* at 200.

[40] This section introduces these topics. There is a plethora of literature and resources available online and elsewhere that should be explored.

[41] Chapter 8 extensively addresses state and local tax laws and related programs from an heirs' property perspective. Common tax relief programs are for agricultural land (property is appraised for agricultural value rather than market value), senior citizens and permanently disabled individuals (often only tax up to a specific value or defer taxes while qualifying person is the owner), and disabled veterans. Check with the local tax authority for information about available programs.

i. Property Taxes

If the property is heirs' property, property taxes can be and often are a huge source of conflict, resentment, and loss of ownership. Each owner is liable for property taxes proportional to his or her share. If any owner pays the share of another owner(s), the paying owner is entitled to reimbursement.[42] However, many landowners have the misconception that they are entitled to additional or exclusive ownership of the property when they pay another owner's share of the property taxes. This underscores the importance of being knowledgeable about property taxes connected to the family real estate. It is also important to develop a strategy for paying property taxes. Such a strategy requires confirmation of the current owners, as well as the percentage share they own in the property.

Equipped with the pertinent property tax and owner shares information, families should seek to develop a payment strategy that optimizes every owner's capacity to pay. Taxes are due once a year and typically people pay in lump sum. However, owners could estimate the annual amount owed by each owner and pay in a series of payments over the year leading up to the due date. Another way to address the imbalance of paying and nonpaying owners is for nonpaying owners to transfer their ownership interests to paying owners.

ii. Mortgages

Some family property, whether heirs' property or not, may have other liabilities attached to the property, such as mortgages. A mortgage is a security interest in the property connected to a loan. The borrower(s) signs a note—a legal document describing the loan terms. They also sign a mortgage or deed of trust, which provides the lender with certain rights related to the property, including the right to force the sale of the property if there is a default. A standard mortgage also provides the lender with the right to accelerate the loan, that is, to demand full payment immediately. One condition for acceleration is a change in ownership. Whether a family is preparing for a change of ownership during the life of the owner/borrower or after their death, it is important to know the terms of the mortgage and develop a strategy for repayment. Although heirs do not inherit the debt, the debt stays tied to the property and the lender can foreclose on the property. Payment must continue until the loan is paid off.

iii. Impact of Personal Debt

Heirs' property owners should also consider the possibility that any individual owner's personal debt could become tied to the property because their share in the property is subject to their debts. This can create a lot of issues for the family—even more reason to do entity-centered succession planning. There are other financial management considerations for family property, including upkeep of the property, which can get expensive. Employing strategies that offer flexibility and support every owner's ability to pay is key.

b. Family Members and Others Using and Managing Residential Real Estate

Families with residential real estate must also consider how to manage owners and other family members living in the home(s) on the property. This is another significant source of conflict for family owners. All heirs' property owners are entitled to use and benefit from the family property.

[42] Owners who pay on behalf of nonpaying owners have a lien on the interest the nonpaying owner has in the property. Enforcing this lien would require court action, such as small claims court in the county where the property is located.

They cannot exclude others from use. As well, any owner using the property to the exclusion of others should compensate the other owners for their use. They should be responsible for the property taxes and upkeep of the property, including paying the mortgage. Failure to establish and follow an agreement in which occupant owners are paying for the upkeep of the home and compensating the nonoccupant owners with rent will most likely create conflict and, thus, significantly increase the risk of loss through partition sale. This is because nonoccupant owners will build resentment—making them more susceptible to predators seeking an interest in the property to force a partition sale. Add to this scenario market demand for the subject property and you have the most vulnerable heirs' property.[43]

It's common for families with real estate to have multiple homes and structures on the property. In fact, it's common for families to own land for the purpose of providing a single source of real estate upon which the family can operate multiple intrafamily households. There is a lot of value in doing this. Essentially, multidwelling parcels of land allow families to more effectively and equitably manage limited resources—extending the benefits of family-owned real estate. Optimizing this potential requires compliance with local zoning, cooperative co-management between family members, and care to avoid physical harm to the land and associated natural resources.

This type of activity would be ideally managed by an entity-centered ownership in which the entity governing documents have provisions for family members dwelling on the property and building on the property. Contracts with the dwelling family members will be very effective and necessary to minimize conflict and provide clear guidance on authority, use, and more. In fact, families should require contracts. Family members who build structures or place mobile or modular homes on the property should be cautious proceeding without a contract with the owner(s) of the property, to ensure their investment belongs to them only and not the owner(s) of the land upon which their building is located. Of course, then, working with a skilled attorney is necessary.

9. *Physical Damage; Hazards and Hazard Insurance; Clear Title and Government Programs*

Families should also consider how to manage their property when there is physical damage or harm to the property. It is common for heirs' property to be uninsured by homeowners insurance and hazard insurance, unless it is required by a mortgage holder. Homeowners insurance is financial protection against theft or damage to the property. Hazard insurance offers financial protection against structural damage caused by natural disasters. State and federal governments also provide financial assistance and loans to help homeowners recover from disasters.

Heirs' property owners face barriers to program eligibility when they do not have clear title or legally confirmed owners and when they cannot produce the documents required for their eligibility. Families, particularly those in disaster-prone areas, should familiarize themselves with the eligibility criteria for financial assistance and take that action one step further by collecting and preparing the documentation required for eligibility. It is essential to do this in preparation for, rather than in response to, a disaster. It is also essential to store the documents in a place where they can be easily

[43] Of course, families can agree to a variety of terms for occupant owners, including no rent. Regardless of the terms, it is prudent to have an agreement in writing and ensure its effectiveness with regular review of terms by the owners and the attorney working with the family.

retrieved if injury or destruction to the property occurs. Fire safes and safe deposit boxes are an option. Digital storage, however, is likely the best option.

a. Stewardship

i. Natural Resources on Family Land

Families owning real estate with natural resources should explore how they steward the land to protect those resources and whether those natural resources can be used for income. Family agricultural land ownership is vital to protection of clean water and wildlife. Traditional farming, for example, produce, livestock, tobacco, and cotton, is very common for family owners. And often where there is a traditional farm, there are trees. Trees are vital to the protection of our environment and to various industries. In my home state of North Carolina, the timber industry generates more than $30 billion a year.

There are many resources for agricultural landowners on the county, regional, state, and national levels. Landowners should educate themselves about the various resources at each level and consider how they might benefit from them. This includes county extension offices, land trusts, agricultural landowner membership organizations, landowner serving organizations[44], land grant universities, state departments of agriculture, and various agencies within the USDA, especially the Farm Service Agency, the US Forest Service, and the Natural Resource Conservation Service. A great resource for agricultural landowners is the Center for Agriculture and Food Systems at Vermont Law School (https://farmlandaccess.org/). This robust website even includes a legal toolkit.

ii. Income Opportunities

As mentioned above, families with agricultural land (regardless of the size) should consider opportunities to derive income from the real estate. The activities are far ranging in type of activity and legal complexity. Working with a lawyer and specialized service providers such as foresters and consultants are key to securing owner rights and optimizing the income potential of the property.

In addition to growing produce, raising livestock, and timber, families can also license (permit) others to use their property. Licensing others to use your real estate is giving them the permission to conduct an activity on the property. Examples of income activities in this category are hunting, event rentals, short-term rentals (e.g., VRBO and Airbnb), fruit harvesting or picking, solar power generation, equipment and livestock rental, and beekeeping.

Leasing your real estate to others provides them with an exclusive interest in the property for a long period of time. Examples of the types of leases are residential and farm leases, oil and gas and mineral leases, and timber leases. Owners should be very knowledgeable and thoughtful about the terms of the lease agreements. They should also be prepared to address issues that arise with leasing their property. It is wise to consult with an attorney before signing any such lease.

iii. Easements

Easements offer yet another opportunity for income. An easement gives a person or organization (e.g., land trust, government, utility company) the right to use someone else's real estate for a specific purpose. A very common form of easement is a "right of way" which permits a landowner to

[44] The American Forest Foundation is an example of an organization providing resources and support for family-owned land. Family-owned forests make up the largest proportion of forests in the United States, which means family-owned forests play a big role in clean water, carbon sequestration, as well as in the wood products industry.

travel across another landowner's property to access their own. Conservation easements are also very common. The most common purpose of a conservation easement is to restrict specific activities on a property in order to protect a natural resource. Both nonprofit organizations and governments buy conservation easements.

When a property is "burdened" by a conservation easement, the market value and tax value are decreased significantly, which could be a benefit or a detriment. Most conservation easements last forever (perpetual). Therefore, conservation easements are most beneficial for intergenerational family property when the family has goals to maintain the property's natural resources and limit development on the property. Doing so could be in exchange for increasing the economic value of the property and, thus, the family's intergenerational wealth.

This discussion of strategies to maintain and steward family real estate is intended to draw attention to elements that heirs and their attorneys need to consider. Other elements are discussed in other chapters of this book.

III. CONCLUSION

For many families, owning real estate is not only a source of wealth or part of the American dream, it is an act of defiance—an act of humanity. The ability to acquire real estate, maintain it, increase its value, and then share that with future generations of your family is incredibly powerful. For too long, family real estate has been undermined by insufficient solutions and reliance on a legal system that does not empower family real estate owners in the positive way it could. There are no one-size-fits-all solutions. What works for some may not work for others. Therefore, building and maintaining intergenerational real estate ownership in families deserves an expansive and creative strategy.

This chapter began with my very sad, unfortunate story that I hope no one else ever has to experience. Yet I know that many people have and will do so. If anything, my own experience opened my eyes to the importance of building resiliency in our lives, including when it comes to family, home, and intergenerational wealth. We may not be able to control the various things that shift our lives, but we do have a measure of control over our own resiliency—our ability to recover, reform, and move on. We have to change the norm for family real estate ownership to enhance the value families derive from their heirs' property, including better preserving and building generational wealth, as well as protecting family heritage and cultural and historic value.

7

Probate and Business Organization Strategies to Minimize Land Loss of Heirs' Property

—David J. Dietrich

I. PROLOGUE

From 2002 to 2008, I co-chaired the Property Preservation Task Force (PPTF), created by the Real Property, Trust and Estate Law (RPTE) Section of the American Bar Association (ABA). The PPTF was formed in response to the 2001 Associated Press articles titled "Torn from the Land" written by Todd Lewan and Dolores Barclay. That award-winning, three-part series chronicled African American land loss due to predatory partition actions and prompted national attention among members of the ABA.[1] Shortly after the PPTF was formed, Professor Thomas Mitchell became a member. I owe him a debt of gratitude for guiding us to the conclusion that partition law, then a "sacred cow" of many real estate lawyers, needed to be reformed. As discussed below, and elsewhere in this book, the PPTF ended up developing a proposal that was submitted, with ABA support, to the Uniform Law Commission (ULC), requesting the ULC to establish a drafting committee to develop a model state statute, or uniform act in the ULC's lexicon, to address partition law abuse. Professor Mitchell served as the reporter of the drafting committee for what ultimately became the Uniform Partition of Heirs Property Act (UPHPA).

A bit of personal history is in order. I grew up in Billings, Montana, where I live and practice law. In the 1970s, when I was a teenager, my family suffered what we experienced as land loss when

---

[1] Todd Lewan & Dolores Barclay, *Torn from the Land,* Associated Press (2001), http://www.hartford-hwp.com/archives/45a/393.html;

a family lake cabin built in the 1930s was lost to a wealthy out-of-state landowner who acquired the entire lake property. The cabin owners around Rock Creek Lake had had a loose "legal license" arrangement for five decades with the previous owner of the lake, a license it turns out that could be terminated at the will of the landowner. The new landowner refused to continue the agreements. My father, John M. Dietrich, a veteran real estate lawyer in Montana's largest law firm, strained to explain to me and my siblings why real estate law provided no remedy. Forty to fifty years of cabin history vanished as twenty cabins went up in smoke after an unsuccessful appeal to the Montana Supreme Court. At that young age, this experience served as my introduction to property law and how people who have certain property rights can lack legal remedies that they understandably assumed they had.

In college, I gained an appreciation for the role legislatures play in our legal system. To this end, in 1978, I marveled at observing the US Congress in action as a Lyndon Baines Johnson congressional intern on Capitol Hill, thanks to the congressman from eastern Montana who afforded me this opportunity. Among other experiences, I observed the power of legislation to solve problems, which left an impression on me.

After graduating from Whitman College in 1979, I was a Peace Corps volunteer in Côte d'Ivoire, West Africa, working on immunization. My time as a volunteer increased my understanding of racism in a profound way. I learned a great deal about the history of racial subjugation in Africa, including details about the European enslavement of Africans. Just as importantly, as a result of the friendships I developed with my fellow Peace Corps volunteers who were African American, friends who mentored me in important ways, I learned a great deal that I had not known before about the crushing reality of racial and economic injustice back in the United States, injustices that remain deeply entrenched more than 150 years after the signing of the Emancipation Proclamation. Unconsciously, I developed a deep, if inchoate, commitment to promote economic justice back home. I decided to go to law school and hoped that I would be able to find some way to apply the legal education I would obtain to do something to promote equality and justice in the United States.

By 1997, as a licensed lawyer in Montana, doing real estate deals and estate planning work for ranchers, I was appointed co-chair of the Estate Planning for Farmers and Ranchers Committee of the RPTE Section of the ABA. As an ABA member, I had written and spoken about using business entities and forming conservation easements to avoid land loss for ranchers. As an ambitious RPTE section member, I learned of hostile partition actions of tenancy-in-common properties.

By then, I also had discovered that many Montana families had not done any estate planning. As a result, many heirs to farm and ranch land became tenants in common, in areas experiencing a rapid appreciation of real estate values, caused by a burgeoning national interest in Montana that the movie *A River Runs Through It* helped generate. The unstable ownership and lure of liquidating land for cash generated significant infighting within many families. These fights pitted family members who wanted to maintain legacy ranches within their families against other family members who wanted to sell the ranches quickly for cash.

But nothing I had encountered in my career approached the legal "Rubik's cube" of African American–owned land in the South known as heirs' property. Such ownership represented "the worst problem no one's heard of," according to John Pollock, who first used this phrase to describe the invisibility of substantial African American land loss attributable to ruinous partition sales. Before the Associated Press series revealed to the public how real estate speculators and developers had used partition law in a patently unjust way to "legally steal" a massive number of acres from African American families that owned land in the South, the African American heirs' property problem had been hiding in plain sight for decades. Important stakeholders who were in a position to address this important, if little-appreciated, civil rights issue mostly turned a deaf ear to the repeated desperate pleas many African American families made for assistance.

Notably, in 2002, Dennis Belcher, the beloved and legendary RPTE section chair and a partner in the elite eastern seaboard firm of McGuireWoods, was thinking aloud about why RPTE leadership had appointed me co-chair of PPTF. He chuckled and said, "David, we needed to pick a small firm lawyer west of the Mississippi who likely has never used partition law techniques, which many of our firms may have used over the years." Dennis twinkled as he said this and exhorted me to "accomplish things" in my co-chair role.

Now, because of the Barclay and Lewan articles, action by the ABA and the Uniform Law Commission, and heirs' property advocacy by Professor Mitchell that has earned him recognition in a MacArthur "Genius Grant," the heirs' property problem is no longer a dirty secret in US real property law. Thanks to the PPTF and the ABA's support, the ULC formed a drafting committee in 2007 to draft what would become the Uniform Partition of Heirs Property Act (UPHPA). In addition to a debt of gratitude to Professor Mitchell, it is important to recognize the contributions of PPTF co-chair Julius J. Zschau of Tampa, Florida, and member Ira Waldman of Los Angeles, California. Ira was unabashed in lobbying the ULC in 2006 to form a scoping committee, which eventually led to formulation of the UPHPA.[2]

Because of the ABA's inclusive "big tent" approach, it played an important role in helping enable many nonprofit organizations in the South that had fought the heirs' property fight for decades to participate in the development of the proposal the RPTE sent to the ULC and ultimately in the drafting of the UPHPA. This was especially true for John Pollock and his advocacy before the ULC, as described in chapter 4.

On a personal level, in 2016 to 2017, I became section chair of the RPTE section of the ABA in part because of the PPTF's work. But my involvement with the UPHPA did not end when the ULC drafted the act. During the 2013 Legislative Session, an heir in Montana asked her state senator, Kendall Van Dyk, to sponsor a bill that would alter the law governing tenancies in common. The heir made this request because her aunt's divorced husband, a real estate developer in Florida, had threatened to sell a jointly owned legacy family cabin and simply divide the proceeds. Senator Van Dyk introduced the Montana Uniform Partition of Heirs Property Act in January 2013. I assisted the ULC in getting the UPHPA passed by the Montana Legislature in the 2013 Session, with a 99–1 vote on the House Floor and a 50–0 vote on the Senate Floor.

---

[2] Speaking of thanks, I owe another great debt of gratitude to Erica Levine Powers, Esq., who tirelessly edited, reviewed, and rereviewed this book chapter. She cajoled and teased many of the aspects of this chapter out of my 36 years of law practice and inspired more recent research. She also tolerated my not-so-veiled humor in allowing Ole and Gina Larsson's family of underplanned Vikings to make their cameo appearance in a legal publication. I also owe a debt of gratitude to Dirk A. Williams, a skilled tax lawyer, back country skier, and friend from Missoula, Montana, whose wise comments are cited occasionally in this outline; thanks to him, I avoided oversimplification and error on many topics.

II. PARTITION IN PROBATE AND BUSINESS ORGANIZATION STRATEGIES TO MINIMIZE LAND LOSS OF HEIRS' PROPERTY

The content of this chapter derives from my law practice from 1984 and from my presentations from 2012 to 2019 for the Skills Training for Estate Planners (STEP) program, an annual program for lawyers transitioning into estate planning, sponsored by the RPTE section of the ABA.[3] In my experience, as chair of the Estate Planning for Farmers and Ranchers Committee of the RPTE, many farmers and ranchers throughout the United States are averse to working with lawyers and planning to preserve the asset value of their land, and there are significant similarities with agricultural estate planning in Montana and heirs' property owners nationally.

In addition, the family dynamics that result from lack of planning can be devastating. This can apply to large families with highly fractionalized shares, as described in chapter 5, as well as to relatively small groups of heirs in one or two generations, as discussed in this chapter.

In chapter 6, picking up on Professor Mitchell's concerns about the lack of estate planning and legal services among African Americans, Mavis Gragg addresses the need for strategic planning by heirs' property heirs, including estate planning and will drafting, for long-term management and use of real property as an asset. She includes criteria for selecting a lawyer and emphasizes the need for carefully crafted documents for creating the entities she suggests. She also refers to this chapter for amplification of the details of such entities and documents, including the risks upon dissolution of a limited liability corporation (LLC).

Heirs' property problems can be avoided or minimized through effective will drafting and effective administration during the probate process and by successful business entity planning, using tenancy-in-common agreements, limited liability companies, and long-term trusts. In other chapters of this book, especially chapters 5 and 6, some of these entities are discussed as they relate to protecting family lands from partition by predatory investors. Chapter 6 is particularly concerned with maintaining a legacy in family real property, including stewardship of the land. Heirs' property problems can also be avoided by effective will drafting and administration during the probate process, which I will discuss first. Please see the following disclaimer.[4]

III. HEIRS PROPERTY AND PROBATE

Based on my law practice experience in a rapidly developing area of Montana, the focus in this chapter is, first, on the intersection of the UPHPA and the rules governing the administration of an estate under the Uniform Probate Code, applicable in Montana,[5] and second, on the pros and cons of

---

[3] My most recent version of this was the 2019 Skills Training for Estate Planners, "Considerations and Strategies in Selecting Business Entities" by David J. Dietrich, Dietrich & Associates.

[4] *Disclaimer.* The emphasis of this book chapter is on protecting heirs' property owners from further fractionalization of real estate, mismanagement, misadministration of estates, with or without wills, and the risks of co-ownership dissolution when real estate is placed into a business entity. This chapter incorporates general strategies involving state or federal income tax and state or federal estate and gift taxation, when real estate is placed into a tenancy-in-common agreement, a grantor trust, or an LLC. The author is aware that techniques used for valuation reduction and estate and gift tax management are sought to be changed by the United States Treasury Department, the Internal Revenue Service (IRS), and its Priority Guidance Plan. Valuation and estate and gift tax planning are outside the scope of this outline. See the IRS's Priority Guidance Plan at https://www.irs.gov/privacy-disclosure/priority-guidance-plan.

[5] Nineteen states have adopted the Uniform Probate Code. *See Probate Code*, UNIF. L. COMM'N, https://www.uniformlaws.org/committees/community-home?CommunityKey=a539920d-c477-44b8-84fe-b0d7b1a4cca8 (last visited Nov. 16, 2021). Montana's version of the Uniform Probate Code is found at MONT. CODE ANN. 72-1-101 et seq (2021).

business entities for asset preservation. Montana is a state with appreciating land values in a lawyer-averse agricultural environment. I provide a factual anchor to this discussion with the Larsson family of Gallatin County, Montana. Please carefully read annex A at the end of the chapter. While the situation described represents a hypothetical case, it demonstrates the estate planning, administration, and asset protection challenges of agricultural heirs' property in Montana, when an estate is "under-planned" and when the real estate values rapidly appreciate. The hypothetical Larssons have not engaged in advance or entity planning, and their land has rapidly appreciated in value due to the nationally famous attractions of the Big Sky country. Before addressing entity planning solutions, a short explanation of tenancy in common or "heirs' property" real estate in Montana and the probate process in a Uniform Probate Code state, Montana, is in order. The purpose of this section is to set out the basic strategies of probate administration when heirs' property comprises a major portion of the probate estate, either (1) because heirs' property is being administered under a probate estate in "intestacy" or (2) by virtue of a will that distributes real estate to heirs in cotenancy, which is often heirs' property under the UPHPA.

A. Intestacy under State Law, Relationship to Heirs' Property, and Tenancy in Common

Heirs' property is real property whereby each of the owners has come into ownership, from inheritance or gifting, in the form traditionally known as tenancy in common. An owner of a cotenancy real estate interest has a vested legal interest that can be transferred by a will or deed, or due to a lack of planning, can be transferred by intestacy, meaning the legal system of transferring real estate when there is no will or other means of transfer at death. Because heirs usually own the tenancy-in-common interest individually, the term "heirs' property" usually excludes ownership in a partnership, LLC, corporation, or trust. If the tenancy-in-common ownership is funded into a partnership, LLC, or trust, this can help to avoid further fractionalization of heirs' property. The protective aspects of entity ownership and planning are detailed later in this chapter.

1. The Larssons as Heirs' Property Heirs under the UPHPA

The Larssons meet the UPHPA definition of heirs' property heirs. "Heirs' property" under the UPHPA is defined as tenancy-in-common real estate having: (1) no agreement governing rights on partition; (2) one or more of the cotenants acquired title from a relative, whether living or deceased; and (3) 20 percent or more of the real estate interests are held by cotenants who are relatives, or 20 percent or more of the real estate interests acquired title from a relative, living or deceased, or 20 percent of the cotenants are relatives.[6]

2. Intestate Transfer of Heirs' Property and the Reverse Buy Sell Provision of the UPHPA

Intestacy often occurs with heirs' property. It is the presumed form of ownership transfer occurring upon the death of an individual that all state legislatures have imposed for deceased individuals, and it may be applied for successive generations. For example, if a tract of real estate, consisting of 60 acres, was owned in 2021 by Ole Larsson, who died without a will or a funded trust and he left

[6] Mont. Code Ann. § 70-29-402(5) (2021).

no spouse but three children surviving him, Ole's 60 acres has fractionalized into ownership equally among his three heirs such that they each now have a 33.33 percent *undivided* interest in the 60 acres. The three heirs do *not* own a divided 20 acres each, absent a partition order for distribution in kind.[7]

The UPHPA allows the cotenant owners (who did not petition a court for court-ordered sale) to buy out the partitioning heirs at appraised value for a limited period of time; this is sometimes referred to as a "reverse statutory buyout."[8] If the sale does not occur as to all interests, then the court "shall order partition in kind" and "shall consider" the six UPHPA "great prejudice" factors if it seeks to avoid a partition in kind:

(1) In determining under [Section 70-29-412(1)] whether partition in kind would result in great prejudice to the cotenants as a group, the court shall consider the following:
   (a) whether the heirs' property practicably can be divided among the cotenants;
   (b) whether partition in kind would apportion the property in such a way that the aggregate fair market value of the parcels resulting from the division would be materially less than the value of the property if it were sold as a whole, taking into account the condition under which a court-ordered sale likely would occur;
   (c) evidence of the collective duration of ownership or possession of the property by a cotenant and one or more predecessors in title or predecessors in possession to the cotenant who are or were relatives of the cotenant or each other;
   (d) a cotenant's sentimental attachment to the property, including any attachment arising because the property has ancestral or other unique or special value to the cotenant;
   (e) the lawful use being made of the property by a cotenant and the degree to which the cotenant would be harmed if the cotenant could not continue the same use of the property;
   (f) the degree to which the cotenants have contributed their pro rata share of the property taxes, insurance, and other expenses associated with maintaining ownership of the property or have contributed to the physical improvement, maintenance, or upkeep of the property; and
   (g) any other relevant factor. See Mont. Code Ann. 70-29-412 (1) (2021).

In making a determination under subparagraph (a) of this statute, often topographical issues such as access to water, access to roads, and the varying nature of grasslands and irrigated property can make the division of even a large tract a difficult fact finding for any court. Accordingly, Montana judges still prefer to appoint referees in partition to make case specific fact findings. See Mont. Code Ann. 70-29-202 (2021), which is preserved under Montana's UPHPA under Mont. Code Ann. 70-29-405 (2021).

In short, the UPHPA modifies traditional partition law by adding valuation and procedural safeguards for all three of the heirs of the ranch: a fair market appraisal of the entire ranch, without discounting any interest; a reverse, statutory buy sell mechanism if any of the heirs seek to buy out the others for values below the appraised price of the ranch, and an open-market sale of the property, if it must be sold, but only after a finding that a distribution in kind is not feasible.

---

[7] *Id.*

[8] Timeframe is 60 days under Montana's statute. *See* Mont. Code Ann. § 70-29-411(5) (2021).

As set out in annex A, the Larsson family example, Ole Larsson's estate also consists of a 3,840-acre ranch, which, due to his investment of labor and capital, Odin wants to receive from his parents' estates. Examining the application of the UPHPA to a highly appreciated 60-acre tract and a much larger 3,840-acre tract, in connection with Montana's Uniform Probate Code (UPC), demonstrates some of the realities and weaknesses of heirs' property ownership in an "under-planned" estate.

B. Probate of an Intestate and Testate Estate in a Uniform Probate Code State

State law on intestacy (an estate without a will or other effective transfer on death plan) and testacy (an estate with a will), rather than federal law, dictates how real property transfers when there is no will, funded trust, or other planning entity that directs the transfer. At least nineteen states have enacted the UPC, including Montana. On the death of an individual owning real property, without a will, his or her assets automatically transfer to the heirs.[9]

See UPC Section 3-901, which states "in the absence of administration, the heirs and devisees are entitled to the estate in accordance with the terms of a probated will or the laws of intestate succession." Upon the passing of Ole and Gina Larsson, if there is no will, each of the Larsson family members will take a 33 percent undivided interest in the 60 acres known as the Alfalfa Field and the 3,840-acre Lazy V Ranch. If the heirs inheriting from Gina and Ole do not plan their estates (and obtain a *divided* as opposed to *undivided* interest[10]), their heirs in turn will obtain a fractional interest of their parent's share. See the intestacy statute of the UPC at Section 2.101.

1. *Probate Administration of Intestate Tenancy-in-Common Property: The "Personal Representative"*

Since its inception in 1969, the UPC has included Section 3-911, which provides as follows:

> **Partition for Purpose of Distribution.** When two or more heirs or devisees are entitled to distribution of undivided interests in any real or personal property of the estate, the personal representative or one or more of the heirs or devisees may petition the court, prior to the formal or informal closing of the estate, to make a partition. After notice to the interested heirs or devisees, the court shall partition the property in the same manner as provided by the Law for civil actions of partition. The court may direct the personal representative to sell any property which cannot be partitioned without prejudice to the owners and which cannot conveniently be allotted to any one party.

In the estate of Ole or Gina Larsson the appointed personal representative owes fiduciary duties equally to all of the owners of the fractional interests who, at the moment of the death of the decedent, are vested in undivided fractional interests in the Alfalfa Field and the Lazy V Ranch. Montana's version of the UPHPA does not affirmatively state that the UPHPA overrides the provisions of the "partition for purpose of distribution" provision of UPC Section 3-911,[11] which is Montana's version

[9] Subject to probate court administration.

[10] Unif. Prob. Code § 3-901 (Unif. L. Comm'n. 1969).

[11] But this provision is not required: Mont. Code Ann., *supra* note 5, which states that whenever possible the statute shall be interpreted to follow legislative intent, and that particular statutes (UPHPA) prevail over general (UPA 3-911).

of the "Probate Partition" Act found in Mont. Code Ann. 72-3-914 (2021). At least nineteen other states have enacted the UPC and many other states have similar provisions.[12]

2. *The Personal Representative's Fiduciary Duty: Unclear Standards under Uniform Probate Code and the UPHPA, and the Potential Adverse Impact on Heirs' Property Heirs*

The personal representative must administer the estate to achieve the best outcome for the heirs, by exercising its "fiduciary duty." "A personal representative is a fiduciary who shall observe the standards of care applicable to trustees." UPC Section 3-703(a). This standard can be modified by the probated will, but it must be in the best interests of the estate. *Id.* In an heirs' property case, it is unclear whether this means maximizing the proceeds from a sale or distributing the property in kind. But the provisions of the Mont. Code Ann. 72-3-914 (cf. UPC Section 3-911, above) uses the default test of "partition by public sale unless there is substantial prejudice" standard.

This is a different approach than that used by the UPHPA, which prefers a "distribution in kind" approach and requires a specific finding by the court to sell the property.[13] But the Montana Probate Code statute is ambiguous because it also states, "the court shall partition the property in the same manner as provided by the Law for civil actions of partition." It does not carve out the UPHPA "facts and circumstances test" of Mont. Code Ann. 70-29-413 (2021); however, the specific statute should control over the general under Mont. Code Ann. 1-2-102 and the UPC does prefer a distribution in kind under UPC 3-906. Accordingly, if a personal representative desires to simply achieve the highest and best sales price for the property, an informally appointed personal representative (meaning that the court is not involved, unless an affected heir so moves the court to be involved) may sell the property, and divide the proceeds, without any court involvement and notice to the heirs; arguably this may be a breach of fiduciary duty, but this is small financial and emotional consolation to an heir who has lost the opportunity to receive a tract of legacy family real estate forever.

This is a serious potential risk in the Larsson estate if Hans Lunder is appointed informally as personal representative, without court supervision, and seeks to liquidate the real estate assets aggressively (see the discussion that follows, regarding his conflict of interest, after Footnote 14). This is potentially a train wreck for heirs' property owners. A deeper examination of the probate court partition process and invoking greater court involvement under the UPC's "supervised administration" is discussed later in the chapter.

C. The Alternative: A Will Providing for Distributing Specific Tracts of Land to Specific Heirs

The foregoing process would likely be used in an intestate estate. Had either Gina Larsson or Ole Larsson provided in their will that *individual,* identifiable tracts, that is, specific devises, of the Lazy V Ranch were to be distributed to Odin, Freya, or the heirs of Thor, each of these heirs would be able to rely on the probate code's protections for distributions in kind. *See* UPC Section 3-906, which

[12] *See Probate Code*, Unif. L. Comm'n, https://www.uniformlaws.org/committees/community-home?CommunityKey=a539920d-c477-44b8-84fe-b0d7b1a4cca8 (last visited Nov. 16, 2021).

[13] UPC (MCA 72-3-902) also provides a preference for in-kind distributions where possible and this approach supports the UPHPA approach.

provides "unless a contrary intention is indicated by the will, the distributable assets of a decedent's estate must be distributed in kind . . ." The UPC also provides that purchases from distributees of real property who have received an instrument or deed of distribution from the personal representative "takes title free of rights of any interested person in the estate." *See* UPC Section 3-910.

Further, any distributions in kind to Freya, Thor's heirs, and Odin could be made subject to an option in the language of the will in favor of Odin for the purchase by him of the ratable fair market value of their interests. This option could be exercised by a certain date (for example, 6 months after any estate tax return, or 18 months from the date of death) in the probate proceeding. If that fails, then the court can direct the personal representative to distribute the property in kind or to sell all of the property *en masse*.

1. *The Plot Thickens: Enter the Personal Representative with a Conflict of Interest—Can the UPHPA Be Used to Slow Down Probate Court Partition of Heirs' Property in a Uniform Probate Code State?*

Assume that Ole and Gina Larsson have both died and Gina, as the second to die, leaves a will that provides that the residuary of her estate is to be divided equally to Thor, Freya, and Odin, "by representation." This results, as to both the Alfalfa Field and the Lazy V Ranch, in one-third undivided interests to Freya and to Odin, and a one-third share to be split among Thor's three children.[14] To serve as personal representative Gina has named in her will one Hans Lunder, a local trust officer from the Norsemen Trust Company, who is Freya's boyfriend. Hans has communicated to Freya and Odin that his intention is to appraise both the Alfalfa Field and Lazy V Ranch properties and file a federal estate tax return within 15 months of Gina's death (to use Gina's estate tax exemption), to pay the estate tax, and distribute the net proceeds to Freya, Odin, and Thor's children. He is an experienced trust officer with a corporate trust company and is known for quickly selling real estate in large estates if there is any dissension among heirs. He is aware of the hotel chain's offer to purchase the Alfalfa Field.

Odin, because of his longstanding contribution of labor and personal resources to the Lazy V Ranch, disagrees with Hans's plan and insists on receiving his one-third share of the ranch in kind. He wants Hans to consider allowing him to buy out the shares of Freya and Thor's children in the ranch. Odin proposes to use the proceeds from the sale of the Alfalfa Field to the hotel chain to purchase Freya and Thor's children's interests. Freya and Thor's children appear to side with Hans and insist on liquidation of both the Alfalfa Field and the Lazy V Ranch as soon as possible after the appraisal.

In a UPC state, Hans can be appointed by a local district court clerk (or the "Registrar" in Sections 3-302 and 305 of the UPC) without a court hearing, within 120 hours after Gina's death, and begin the process of valuing and listing the property, all without a court order authorizing the sale. (This is known as an unsupervised or nonintervention probate statutory scheme.) But any of the heirs are entitled to seek "supervised administration," which automatically converts the case to a proceeding requiring court orders to authorize the personal representative's actions. See Section 3-501 of the UPC.

The UPC allows for a court proceeding for a partition action "in the same manner as provided by the Law for civil actions of partition." In Montana, the statutory default is that three referees in

[14] Unif. Prob. Code § 2-106 (Unif. L. Comm'n. 1969) if intestate; § 2-709 if there is a will, as here.

partition are appointed as fact finders (unless the parties stipulate on one referee) to assist a court in rendering a determination of whether the property cannot be sold without great prejudice to the owners. Mont. Code Ann. 70-29-202 (2021). The use of referees is incorporated into the UPHPA heirs' property scheme. Mont. Code Ann. 70-20-405 (2021).

If the personal representative of the Gina Larsson estate insists on a partition by sale, for the benefit of Freya and Thor's children, but over the objection of Odin, then the "Buyout by Cotenant" statute of the UPHPA should apply. See Mont. Code Ann. 70-29-411 (2021). This would allow Odin the option to purchase Freya's and Thor's interests, unless they would suffer "great prejudice as a group" under Mont. Code Ann. 70-29-412 (2021). Sale of the Alfalfa Field may suffer from a distribution in kind, but the sale of the Lazy V. Ranch, if coordinated with the sale of the Alfalfa Field, may result in a distribution in kind of the entire tract of the Lazy V to Odin.

D. The UPHPA "Relevant Factors and Circumstances Test"

To support this conclusion and recommendation to the personal representative, the referees can be instructed by the personal representative or a probate court to use the UPHPA "relevant factors and circumstances" test under Mont. Code Ann. 70-29-413 (2021). That statute provides as follows:

(1) In determining under [the partition alternatives statute] whether partition in kind would result in great prejudice to the cotenants as a group, the court shall consider the following:
  - (a) whether the heirs' property practicably can be divided among the cotenants;
  - (b) whether partition in kind would apportion the property in such a way that the aggregate fair market value of the parcels resulting from the division would be materially less than the value of the property if it were sold as a whole, taking into account the condition under which a court-ordered sale likely would occur;
  - (c) evidence of the collective duration of ownership or possession of the property by a cotenant and one or more predecessors in title or predecessors in possession to the cotenant who are or were relatives of the cotenant or each other;
  - (d) a cotenant's sentimental attachment to the property, including any attachment arising because the property has ancestral or other unique or special value to the cotenant;
  - (e) the lawful use being made of the property by a cotenant and the degree to which the cotenant would be harmed if the cotenant could not continue the same use of the property;
  - (f) the degree to which the cotenants have contributed their pro rata share of the property taxes, insurance, and other expenses associated with maintaining ownership of the property or have contributed to the physical improvement, maintenance, or upkeep of the property; and
  - (g) any other relevant factor.

(2) The court may not consider any one factor in [above set of considerations] to be dispositive without weighing the totality of all relevant factors and circumstances.

If Odin seeks supervised administration, these factors can and should dictate how Hans, the personal representative, having valuable real estate at his discretion, must exercise his fiduciary duty. They also provide a basis for influencing a probate court that the sale for the highest cash price is a simplistic interpretation of fiduciary duty by Hans. But this will not happen in a UPC state unless the heirs are actively represented and move the court for supervised administration and make the specific motion to the court. The importance of heirs' property owners' access to informed legal counsel, willing to cause court intervention by motion or other affirmative action in a system premised on nonintervention, cannot be overstated.

Further, the UPHPA's fair market value provision and open market value provisions may assist Odin in ensuring that the sale of the Alfalfa Field is sold at fair market value and not at a fire-sale price. *See* UPHPA Mont. Code Ann. 70-29-410 and 414 (2021). Not only can Odin seek a distribution in kind, but also, he may influence an "offset" buyout from his share in the sale of the Alfalfa Field to purchase Freya and Thor's children's interests in the Lazy V Ranch. The UPHPA has a clear buyout process to ensure that Freya and Thor's children's shares are paid at appraised value in accordance with their proportionate interests. See Mont. Code Ann. 70-29-410 (2021).

Hans's plan for a mechanical distribution of the net sales proceeds to Freya ignores the flexibility of the UPC's provision promoting private agreements among successors to the decedent (the living heirs), which are binding on the personal representative under UPC Section 3-912:

> Subject to the rights of creditors and taxing authorities, competent successors may agree among themselves to alter the interests, shares, or amounts to which they are entitled under the will of the decedent, or under the laws of intestacy, in any way that they provide in a written contract executed by all who are affected by its provisions. The personal representative shall abide by the terms of the agreement subject to the obligation to administer the estate for the benefit of creditors. Freya's Chapter 7 Bankruptcy Trustee could have standing to participate in the estate settlement agreement as one of her creditors under the hypothetical lien creditor provisions of federal bankruptcy law, namely, 11 USC Section 544.

E. Assume the Real Estate Is Transferred to the Larsson Heirs Equally as Tenants in Common: Goals of the Cotenants That Diverge

Assuming the personal representative deeds the real estate to the Larsson children and grandchildren from the estate, without a sale at the estate level, a second problem arises: do the goals of the cotenants diverge? Some owners may want to conserve the property, others may want to develop it, others may want to liquidate it, and others may want to rent it to third parties. As is discussed in chapter 5, a mediated discussion among tenants in common will be essential for them to arrive at a decision.

From a practical standpoint, the estate planner or real estate lawyer assisting the heirs' property owners will need to identify the various factions of the co-owners whose goals align. If, for example, the Larsson 60-acre tract known as the Alfalfa Field real estate is owned by Odin, Freya, and Thor's three children as joint owners, can any one of them force a "distribution in kind" under Montana's

UPHPA? With respect to the Lazy V ranch, a 3,840-acre ranch, can any one of them, or a combination of them, achieve a "distribution in kind" of part or all of the property under Montana's UPHPA?

Assuming there is no forced sale in the probate proceeding and there is a distribution from the personal representative out to the Larsson heirs in undivided interests, the forced cotenancies are likely to create disputes in the future, which might manifest in, among others, one or more of the following (none of these problems standing along is inevitable, and the list is not exclusive):

1. There is a practical disincentive of the cotenant owners to make improvements because no one of them is in control; in fact, many lending institutions will not advance loan proceeds for improvement of tenancy-in-common ownership without the consolidation of title into a limited liability company or other business entity or trust.[15]
2. Lenders may require all of the owners to guaranty loan obligations, and this may become unworkable if ownership is highly fractionalized.
3. The cotenant owner who remains on the farm and expends substantial sums of his or her own money for taxes, insurance, and maintenance may not be reimbursed for these expenditures.
4. The consolidation of ownership by one co-owner acquiring the interests of other co-owners may be difficult or impossible because other co-owners are either not available or have predeceased the co-owner seeking to consolidate title.
5. Possible "adverse possession." An owner who owns and occupies property in an open, continuous, notorious and obvious fashion to the exclusion of nonfamily members for the requisite period of years (often 5 to 15 years), may acquire "title" to real estate by adverse possession.[16] However, a cotenant owning with cotenant relatives cannot assert adverse possession unless the occupying cotenant affirmatively communicates "ouster" to the other cotenants, that is, "I intend to oust you from the property and obtain your title by adverse possession."

The practical impact of this rule is that title to co-own real property remains in limbo in the names of fractional owners, now alive and who have predeceased, preventing the occupying cotenant seeking to consolidate ownership by adverse possession. Because of the limitations on the doctrine of adverse possession, the Larsson family heirs will not be able, absent partition by agreement or court order, to achieve clear divided ownership of any of their fractional ownership interests in either the Alfalfa Field or the Lazy V Ranch.

F. The Opportunities and Limitations of the UPHPA

As Professor Mitchell points out in chapter 1, among African American heirs who initially had no access to making wills, the absence of a will may be attributable to a number of factors, including an initial lack of access to lawyers, lack of trust in lawyers, and a serious paucity of African American lawyers with experience in trusts and estates law. In a lawyer-averse agricultural state like Montana, landowners like the Larsson family also have problems with the absence of a will, which puts

---

[15] Consolidated ownership in a corporation, trust, LLC or other entity is preferred by lenders based on the author's 36 years of observing agricultural lenders [not] issue loans in Montana; *see also elending Program*, Farmers.gov (last visited Nov. 16, 2021), https://www.farmers.gov/working-with-us/heirs-property-eligibility/relending.

[16] 3 Am. Jur. 2d *Adverse Possession* § 9 (2021).

members of the family at risk of land loss by liquidation or sale to a third party when the temptation of liquidation and sale overrides any goal to retain the legacy of retaining the real estate. In Montana, this is also due to a lack of legal resources, with landowners choosing not to seek legal resources when a will, trust, or probate avoidance device could easily override the inherent instability of heirs' property.

Chapter 6 makes an eloquent case for the need for strategic planning, including estate planning and entity planning, for current heirs' property heirs to transform their real property interests away from tenancy in common. From its initial analysis by the Uniform Law Commission, a fundamental premise of the UPHPA was that state partition law required reform to curb partition law abuses.[17]

G. "Buyout" Provision in a Will or Trust

An owner's will or trust may dispose of real estate to multiple heirs and grant an option to one or more heirs to purchase out the remaining owners or allow one heir a right of first refusal to buy out the remaining heirs. The varieties of these provisions depend on the quality of the will or trust and vary widely. A clearly drafted buyout right in a will or trust, if its exercise lies in the hands of a competent personal representative or trustee, can be a powerful tool for transferring title to a single heir, over multiple heirs. However, the asset still remains subject to the creditors' claims of the original owner and the creditors of the next generation of owners. In the case of the Larssons, a clearly drafted buyout provision could provide for Odin's purchase of Freya's and Thor's children's interest in the Lazy V Ranch. But after the buyout, Odin's interests would remain subject to his creditors. Odin should form a limited liability company or grantor trust to protect his interests and the interests of his heirs in the real estate.

The remainder of this chapter considers various forms of business arrangements or entities that can override traditional state real property partition and enhance or complement the provisions of the UPHPA.

IV. SOLUTIONS INVOLVING LIMITED LIABILITY COMPANIES, TRUSTS, AND OTHER BUSINESS ORGANIZATIONS

Jointly owned property forces consideration of the fundamental reality that real estate capital in its most basic form is never inert and will inexorably move from owner to owner and generation to generation. Using simplistic transfer on death deeds, beneficiary designations, or survivorship designations creates a thin-layered and temporary solution that serves only the initial owner(s). Discovering the long-term goals of the successor owners with respect to the real estate and creating a trust or, better yet, a well-drafted and -managed limited liability entity that can last for generations, may help avoid dissension and land loss through partition. But such a business organization will only last if the inexorable changes to the real estate owned by the business organization can be adapted to the owner's goals, through good succession planning and proactive business management. Individual humans' objectives change through time, as does the character and value of real estate. Wise control and measured flexibility can be achieved with good planning.

---

[17] *See* November 12, 2005, minutes of the Joint Editorial Board of the Uniform Real Property Acts of the National Council of Commissioners of Uniform State Laws, now the Uniform Law Commission (herein "ULC").

Entity planning is used for asset protection and management, as well as enhancement, based on various criteria, including considerations of owner liability, transferability of ownership, allocation of income, taxation on formation, basis increases on death, deductibility of losses, and liquidation of the entity. In selecting the business entity, the estate planner must identify the long-term goals of the client, which for real estate owners of heirs' property likely includes whether the real estate is to be developed or protected in the long term.

Identifying which of the tax and nontax issues emerge as important, and planning the foregoing, can be a complex, multilevel process and may require the planner to use "the team approach" in coordinating with the trust officer, CPA, real estate developer, or other key business decision makers of the client who have influence on how the real estate will be managed and transferred.

Here are some fundamental considerations:

1. Do the owners of the fractional interests have existing credit problems or threatening claims prior to the transfer of their real estate into a business entity?
2. What is the likelihood that potential investors in the business entity may include non-family members?
3. If non-family members may be involved, then heightened awareness should be taken to confirm that the ownership and control of the entity will not be lost to strangers by reason of dilution of less wealthy owners' interests by an investor who is demanding capital calls that not all owners can make.
4. The determination of the value of the interest for buyout or liquidation purposes if a member wants to sell or dies.
5. The liability of the entity for members' preformation debts and for the entity's debts, obligations, and ongoing maintenance.
6. Control over the entity, including day-to-day operations and the voting power for amendment or liquidation of the entity.
7. The requirements of cash contributions necessary to establish and maintain the operations of the entity.
8. Liquidation and dissolution requirements.

A. The Grid: Annex B

A grid comparing various business organizations is appended to this chapter as annex B. It contrasts a variety of business organizations (a sole proprietorship, partnership, C corporation, S corporation, and LLC are compared) that form the core types of organizations for "entity planning."[18] Although the grid is not comprehensive, it does include the major entities that should be considered in this chapter: LLCs, trusts, and tenancy-in-common agreements (TICs). What emerges from this comparison, based on both federal and state law, is that the LLC is the preferred entity of choice, and it can be combined with the use of certain forms of trusts.

[18] As shown in the grid, each of the entities has varying levels of asset protection from existing or future creditors, different types of management structures (boards of directors or managers), requirements of waiver of partition, provisions for distribution in kind to the owners in the event of liquidation, and provisions providing for protection from the dilution or from the adverse income tax consequences on voluntary or court-ordered liquidation. The grid includes citations to various Uniform Acts.

B. Entities to Avoid Land Loss for Tenancy-in-Common Real Estate Owners: Limited Liability Corporations, Irrevocable Grantor Trusts, and Tenancy-in-Common Agreements

This chapter proposes the following solutions to avoid land loss in order of preference for real estate owners:

1. (Highest preference): Limited liability company, established and funded either by the testator during his or her life or the heirs' property owners following the owner's death, which gives control to managers or members, creates a partnership business structure for the ongoing ownership of the real property, and sets out day-to-day control, amendment, voting, and liquidation voting provisions.
2. (Medium preference): Irrevocable grantor trusts formed by the heirs' property owner or owners to define who serves as trustee, who are or will become beneficiaries, and the rights and limitations the beneficiaries have in their continuing beneficial ownership of the real property owned by the trust.
3. (Lowest preference): Tenancy-in-common agreements funded by the heirs' property owners to preserve the real estate nature of the heirs' property ownership, providing a management structure and restrictions on transfers of the real estate interests.

V. GENERAL CAUTIONS ON FORMING AND MAINTAINING LLC'S AND TRUSTS

A. General Cautions on Forming and Maintaining LLC's and Trusts

1. *General Risk of Conversion of a Real Estate Interest to a Personal Property Interest*

A very important word of caution: placing heirs' property owners into a limited liability company, limited partnership, trust, or corporation (very rarely used for holding real estate), converts the heirs' property real estate interest into an interest in personal property. No heirs' property owner should consider forming a limited partnership, limited liability company, trust, or other entity, including a tenancy-in-common agreement, without first securing an experienced real estate and tax lawyer and an experienced accountant.[19] Further, heirs' property owners should not rely on the law firm or accountant selected by the promoter or the developer; the heirs' property owner needs his or her own lawyer and accountant.

2. *Dangers of Loss of Real Estate Tax Deferral under Internal Revenue Code Section 1031 and Dilution*

Internal Revenue Code (IRC) Section 1031 is an important tax provision enabling an owner of a real estate interest to defer paying capital gains on property held for investment if the owner replaces that property for like-kind real estate within approximately 6 months of the date of sale. If the owner of the property passes away, the property achieves a new basis measured as of the date of the owner's

---

[19] *See* LLCs, Partnerships, and Unincorporated Entities Committee, ABA, https://www.americanbar.org/groups/business_law/committees/llcs/. Other good sources of LLC state law are Philip J. Jelsma & Pamela Everett Nollkamper, The Limited Liability Company I & II (2019); Carter G. Bishop & Daniel S. Kleinberger, Limited Liability Companies: Tax and Business Law (2021).

death. See IRC Section 1014 (a). If real estate is funded into an LLC, this converts the real property interest into a personal property interest and disqualifies that asset from tax deferral under IRC Section 1031 in the event of a later sale, unless more sophisticated "Drop and Swap, Swap and Drop, or Partnership Division" planning is used.[20]

3. *Danger of Dilution of Converted Personal Property Interest*

If a contributed real estate interest is converted to a personal property interest, and the remaining owners seek an equivalent cash or noncash contribution via a capital call, this may result in dilution of the converted interest. Becoming co-owners in an LLC or other partnership entity with liquid, wealthy co-owners or partners may dilute heirs' property owners' interests during the business life of the LLC. The LLC operating agreement needs to be reviewed carefully to ascertain what is the effect of an unpaid capital contribution.

4. *Danger of Income Taxation to a Contributing Partner who Receives a Capital Interest on Formation*

Partners' or shareholders' initial contributions to a business organization can consist of land or cash or services. If a promoter or manager of an LLC wants an LLC interest but contributes no land or other capital contributions, he may be taxed on the value of the interest immediately as income.[21] See IRC Section 83(a) and Treasury Reg. 1.721-1(b)(1). Likewise, if services are contributed to a partnership or corporation solely for a capital interest, then an immediate income tax may be imposed on the contributor of the services who received the capital, that is, the stock or an LLC membership interest.[22]

5. *Danger of Administrative Dissolution by Failure to File or Renew Annual Reports with State Secretary of State, by Agreement, or by Application of a Member Claiming Unlawful Conduct of Business*

A corporation, limited partnership, LLC, limited liability partnership, or other entity granted a state "certificate" or "charter" of limited liability can fail due to a failure to file an annual report with the

---

[20] See Paragraph 9.3, Long and Foster Tax Free Exch. under IRC Section 1031, Current Problems in Exchanges: (Thomson Reuters) § 9:3 Partnership Split-ups:

> Partners owning real property together may want to go their separate ways but may also wish to take advantage of the tax-deferral provisions of I.RC. § 1031 by exchanging the equity in their partnership interest into real properties to be held by each of them separately. Such an exchange can be structured in several ways:
>
> (1) Drop and Swap. If all of the partners want to split up, the partnership can distribute its property to the partners pro rata as cotenants. The distribution by the partnership is generally tax-free under I.RC. § 731. Each cotenant then exchanges his or her real property interest for a separate property under I.RC. § 1031. This is sometimes called the "drop and swap."
>
> (2) Swap and Drop. Each partner can designate a separate replacement property and the partnership can exchange its property for the designated replacement properties. The partnership can then dissolve at some point, distributing the replacement properties to the respective partners in a taxfree liquidation under I.RC. § 731 of their partnership interests. This is sometimes called the "swap and drop."
>
> (3) Partnership Division. The partnership undergoes a partnership division and divides into two separate partnerships, each owned by at least two of the partners. The partnership can divide into two or more partnerships under the partnership division rules of I.RC. § 708(b)(2) before, after, or perhaps even during the exchange.

[21] *See* I.R.C. § 83(a); *See also* Treas. Reg. § 1.721-1(b)(1) (1960).

[22] *See* Ted D. Englebrecht, *Receipt of Partnership Interest for Services: Income or Not?* THE CPA JOURNAL ONLINE, May 1992; *See also* I.R.C. § 83(b).

secretary of state of the state of formation.[23] State acts often allow for reinstatement, sometimes retroactively, to the date of dissolution, to preserve or resurrect the liability protection.

An example of a state statute setting out the numerous means of dissolution for LLCs is Section 701 of the RULLCA,[24] which provides the following bases for dissolution of an LLC:

(a) A limited liability company is dissolved, and its activities and affairs must be wound up, upon the occurrence of any of the following:
  (1) an event or circumstance that the operating agreement states causes dissolution;
  (2) the affirmative vote or consent of all the members;
  (3) the passage of 90 consecutive days during which the company has no members unless before the end of the period:
    (A) consent to admit at least one specified person as a member is given by transferees owning the rights to receive a majority of distributions as transferees at the time the consent is to be effective; and
    (B) at least one person becomes a member in accordance with the consent;
  (4) on application by a member, the entry by [the appropriate court] of an order dissolving the company on the grounds that:
    (A) the conduct of all or substantially all the company's activities and affairs is unlawful;
    (B) it is not reasonably practicable to carry on the company's activities and affairs in conformity with the certificate of organization and the operating agreement; or
    (C) the managers or those members in control of the company:
      (i) have acted, are acting, or will act in a manner that is illegal or fraudulent; or
      (ii) have acted or are acting in a manner that is oppressive and was, is, or will be directly harmful to the applicant; or
  (5) the signing and filing of a statement of administrative dissolution by the [secretary of state] under Section 708.

(b) In a proceeding brought under subsection (a)(4)(C), the court may order a remedy other than dissolution.

Contested dissolutions often involve a court order to stay the dissolution pending an accounting among the various LLC members, which may include an assessment of obligations of the third-party creditors, the relative contributions of the members, member loans to the LLC, and a determination whether money or capital paid or contributed to the LLC was a loan or a capital contribution.[25] The real estate owned by the heirs' property owners originally contributed to the LLC will rarely emerge

[23] State charters or certificates granting limited liability are not provided for general partnerships, trusts, or tenancy-in-common agreements. Each state, by virtue of its power to allow filings to grant limited liability has the power to revoke the issued "charter." Further, judicial proceedings to "pierce the corporate or LLC veil" also can cause dissolution in the event a court finds that owners committed fraud, mismanagement, or oppression. *See* Revised Unif. Ltd. Liab. Co. Act § 701 (Unif. L. Comm'n. 2006).

[24] *Id.* RULLCA refers to Revised Uniform Limited Liability Company Act of 2006, as Amended in 2013. See uniformlaws.org for the complete text and comments.

[25] An excellent discussion of various issues involved in LLC litigation is set out in Phillip L. Jelsma & Pamela E. Nollkamper, The Limited Liability Company, Litigation § 11: 140-200, James Publishing Co, (2019). ISBN 978-1-949517-54-5;

from a dissolution in its original tenancy-in-common ownership. Further, courts often award relief other than dissolution and enable one member to buy out the other.[26]

6. *Danger of Judicial Dissolution or Veil Piercing on Determination of Oppression or Economic Frustration, and Buyout Remedies*

The consequences of a failed LLC receiving heirs' property can be disastrous to the original contributors of heirs' property. Once formed and funded with heirs' property real estate, if a member seeks dissolution, judges are given the flexibility to force a buyout from one member to the other under RULLCA Section 701(b) to preserve the veil of limited liability and avoid income tax issues on dissolution. But if the LLC has been poorly maintained (no operating agreement, no tax returns, failure to maintain accountings of contributions and withdrawals, failure to document member-to-member loans, or inadequate records of voting), judges may also allow for piercing the LLC veil or dissolving the LLC using principles of veil piercing from the corporate context; this is particularly true if a member makes a showing of fraud or oppression.[27]

7. *Danger of Do-It-Yourself Operating Agreements Obtained From On Line Sources*

Many "off-the-shelf" operating agreements, purchased through online services, are actually more dangerous than not having an operating agreement at all. This is because the default provisions of a state having enacted the RULLCA statute, or many other state statutes, often provide a more rational default scheme for governance, buyouts of members, and dissolution, then an off-the-shelf operating agreement. This is particularly true with heirs' property because few if any off-the-shelf LLC operating agreements will allow for distributions in kind of real estate after the funding and forming of the LLC, and few if any will provide for protections against the dilution of members' interests for unpaid capital calls.

B. Advantages of Limited Liability Companies

1. *Why the Limited Liability Company Is a Preferred Business Entity*

LLCs were originally formulated in Wyoming in 1978 and combine corporate-like liability protection with the benefits of very flexible partnership taxation.[28] LLCs are the preferred vehicle for holding real estate, although limited partnerships have been used for decades for development real estate. Forming, funding, and operating LLCs requires a working knowledge of state enabling acts for the chosen LLC law state, which may vary from the location of the LLC (often a Delaware LLC is used, due to the management-friendly provisions of that state). The Business Law section of the ABA has a very famous committee, the LLCs, Partnerships and Unincorporated Entities Committee, which provides invaluable Delaware and non-Delaware case law updates on the liquidation, fiduciary duty application, and LLC governance issues.[29]

---

[26] *See* Jelsma & Knollkamper, *supra* note 19.

[27] *See* Jelsma & Nollkamper, *supra* note 19 at § 11:140.

[28] Rev. Rul. 88-76, 1988-2 C.B. 360 launched the LLC revolution by allowing partnership taxation for entities with limited liability features, like a corporation.

[29] *See* LLCs, Partnerships, and Unincorporated Entities Committee, ABA, https://www.americanbar.org/groups/business_law/committees/llcs/.

a. Advantage One: A Member's Liability Can Be Limited to Their Capital Investment, Unlike a Cotenancy Agreement or a General Partnership

A hallmark provision of an LLC is Section 304 of RULLCA, universally found in LLC state acts:

> **SECTION 304. LIABILITY OF MEMBERS AND MANAGERS.**
>
> (a) A debt, obligation, or other liability of a limited liability company is solely the debt, obligation, or other liability of the company. A member or manager is not personally liable, directly or indirectly, by way of contribution or otherwise, for a debt, obligation, or other liability of the company solely by reason of being or acting as a member or manager. This subsection 83 applies regardless of the dissolution of the company.

Notwithstanding its partnership taxation structure and taxation (by default), this provision provides a liability shield for LLC members and managers. This insulates the owners from personal liability for LLC contracts and tort claims, unless grounds exist for piercing the LLC veil or unless the members or managers have directly guaranteed the LLC's obligations.

b. Advantage Two: An LLC Can Have a Flexible Operating Agreement and Capital Structure

The LLC is the preferred business entity to avoid land loss for fractionalized tenancy-in-common ownership. Transferring all or even some tenancy-in-common interests (whether highly fractionalized or not) achieves the advantage of protecting the fractional owners' interests from their own or other creditors (after formation), centralizes management, and provides for easier ownership succession. But it is critical to have a clear operating agreement that establishes mathematical (like stock) ownership, often in the form of "units." This often is set at the time of the members agreed-upon relative initial capital contributions. The operating agreement may also establish whether the members' units are voting or nonvoting, and whether, on certain events, the managing members have the right to alter the unit numbers (which should not be expressed merely as initial percentages of ownership but rather as units, like stock certificates). This is critical if one or another of them contributes capital after the formation of the LLC and the number of units need to be recalculated after formation. This will also be important in calculating voting and how assignments of units, amendment of the agreement, or dissolution of the LLC can be voted upon by the members.

The amounts or required voting percentages for operational voting, assignment of units, amendment of the operating agreement, and liquidation of the company should be clearly expressed in the operating agreement. Members may have certain rights for "preferred returns" where the distributions from the LLC are preferentially paid to one member (for example, a founding member contributing cash) and not to another member who contributes land only. Capital calls requiring members to provide additional cash can also be included in the operating agreement, with a determination of the consequence if a member cannot make the capital call.[30]

[30] Because of the flexible capital structure of the LLC, the LLC has replaced subchapter S and subchapter C corporations as preferred entities to hold real estate, as well as for reasons related to the adverse income tax effect of liquidating and distributing subchapter C corporations and the inflexible capital structure of a subchapter S corporation.

c. Advantage Three: The Limited Liability Company Has Been Adopted in All States and the RUCCLA Is Widely as a Good Model Act

Each state has individual LLC acts and most of these acts require managers or members in control to exercise minimum fiduciary or trust-like duties in the operating of the LLC, although the Delaware Act offers a nonfiduciary contractual basis for LLC management that attracts LLC formation in that state.[31] The ULC reports that nine states adopted the first Uniform Act of 1996 and another twenty-one have adopted the 2006 version (amended in 2011 and 2013). The ULC website, uniformlaws.org, and the Comments on the various iterations of LLCs since 1996, are an excellent introduction to the "big issues" in state laws on LLCs and contain detailed information on the history and status of key state law issues on LLCs.

A multi-member LLC can elect to be taxed as a partnership for federal and state income tax purposes or as a subchapter S corporation.[32] This distinction is important for self-employment tax reduction.[33] Subchapter S corporations can be owners of an LLC, which offers further opportunities for self-employment tax reduction,[34] often with the S corporation serving as the manager of the LLC. But caution should be used here because using an entity, whether a subchapter S corporation or an LLC, can reduce contributions due under the Federal Insurance Contributions Act (FICA) and reduce available government benefits under Social Security Disability.

d. Advantage Four: Limited Liability Companies Can Have Corporate-Like or Partnership-Like Management Structures as Either Manager or Member Managed

The control provisions of an LLC can be "manager managed" or "member managed". In a manager-managed LLC, the manager, or managers, notwithstanding the fact that they may own less than 50 percent of the LLC membership interests, control the day-to-day operations and distribution in kind of LLC property, over the possible objection of other members of the LLC who own more than 50 percent of the LLC membership interests. The level of fiduciary duties owed to the members by

---

[31] *See* Revised Unif. Ltd. Liab. Co. Act § 409 (Unif. L. Comm'n. 2006).

[32] *See* Treas. Reg. 301.7701-3.

[33] *See* https:// www. fundera.com/blog/ llc-v.- s-corp and the authorities cited therein.; *see also* Bloomberg Tax Management Portfolio: Portfolio 701 1st at Section VII Compensation Issues A. Reasonable Compensation Issues; *see also, Ibid,* at Section VII at E 2. Self-Employment Tax; *see also,* IRC Section 1402 (a)(13).

[34] According to Dirk Williams, JD and LLM, of Missoula, Montana, "Using entities to reduce self-employment tax in Mom-and-Pop businesses often is a trap, encouraged by well-meaning accountants who do not see the whole picture. Too often a couple will build a business, and following the accountant's advice attribute all income to one spouse (usually the husband) in order to avoid paying self-employment tax above the FICA cap amount for a single individual. The couple later divorces, and divides the business (or the business has closed). The spouse who did not have any of the business income attributed to her subsequently encounters serious health issues, and applies for Social Security Disability Income. Because all the self-employment income was attributed to the other spouse, the ill spouse has made insufficient FICA contributions, and therefore is not eligible for SSDI, even though she worked in the business and now meets medical disability requirements. Worse yet, if the 'non-contributing' spouse becomes ill, then the couple divorces, then she applies for SSDI, she is ineligible due to her lack of FICA contributions, AND she is ineligible for Supplemental Security Income (a much less robust means-tested benefit) until she has spent down the property she received in the divorce settlement."

the manager can be refined, and in some states even eliminated, which may attract real estate developers who often want their duties to be contractual, not fiduciary.[35]

Manager-managed LLCs offer a central means of decision making for highly fractionalized heirs' property, often because all or a significant percentage of the tenancy-in-common owners have deeded their interests into the LLC or because heirs' property owners have inherited their LLC interests by a will, trust, or intestacy transfer in an LLC that has converted heirs' property to LLC ownership. A manager-managed LLC is very similar to a limited partnership, with a general partner controlling the operation even though that general partner may own merely a one percent interest in the limited partnership. Like a general partner in a limited partnership, the manager of a manager-managed LLC is like an airline pilot in the cockpit of a large aircraft, with the remaining passengers as limited partners or, in the LLC, the nonmanaging members.

On the other end of the spectrum, an LLC may be "member managed," whereby each of the members own a pro rata percentage of the LLC membership interests and the LLC is essentially operated by majority, egalitarian vote, based on pro rata ownership.[36]

e. Advantage Five: Limited Liability Companies Have Superior Protection of Assets from Creditors

LLCs achieve a level of asset protection that is superior to a self-settled trust or tenancy-in-common agreement because of a unique feature of LLC law that provides that a creditor's sole recourse (when it levies on or attaches its judgment against the LLC) is a charging order against income or distributions flowing out of the LLC to individual LLC members.[37] This means that a creditor of an individual member of the LLC can only levy on income payable to that LLC member and may not levy or attach the real estate owned by the LLC. In the words of the Uniform Law Commissioners:

> . . . the judgment creditor of a member or transferee is entitled to a charging order against the relevant transferable interest. While in effect, that order entitles the judgment creditor to whatever distributions would otherwise be due to the member or transferee whose interest is subject to the order. However, the judgment creditor has no say in the timing or amount of those distributions. The charging order does not entitle the judgment creditor to accelerate any distributions or to otherwise interfere with the management and activities of the limited liability company.[38]

For example, if Freya Larsson had received an LLC membership interest before her gambling judgment, the judgment creditor would not be able to reach her membership interest, only distributions

[35] *See* Revised Unif. Ltd. Liab. Co. Act § 409 (Unif. L. Comm'n. 2006); *See also* LLCs, Partnerships, and Unincorporated Entities Committee, ABA, https://www.americanbar.org/groups/business_law/committees/llcs/.

[36] Section 407 of RULLCA makes member management, as opposed to manager management, the default unless the operating agreement provides otherwise. Note that many states require the articles of organization to state whether the LLC is a manager- or member-managed entity. This is a holdover from the 1996 Uniform Limited Liability Company Act. *See* Mont. Code Ann. § 35-8-202 (2021).

[37] *See* Revised Unif. Ltd. Liab. Co. Act § 503 (Unif. L. Comm'n. 2006).

[38] Revised Unif. Ltd. Liab. Co. Act § 503, cmt. 1 (Unif. L. Comm'n. 2006).

paid to her, and its remedies with respect to Freya's membership interest in the LLC would be limited to distributions paid to her.

f. Advantage Six: Limited Liability Company Operating Agreement; Distributions in Kind for Real Estate Contributions

LLCs are highly flexible and may provide for "distributions in kind" of LLC owners' real property. But the default rule under RULLCA is that a member may only receive a distribution in cash, not in kind, in the form of real estate.[39]

This means that the operating agreement must be absolutely clear to allow a real estate interest once contributed into an LLC to be distributed back out in the form of a "distribution in kind." Further, the real estate interest, once contributed into an LLC with a distribution in kind provision, generally cannot be simply deeded out of the LLC until after an accounting of all internal and external obligations of the LLC.[40]

Further, even if the operating agreement allows for a distribution in kind, a member dissociating and demanding receipt of a tract of real estate, for example, stands in the status of a creditor and its right to receive the asset is subject to offset "for any amount owed to the company by the member or person dissociated as a member on whose account the distribution is made."[41] This means that upon the vote of the managing members or the requisite percentage of member managers, the LLC may distribute a portion of the real estate out to individual members on certain events.

This provision is intended to override a common state law provision that the law of partition is automatically waived by all LLC members upon the formation of an LLC (the legal effect of this means that a real estate interest contributed into an LLC is converted from a real estate interest to an interest in personal property and is not subject to partition in kind, that is, a deed to a specific tract of real property).

In short, a distribution-in-kind provision may be extremely helpful if ever the parties wish to transfer tracts of LLC real property back to individual owners at some future date, but the member getting a distribution in kind of LLC real estate will not get it out of the LLC without an accounting as stated above, and this may affect the amount of real estate transferred back from the LLC.

---

[39] *See* Revised Unif. Ltd. Liab. Co. Act § 404 (Unif. L. Comm'n. 2006). Contrast the choice of a real estate corporation: According to attorney Dirk Williams, "This is why since the repeal of the General Utilities Doctrine in TRA 1986 the corporate form has been a generally poor entity choice for holding real estate. For example, farming parents whose farmland is held in a corporation, of which they own a majority of the stock, cannot help their child who is a minority shareholder get started with his or her own farm by redeeming the child's stock in exchange for a fraction of the corporation's farmland without triggering recognition of any built-in gain. The LLC form, on the other hand, facilitates nonrecognition if the redemption is properly organized and executed. The same reasoning applies to discourage the LLC organizer from election to treat a real estate LLC as an S Corp under the check the box regulations." See Bloomberg Tax Management Portfolios: US Income Portfolios: Portfolio 701 1st Choice of Entity: Operational Issues, IV Taxable Disposition/Liquidation of Entity Ownership Interest, subparagraphs C and D.

[40] *See Id.*, cmt. 1; *See also Id.* at § 701. See the discussion of dissolution in section V.A.3.

[41] *See Id.* at § 404(d).

g. Advantage Seven: Disproportionate Contributions Can Alter Ownership Percentages

Furthermore, LLCs can have features that will reward LLC members who make disproportionate capital contributions for the ongoing maintenance or repair of LLC property. For example, should one LLC member, say, Odin Larsson, advance significant sums for the repair or improvement of LLC properties, Odin's contribution may be rewarded with an increase in that LLC member's percentage ownership. Contrarily, other noncontributing members, say, Freya or Thor's children, may see their membership interest percentages diluted if they do not answer an LLC manager's "capital call" for unpaid contributions for maintenance of the LLC property.[42] This feature can be manipulated by "cash-rich" LLC members to achieve control over and dilution of noncontributing members' interests, thus owning the real estate (LLC operating agreements need proactive legal and accounting advice!). How the LLC will be managed and governed will influence how this powerful feature is used during the life of the LLC.

This is to be contrasted with traditional trust law, which provides that beneficiaries may have no liability for capital contributions at all, or, if they are asked to contribute, those unpaid contributions may be deemed loans by one beneficiary without the automatic dilution of the remaining nonpaying beneficiaries' interest in the trust. Trusts are discussed in section VII.

h. Advantage Eight: Ability to "Pick Your Partner"

LLCs may also restrict the transferability of membership interests and differentiate between "permitted transferees and unpermitted transferees." This means that an LLC operating agreement allows the members "to pick their partners" and an unpermitted transferee has no rights to management or information.[43] *See* ULC Uniform Limited Liability Company Act Section 502 and Comments.[44]

For example, should a Larsson family LLC formed by Ole and Gina limit the "permitted transferees" of the LLC to lineal descendants of Ole and Gina, then Thor's children's spouses, or Freya's autumn romance with and marriage to Hans Lunder, the trust officer, would pose no threat to Odin. This means a transfer to Freya's new spouse of her membership would trigger the right of the LLC or other members to purchase the membership interests being assigned, with the possibility of the application of significant discounts and devaluation of those interests.

The flexibility of the laws governing LLCs in allowing the organizing party or members to provide in the operating agreement a procedure for limiting or allowing new members is a critical

---

[42] *See Id.* at § 403 and Comments, as follows:

> SECTION 403. LIABILITY FOR CONTRIBUTIONS. (a) A person's obligation to make a contribution to a limited liability company is not excused by the person's death, disability, termination, or other inability to perform personally. (b) If a person does not fulfill an obligation to make a contribution other than money, the person is obligated at the option of the limited liability company to contribute money equal to the value of the part of the contribution which has not been made. (c) The obligation of a person failing to make a contribution may be compromised only by the affirmative vote or consent of all the members. If a creditor of a limited liability company extends credit or otherwise acts in reliance on an obligation described in subsection (a) without knowledge or notice of a compromise under this subsection, the creditor may enforce the obligation.

[43] *See Id.* at § 502 and Comments.

[44] *Id.*

benefit of the LLC as an entity choice. Indeed, the members of the Larrson family's LLC could even, if so inclined, modify the agreement to allow admission of Hans as a full member.

i. Advantage Nine: Provisions on Voting in a Well-Drafted Operating Agreement Can Be Clear and Avoid Controversy and Can Fine-tune What Fiduciary Duties Are Owed by the Manager

The LLC operating agreement should clearly define what voting percentage is required to initiate a capital call and what will be the consequences of a duly authorized but unpaid capital call. Is the noncontributing heirs' property owner automatically diluted or is there a "deemed" loan to that heir, from the more-wealthy heir, which may later result in a forfeiture of that heir's interest? Has the heir jumped from the partition law frying pan into the dilution fire?

The operating agreement should also describe the requisite percentage of member votes for the admission of new LLC members, the amendment of the agreement itself, and the liquidation of the LLC. Because LLCs are sanctioned by state statutes, judges in state courts have jurisdiction to determine whether members' interests should be bought out or whether the LLC should be liquidated and the net assets distributed out to the owners after payment to the LLC creditors. Because these provisions often arise due to internecine disputes among members, LLC liquidation cases are often matters of accounting. These disputes often also involve damages arising from breach of fiduciary duty by members in control positions. The extent to which members in control of an LLC owe fiduciary duties to the others can be defined in the operating agreement and are addressed in RULLCA 2006 Section 105 and its Comments.[45]

An LLC operating agreement in most states is not simply a contract among members, but rather imposes certain trust-like duties to the managing member or members in control. This may become important where the objectives of various members of the LLC conflict, such as conserving real estate versus developing real estate, or other governance issues arising from the ownership of real estate. An example of trust-like duties would be the avoidance of a conflict of interest by a person serving as a manager. In our example, if Hans Lunder, Freya's fiancé and soon-to-be husband, is also actively managing other real estate ventures, is that not a conflict of interest preventing him from serving as a manager for the Larsson LLC?

j. Advantage Ten: Alternative Dispute Language Can Be Tailored to the Needs of the Limited Liability Company

Finally, LLC operating agreements can include alternative dispute resolution mechanisms such as mandatory arbitration, which replace expensive litigation requiring the use of a delayed court system. Because of the complexity of LLC management and operations, arbitration of accounting

---

[45] The ULC Comments to Section 105 of the ULLCA (2006) Act explain the issue:

> The Operating Agreement and the Fiduciary and Other Duties of Those Who Manage. One of the most complex questions in the law of unincorporated business organizations is the extent to which an agreement among the organization's owners can affect the fiduciary and other duties of those who manage the organization (e.g., members in a member managed LLC; managers in a manager managed LLC). As explained in detail in the comment to Subsection (d)(3), this act rejects the notion that a contract can completely transform an inherently fiduciary relationship into a merely arm's length association. Within that limitation, however, this section provides substantial power to the operating agreement to reshape, limit, and eliminate fiduciary and other managerial duties.

and operational issues, including dissolutions or buyouts, should be done by arbitration, but items requiring injunctive relief to avoid irreparable harm can be carved out of the operating arbitration provision.

An example of a manager-managed LLC operating agreement intended for multiple future heirs' property owners is included as annex C.

VI. LESSONS LEARNED: ENTITY PLANNING AND THE LARSSONS

Returning to the Larsson example, if Ole and Gina Larsson had used entity planning for their transfer of real estate wealth, the family might have enjoyed significant benefits. Recall that Odin wishes to purchase Freya's and Thor's children's two-thirds ownership interests in the Lazy V Ranch with his share of the sales proceeds from the Alfalfa Field to the hotel chain. Here are the benefits they might have enjoyed:

1. Freya's judgement creditor would not be able to levy on or attach her undivided LLC membership interest, because her creditors are only entitled to a charging order of her income interest.
2. Odin's goal of obtaining full interest in the Lazy V Ranch, while using his interest in the Alfalfa Field as a cash source to buy out Freya and Thor's children, could occur in the form of a membership purchase agreement or redemption from the sales proceeds from the Alfalfa Field.
3. The member managers of the Larsson Family LLC, possibly Ole, Gina, or Odin, or Hans Lunder as trustee of the Norseman Trust, could control the negotiation for the sale of the Alfalfa Field to the hotel chain and offset the sales proceeds to Odin to purchase Freya's and Thor's children's interest in the Lazy V Ranch.
4. Fractional ownership would be avoided but the definition of transferability of LLC membership interest to the heirs of Thor, Freya, and Odin could be articulated as "permitted transfers to further generations."
5. Estate and gift taxes, if any, may be reduced in Ole's and Gina's estates.
6. Odin's disproportionate capital contributions for his labor and capital improvements at both the Alfalfa Field and the Lazy V Ranch could increase his percentage interest or be compensated in a buyout of Freya's and Thor's children's interest in the Lazy V Ranch.

The following is a checklist for good practices when heirs' property is deeded into an LLC. It is critical to:

1. File annual reports consistently with the secretary of state of the state of formation.
2. Have a written operating agreement signed by all members, or acknowledged by them, with clear voting language (by units) for operational control, the percentage of votes required for assignment of LLC membership interest, the required member votes required for amendment of the operating agreement, and the required member votes for liquidation of the entity.
3. Maintain records of contributing LLC members or heirs' property owners' initial capital contributions.

4. Document whether distributions in kind of contributed real property will be allowed and how the tax attributes to other members of the distributed real estate will be calculated in light of an LLC accounting.
5. Document records of the withdrawals of income or other assets from the LLC.
6. Document records of all loans advanced by LLC members.
7. Document records of all loans advanced by third-party creditors.
8. Document any amendments to the operating agreement.

If a judge perceives that the members will not maintain the LLC, the judge may likely conclude that it is "not reasonably practicable to carry on the company's activities and affairs in conformity with the certificate of organization or the operating agreement."[46] See RULLCA Section 701. The 1996 version of the Uniform Limited Liability Company Act is even broader: "that the economic purpose of the company is likely to be unreasonably frustrated.[47]"

In the event the LLC is dissolved, third-party creditors are paid in advance of any members' loans and the restoration of deficit capital accounts.[48] If there are disproportionate capital accounts of members, those can be restored but there can be serious federal income tax consequences with operating agreements omitting capital account restoration and qualified income offset language.[49]

Beside LLCs, trusts are also used by skilled planners as vehicles to hold heirs' property. Trusts can be used as substitutes for LLCs or in combination with LLCs. We now turn to a discussion of trusts.

VII. GRANTOR TRUSTS

Trusts are commonly used to hold real estate because control can be vested in a single trustee who has control over all the heirs' property real estate funded into the trust, often by the senior generation. An example would be Ole and Gina Larsson funding their Alfalfa Field and Lazy Ranch into a joint revocable trust or mirror-image, single-person revocable trusts, choosing each surviving spouse as initial beneficiary and then pro rate to their children, likely with intermediate trusts for estate tax reduction.[50]

The trustee is subject to fiduciary standards for the benefit of the multiple beneficial owners, which is good for beneficiaries, but it may be difficult to locate a trustee willing to manage heirs' property, because of the inherent conflicts of interest among the various beneficiaries and the inherently high-risk nature of real estate (toxic waste, premises liability). Consider the conflicting goals of the Larsson family heirs: Freya and Thor's children want to sell the Alfalfa Field and the Lazy V Ranch.

---

[46] *See* Revised Unif. Ltd. Liab. Co. Act § 701 (Unif. L. Comm'n. 2006).

[47] *See* Unif. Ltd. Liab. Co. Act § 801 (4) (i)_; *See also* Mont. Code Ann. § 35-8-902 (2021).

[48] *See* Revised Unif. Ltd. Liab. Co. Act § 707(a & b) (Unif. L. Comm'n. 2006).

[49] IRC § 704(b) and related Treasury Regulations; Carter G. Bishop & Daniel S. Kleinberger, Limited Liability Companies: Tax and Business Law, paragraph 9.06.

[50] Estate planning is beyond the scope of this chapter, but each of them would likely use "credit shelter" or "exemption equivalent" trusts, possibly qualified terminable interest trusts or QTIP trusts, or spousal lifetime access trusts, to maximize their federal estate tax exemptions of approximately $11,580,000 each for 2020; this amount may decline radically in 2023 to $6,000,000 each.

Odin wants to buy out their interests in the Lazy V Ranch.[51] Further, the beneficial owners enjoy limited liability and asset protection, but their beneficial interests in the trust cannot be used for loan collateral and are often not assignable or transferable (although the trust as a whole may be able to obtain loans). Contributions advanced by beneficiaries do not increase their percentage ownership and are usually characterized as loans to the trust.

The most common trust form is a revocable trust used as a probate avoidance device and an estate planning tool. Trusts can be used to avoid fractionalization of both the surface estate and, often, subsurface mineral estate owners.[52]

A popular form of trust planning for income and estate tax planning used by many estate planning professionals is an intentionally defective grantor trust. If a trust is irrevocable, with the result that the trust has its own employer identification number, and is irrevocable under state law, the trust-generated income may be structured to be taxed to the grantor, not the trust, which would pay much higher income tax rates.[53] The trust can also be drafted so the assets are beyond the reach of the grantor's federal estate tax, if any. This assumes that the trust grantor has removed, by gift, transfer, or sale, the assets transferred to the trust and does not have powers over the trust under IRC Sections 2036 and 2038. A trust that is both irrevocable (based on state trust law) and taxed, on an income tax basis, to the grantor is often known as an intentionally defective grantor trust.[54]

One goal of the advanced planning method using an intentionally defective grantor trust for heirs' property owners will allow the grantor/owner to "freeze" values of potential future appreciation of heirs' property real estate by excluding the real estate assets from the grantor's estate (granting the real estate into the trust), yet allowing the family of the grantor to retain and enjoy the benefits of trust ownership for successive generations with trustee asset management and trust protection.[55] See also the discussion that follows on "Advance Planning with Trusts and Heirs' Property."

Trusts consist of three parties: (1) the original grantor or settlor who conveys real estate into a trust; (2) the trustee who governs day-to-day long-term management of the trust, often the original grantor until he or she dies or becomes incapacitated (the trustee can be either an individual or a

---

[51] Just as a personal representative in the probate context can be influenced by the UPHPA situation, so might a trustee who is acting after Ole and Gina's death, if a beneficiary seeks court management of the trustee's conduct. Although the property may be trust property and technically not heirs' property, the trustee's exercise of its fiduciary duty could be strongly influenced by the valuation and open-market sale provisions of the UPHPA. See section 1 of this chapter.

[52] "Illinois Land Trusts" flip control from a trustee to multiple beneficiaries by virtue of a beneficiary agreement and as such can be used for highly fractionalized heirs' property. Such trusts were considered as a solution to heirs' property but the idea was rejected by the Drafting Committee of the Uniform Law Commission Joint Editorial Board.

[53] If the trust gives the grantor certain powers over the trust (such as the power to substitute assets of equal worth), the income from the trust will be taxed to the original grantor rather than to the trust itself, avoiding trust income taxation at a substantially higher trust income tax rate. IRC Section 675.

[54] The term "defective" is a misnomer because nothing is actually defective about the trust; it fails the attributes of stand-alone trust income taxation and because the grantor has retained powers to substitute trust assets of equal worth, or other powers under IRC 675, the income is taxed to the grantor and not the trust itself, which is a good result because irrevocable trust tax rates often exceed the individual grantor's tax rate. If real estate is conveyed into a trust, its income and capital gains will be taxed to the grantor, not the trust or the beneficiaries.

[55] This technique is a very complex planning tool; an excellent source of information on irrevocable grantor trusts is HOWARD M. ZARITSKY, THOMSON REUTERS, TAX PLANNING FOR FAMILY WEALTH TRANSFERS DURING LIFE: ANALYSIS WITH FORMS (5th ed chapter 3).

corporate trust company); and (3) the beneficiary or beneficiaries, who can be the original settlor, a spouse, children, or distant grandchildren and great-grandchildren.

A. Disadvantages to Trusts

Here are some general disadvantages to trusts. Beneficial interests in trust, depending on the trust document, may be transferable only to the lineal descendants of the original grantor. Those beneficiary interests may not enjoy "step up" in basis at the time of the passing of the beneficiary unless the beneficiary is granted a general power of appointment to assign the interest to a broad class of people. Loans advanced by the beneficiaries for capital improvements may not increase the creditor beneficiary's percentage ownership and are often not available. Depending on the experience and sophistication of the trustee, an irrevocable, long-term RAP (Rule Against Perpetuities—see the next section) trust, may or may not have been well administered and may have lurking claims against the successor trustee. Finally, corporate trustees may be reluctant to incur the risk of managing hard to value and hard to administer heirs' property assets.

B. Advance Planning with Trusts and Heirs' Property

1. *The Rule Against Perpetuities (RAP) and the Seven non-RAP States Create Opportunities for Heirs' Property Trusts in States Not Governed by the RAP*

If avoidance of land loss is the primary objective, then long-term trust administration should be considered. If the trust is to last more than approximately 90 years, then planning is required. In all but seven states,[56] US trust law prevents long-term, multigenerational trust ownership because of the Rule Against Perpetuities (RAP). The RAP creates a fundamental limitation on the duration of a trust. If perpetual or long-term ownership is sought through generations, the trust may be void from the beginning because the RAP prohibits ownership beyond a "life in being (at the time of the trust creation or the time the interest is granted), plus twenty-one (21) years." If there is any possibility that this will occur, the trust may be void from the outset. However, a modified statutory rule under the so called "wait and see" approach is applicable in thirty-one states that have adopted the Statutory Rule Against Perpetuities.[57] But this rule provides little relief.

Accordingly, at least twenty states, to various extents, have modified the common law RAP, which provides an opportunity to form long-term trusts for heirs' property.[58] If long-term trust ownership is a goal of the heirs' property owners, then the following advance planning should be considered: (1) the heirs' property owners should form a dynasty trust in a non-RAP state, (2) the heirs' property owners should contribute their heirs' property interests to an LLC in exchange for membership interests in the LLC; and (3) the heirs' property owners should contribute their new

---

[56] See statutes for Alaska, Colorado, Delaware, Florida, Idaho, Illinois, Maine, Maryland, Massachusetts, Nevada, New Jersey, New Hampshire, Ohio, Pennsylvania, Kentucky, Rhode Island, Tennessee, South Dakota, Utah, Washington, and Wyoming.

[57] *See Statutory Rule Against Perpetuities*, Unif. L. Comm'n, https://www.uniformlaws.org/committees/community-home?CommunityKey=addf3263-af92-4421-a83c-2ef7bc9a1b94.

[58] See summary sources at ieds.online and oshins.com.

LLC membership interests to the new dynasty trust; this arrangement may provide a powerful source of asset protection and land loss prevention.[59]

2. *The Self-Settled Trust Doctrine and the Domestic Action Protective Trust in a Long-Term Trust Administration Estate*

As important as the RAP is the "self-settled trust doctrine." The traditional common law rule provides that a trust created by a grantor or settlor for his or her benefit does not achieve asset protection for claims against the original grantor if he or she is to be a beneficiary.[60] The Uniform Trust Code incorporates the self-settled trust doctrine, and the rule applies in some form or another in all fifty states.

But approximately sixteen states have now adopted exceptions to the self-settled trust doctrine, thus allowing for "Domestic Asset Protection Trusts ('DAPT')," whereby if a settlor grants or transfers property into a trust, has no claims at the time of transfer, and otherwise complies with the applicable state DAPT statutes, assets in the DAPT are protected from the grantor's creditors, even as the grantor retains some rights to receive trust distributions.[61] Although each DAPT-friendly state has adopted its own unique statutory scheme, the DAPT laws typically have as their cornerstone a statute that spells out specific requirements for a spendthrift clause and trust situs clause to be included in the trust instrument to invoke the state's DAPT statutes. A well-known chart known as the "Domestic Asset Protection Trust State Rankings Chart" ranks various state statues and weighs factors such as the impact of that state's Uniform Voidable Transfers Act, if any, statutes of limitations for future or past creditors, the strength given to spousal or child support creditors' rights, the strength given to tort claim creditors, and the ease of use of the statute.[62]

In short, the original grantor may want to form a long-term trust in a non-RAP state, extending the administration as long as is allowable under that state's law. This strategy can be combined with using a trust that complies with the requirements of that same state's DAPT statute; if the heirs' property owners do not have creditors' claims before the formation, this may be a very powerful means to

---

[59] For example, an LLC from Montana, where the Rule Against Perpetuities is enshrined in the state constitution, could be formed and funded with heirs' property located in Montana. The LLC interests would be owned by the South Dakota trust and could be formed and administered in South Dakota, a non-RAP state, which also has no state income tax. Montana's income tax will be payable for Montana source income, but the real estate may be protected in perpetuity and any post-LLC-formation creditors of the individual heirs' property owners will likely have no recourse to the heirs' property owners, the Montana LLC, or the South Dakota trust. South Dakota also has no state income tax so any accumulated income tax will not be taxed at the state tax level. The trust can last perpetually under South Dakota law; *See also* the discussion of the self-settled trust doctrine, below; *See also* Howard Zaritsky, Tax Planning for Family Wealth Transfers During Life, § 8.06(3)(b) (2021); *See also* Steve Oshins, Oshins & Associates, LLC, State Rankings Charts, oshins.com/state-rankings-charts, Dynasty Trust State Rankings chart, which weighs the impacts of that state's Rule Against Perpetuities, state income tax, spendthrift trust protections, protecting against a divorcing spouse or child support claim, the presence of a domestic asset protection trust statute in the state, a decanting statute in that state, and the availability of nonjudicial settlement agreements.

[60] *See* Unif. Trust Code § 505(1) (Unif. L. Comm'n. 2000).

[61] *See* Oshins, Domestic Asset Protection Trust State Rankings Chart, oshins.com/state-rankings-charts; *see also* Duncan E. Osborne & Elizabeth L. Morgan, Thomson Reuters, Asset Protection: Domestic and International Law and Tactics (1997–2021 paragraph 5.4).

[62] As demonstrated in the example above, South Dakota is a DAPT state. If funded with the interests of a South Dakota LLC owning heirs' property, the trust could exist perpetually and have very powerful asset protection. It is to be noted that this is a fast-moving area of trust law and federal estate taxation. It is vital to consult an expert attorney in a DAPT state and do business with a trust company in a non-RAP state having also a domestic asset protection trust statute in place.

protect heirs' property.[63] Again, using an LLC to fund the trust may provide valuable asset protection benefits.[64]

Warning: this is a complex and fast evolving area. Pre-LLC-formation creditors and creditors in federal bankruptcy can upset much of this planning.[65] It is critical to obtain lawyers with estate and income tax and asset protection planning expertise.

3. *Using a Domestic Asset Protection Trust in a Long-Term Trust Administration State with a Directed Trust*

A recent development in state trust law also allows the trustee of a trust containing heirs' property to limit the trustee's liability by cabining off the trustee's duties for administering real estate from the trustee's duties to manage more liquid assets, with the use of a "trust director" and a "directed trustee."[66] This can greatly alter a trustee's fiduciary duty and increase the pool of trustees willing to administer heirs' property. This is advanced trust planning and experienced lawyers and trust companies using directed trusts should be consulted.[67]

C. Critical Trust Considerations

In general, when considering a trust as a vessel for holding heirs' property, the analysis should consider the following:

1. Is the trust located in a favorable jurisdiction for income tax purposes, including a statute involving domestic asset protection features?[68]
2. Should the trust utilize the Uniform Directed Trust Act or other state laws that facilitate the division of trustee duties, such as a committee to instruct the trustee regarding trust investment decisions and/or distributions.[69]
3. Who will be the trustee (an individual, a group of individuals, or a corporate trust company) and what will be their fiduciary duties?
4. Consider special language for using the UPHPA to define how the fiduciary trustee sells or holds heirs' property.

---

[63] *See* Steve Oshins, Oshins & Associates, LLC, Dynasty Trust State Rankings, oshins.com/state-rankings-charts, which, like the Domestic Asset Protection Trust State Rankings Chart, weighs the impacts of that state's Rule Against Perpetuities, state income tax, spendthrift trust protections, protecting against a divorcing spouse or child support claim, the presence of a domestic asset protection trust statute in the state, a decanting statute in that state, and the availability of nonjudicial settlement agreements.

[64] *See* note 62 above

[65] *See* Waldron v. Huber (In re Huber), 493 B.R. 798 (Bankr. W.D. Wash. 2013); *see also* Jason S. Scott, Thomson Reuters, Asset Protection: Domestic and International Law and Tactics § 25:5. Legal Grounds for Attacking APTs—Public Policy Argument (2021).

[66] *See* Directed Trust Act (Unif. L. Comm'n. 2017).

[67] One such trust company is First Trust of Rapid City, South Dakota. *See* First Trust Company, www.firsttrustcompany.com (last visited Nov. 16, 2021).

[68] *See* Oshins, *supra* note 61.

[69] *See* Comments to Directed Trust Act (Unif. L. Comm'n. 2017).

5. How will trustee succession be arranged in the future?
6. Will the trust have certain provisions that can be modified by the beneficiaries, such as refusing to allow or allowing the distribution in kind of trust property, or other provisions which, if described and deemed "material purposes," are not subject to court modification in the future?[70]
7. Does the trust have alternative dispute resolution language, provisions allowing for trust divisions if the beneficiaries cannot own property together in the trust, or provisions allowing for deeding out of real estate if a beneficiary wants to receive real estate outside of the trust's ownership?
8. What are the consequences of one beneficiary making capital contributions or loans to the trust while others do not? Does a loan allow for reallocation of beneficial interests or forfeiture if not paid?
9. Can the beneficiaries, by majority vote or otherwise, force the sale of the trust assets in the event the beneficiaries and the trustee dispute the operating or maintenance of the trust?

An example of an irrevocable trust in a RAP state used for a family cabin with blended trustee and beneficiary control is included as annex D.

VIII. USE OF TENANCY-IN-COMMON AGREEMENTS

The third entity is the tenancy-in-common agreement (TIC); this is very valuable to preserve the real estate nature of the heirs' property for tax deferral treatment under IRC 1031.

The use of a TIC may be critical to heirs' property owners if their goal is to retain the real estate nature of their ownership and avoid characterization as a partnership interest under state law. To retain the real estate character, as opposed to personal property character, of appreciating land investments, TICs became popular in the mid-2000s. They also describe how capital calls are to be made by the co-owners, the consequences of a contributing versus noncontributing member not making a capital call, rights of first refusal, and preserving the right of partition of the property and waiver of any intention to become partners under state law or federal tax law.

Commercial "TIC Properties" were sanctioned by IRS Rev. Proc. 2002-22, which established for federal tax purposes the basis upon which the IRS will *not* characterize a tenancy-in-common agreement as a partnership. The goal is to preserve tax deferral treatment under IRC Section 1031 and deductibility of rental real estate expenses against income.

State law can convert tenancy-in-common real estate to partnership property. Under the Revised Uniform Partnership Act (RUPA) Section 204(c), property is presumed to be partnership property if it is purchased with partnership assets, *even if not acquired in the name of the partnership*, or if one or more of the partners acquires title with an indication, when transferring title to the property, of the person's capacity as a partnership or the existence of a partnership. Furthermore, should the parties file a partnership return *reporting the income derived from the TIC property as partnership*

---

[70] This is a critical provision under the Uniform Trust Code, Sections 410 and 411, which allow broad modification unless the provision sought to be modified is a "material purpose" under those sections. *See* UNIF. TRUST CODE § 410 & 411 (UNIF. L. COMM'N. 2000).

income, this could convert the TIC real estate to partnership real estate and subject the real estate to the mandatory buyout provisions of RUPA Section 701. This applies among the partners, and not third-party creditors relying on real estate records. See Comments to RUPA Section 204. The buyout provision is RUPA Section 701 and might result in a requirement that the other TIC owners buy out a deceased (dissociated) TIC property owner. This would be fatal to any claim that the property is in fact tenancy-in-common property.

Further, while TICs provide for limitations of transferability of the tenancy-in-common interest, they nevertheless expose the property to creditor problems of each of the cotenancy owners.

The following are common features of a tenancy-in-common agreement, an example of which is shown in annex E:

1. The agreement specifies a specific term of the agreement.
2. The agreement specifies that an entity, usually a limited liability entity, may manage the property to handle the leasing operation and maintenance of the property.
3. The agreement provides that if additional operating capital be needed from the owners to operate, improve, or otherwise manage the property, the manager may notify the owners of the requirement of such additional funds. The failure of any owner to make such additional contributions within an agreed notice period may constitute a default under the agreement. Any nondefaulting owner has the right, not the obligation, to pay the defaulting owner's pro rata share of the requested contribution.
4. In the event a nondefaulting owner elects to pay the defaulting owner's share, the nondefaulting owner may be entitled to a percentage of the defaulting owner's interest.
5. In the event of sale, the owner shall have the right to sell or exchange their interest in the property but must first offer to sell such property to other owners. The selling owner shall first offer to the other owners the property for a period of 30 days. In the event the nonselling owners reject the offer, then the selling owner shall be free to sell his or her interest in the property. In the event the nonselling owners accept the offer to purchase the property, then the nonselling owners shall have 60 days within which to purchase the property.
6. All owners shall have the right to partition the property provided that they first offer to sell their interest to the other owners for the appraised value. In the event the nonselling owners decide to name their own appraiser, they may do so, and those two appraisers may identify a third appraiser to appraise the property.
7. The sale price carries with it an agreed discount from the value of the selling owner's percentage ownership. In the event that the nonpartitioning owner rejects the offer, the partitioning owner is free to initiate a partition action in the appropriate court.
8. The agreement often contains an express waiver or statement that the parties do not intend to become partners under the agreement and waive any mandatory buyout provisions under state partnership law.

If preservation of the real estate character of the heirs' property is not a primary goal, it is highly likely that an LLC or grantor trust, discussed earlier, are superior vehicles over a tenancy-in-common agreement.

IX. ADVANCED STRATEGIES COMBINING ESTATE PLANNING PROVISIONS WITH TRUSTS, LIMITED LIABILITY COMPANIES, AND CONSERVATION EASEMENT RESTRICTIONS

The penultimate form of asset protection outside an LLC or trust as described in this chapter is a perpetual conservation easement monitored by a state or federal agency or a private conservation easement land trust, such as the Nature Conservancy. If the heirs' property falls under a conservation purpose, such as a place of "relatively natural habitat," then long-term use and development restrictions for a conservation easement may be a valuable tool for heirs' property. [71]

But this necessarily means all of the heirs agree to perpetual restrictions. If all owners can grant the fractionalized real estate under a conservation easement and grant the easement to a land trust or other "qualified organization," that act alone may do more to avoid land loss of fractional interests than any other planning.

Conservation easements are popular not only for preservation of natural habitat and open space, but also for the purposes of achieving public access to areas where public ownership is minimal.[72] Conservation easements may result in significant charitable income tax deductions for the owners of the underlying real estate or may generate revenue, whether through private fundraising or governmental programs such as the Agricultural Land Easement program of the US Department of Agriculture. Nevertheless, conservation easements should be approached carefully, with the idea that the conservation easement, once imposed on the property and restricting its further subdivision or limiting its commercial use, will not likely be amended by consent of the land trust or other entity that is named as beneficiary of, and endowed with the duty and power to enforce, the covenants of the conservation easement. Judicial action will likely be required and will likely not be successful.[73]

The objectives of the individual fractional owners must be carefully identified prior to the placement of conservation easement restrictions on the property. Again, the restrictions can be placed on the property even though, and perhaps only after, it is placed in a limited liability company.

The value of a conservation easement for fractional owners seeking to preserve their property is that a permanent nonprofit organization will have the power to monitor any violation of the conservation easement restrictions. (The membership interests or actual real estate ownership interests are nevertheless transferable to heirs of the individual fractional owners but are made subject to the conservation easement restriction.) Conservation easements often involve predetermined "splits" where a large conservation easement tract may be further subdivided in a limited fashion that does not materially impair the conservation values (natural habitat, or open space, for example) for which the conservation easement was formed. What is important is that unless all owners are willing to place their real estate interests under a conservation easement, the conservation easement may not be appropriate, and one owner's retention of a tenancy-in-common interest may subject the entire tract to sale or distribution in kind under that state's partition laws.

---

[71] David J. Dietrich & Christian Dietrich, *Introduction*, Conservation Easements: Tax and Real Estate Planning for Landowners and Advisors XII–XXIX (2011).

[72] *Id.*

[73] *Id.*

X. CONCLUSION

Discovering the long-term goals of heirs' property owners with respect to the real estate and creating a trust or, better yet, a well-drafted and -managed limited liability entity that can last for generations may avoid dissention and land loss through partition. But such a business organization will last only if the inexorable changes to the real estate owned by the business organization can be adapted to the owner's goals, through good succession planning and proactive business management. Individual humans' objectives change through time, as does the character and value of real estate. Wise control and measured flexibility can be achieved with good planning.

Annex 7A

To illustrate entity planning issues for heirs' property owners, meet the (under-planned) Larsson family of Gallatin County, MT.

Ole and Gina Larsson, in their seventies but both deceased, sequentially, in 2021, inherited 80 acres of Gallatin County real estate in 1980. Ole inherited the land from his late father Sven. Ole also inherited the Lazy V Ranch in Sweetgrass County, Montana, consisting of 3,840 acres of improved grassland with a strong recreational value. It is near the site of the filming of *The Horse Whisperer*.

Due to its proximity to the Big Sky ski resort and the Belgrade Bozeman International Airport, the 80 acres in Gallatin County now may be worth $8 million, because a luxury hotel chain wants to purchase it.

Of the original 80 acres of the Gallatin County property, 60 acres are undeveloped; it is referred to as "the Alfalfa Field."

Ole did not transfer any of the acres of the Lazy V. Ranch but planned to leave it first to Gina and then in equal one-third shares to their children Freya and Odin, and in one-ninth shares to each of their son Thor's children. It is valued at $3,000 per acre or $11,520,000.

Ole and Gina left simple wills transferring the property first to each other and then to their children equally, by representation. Odin died first, and Gina a few months later.

In 2020, Thor was killed while serving in the US Marine Corps. He was divorced in 2018, and he left his real estate interest to his three children, who have inherited in equal shares. One of Thor's children is under the age of majority.

Etta is married to Odin, who is the "on the farm" heir and has been actively operating it, harvesting alfalfa from the Alfalfa Field with Ole. Odin also does all of the work on the Lazy V Ranch.

Freya is a legal support paralegal and has had an independent contractor business for paralegal work in her home since the early pandemic days of February 2020. She has a gambling problem and may need to file for bankruptcy. She is engaged to be married to Hans Lunden, who Gina has named in her will as personal representative for her estate. Hans's personality and administrative style are described in the conflict-of-interest discussion that follows footnotes 13 and 14 of this chapter.

The 60-acre Alfalfa Field is prime development property. A luxury hotel chain's developer has approached Ole and the family, and wants to purchase the full 80 acres. The chain has offered to purchase the property for $8 million. The hotel chain plans to allow for 20 of the 80 acres to remain in a conservation easement with a Nordic ski track and skijoring and Viking theme.

Thor's children strongly support the idea of sale to the hotel chain. Freya needs the money. She has been served with a $233,000 gambling debt from her last trip to Las Vegas.

Both Ole and Gina died in 2021. What can be done in their estates?

Should Gina and Ole's heirs form a trust, a limited liability company, or a tenancy-in-common agreement?

Annex 7B

	Sole Proprietorship	General Partnership	Limited Partnership	Limited Liability Company	C-Corporation	S-Corporation	Revocable Trust	Irrevocable Trust	Tenants-in-Common Agreement
Management and Control	Sole owner	Each partner is an agent for the partnership and creates joint and several liability; see limitations under RUPA Section 307	Vested in general partners for most decisions; limited partners have reserved voting for major decisions; see RULPA Sections 402 and 305	Manager-managed LLC allows board of directors (BOD)-type governance; member-managed LLC allows pro rata voting without BOD; other members can have reserved powers under either form of management; member managed is the default under the RULLCA at Section 407 but this statute is easily modified for manager management	Board of directors regardless of ownership; but statutory close corporation can eliminate BOD and have partnership-like shareholders agreement	Board of directors regardless of ownership; but statutory close corporation can eliminate BOD and have partnership-like shareholders agreement	Trustee or successor trustee; also, trust director; but agreement can allow beneficiary consent for certain actions; see nonwaivable duty of trustee to act for beneficiaries under UTC's Section 105, unless the trust is a directed trust	Trustee or successor trustee; also, trust director; but agreement can allow beneficiary consent for certain actions; see nonwaivable duty of trustee to act for beneficiaries under UTC's Section 105, unless the trust is a directed trust	Usually through a designated manager, which can be a corporation or a limited liability company

Ownership Limitations	Sole owner only	State law allows single class but the partnership agreement can provide otherwise	State law allows single class but the partnership agreement can provide otherwise	Can have multiple classes of ownership; no limit on number of owners	None	Limited to natural persons or special trusts (ESBTs or QSSTs); limited to 100 shareholders for S-corporations formed after 2004	None	None	See Rev. Proc. 2022 to avoid TIC being taxed as a partnership
Limited Liability Features	None	Partners are jointly and severally liable, unless a limited liability partnership is elected	Limited partners have limited liability unless they act like a general partnership; general partnership has unlimited liability but can elect to limit liability in states having an LLLP statute	Charging order against distributions is the exclusive remedy for creditor and there is no right of a creditor to become member absent consent of remaining members	Stock can be levied upon; corporate veil protects stockholders from individual liability but corporate assets are subject to claims	Stock can be levied upon; corporate veil protects stockholders from individual liability but corporate assets are subject to claims	None	Yes, state spendthrift laws can provide protection for beneficiaries' interests from creditors; trustees have broad liability as fiduciaries	Individual owners' real estate interests are subject to individuals' creditors; manager should be a corporation or an LLC; the entire tract is subject to state partition laws unless the agreement contains a waiver of partition

	Sole Proprietorship	General Partnership	Limited Partnership	Limited Liability Company	C-Corporation	S-Corporation	Revocable Trust	Irrevocable Trust	Tenants-in-Common Agreement
Ownership Limitations	Individual only	No limitations; corporations, LLCs and other entities can be partners	No limitations; corporations, LLCs and other entities can be partners	No limitations; corporations, LLCs and other entities can be partners	None under state law	Limited to natural persons or special trusts (ESBTs or QSSTs); limited to 100 shareholders; IRC Section 1361 (b)	None	None	Cannot have partnership features; if so, it will be taxed as such; see Rev. Proc. 2022
Duration of Life	Depends on sole owner	Not perpetual; depends on duration of partners' existence or agreement	Can be short-lived if certificate of limited partnership lapses; then reverts to general partnership	Can be term or perpetual	Perpetual	Perpetual	Per trust agreement	Per trust agreement and state law Rule Against Perpetuities	Based on individual owners
Income Tax Rates	Individual only	Pass through to individual rates	Pass through to individual rates	Pass through to individual members' rates	Maximum of 21%	Pass through to individual shareholder	Taxed at grantor's tax rate	Taxed at 39% and higher, unless it is deemed a grantor trust under IRC 671 to 679	Individual only
Self-Employment Tax	All income is subject to self-employment tax	All income is subject to self-employment tax	Self-employment and non-self-employment distributions can be structured	All distributions are subject to self-employment tax	Self-employment wages and non-self-employment distributions can be structured	Self-employment wages and non-self-employment distributions can be structured	All income is subject to self-employment tax	Self-employment and non-self-employment distributions can be structured	All income is subject to self-employment tax

IRC 1031 Tax Deferral	Yes	No; partners' interests are personal property	No; partners' interests are personal property	No; LLC membership interests are personal property	Only at corporate level; stock interest is not a 1031 asset	Only at corporate level; stock interest is not a 1031 asset	Yes		Yes
Modification of Governing Documents	Not Applicable	Per Agreement or by majority of partners' interests		Per agreement	Per bylaws	Per bylaws	Per trust agreement or UTC provision 411	Per trust agreement or UTC provision 411	Yes, per TIC agreement
Liquidation of Entity	Not applicable	Per agreement but court can liquidate; see also state law mandatory or discretionary court-ordered buyout	Per agreement but court can liquidate; see also state law mandatory or discretionary court-ordered buyout	Per agreement but court can liquidate; see also state law mandatory or discretionary court-ordered buyout	Often requires a supermajority interest of 67% to 75% of stockholder interest in older corporations; unless the BOD or the articles require otherwise, the new version of the Model Business Corporation Act allows dissolution by a majority of a duly noticed quorum of shareholders	Often requires a supermajority interest of 67% to 75% of stockholder interest in older corporations; unless the BOD or the articles require otherwise; but the new version of the Model Business Corporation Act allows dissolution by a majority of a duly noticed quorum of shareholders	Upon distribution of trust, as limited by state Rule Against Perpetuities; or upon amendment, revocation, or termination of trust under UTC Section 410	Upon distribution of trust, as limited by state Rule Against Perpetuities; or upon amendment, revocation, or termination of trust under UTC Section 410	No entity to liquidate, only real estate assets; if a liquidation is ordered, it is usually due to a partition action; courts vary in applying "partition by public sale"with "partition by distribution in kind of real estate assets"; see UPHPA

	Sole Proprietorship	General Partnership	Limited Partnership	Limited Liability Company	C-Corporation	S-Corporation	Revocable Trust	Irrevocable Trust	Tenants-in-Common Agreement
					voting; see Section 14.02 of the 2016 Model Business Corporation Act	voting; see Section 14.02 of the 2016 RMBCA			Comments on Uniform Law Commission website
Assignment of Interests in Entity	Not applicable	The assignee becomes a mere transferee unless it is admitted to the partnership and consents to partnership agreement	The assignee becomes a mere transferee unless it is admitted to the partnership and consents to partnership agreement	The assignee becomes a mere transferee unless it is admitted or permitted under the operating agreement	Assignable, unless restricted under a stock purchase agreement	Assignable, unless restricted under a stock purchase agreement	Can be transferred to descendants	Can be transferred to heirs, often with limited or general power of appointment	As a real estate interest, undivided interest can be transferred; often subject to contractual right of first refusal in remaining owners

1. **RMBCA** = the Revised Model Business Corporation Act (2016 Revision); see https://www.americanbar.org/content/dam/aba/administrative/business_law/corplaws/2020_mbca.pdf; see also https://businesslawtoday.org/2017/01/model-business-corporation-act-2016-revision-launches/
2. **RUPA** = the Revised Uniform Partnership Act (1997); see https://www.uniformlaws.org/ and Official Comments
3. **RULLCA** = the Revised Uniform Limited Liability Company Act; see https://www.uniformlaws.org/ and Official Comments
4. **RULPA** = the Revised Uniform Limited Partnership Act; see https://www.uniformlaws.org/ and Official Comments
5. **TIC** = tenancy in common; see https://www.law.cornell.edu/wex/tenancy_in_common; see also: https://andysirkin.com/tenancy-in-common-tic/general-information/tenancy-in-common-primer/
6. **UTC** = the Uniform Trust Code; see https://www.uniformlaws.org/ and Official Comments

Annex 7C
Operating Agreement

OF

____

A MONTANA LIMITED LIABILITY COMPANY
EFFECTIVE MARCH 12, 2021.

SECTION 1
Organization

1.1 Agreement. The Members hereby enter into this Operating Agreement ("Agreement") to regulate the affairs of the Company and the conduct of its business, and to govern relations among the Members and the Company upon the terms and conditions set forth herein, subject to the provisions of the Montana Limited Liability Company Act (the"Act"), Title 35, Chapter 8 of the Montana Code Annotated, as amended from time to time.

1.2 Formation. The Members formed a limited liability company on **March 12, 2021**, upon the terms and conditions provided in this Agreement, subject to the provisions of the Montana Limited Liability Company Act (the "Act"), Title 35, Chapter 8 of the Montana Code Annotated as amended from time to time.

1.3 Name. The name of the Limited Liability Company is ________________ ("Company"). It is a **manager managed** limited liability company.

1.4 Principal Place of Business. The principal place of business of the Company is ________________________
____________________________________.

1.5 Term. The Company shall begin on the date of filing its Articles of Organization with the Secretary of State, and shall be perpetual, or until otherwise dissolved in accordance with this Agreement.

1.6 Manager and Members. The Co-Managers of the Company are _____________and _____________. The Members of the Company are **as Trustee of the _____________ Revocable Trust dated March 11, 2021,** _____________ **as Trustee of the _____________ Revocable Trust dated March 11, 2021,** ______________, ______________, _______________ **and** ________________.

SECTION 2
Purposes of the Business

2.1 Purpose. The Company will engage in general business services through the supervision of Co-Managers to hold, protect, and manage recreational real estate and related business ventures for which the Members owning the majority of the Company Ownership Units may agree.

SECTION 3
Contributions and Capital Accounts

3.1 Contributions. Upon execution of this Agreement, the Members have contributed or will contribute the property more particularly described on Exhibit A and shall receive the initial Ownership Units as set forth in Section 4.1. No member shall have any further obligation to contribute cash, property, or services to the Company except as otherwise expressly provided in this Agreement.

3.2 Additional Contributions. The Members may, but are not required to, contribute additional capital deemed necessary by a vote of a majority of the Ownership Unit holders of the Company. After receiving Thirty (30) days' written notice, in the event that any Member fails to contribute their proportionate share of any or all of the additional capital requested by a majority of Ownership Unit holders, then other Members, or any one of them, may contribute the additional capital not paid in by such refusing Member, and shall receive an increase in the proportionate share of the Ownership Units in the entire Company in direct proportion to the additional capital contributed. The right to make up additional capital contributions of a refusing Member and the consequent right to an increase in Ownership Units shall be available in the same order as the right to share in distributions of the remaining Members on a pro rata basis. Any reallocation of capital accounts necessary as a result of additional capital contributions shall be made on the books within One Hundred Eighty (180) days of the additional contribution.

SECTION 4
Profits and Losses

4.1 Determination and Allocation. Profits and losses shall be determined annually. Except as provided in Section 5, profits and losses shall be allocated and shared between or among the Members in accordance with the following Ownership Units:

Member	Initial Ownership Percentage	Ownership Units
__________ as Trustee of the __________ Trust dated March 11, 2021	40%	4,000
__________ as Trustee of the__________ Trust dated March 11, 2021	40%	4,000
__________________	5%	500
__________________	5%	500
__________________	5%	500
__________________	5%	500

SECTION 5
Tax Matters

5.1 General. For income tax purposes, except as provided in this Section 5, all items of Company income, gain, loss, and deduction shall be allocated and shared between or among the Members in the same manner that profits and losses are allocated and shared pursuant to Section 4.1.

SECTION 6
Distributions

6.1 Non-Liquidating Distributions. Except as prohibited by the Act, distributions of the Company (other than distributions specified in Sections 6.2, 6.3, and 4.1) shall be made between or among the Members in accordance with the Ownership Units and shall be distributed at least annually.

6.2 Liquidating Distributions. All distributions made in connection with a winding up of the Company shall be made in the following order of priority:

A. To Company creditors, including Members who are creditors, to the extent otherwise permitted by law, in satisfaction of liabilities of the Company, whether by payment or by the making of reasonable provision for payment, other than liabilities to Members for distributions under Sections 35-8-605 of the Act;

B. To Members and former Members of the Company in satisfaction of liabilities for distributions under Sections 35-8-605 of the Act; and

C. Between or among the Members in accordance with the relative balances of their positive Capital Accounts until the Capital Accounts of all of the Members have been reduced to zero under this Section 6.2(C).

Notwithstanding the foregoing sentence, such distributions shall in all events be made in accordance with Treas. Reg. § 1.704-1(b)(2)(ii)(b)(2). For purposes of this Section 6.2, the Capital Accounts shall be determined after allocating all profits and losses under Section 4 through the date of the distribution.

6.3 Tax Payment Distributions. The Company shall make distributions to Members in an amount sufficient to pay the *maximum* estimated state and federal tax liability of each Member calculated as the product of: (a) the amount of the *maximum* estimated, projected distributions reportable on each Member's respective K-1 attachments to their respective tax returns for the current tax year (b) multiplied by an imputed tax rate of Forty Percent (40%). In addition, because the Company has elected to be categorized as a partnership for both federal and state tax purposes, the Members will be taxed on a share of items of profit or loss of the Company. The Members desire that the Company make tax distributions in order to provide all Members the cash necessary to avoid the imposition of penalties by federal and state taxing authorities. The Company shall make tax distributions to all Members on or before March 15, June 1, September 1, and December 1 of each year in proportion to their Ownership Units. The amount of the tax distribution shall be determined by the Company, but shall be in an amount reasonably calculated to ensure each Member (or if any Member is a limited liability company, the members of such constituent limited liability company, as the case may be) shall be able to make quarterly estimated tax payments on the estimated income derived from the Company in an amount equal to the lowest amount required to be paid by an individual pursuant to Code Section 6654 to avoid the assessment of any penalty. For the purpose of computing the tax distributions, it shall be assumed that all income deemed to be received by all Members is taxable at the highest marginal tax rate imposed on the ordinary income of individuals under the Federal Income Tax laws.

6.4 Partnership Representative. Member, ___________________ shall serve as the **Partnership Representative** ("partnership representative" as defined in Section 6223 of the Code, as amended by the Bi-partisan Budget Act of 2015) by executing this Agreement. The Partnership Representative is authorized and required to represent the Company (at the Company's expense) in all disputes, controversies, or proceedings with the Internal Revenue Service, and, in its sole discretion, is authorized to make any available election with respect to the BBA Partnership Audit Rules and take any action it deems necessary or appropriate to comply with the requirements of the Code and to conduct the Company's affairs with respect to the BBA Partnership Audit Rules. Each Member and former Member will cooperate fully with the Partnership Representative with respect to any such disputes, controversies, or proceedings with the Internal Revenue Service, including providing the Partnership Representative with any information reasonably requested to comply with and make elections under the BBA Partnership Audit Rules.

SECTION 7
Management

7.1 Management of Company by Manager.

A. Manager. _______________ and _________________ (collectively referred to as "the Manager") shall manage the Company. The Manager shall have such rights, duties and powers as are specified in this Agreement, or conferred upon the Manager by the Members. The Members acknowledge and agree that, except as expressly provided in Section 7.2, it is the intention of the Members to confer upon the Manager full, complete, and absolute power and authority to manage and conduct the business and affairs of the Company to the maximum extent permitted by the Act. A Member, unless also appointed (or hired) as a Manager, officer, or other employee, shall not participate in the day-to-day operations of the business affairs of the Company and, if so appointed (or hired), shall participate only within the scope of authority of such position as set forth in the Agreement or elsewhere. A Manager need not be a Member.

B. Duties of Manager. The Manager shall have the general supervision, direction, and control of the business of the Company. They shall preside at all meetings of the Members. The Manager shall have the general powers and duties of management typically vested in the office of president and vice president of a corporation, and such other powers and duties as may be prescribed by the Members. Subject to the limitations and restrictions set forth in this Agreement, they shall act on behalf of the Company in all matters affecting the day-to-day management and supervision of the Company and its business affairs, and shall have all rights and powers generally conferred by law or otherwise necessary, advisable or consistent therewith.

C. Election. Upon the removal, resignation, or other event causing ____________ or ______________ to cease to be the Co-Manager, ____________ shall serve as Co-Manager. If both ____________ and ______________ cease to act as Manager, _____________shall serve as sole Manager. If _______________ shall cease to act, a successor Manager may be chosen by an affirmative vote of the Members who own seventy percent (70%) of the total Voting Ownership Units of the Company as set forth in Section 4.1. A Manager shall hold office until the Manager resigns or shall be removed or otherwise disqualified to serve, or the Manager's successor is elected and qualified.

D. Removal and Resignation. Any Manager may be removed, with or without cause, by an affirmative vote of the Members who own seventy percent (70%) of the total Voting Ownership Units of the Company as set forth in Section 4.1.

E. Powers of Manager. Without limiting the generality of Section 7.1, but subject to Section 8.4 and to the express limitations set forth elsewhere in this Agreement, the Manager shall have all necessary powers to manage and carry out the purposes, business, property, and affairs of the Company, including, without limitation, the power to exercise on behalf and in the name of the Company all of the powers a Manager of a limited liability company is authorized to exercise under Montana law.

F. Fees and Costs. The Company shall pay to the Manager only such compensation for services performed for the Company as may be approved by a Majority Interest. The Company shall reimburse the Manager for any expense paid by the Manager that the Company properly should bear.

7.2 Officers.

A. Appointment of Officers. The Manager may appoint officers at any time with such duties and powers as set forth in this Section 7.2 or as otherwise determined by the Manager. The officers of the Company shall serve at the pleasure of the Manager, subject to all rights, if any, of an officer under any contract of employment. Any individual may hold any number of offices. The officers shall exercise such powers and perform such duties as specified in this Agreement and as shall be determined from time to time by the Manager. The Manager may appoint himself or herself to fill one or more offices.

B. Removal, Resignation, and Filling of Vacancy of Officers. Subject to the rights, if any, of an officer under a contract of employment, any officer may be removed, either with or without cause, by a Manager at any time. A vacancy in any office because of death, resignation, removal, disqualification, or any other cause may be filled by the Manager.

C. Salaries. The Company may pay such compensation to an officer or employee of the Company pursuant to an employment agreement or other arrangement as may be determined by the Manager.

D. Signing Authority of Officers; termination of Authority. The Manager may authorize any officer or officers to endorse checks, drafts, and other evidences of indebtedness made payable to the order of the Company. Such officer or officers may sign all checks, drafts, and other instruments obligating the Company to pay money.

7.3 Performance of Duties, Limited Liability to Company, Members, and Assignees. The Manager shall not be liable to the Company or to any Member or Assignee for any loss or damage sustained by the Company or any Member or Assignee, unless the loss or damage shall have been the result of fraud, deceit, gross negligence, reckless or intentional misconduct, or a knowing violation of law by the Manager or officer. The Manager shall perform his or her duties in good faith, in a manner it reasonably believes to be in the best interests of the Company and its Members and Assignees, and with such care, including reasonable inquiry, as an ordinarily prudent person in a like position would use under similar circumstances. If the Manager or officer so performs his or her duties as the Manager or officer, as the case may be, the Manager or officer shall not have any liability by reason of being or having been the Manager or an officer.

In performing his or her duties, the Manager and each officer shall be entitled to rely on information, opinions, reports, or statements, including financial statements and other financial data, of the following persons or groups unless the Manager or officer has knowledge concerning the matter in question that would cause such reliance to be unwarranted and provided that the Manager or officer acts in good faith and after reasonable inquiry when the need therefor is indicated by the circumstances:

A. One or more officers, employees, or other agents of the Company whom the Manager or officer reasonably believes to be reliable and competent in the matters presented; or

B. Any attorney, independent accountant, or other person as to matters which the Manager or officer reasonably believes to be within such person's professional or expert competence.

7.4 Indemnification of the Manager.

A. Unless otherwise provided in Section 7.4(d), the Company, its receiver, or its trustee (in the case of its receiver or trustee, to the extent of Company Property) shall indemnify, save harmless, and pay all judgments and claims against any Manager relating to any liability or damage incurred by reason of any act performed or omitted to be performed by any Manager in connection with the Business, including reasonable attorneys' fees incurred by the Manager in connection with the defense of any action based on any such act or omission, which attorneys' fees may be paid as incurred.

B. Unless otherwise provided in Section 7.4(d), in the event of any action by a Member against any Manager, including a Company derivative suit, the Company shall indemnify, save harmless, and pay all expenses of such Manager, including reasonable attorneys' fees incurred in the defense of such action.

C. Unless otherwise provided in Section 7.4(d), the Company shall indemnify, save harmless, and pay all expenses, costs, or liabilities of any Manager, if for the benefit of the Company and in accordance with this Agreement said Manager makes any deposit or makes any other similar payment or assumes any obligation in connection with any Property proposed to be acquired by the Company and suffers any financial loss as the result of such action.

D. Notwithstanding the provisions of Sections 7.4(a), 7.4(b), and 7.4(c) above, such Sections shall be enforced only to the maximum extent permitted by law and no Manager shall be indemnified from any liability for the fraud, intentional misconduct, gross negligence or a knowing violation of the law which was material to the cause of action.

E. The obligations of the Company set forth in this Section 7.4 are expressly intended to create third party beneficiary rights of each of the Managers and any Member is authorized, on behalf of the Company, to give written confirmation to any Manager of the existence and extent of the Company's obligations to such Manager hereunder.

SECTION 8
Role of Members

8.1 Rights or Powers. The Members shall not have any right or power to take part in the management or control of the Company or its business and affairs or to act for or bind the Company in any way. Notwithstanding the foregoing, the Members have all the rights and powers specifically set forth in this Agreement and, to the extent not inconsistent with this Agreement, in the Act.

8.2 Voting Rights. No Member has any voting right except with respect to those matters specifically reserved for a Member vote which are set forth in this Agreement and as required in the Act.

8.3 Meetings of the Members.

A. Meetings of the Members may be called upon the written request of any Member. The call shall state the location of the meeting and the nature of the business to be transacted. Notice of any such meeting shall be given to all Members not less than seven (7) business days nor more than thirty (30) days prior to the date of such meeting. Members may vote in person, by proxy or by telephone at such meeting and may waive advance notice of such meeting. Whenever the vote or consent of Members is permitted or required under the Agreement, such vote or consent may be given at a meeting of the Members or may be given in accordance with the procedure prescribed in this Section 8.3. Except as otherwise expressly provided in the Agreement, an affirmative vote of the Members who own more than fifty percent (50%) of the total Voting Ownership Units of the Company shall be required to constitute the act of the Members.

B. For the purpose of determining the Members entitled to vote on, or to vote at, any meeting of the Members or any adjournment, the Manager or the Member requesting such meeting may fix, in advance, a date as the record date for any such determination. Such date shall not be more than thirty (30) days nor less than ten (10) business days before any such meeting.

C. Each Member may authorize any person or persons to act for it by proxy on all matters in which a Member is entitled to participate, including waiving notice of any meeting, or voting or participating at a meeting. The Member or its attorney-in-fact must sign every proxy. No proxy shall be valid after the expiration of eleven (11) months from the date unless otherwise provided in the proxy. Every proxy shall be revocable at the pleasure of the Member executing it.

D. Each meeting of Members shall be conducted by the Manager or such other individual person as the Manager deems appropriate.

E. Notwithstanding this Section 8.3, the Company may take any action contemplated under this Agreement as approved by the consent of the Members, such consent to be provided in writing, or by telephone or facsimile, if such telephone conversation or facsimile is followed by a written summary of the telephone conversation or facsimile communication sent by registered or certified mail, postage and charges prepaid, to such address as such person may from time to time specify by notice to the Members and the Manager.

8.4 Required Member Consents. Notwithstanding any other provision of this Agreement, no action may be taken by the Company (whether by the Manager or otherwise) in connection with any of the following matters without the written consent of the Members who own at seventy-five percent (75%) of the total Voting Ownership Units of the Company as set forth in Section 4.1.

A. Confession of a judgment against the Company;

B. Any sale of assets of the Company involving total consideration in excess of Twenty-Five Thousand and No/100 Dollars ($25,000.00);

C. Any transaction by the Company involving the incurrence of any indebtedness for borrowed money in excess of Twenty-Five Thousand and No/100 Dollars ($25,000.00) or the issuance of any equity or any equity-based security by the Company;

D. Any capital expenditures in excess of Twenty-Five Thousand and No/100 Dollars ($25,000.00);

E. Any transaction to liquidate or dissolve the Company;

F. Any transaction involving the sale of all or substantially all of the Company's assets and transfer of membership interest in ____________________;

G. Any transaction by the Company to merge, consolidate, or reorganize its business.

8.5 Withdrawal/Resignation. Except as otherwise provided in Sections 6 and 11, no Member shall demand or receive a return on or of its Capital Contributions or withdraw from the Company without the consent of all Members.

8.6 Member Compensation. No Member shall receive any interest, salary, or drawing with respect to its Capital Contributions or its Capital Account or for services rendered on behalf of the Company, or otherwise, in its capacity as a Member, except as otherwise provided in this Agreement.

8.7 Members' Liability. No Member shall be liable under a judgment, decree, or order of a court, or in any other manner for the debts or any other obligations or liabilities of the Company. A Member shall be liable only to make its Capital Contributions and shall not be required to restore a deficit balance in its Capital Account or to lend any funds to the Company or, after its Capital Contributions have been made, to make any additional contributions, assessments, or payments to the Company. The Manager shall not have any personal liability for the repayment of any Capital Contributions of any Member.

8.8 Partition. While the Company remains in effect or is continued, each Member agrees and waives its rights to have Company Property partitioned, or to file a complaint or to institute any suit, action or proceeding at law or in equity to have Company Property partitioned, and each Member, on behalf of itself, its successors and its assigns hereby waives any such right.

8.9 Transactions Between a Member and the Company. Except as otherwise provided by applicable law, any Member may, but shall not be obligated to, lend money to the Company, act as surety for the Company and transact other business with the Company and has the same rights and obligations when transacting business with the Company as a person or entity who is not a Member. A Member, any affiliate or an employee, stockholder, agent, director, or officer of a Member or any affiliate, may also be an employee or be retained as an agent of the Company. The existence of these relationships and acting in such capacities will not result in the Member being deemed to be participating in the control of the business of the Company or otherwise affect the limited liability of the Member.

8.10 Other Instruments. Each Member hereby agrees to execute and deliver to the Company within five (5) days after receipt of a written request therefore, such other and further documents and instruments, statements of interest and holdings, designations, powers of attorney and other instruments and to take such other action as the Manager deems necessary, useful or appropriate to comply with any laws, rules or regulations as may be necessary to enable the Company to fulfill its responsibilities under this Agreement.

SECTION 9
Banking, Books

9.1 Banking. All funds of the Company shall be deposited in the name of the Company in such checking or savings account(s) as the Manager shall designate. Withdrawals therefrom shall be as designated by the Managers.

9.2 Books. The Company books shall be maintained at the principal office of the Company, and each Member shall at all times have access thereto.

SECTION 10
Non-Transferability of Members Interest

10.1 Non-Transferability of Members Interest. No Member shall assign, encumber, mortgage, pledge, transfer, or dispose of any or all of its Ownership Units in the Company, now owned or hereafter acquired except in connection with the following:

A. An inter vivos or testamentary transfer of the Ownership Units to a surviving spouse, lineal descendant, or other heir, pursuant to a natural person's Member's estate planning; or

B. With the express written consent of seventy-five percent (75%) of the Members of this Company.

Any assignment, transfer or attempted transfer, of an Ownership Unit in violation of this Agreement shall be void.

10.2 Consent of Transferee. Any proposed transferee of any Membership Interest must agree, in writing, to be bound by the terms of this Operating Agreement.

SECTION 11
Events Triggering Option or Obligation to Purchase

11.1 Events of Dissociation. The following shall be considered events of dissociation:

A. A Member filing a voluntary petition in bankruptcy;

B. A forced levy or attachment against a Member's Interest;

C. An individual natural person Member's death;

D. The appointment of a guardian or general conservator for an individual natural person Member;

E. A determination by two licensed physicians that an individual natural person Member is disabled and unable to perform their duties under the Operating Agreement;

F. The Member seeking, consenting to, or acquiescing in the appointment of a trustee, receiver, or liquidator of all or substantially all of the Member's property;

G. A Member giving the Company notice of the Member's express will to withdraw;

H. The Member's expulsion, pursuant to this Operating Agreement;

I. The Member's expulsion by judicial determination that the Member:

i. Engaged in wrongful conduct that adversely and materially affected the Company's business;

ii. Willfully or persistently committed a material breach of the Operating Agreement or of a duty owed to the Company or other Members under Mont. Code Ann. § 35-8-310; or

iii. Engaged in conduct relating to the Company's business that makes it not reasonably practicable to carry on the business with the Member.

J. In the case of a Member that is a Trust or is acting as a Member by virtue of being a trustee of a trust, distribution of the trust's entire rights to receive distributions from the Company, except in the case of the substitution of a successor trustee;

K. In the case a Member that is an estate or is acting as a Member by virtue of being a personal representative of an estate, distribution of the estate's entire rights to receive distributions from the Company, except in the case of the substitution of a successor personal representative;

L. Any other event of dissociation under Mont. Code Ann. § 35-8-803; and

M. If a Member becomes incarcerated for any crime. The Member or its successor which is affected by any of the events set forth in the preceding sentence shall give written notice to the Company within thirty (30) days of the event causing dissociation; but failure to give such notice shall not avoid the dissociation event, however.

11.2 Effect of Dissociation. If a Member becomes dissociated (except by a transfer of their Ownership Units under Section 10.1A or B), the Company shall have the option to purchase the dissociated Member's Ownership Units for the price and on the terms as set forth in Section 12, herein.

11.3 Closing. If the Company elects to purchase the dissociated Member's interest, the closing of such purchase and sale shall take place at the office of the Company at a date designated by the Company which shall not be more than one hundred twenty (120) days following the date of dissociation.

11.4 Terms of Payment. A minimum of twenty-five percent (25%) of the purchase price shall be paid to the dissociated Member or his or her representative in cash at closing. Any balance shall be paid in cash in equal monthly payments over a period of five (5) years, the first such monthly payment to be due and payable one (1) month from the date of the down payment, with interest on the unpaid balance at the prime rate as published in the money rates section of the *Wall Street Journal* on the date of closing (or the first immediately preceding business day, if the date of closing is not a business day) (the "Prime Rate"); provided, however, that this interest rate shall not exceed the maximum rate allowed by the laws of the State of Montana. The Company shall have full prepayment privileges to pay the outstanding balance in full or in part at any time.

11.5 Promissory Note. The obligation set forth in Section 11.4 shall be represented by a Promissory Note made by the Company which shall be delivered to the dissociated Member or his or her representative at the time of the down payment. Such Promissory Note shall, at the option of the dissociated Member or his or her representative, carry the personal guaranty of the remaining Members or shall be secured by Company property, and shall require that the entire unpaid balance may, at the election of the obligee, become immediately due and payable in the event that the obligor is late in making a payment and has not made such payment after ten days' written notice thereof.

SECTION 12
Valuation of Member's Interest

12.1 Valuation of Member's Interest upon Involuntary Dissociation. The dissociated Member's Ownership Unit interest in the Company shall be valued according to its fair market value, if the dissociation is due to a Member's dissolution.

12.2 Valuation of Member's Interest upon Voluntary Dissociation. In the event that a Member dissociates for any reason other than those listed in Section 11.1 the value of the Member's Ownership Units will be determined by multiplying the fair market value of the Member's Ownership Units by 1.0.

12.3 Value of Interest in Certain Events. In the event a selling or purchasing Member and the Company do not agree upon the valuation of a Member's interest, each party shall select an appraiser. These appraisers, in turn, shall select a third appraiser. The appraisers will be charged with the task of valuing the Membership interest in accordance with Section 12.1 and Section 12.2 above. The parties shall bear the costs of their individual appraisers and shall split the cost of the third appraiser. If the two appraisers are unable to select a third appraiser, the senior district judge in service of the __________ Judicial Court in and for __________County, __________ shall select the third appraiser. The fair market value shall be the fair market value determined by any two of the three appraisers. If two of the three appraisers are unable to agree upon the fair market value, the fair market value shall be the average of the three appraisers', provided that the lowest appraisal is at least 80% of the highest appraisal. If the lowest appraisal is not at least 80% of the highest appraisal, the fair market value shall be determined by a fourth appraiser appointed by the senior district judge in service for the __________ Judicial Court in and for __________ County, __________. Any buyout price of Company property shall be reduced by the amount of indebtedness owed by the Member to the Company.

SECTION 13
Dispute Resolution

No party to this Agreement shall institute a proceeding in any Court to resolve a dispute with any other party to this Agreement concerning the representations, warranties, covenants, and agreements contained herein, but agree that any such dispute shall be resolved in accordance with the dispute resolution provisions in this Section. Initially, the parties to the dispute shall attempt to resolve the dispute through direct negotiation. If the dispute is not resolved within two (2) weeks after a demand for direct negotiation, the parties shall attempt to resolve the dispute through mediation, with a mediator jointly chosen by the parties. If the mediator is unable to facilitate a settlement of the dispute within a reasonable period of time, as determined by the mediator, the mediator shall issue a written statement to the parties to that effect and any unresolved dispute arising under or in connection with this Agreement shall be settled exclusively by the District Court of the __________ Judicial District, __________ County, State of __________.

SECTION 14
Dissolution

14.1 Events of Dissolution. The Company is dissolved upon the happening of one of the following events:

A. At the time or upon the occasion of events specified in the Company's Articles of Organization or this Agreement;

B. Members owning at least eighty-five percent (85%) of the Ownership Units of the Company consent to a dissolution;

C. The entry of a decree of judicial dissolution.

14.2 Articles of Dissolution. Upon the dissolution and the commencement of winding up of the Company, the Company shall file the required documents with the Secretary of State.

14.3 Procedure. Upon dissolution, the affairs of the Company will be wound up, and the assets of the Company distributed, according to the provisions of Section 9 of the Act.

SECTION 15
Assignment

15.1 General Rules Regarding Assignment. If an assignment of a Membership Interest has not been consented to by Members owning at least eighty-five percent (85%) of the Ownership Units of the Company, the following rules apply:

A. An assignment entitles the assignee to receive, to the extent assigned, only the distributions to which the assignor would be entitled;

B. An assignment of a Member's interest does not entitle the assignee to participate in the management and affairs of the Company or to become a Member or to exercise any rights of a Member;

C. Until the assignee becomes a Member, the assignor continues to be a Member and to have the power to exercise rights of a Member, subject to the Member's or Company's right to remove the assignor pursuant to this Operating Agreement;

The foregoing limitations shall not apply the transfer of an individual Member's Ownership Units to an inter-vivos or testamentary transfer to a surviving spouse, lineal descendant, or other heir of an individual Member, including a trust for the benefit of the surviving spouse or lineal descendants of the individual Member.

SECTION 16
Indemnification

16.1 Mandatory Indemnification. Subject to Section 16.2, the Company shall indemnify a Member from judgments, settlements, penalties, fines, or expenses incurred in a proceeding to which an individual is a party because the individual is or was a Member.

16.2 Limitations on Indemnification. The Company may not indemnify a Member from liability for:

A. The amount of a financial benefit received by a Member to which the Member is not entitled;

B. An intentional infliction of harm by the Member on the Company or its Members;

C. An intentional violation of criminal law by the Member;

D. An unlawful distribution by a Member.

SECTION 17
Investment Purpose

17.1 Investment Purpose. In acquiring a membership interest in the Company, each Member represents and warrants that he or she is acquiring such membership interest for his or her own account for investment and not with a view to its sale or distribution. Each Member recognizes that an investment in a membership interest in the Company is speculative and involves substantial risk. Each Member further represents and warrants that neither the Company nor any other Member has made any guaranty or representation upon which he or she has relied concerning the possibility or probability of profits, losses, or distributions as a result of his or her acquisition of a membership interest in the Company.

17.2 Investment Restriction. Each Member recognizes that: (a) the membership interests in the Company have not been registered under the Securities Act of 1933, as amended (the"Securities Act") and Montana securities laws, in reliance upon exemptions from such registration, (b) a Member may not sell, offer for sale, or transfer all or any part of his or her membership interest in the Company in the absence of an effective registration statement covering such membership interest under the Securities Act and Montana securities laws unless such sale, offer for sale, or transfer is exempt from registration under the Securities Act and Montana securities laws, (c) the Company has no obligation to register any Member's interest for sale, or to assist in establishing an exemption from registration for any proposed sale, offer for sale, or transfer and (d) the restrictions on transfer under this Agreement may severely affect the liquidity of a Member's investment.

SECTION 18
Miscellaneous

18.1 Notices. All notices required or permitted under this Agreement or related to this Agreement or the Company shall be deemed sufficient if in writing and delivered personally or sent by certified mail, return receipt requested, to the Company or a Member, at their last known address. All notices shall be effective on the date of personal delivery, or in the case of mailing, on the date set forth on the receipt of certified mail. In computing any time under this Agreement, the day of the act, event, or default from which the designated period of time begins to run shall not be included, and the last day of the period so computed shall be included unless it is a Saturday, Sunday, or legal holiday in Montana, in which event the period shall run until the end of the next day which is not a Saturday, Sunday, or legal holiday in Montana.

18.2 Entire Agreement. This Agreement embodies the entire understanding and agreement among the Company and the Members concerning the Company and supersedes any and all prior negotiations, understandings or agreements in regard thereto.

18.3 Amendment. This Agreement shall not be amended nor shall any rights under this Agreement be waived except by unanimous written consent from the owners of eighty-five percent (85%) of the Ownership Units.

18.4 Applicable Law. This Agreement shall be construed in accordance with and governed by the laws of the State of Montana.

18.5 Construction. References to a Member, including by use of a pronoun, shall be deemed to include masculine, feminine or neutral, singular or plural, and any person where applicable. References in this Agreement to capitalized terms shall have the same meaning whether in the singular or plural form.

18.6 Severability. The invalidity or unenforceability of any term or condition of this Agreement shall not affect the other terms or conditions of this Agreement, and this Agreement shall be construed in all respects as if such invalid or unenforceable terms or conditions were omitted.

18.7 Headings. The headings of sections of this Agreement are for convenience of reference only and are not intended to restrict, affect, or be of any weight in the interpretation or construction of the terms and conditions of such sections.

18.8 Further Assurances. After execution of this Agreement, the Company and the Members shall execute, acknowledge, and deliver such further documents and do such further acts as may be required to carry out the intent and purposes of this Agreement, including such documents and actions as may necessary or advisable to comply with the requirements of law for the formation and operation of limited liability companies wherever the Company carries on its business.

18.9 Attorneys' Fees. In the event of a default by the Company or a Member under this Agreement, the nondefaulting parties under the Agreement shall be entitled to recover from the defaulting party all costs and expenses incurred by the nondefaulting parties by reason of such default, including, without limitation, reasonable attorneys' fees and costs and court costs, whether such amounts are incurred with or without legal action.

18.10 Binding Effect. This Agreement shall bind, inure to the benefit of, and be enforceable by the parties and their respective successors, which for purposes of this Agreement shall include, without limitation, heirs, devisees, personal representatives, and assignees.

18.11 Effective Date. This Agreement shall become effective when all parties to this Agreement have executed it and once effective shall relate back to the time the Articles of Organization for the Company were filed by the Montana Secretary of State.

18.12 Counterparts. The parties to this Agreement may execute it in one or more counterparts, each of which shall be deemed an original, and all of which together shall constitute one and the same agreement. A facsimile copy of the signature on this Agreement of any party to this Agreement shall have the same force and effect as an original of such signature, the copy of this Agreement to which such facsimile copy of the signature has been attached shall be deemed to have been duly and legally signed and delivered, and such copy of this Agreement to which such facsimile copy of the signature has been attached may be admitted into evidence without the necessity of producing the original of such signature or proving delivery of this Agreement. Notwithstanding the foregoing sentence, the parties to this Agreement shall promptly mail signed originals of this Agreement which have been telecopied to the appropriate parties as soon as possible after signing. This Section shall apply to any amendments or supplements to this Agreement.

IN WITNESS WHEREOF, this Operating Agreement is made and entered into this ____ day of April, 2021.

____

______________________________ ______________________________
Co-Manager Co-Manager

______________________________ ______________________________
Member, Member

______________________________ ______________________________
Member Member

______________________________ ______________________________
Member Member

STATE OF ____________)
:ss
County of ____________)

This instrument was acknowledged before me on the ____ day of April, 2021, by ______________________________ known to me as the Co-Managers of ________________.

____
Notary Signature

STATE OF ____________)
:ss
County of ____________)

This instrument was acknowledged before me on the ____ day of April, 2021, by ______________________________ ___known to me as a Member of ___________________.

____
Notary Signature

STATE OF ____________)
:ss
County of ____________)

This instrument was acknowledged before me on the ____ day of April 2021, by ____________ **dated March 11, 2021,** known to me as a Member of ____________________.

____
Notary Signature

STATE OF ____________)
:ss
County of ____________)

This instrument was acknowledged before me on the ____ day of April, 2021, by ____________ known to me as the Member of ________________.

____

Notary Signature

STATE OF _____________)
:ss
County of ________________)

This instrument was acknowledged before me on the ____ day of April, 2021, by ___________________ known to me as the Member ___________________________.

____

Notary Signature

STATE OF _____________)
:ss
County of ________________)

This instrument was acknowledged before me on the ____ day of April, 2021, by ____________________known to me as the Co-Managers of _____________________.

____

Notary Signature

STATE OF _____________)
:ss
County of ________________)

This instrument was acknowledged before me on the ____ day of April, 2021, by _____________________known to me as the Co-Managers of ___________________.

____

Notary Signature

Exhibit A

Member	Property Contributed
	Legal Description: PropertyAddress:

Exhibit B
Additional Tax Matters

B.1 Loss Limitations. Notwithstanding Section 4.1, losses shall not be allocated to the Members in an amount which is greater than the maximum amount of losses that can be so allocated without causing any Member to have a deficit Capital Account balance, determined at the end of the Company's tax year, after giving effect to the following adjustments:

A. Crediting to such Capital Accounts any amounts which each Member is obligated to restore pursuant to this Agreement or is deemed to be obligated to restore pursuant to the penultimate sentences of Treas. Reg. §§ 1.704–2(g)(1) and 1.704–2(i)(5); and

B. Debiting to such Capital Accounts the items described in Treas. Reg. §§ 1.704–1(b)(2)(ii)(d)(4), (5), and (6).

If some, but not all, of the Members would have a deficit Capital Account balance as described in the foregoing sentence, the limitations set forth in this Section B.1 shall be applied on a Member by Member basis so as to allocate the maximum permissible losses to each Member under Treas. Reg. § 1.704(b)(2)(ii)(d). The foregoing loss limitation is intended to comply with the provisions of Treas. Reg. § 1.704–1(b)(2)(ii)(d) and shall be interpreted consistently with said Regulation.

B.2 Minimum Gain Chargebacks. Notwithstanding Section 4.1, profits (including any gross income or gains) shall be allocated and shared between or among the Members so as to comply with the"minimum gain chargeback" provisions in Treas. Reg. § 1.704–2 (applicable to partnership non-recourse debt or partner non-recourse debt, as the case may be).

B.3 Qualified Income Offset. Notwithstanding Section 4.1, profits (including any gross income or gains) shall be allocated and shared between or among the Members so as to comply with the"qualified income offset" provisions in Treas. Reg. § 1.704–1(b)(2)(ii)(d). Accordingly, if a Member unexpectedly receives an adjustment, allocation, or distribution described in Treas. Reg. §§ 1.704–1(b)(2)(ii)(d)(4), (5), or (6), and such unexpected adjustment, allocation, or distribution puts such Member's Capital Account into a deficit balance or increases such deficit balance, such Member will be specially allocated items of profits (consisting of a pro rata portion of each item of Partnership income, including gross income and gains for such year) in an amount and manner sufficient to eliminate such deficit balance as quickly as possible.

B.4 Gross Income Allocation. Notwithstanding Section 4.1, if any Member has a deficit Capital Account at the end of any tax year which is in excess of the sum of (a) the amount such Member is obligated to restore pursuant to this Agreement, and (b) the amount the Member is deemed to be obligated to restore (pursuant to the penultimate sentences of Treas. Reg. §§ 1.704–2(g)(1) and any gross income and gains) in the amount of such excess as quickly as possible, provided that an allocation pursuant to this Section B.4 shall be made only if and to the extent that such Member would have a deficit Capital Account in excess of such sum after all other allocations provided for in Sections 4 and 5 and Exhibit B have been made as if Section B.3 and this Section B.4 were not in the Agreement.

B.5 Recapture. For income tax purposes, to the extent of any Recapture Income resulting from the sale or other taxable disposition of Company assets, the amount of any gain from such disposition allocated to a Member shall be deemed to consist of Recapture Income to the extent such Member has been allocated or has claimed any deduction directly or indirectly giving rise to the treatment of such gain as Recapture Income.

B.6 Section 754. For income tax purposes, all items of Company income, gain, loss, and deduction allocated and shared between or among the Members in accordance with this Exhibit B and all basis allocations to the Members shall first be determined without regard to any election under Section 754 of the Code; provided, however, such allocations, once made, shall be adjusted as necessary or advisable to take into account the adjustments permitted by Sections 732, 734, and 743 of the Internal Revenue Code.

B.7 Tax Credits. For income tax purposes, all income tax credits with respect to Company assets or business shall be allocated and shared between or among the Members in the same manner that losses are allocated and shared between or among the Members pursuant to Section 4.1 and Section B.1.

B.8 Section 704(c). The Members recognize that with respect to assets contributed to the Company by a Member and with respect to Company assets revalued in accordance with Treas. Reg. § 1.704–1(b)(2)(iv)(f), there may be a difference between the Carrying Value of such assets at the time of contribution or revaluation and the adjusted basis of such assets for income tax purposes at that time. Therefore, all items of Company depreciation, depletion, amortization, and gain or loss, as computed for income tax purposes with respect to such assets, shall be allocated and shared between or among the Members to take into account the variation between the book-tax disparities in accordance with the provisions of Sections 704(b) and 704(c) of the Code and the Treasury Regulations under those Sections, all as shall be determined by the Members owning 50 percent of the Ownership Percentages of the Company.

B.9 Carrying Values. The Carrying Values of Company assets shall be adjusted in accordance with Treas. Reg. § 1.704–1(b)(2)(iv), as determined by the Members owning 50 percent of the Ownership Units of the Company; provided, however, that if 50 percent of the Ownership Units of the Company make any such adjustments, the Capital Accounts shall also be adjusted to comply with Treas. Reg. § 1.704–1(b)(2)(iv)(f) or (g) and 1.704–1(b)(4). The Carrying Values of Company assets shall be increased or decreased to reflect any adjustments to the adjusted basis of such assets for income tax purposes pursuant to Sections 732, 734, and 743 of the Code, but only to the extent such adjustments are taken into account in determining Capital Accounts pursuant to Treas. Reg. § 1.704–1(b)(2)(iv)(m).

B.10 Curative Allocations. The allocations set forth in Sections B.2, B.3, and B.4 (the "Regulatory Allocations") are intended to comply with the requirements of Treas. Reg. §§ 1.704–1(b) and 1.704–2. Notwithstanding any other provision of this Exhibit B (other than the Regulatory Allocations), Members shall make such offsetting special allocations of Company income, gain, loss, or deduction in whatever manner and at whatever time they determine to be appropriate so that, after such offsetting allocations are made, each Member's Capital Account balance is, to the extent possible, equal to the Capital Account balance such Member would have had if the Regulatory Allocations were not part of this Agreement.

Annex 7D

Trust Agreement

This Second Restatement is made this _______ day of _________________, 2021, by and between _____________ and _____________ (hereinafter referred to as the "Settlors"), as Settlors of the ____________________Trust dated December 12, 2002, and _________________of _____________ County, ___________and ______________ of ___________ County, ___________, as Co-Trustees of the ______________ Trust dated December 12, 2002 (hereinafter referred to as the "Co-Trustees" or "Trustees").

A. WHEREAS, the Settlors of this Trust Agreement are: ________________ (a/k/a _________________) of _____________ County,__________ and ______________of_____________ County, ___________.

B. WHEREAS, real property and personal property (the Property herein) has been conveyed to the _______________Trust dated by the Settlors; it is the Co-Trustees' intention to include all of that Property as trust property under the terms of this Trust, without necessity of any further conveyance. Settlors each transferred into said Trust and allocated to the separate trust share of the Settlor who made the transfer, his or her undivided one-half (1/2) leasehold interest in the real property located in ____________ County, ___________, and more particularly described as _____________________________________ _____. In addition, _____________________ transferred to his separate trust share, all of his interest in the ___________________________ by an assignment document, which provides that upon the death of _______________ (or upon the death of his wife, _______________________, if she survives him) one-half (1/2) of the interest in such addition shall be allocated to the separate trust share of ____________________ pursuant to the terms of the assignment document. **The Property** described in Schedule "A", annexed hereto shall be made a part hereof and all of those assets shall be held and administered as set forth in this Second Restatement of the ____________________ Agreement.

C. WHEREAS, notwithstanding the disproportionate contributions of the Settlors as set forth immediately above, the Settlors intend to clarify that the Beneficiaries, as set forth in this Second Restatement, shall each hold an equal undivided one-half interest in the entirety of the Trust estate, which includes, but is not limited to, all of leasehold interest in the real property located in __________ County, ________________, and more particularly described as __________________________________ and all property included in the hereto attached Schedule "A."

D. WHEREAS, because of the immediately foregoing, the parties agree to waive any and all claims for disproportionate Settlor Contributions, forever, and desire the entirety of the Trust estate to be divided equally among the beneficiaries upon any distribution thereof, and agree to execute any and all documents, deeds, or instruments of conveyance necessary to effectuate the immediately preceding Paragraph C;

E. WHEREAS pursuant to Article VII, Paragraph C of the original Trust Agreement, the Settlors reserved the right, at any time and from time to time during their joint lifetimes, to amend the original Trust Agreement, in whole or in part, by an instrument duly executed by both Settlors and delivered to the Trustee;

F. WHEREAS, the Settlors desire to execute this Restatement of the ________________ Trust Agreement and intend to revoke and replace any and all previous Agreements in their entirety;

THIS TRUST SHALL CONTINUE TO BE KNOWN AS THE "TRUST AGREEMENT Dated December 12, 2002" (hereinafter the "Trust" or "Agreement").

WHEREFORE, in consideration of the foregoing, the Settlors acknowledge and agree:

1. That the representation and warranties, A through H, as recited above, are true and intended to be incorporated into the Trust.

2. In full recognition of their rights to receive an undivided one-half (1/2) interest in the Property described in Paragraph B above, all of the Beneficiaries nevertheless agree to hold the Property in the ____________________ TRUST until December 31, 2090, unless earlier terminated pursuant to the terms hereof or under Montana law.

3. The parties agree that the following shall constitute the Beneficiaries of this Trust:

   A. ________________ and ______________, of ________ County, ____________ and their lineal descendants; and

   B. ________________ and ______________, of ________ County, ____________, and their lineal descendants.

____________ has two children, ______________ and ____________, and ____________ has two children, ______________ and ______________. Lineal descendants shall include any person who is legally adopted by any child or other descendant of ____________ or ______________ prior to age eighteen (18) and such person's descendants.

4. The parties agree that the following individuals shall continue to serve as initial Co-Trustees of this Trust:

   A. ________________, of __________ County, ________; and

   B. ________________, of __________ County, ________.

The Co-Trustees acknowledge their legal duty to cooperate in the administration of the Trust, which shall include prompt responses to communications between them. ____________ and each of his successor Trustees is referred to as the "________ Trustee" during the time such Trustee(s) are acting, and ____________ and each of her successor Trustees is referred to as the "_________ Trustee" during the time such Trustee(s) are acting.

5. In the event that ________________ is unable or unwilling to serve as Co-Trustee, ________________ and ________________ shall be his Successor Co-Trustees. In the event that either ______________ or ________________ is unable or unwilling to serve as Co-Trustee, the other one of them shall be the Successor Co-Trustee. In the event that ______________ is unable or unwilling to serve as Co-Trustee, ______________ and ______________ shall be her Successor Co-Trustee. In the event that either ______________ or ______________ is unable or unwilling to serve as Co-Trustee, the other one of them shall be the Successor Co-Trustee. No bond shall be required of the trustees designated herein.

If there is more than one person acting as the __________ Trustee or as the ________ Trustee, such persons shall act by majority vote and if only two persons are acting, such persons must act unanimously. During any time a ________ Trustee or a __________ Trustee is acting, such ________ Trustee and such ________ Trustee shall each hold no less than fifty percent (50%) of the trustee voting power. Any individual Trustee may appoint one or more successor Trustees to act in the place of such Trustee, to be effective immediately or in the future upon any stated contingency.

6. The children of the Settlors, acting by majority vote, may remove any Co-Trustee or both Co-Trustees no more frequently than one (1) time every three (3) years commencing upon the death or incapacitation of last surviving Settlor. If a child of either Settlor is deceased, such child's adult descendant(s), if any, shall by majority vote exercise the voting rights of such deceased child. In voting to remove a Co-Trustee, such voting group shall appoint a successor individual or corporate trustee having the following qualifications:

   A. Experience in the management of residential or commercial real estate, preferably in ____________ County, Montana;

   B. Experience in the administration of business organizations including trusts with multiple owners or beneficiaries;

   C. Being insured by a commercial insurance company for errors and omissions in the exercise of the fiduciary duties of a trustee; and

   D. Sufficient other business, real estate, or fiduciary management experience creating expertise sufficient to manage the Trust assets.

7. ____________ (during her lifetime) and her husband and/or descendants (after her death) shall be required to pay one-half (1/2) of the expenses to maintain the Property, including lot lease payments, reserve and operating assessments and special assessments of the ________________ Association, insurance premiums, real estate taxes and utilities (collectively the"maintenance expenses"), and ______________ (during his lifetime) and his wife and/or his descendants (after his death) shall be required to pay one-half (1/2) of the maintenance expenses. The ___________Trustee shall be responsible for collecting such funds from _____________ or her husband and/or her descendants and the __________ Trustee shall be responsible for collecting such funds from ___________ or his wife and/or his descendants. Either of the Co-Trustees is authorized to engage in normal and ordinary day-to-day decisions acting unilaterally, including without limitation, payment of any insurance, utilities, or maintenance items relative to the Property; provided, however, should any expenditure exceed the sum of One Thousand Dollars ($1,000.00) then the Co-Trustees shall agree unanimously on any such expenditure. The Co-Trustees shall confer with each other regarding management decisions, investment decisions, and for an annual budget at least annually on or about February 28 of each year. The ___________ Trustee may deny access to the Property to any descendant of ____________ during the period any such descendant does not contribute to the payment of such expenses as requested by the ___________ Trustee, and the __________ Trustee may deny access to the Property to any descendant of ___________ during the period any such descendant does not contribute to the payment of such expenses as requested by the __________ Trustee.

8. The Co-Trustees shall hold, administer, and manage the Property, and associated outbuildings, structures, and equipment in accordance with the terms of this Second Restatement.

9. Without limitation of the foregoing paragraphs, the signature of both Co-Trustees shall be required for the following:

   A. Acquiring any personal property for the Trust at a cost in excess of One Thousand Dollars ($1,000.00);

   B. Signing any lease, sub-lease, short term rental, license, easement, or other arrangement involving the use and occupancy of the assets of the Trust;

   C. Making any capital improvement, repairs, alterations, or changes in or to any part of the real property assets in excess of One Thousand Dollars ($1,000.00);

   D. Implementing a daily, weekly, or other periodic use schedule of the Property which shall include the ________ and the __________ each having use of the Property either the month of July or the month of August annually and adopting instructions for the use of the Property, including responsibility for seasonal opening and closing of the Property, procedures for opening and closing, periodic purging of unneeded items and requirements of vacating the Property, including leaving the Property clean and orderly and removing all personal items; and

   E. Establishing an annual budget for all Trust-related expenses, including but not limited to taxes, cabin maintenance, association fees, assessments, and capital improvements.

10. The Trust's assets shall not be subject to the personal creditors of either Co-Trustee or the creditors of any Beneficiary. All interests of any Beneficiary of this Trust shall not be subject to assignment, levy, execution of hypothecation, pledge, sale, or distribution to any creditor of any Beneficiary or Trustee hereunder; nor may any Beneficiary voluntarily or involuntarily transfer their interest in the Trust.

11. The Co-Trustees shall keep adequate records of the administration of the Trust, keep the Property separate from the Co-Trustees' own real or personal property and shall inform and report to any qualified Beneficiary financial information regarding the administration of the Trust in accordance with MCA 72-38-813 (2019).

12. All of the children of ______________ and ___________ are qualified Beneficiaries entitled to receive information and reports under MCA 72-38-813 (2019). This extends to the lineal descendants of ____________ and ______________.

13. Should the Co-Trustees deadlock on any issue of trust administration, then the Co-Trustees agree to engage in good faith mediation for a period of at least thirty (30) days, unless there exists the threat of immediate and irreparable harm to the Property, in which case, any Trustee or Beneficiary may petition for injunctive relief with the ____________ County District Court.

14. Should the Co-Trustees be unable to reach agreement on the expenditure of any item in excess of One Thousand Dollars ($1,000.00) or the incurrence of debt for the maintenance and improvement of the Property or otherwise, then the Co-Trustees agree that they should submit any dispute which may arise between them to mediation and eventually, if necessary, the determination of the sitting District Court Judge in _____________ County, Montana.

15. Should mediation be unsuccessful, the Co-Trustees may file a petition for a determination including, but not limited to, any of the following:

    A. to resolve which Beneficiary is entitled to purchase the other Beneficiary's interest in this Trust;

    B. the buy-out of any individual Beneficiary;

    C. for recommendations regarding the ongoing operation and maintenance of the Property, without the necessity of the buy-out of any individual Beneficiary; or

    D. for the sale of all or substantially all of the Property first to some or all of the Beneficiaries and second to a non-___________ or non-_________ family member.

16. In the unlikely event a Beneficiary's interest is sold or purchased, the Court shall avoid discounts on valuations. Each Beneficiary may make a recommendation to the District Court regarding a formula to determine the value of his or her interest in the Trust and by accepting his or her position as a Beneficiary under the Trust, agree to accept the District Court's valuation determination. The Beneficiaries shall be entitled to a one (1) year period within which to purchase each other's interests; should they be unable to come to a determination within one (1) year from the date of the filing of a petition, the Court or the Co-Trustees may list the Property and all Trust assets for sale and distribute the sale proceeds to the Beneficiaries. Further, in the unlikely event of the sale of all of the Trust property, the property should be listed over a lengthy period of time to avoid highly discounted sales values of the real estate.

17. The Co-Trustees shall have all the powers under Mont. Code Ann. Sections 72-38- 815 and 816, (2019); furthermore, the Co-Trustees may petition the Court for guidance as to the exercise of their powers as to the Trust property specifically.

18. In case the income or principal payment under any trust created hereunder or any share thereof shall become payable to a person under the age of eighteen (18) years, or to a person under legal disability, or to a person not adjudicated incompetent, but who, by reason of illness or mental or physical disability, is, in the opinion of the Trustee, or his or her successors, unable properly to administer such amounts, then such amounts shall be paid out by the Co-Trustee, or his or her successors, in such of the following ways as the Co-Trustee, or his or her successors, deems best: (1) directly to such beneficiary; (2) to the legal appointed guardian of such beneficiary; (3) to a relative or friend for the care, support, and education of such beneficiary; (4) by the Co-Trustee using such amounts directly for such beneficiary's care, support, and education; and (5) to a custodian for the beneficiary

under the Montana Uniform Transfers to Minors Act. The Co-Trustee, or his or her successors, shall be fully indemnified for any such expenditure made in good faith.

19. The Co-Trustees, or his or her successors, shall at least annually, on or before the 30th day of April of the following year during the term of this Trust, furnish the Beneficiaries with a full accounting of all receipts and disbursements of this Trust for the prior calendar year and shall furnish to such persons any information in connection with the ______________ Cabin Trust estate as shall be requested by them in writing.

20. This ________________ Cabin Trust Agreement merges all oral and written negotiations of the subject matter thereof and shall not be modified except in writing and signed by the Co-Trustees and all of the then living adult Beneficiaries.

21. Should any qualified Beneficiary file any action to sell the Property to forfeit the interest of any Beneficiary, or to surcharge or penalize any Trustee or Beneficiary serving or owning any assets in the Trust, which the Court concludes is vexatious or frivolous, then the party filing such action shall forfeit their interest beneficial, legal or otherwise in the Property and their interest shall be distributed equally between and among all other Beneficiaries.

22. No person or corporation dealing with the Co-Trustees, or their successors, shall be required to investigate the Co-Trustees' authority for entering into any transaction or to see to the application of the proceeds of any transaction.

23. The Beneficiaries may hereafter, from time to time, pay over or deliver additional sums of money, securities, or other real or personal property to the Co-Trustees, or their successors, to be held, managed, invested, reinvested, and distributed by the Co-Trustees, or their successors, as an addition to said trust estate and in all respects as herein provided.

24. The Co-Trustees, and their successors, shall be reimbursed for any out-of-pocket expenses incurred by either of them in the administration of this Trust. The Co-Trustees shall reconcile and reimburse such out-of-pocket expenses at least three times annually, on or before February 28, June 30, and November 30. No compensation shall be paid to the Co-Trustees, or their successors, unless a corporate successor trustee is appointed by the Court as hereinafter provided who may then be paid a reasonable compensation for its services.

25. No interest in the ________________ Trust, or any trust created therein, shall be subject to a Beneficiary's liabilities or creditor claims, assignment, or anticipation, voluntary or involuntary. Any creditor or assignee of either of the Beneficiary's beneficial interest may only reach the maximum amount that could be distributed to or for the individual Beneficiary's benefit. If the Co-Trustees shall determine that a Beneficiary would not benefit as greatly from any outright distribution of Trust income or principal because of the availability of the distribution to his or her creditors, the Trustee shall instead expend those amounts for the benefit of the Beneficiary. This direction is intended to enable the Co-Trustees to give the Beneficiary the fullest possible benefit and enjoyment of all of the Trust income and principal to which he or she is entitled. This spendthrift clause is a **material purpose** of this ____________ Cabin Trust.

26. This _______________ Cabin Trust may be amended or revoked during the joint lifetimes of the Settlors by a written instrument signed by both Settlors. After the death of the first Settlor to die, the Trust shall be irrevocable and may only be modified as provided in Paragraph 20 of this Agreement. While both Settlors are living, either Settlor may revoke this Agreement with respect to his or her separate trust share. A Court shall have the authority to modify the __________________ Trust Agreement to modernize the Trust in accordance with changes in state trust law, to allow that the Trust may be further reformed to achieve the Beneficiaries' tax objectives, and that any trust created herein may be further combined or divided all in accordance with Mont. Code Ann. § 72-38-415 through Mont. Code Ann. § 72-38-417 (2019), as appropriate.

27. A Trustee may resign by giving sixty (60) days written notice specifying the effective date of the resignation to the Co-Trustee(s) and to the Beneficiaries.

28. No successor Trustee shall be personally liable for any act or omission of any predecessor Trustee. Any successor Trustee shall accept, without examination or review, the accounts rendered and the property delivered by or for a predecessor Trustee without incurring any liability or responsibility. Any successor Trustee shall have all the title, powers, and discretion of the Trustee succeeded, without the necessity of any court order or conveyance or transfer.

29. The substantive laws of the State of Montana (without consideration of any Montana choice of law provisions) shall govern all aspects of this ____________ Cabin Trust, including the construction, validity, and effect of the provisions thereof. The venue for any disputes related to the terms of this instrument shall be the Montana District Court, ____________ County or the United States District Court for the District of Montana.

30. This TRUST shall terminate upon the first of the following to occur: 1) the death of all the Beneficiaries; 2) at such time when no Beneficiaries seasonally occupy or use the Property; or 3) ninety (90) years after the date of creation of the ______________________ TRUST. Upon such termination, the Trust's assets, including corpus and accumulated income, shall be distributed or retained in trust as follows:

    A. The assets of the ______________ trust share shall be distributed to or held in trust for the lineal descendants of ______________, per stirpes, as determined by the ____________ Trustee or Trustees, upon providing notice to the Beneficiaries or any interested party as required by law. If ____________, ____________ and all the lineal descendants of ____________ are deceased, the assets of the ______________ trust share shall be distributed as provided in subparagraph B of this Paragraph 30.

    B. The assets of the ______________ trust share shall be distributed to or held in trust for the lineal descendants of ______________, per stirpes, as determined by the ____________ Trustee or Trustees, upon providing notice to the Beneficiaries or any interested party as required by law. If ______________, ____________ and all the lineal descendants of ____________ are deceased, the assets of the ______________ trust share shall be distributed as provided in subparagraph A of this Paragraph 30.

31. Any individual acting as Trustee shall be indemnified and reimbursed from the trust for any loss, damage, liability, or expense incurred or sustained by the Trustee, in an individual or fiduciary capacity, by reason of any act or failure to act of the Trustee for or on behalf of and in furtherance of the trust. However, the protection provided by this paragraph shall not apply to any loss, damage, liability, or expense incurred or sustained by reason of such Trustee acting in bad faith or with reckless indifference to the fiduciary duties of the Trustee.

SETTLORS

____

____

TRUSTEES

____

, Co-Trustee

____

, Co-Trustee

Schedule "A"

[REAL PROPERTY DESCRIPTION]

[PERSONAL PROPERTY VIA BILL OF SALE]

Annex 7E

Tenants-in-Common Agreement

This Tenants-in-Common Agreement is entered into this ____ day of __________, 2021, by and between Jones Family LLC ("Jones" herein) and Smith Family LLC ("Smith" herein); collectively referred to as "Owners" and individually as "Owner" or "Smith" or "Jones" and AAA Property Management, Inc, herein referred to as "Corporation."

WITNESSETH:

WHEREAS, Smith and Jones have, simultaneous with the execution hereof, each acquired a Fifty Percent (50%) undivided interest as tenants in common in and to that certain real property described generally as______________ (the "Property") as described on Exhibit "A"; and

WHEREAS, the Smith and Jones families own their respective interests in the Property as tenants in common, subject to the terms, covenants and conditions set forth below, which terms are necessary to ensure the proper and orderly management and operation of the Property during the period of the Owners' co-ownership;

WHEREAS, Smith and Jones own and control Corporation which will receive rents and pay capital for the maintenance and improvements of the Property and act as the manager of the Property.

NOW, THEREFORE, for good and valuable consideration, the receipt and sufficiency of which are hereby acknowledged, the parties hereto agree as follows:

1. Term. This Agreement shall be for a term of five (5) years, commencing on the date of execution hereof, unless sooner terminated by (i) sale of the Property by the Owners; or (ii) termination of this Agreement by both parties.

2. Management. Smith and Jones shall execute a Management Agreement naming Corporation as manager of the Property, on a renewable annual basis, to handle such matters as the lease, operation, and maintenance of the Property as more fully set forth in said agreement, a copy of which is attached hereto as Exhibit "B." Said agreement shall provide a twelve-month termination provision. Instructions to Corporation may be issued by either of the Owners, except that, in the event of the sale or refinancing of the Property, the consent of both Owners shall be required.

3. Operating Capital and Expenses. In the event Corporation determines, from time to time, that additional capital from the Owners is required (whether for capital improvements or ordinary and routine operating expenses, including insurance, taxes, snow removal, utilities, and furniture for the Property) to operate, improve, or otherwise manage the Property, Corporation shall so notify the Owners, in writing, of the total additional sum required, and request that each Owner submit Fifty Percent (50%) (or the amount of each Owner's proportionate share of said total, if different), within ten (10) days after receipt of said written notice.

The failure of any Owner to make such additional contribution within ten (10) days after receipt of notice requesting same shall constitute a material breach of this Agreement and the noncontributing Owner shall be considered in default hereunder. The amount of any delinquent additional contribution plus interest at the prime rate as published from time to time in the *Wall Street Journal* plus three percent (3%), shall be offset against any further distributions due the defaulting Owner.

The nondefaulting Owner shall have the right, but not the obligation, to pay the defaulting Owner's pro rata share of such additional contribution. The nondefaulting Owner so electing to pay the defaulting Owner's share shall be entitled to a percentage of the defaulting Owner's interest. A portion of the defaulting Owner's interest shall be transferred to the nondefaulting Owner who has made said payment under the following formula: the percentage of the defaulting Owner's interest that will be transferred to the nondefaulting Owner shall be the quotient wherein the dividend is the amount paid by the nondefaulting Owner and the divisor is the current amount of all sums paid, to date, by the defaulting Owner for the purchase or operation of the Property. For example, if the amount paid by the nondefaulting Owner is $10,000.00 and the current total sums paid by the defaulting Owner for the purchase and operation of the Property is $200,000.00, then five percent (5%) of the defaulting Owner's interest will be transferred to the nondefaulting Owner. The defaulting Owner shall have a period of sixty (60) days from the date of said payment to redeem its interest from the nondefaulting Owner by paying to said nondefaulting Owner the amount of the funds advanced by the nondefaulting Owner together with interest thereon at the *Wall Street Journal* prime rate plus three percent (3%).

4. Right of First Refusal as Condition Precedent to Sale to Third Party or Partition of the Property.

   a. Sale of the Property. Either Owner shall have the right to sell, exchange, or otherwise transfer its interest in the Property, or any part thereof, after having first offered to sell said interest to the other Owner in accordance with the following procedure:

      (i) The interest in the Property which the transferring Owner intends to sell, exchange, or otherwise transfer (whether such interest includes all or a portion of the Owner's interest) shall first be offered in writing to the other Owner at the stated price at which the interest is proposed to be sold to a third party. The other Owner shall have a period of thirty (30) days after receipt of such notice in which to accept or reject said offer, in writing.

      (ii) In the event the nontransferring Owner rejects the offer, then the transferring Owner shall be free to sell its interest in the Property on the terms set forth in the notice and on no other terms. In the event the nontransferring Owner accepts the offer, then the nontransferring Owner shall purchase the interest of the transferring Owner on the terms set forth in said notice within sixty (60) days after the acceptance of said offer. The selling Owner shall pay any and all title insurance premiums and reasonable closing costs associated with said transfer.

   b. Partition of the Property. Either Owner shall have the right to partition the Property, after having first offered to sell his interest therein to the other Owner in accordance with the following procedure:

      (i) The Owner desiring to partition the Property shall notify the other Owner, in writing, of such desire. In such notice, the Owner seeking partition shall name an appraiser active in the appraisal of recreational property in Carbon or Yellowstone County, Montana. The nonpartitioning Owner shall have twenty (20) days to consent to such appraiser, or identify another appraiser active in Carbon or Yellowstone County, Montana. Failure to submit an alternative appraiser's name within the twenty (20)-day period constitutes consent to the initial named appraiser. If the nonpartitioning Owner identifies a second appraiser, then the two identified appraisers shall promptly designate a third appraiser to appraise the Property. The partitioning Owner shall pay the cost of an appraisal of the Property conducted by the designated or agreed appraiser. Within five days after receipt of the appraisal report, and prior to the initiation of any partition action, the partitioning Owner shall offer to sell his interest in the Property to the nonpartitioning Owner, in writing, at a discounted price equal to (i) the Property's appraised value, times (ii) the partitioning Owner's percentage ownership interest in the Property, times (iii) 1.0; (provided, however, for a period from November 1, 2021 to October 31, 2026, such multiplier shall be 0.70, to reflect a Thirty Percent (30%) Discount negotiated by the parties for the initial phase of ownership of the Property). The other Owner shall have a period of thirty (30) days after receipt of such written offer in which to accept or reject said offer, in writing. Failure to follow the procedures set forth in this section shall constitute a complete defense to any partition action brought by any Owner.

(ii) In the event the nonpartitioning Owner rejects the offer, then the partitioning Owner shall be free to initiate a partition action in the appropriate court. In the event the nonpartitioning Owner accepts the offer, then the nonpartitioning Owner shall purchase the interest of the other Owner at the price set forth in said notice within one hundred twenty (120) days after the acceptance of said offer. The selling Owner shall pay any and all title insurance premiums and reasonable closing costs associated with said transfer. The parties acknowledge and agree that, in the event of default under the terms of this Agreement by either Owner, the nondefaulting Owner shall have the right to seek specific performance of the terms of the Agreement by the defaulting Owner and money damages.

5. Status of Relationship. The parties acknowledge that it is their intention to hold the Property as tenants in common and that they have expressly elected not to become partners and that neither this Agreement nor any provision of this Agreement shall be interpreted to impose a partnership relationship at either law or equity on the parties. Accordingly, no Owner shall have any liability for the debt or obligation of any other Owner.

6. Notice. Any notice required or desired to be given under this Agreement shall be deemed given, if in writing and hand delivered or sent by United States certified mail, to the other party at the address shown for said party below:

To the Corporation: With Copy to:

To:

7. Dispute Resolution/Attorneys' Fees. Any disputes arising under this Agreement shall be submitted to binding arbitration in the ______________County, by an arbitrator chosen from the list maintained by the American Arbitration Association. In the event of any dispute hereunder, the party prevailing in such arbitration shall be entitled to recover, in addition to all other remedies or damages, reasonable attorneys' fees incurred in such action.

8. Counterparts. This Agreement may be executed in counterparts, each of which will be deemed to be an original and all of which together will constitute one and the same instrument.

9. Governing Law. This Agreement is entered into in the State of and shall be governed in all respects by the laws of such State.

10. Subordination. The parties hereto agree that the rights and interest granted to each hereunder shall, in all respects, be subject and subordinate to the interest of [insert Bank name] of in and to the Property.

dated _______________, 2021.

IN WITNESS WHEREOF, the undersigned have set their hands and seals on the date and year first above written.

8

Heirs' Property, Property Tax Relief, and the Further Undermining of Black and Latino Homeowners' Housing Stability

—Heather K. Way*

I. INTRODUCTION

This chapter examines how state and local property tax relief programs for homeowners in the United States routinely exclude homeowners who reside on "heirs' property." The discriminatory structure of these programs increases the property tax burdens and overall housing instability of heirs' property homeowners, exacerbating this country's vast racial divides.

As described in chapter 1, heirs' property is a common type of real property ownership that forms when family members inherit property. Family members share ownership of the property as tenants in common and often lack legal documentation that establishes their ownership. Heirs' property is particularly prevalent among Black landowners in the rural South and older urban communities with historically high concentrations of Black and Latino landowners.[1]

* My thanks to Ruthie Goldstein, Lauren Richter, Amy Das, and Eric Newman for their research assistance; Mechele Dickerson, Thomas Mitchell, and Jim Kelley for their thoughtful feedback; and Mia Loseff and Benjamin Vergil for their assistance with the GIS maps appearing in figures 8.1–8.3, which can be viewed at http://ambar.org/heirs-property-supplement.

[1] *See, e.g.*, Maps of Likely Heirs Property in Texas' Largest Urban Areas by Race and Ethnicity (a collection of GIS maps on file with author); Dan Geringer, *The Problem of Tangled Titles*, Philadelphia Inquirer (Mar. 7, 2021), https://www.inquirer.com/news/inq/changing-philadelphia-20141023.html (discussing how "[t]angled titles threaten the homes of 14,000 residents throughout the city" and presenting a map with the location of these properties); Ann Carpenter, et al., *Understanding*

Although not all heirs' property is occupied, heirs' property parcels often include homes that one or more of the heirs occupy as their primary residence. This chapter focuses on these occupied residential heirs' property parcels, enhancing our understanding of the unique challenges facing the owners of this subset of heirs' property.

Although a small number of legal scholars and a larger number of journalists have addressed some of the challenges heirs' property owners face, many critical issues impacting owners of heirs' property—both residential and nonresidential properties—have not been addressed adequately. Most publications on heirs' property have focused on partition laws that have enabled speculators, developers, and others to strip millions of acres of land from Black families.[2] By focusing on property tax relief programs that exclude homeowners with heirs' property, this chapter presents new research on another set of public policies that contributes to the vulnerability of heirs' property ownership and erosion of Black as well as Latino wealth.

Section II presents an overview of state and local government programs that reduce the property taxes on homeowners' primary residences, also known as homesteads, and the important role the programs play in increasing the housing stability of homeowners—especially those who are financially insecure. Cumulatively, these programs deliver billions of dollars in property tax savings to homeowners across the country. Many state and local governments also protect homeowners from foreclosure when they fall behind on their property taxes.

Section III shows how exclusionary policies, such as strict titling record requirements and criteria governing cotenants, cut off homeowners with heirs' property from these important property tax relief protections. Section III also demonstrates the impacts of these exclusionary polices on Black and Latino homeowners, through research on inherited homesteads in Texas. Black and Latino homeowners are already penalized in other ways by systemic racism embedded in property tax policies, such as through inflated property tax assessments.[3] The exclusion of heirs' property homeowners from property tax relief programs on their homesteads exacerbates these inequities, further saddling Black and Latino homeowners with excessive property tax burdens, imperiling their housing security, and eroding their wealth. To help remedy these structural inequities, Section IV proposes a series of fairly simple statutory reforms that states

Heirs' Properties in the Southeast, FED. RSRV. BANK OF ATLANTA (Apr. 19, 2016), https://www.atlantafed.org/community-development/publications/partners-update/2016/02/160419-understanding-heirs-properties-in-southeast (discussing how heirs' property is "disproportionately found in low-income ethnic and racial minority families").

[2] *See, e.g.*, Thomas W. Mitchell, *From Reconstruction to Deconstruction: Undermining Black Landownership, Political Independence, and Community through Partition Sales of Tenancies in Common*, 95 NW. U.L. REV. 505 (2001); Michelle Chen, *Black Lands Matter: The Movement to Transform Heirs' Property Laws*, THE NATION (Sept. 25, 2019), https://www.thenation.com/article/archive/heirs-property-reform; Thomas W. Mitchell, *Restoring Hope for Heirs Property Owners: The Uniform Partition of Heirs Property Act*, 40 ST. & LOC. L. NEWS 6 (2016), https://www.americanbar.org/groups/state_local_government/publications/state_local_law_news/2016-17/fall/restoring_hope_heirs_property_owners_uniform_partition_heirs_property_act.

[3] Teresa Wiltz, *Black Homeowners Pay More Than 'Fair Share' in Property Taxes*, STATELINE (June 25, 2020), https://www.pewtrusts.org/en/research-and-analysis/blogs/stateline/2020/06/25/black-homeowners-pay-more-than-fair-share-in-property-taxes; Andrew Kahrl, *More for Less: How Property Taxes Fuel Racial Inequity*, TAXNOTES (Jan. 21, 2021), https://www.taxnotes.com/special-reports/tax-history/more-less-how-property-taxes-fuel-racial-inequality/2021/01/21/2l6gq.

could enact to help heirs' property homeowners access the property tax relief protections that other homeowners have.[4]

II. PROPERTY TAX TAX RELIEF PROTECTIONS FOR HOMEOWNERS

Along with the sales and income tax, the property tax is one of the three major types of taxation in the United States, and the property tax is the primary source of revenue for local governments such as cities, counties, and school districts. Property taxes are usually administered at a local level, but most states impose restrictions on how local governments tax property.[5]

Single-family homeowners in the United States pay an average of $3,561 in property taxes annually,[6] but the property tax burden for homeowners varies widely across the United States, depending on home values, tax rates, and reductions available to homeowners. In 2018, the tax bill on the median home value in the largest city of each state ranged from $578 (Birmingham, Alabama) to $10,497 (Portland, Oregon).[7] While almost half of US taxpayers pay less than 2.5 percent of their income on property taxes, close to 10 percent pay more than 10 percent of their income in property taxes, and 4 percent pay 20 percent or more.[8] Those with the highest property tax burdens are far more likely to be low income: Of the households paying more than 20 percent of their income in property taxes, more than nine in ten make less than $40,000.[9]

Every state in the United States and many local governments have adopted laws that lower homeowners' property tax bills on their homestead, while many also offer protections for homeowners who fall behind on their taxes, such as payments plans or protections from foreclosure. These property tax relief programs for homesteads are a key feature of property tax systems, and governments adopt them to advance a number of goals, including making property taxes more politically palatable for voters, creating a more fair and progressive distribution of property tax burdens, and limiting the destabilizing impacts of property taxes on homeowners—especially for those who are financially insecure. After presenting an overview of property tax relief programs commonly available in the

---

[4] *See* note 66 for a discussion of the methodology used in identifying heirs' property homeowners impacted by these exclusionary policies in Texas and opportunities for future research to quantify these impacts nationwide.

[5] Jacqueline Byers, *Property Taxes: A Look at Exemptions, Tax Limits and Assessment Cycles*, NAT'L ASS'N OF CNTYS 3–5, 13–14 tbl.2 (2012), https://www.naco.org/sites/default/files/documents/Property%20Taxes%20A%20Look%20at%20Exemptions,%20Tax%20Limits%20and%20Assessment%20Cycles.pdf.

[6] Brenda Richardson, *Residents Pay the Lowest Property Taxes in These States*, FORBES (Apr. 9, 2020, 1:00 AM), https://www.forbes.com/sites/brendarichardson/2020/04/09/residents-pay-the-lowest-property-taxes-in-these-states/?sh=6fb2f1675834 (providing data for 2019).

[7] *50-State Property Tax Comparison Study for Taxes Paid in 2018*, LINCOLN INST. OF LAND POL'Y & MINN. CTR. FOR FISCAL EXCELLENCE 60 tbl.2a (2019), https://www.lincolninst.edu/sites/default/files/pubfiles/50-state-property-tax-comparison-for-2018-full_3.pdf.

[8] John H. Bowman, et al, *Property Tax Circuit Breakers: Fair and Cost-Effective Relief for Taxpayers*, LINCOLN INST. OF LAND POL'Y 5 (2009), https://community-wealth.org/sites/clone.community-wealth.org/files/downloads/report-bowman-et-al.pdf.

[9] *Id.*

United States, I focus on this latter goal: the role of property tax relief programs in promoting housing stability for those who are financially insecure.[10]

A. Types of Property Tax Relief Programs

The types of local and state property tax relief programs for homeowners and their homesteads vary widely. Many programs are limited to homeowners who are senior citizens, while others apply to lower-income households, persons with disabilities, veterans, or other classes. Some programs require homeowners to submit an application to qualify, while others are self-implementing.

The following is an overview of some of the most common categories of state and local programs that lower homeowners' property tax bills:[11]

- **Property tax exemptions**, together with credits, are the most widely adopted form of property tax relief, available in forty-seven states and the District of Columbia.[12] Property tax exemptions reduce the taxable amount of a homestead's value by either a fixed dollar amount or a percentage of the homestead's value. For example, South Carolina's homestead exemption law exempts the first $50,000 of a home's appraised value from taxation if the homestead is owned by a senior.[13] As a result, if a home is valued at $125,000, only $75,000 is subject to taxation.
- **Property tax credits** reduce a homeowner's overall tax bill by a fixed dollar amount or percentage, or allow a homeowner to deduct a portion of the property taxes on their residence from their state income tax bill. For example, Illinois' property tax credit reduces a homeowner's state income tax bill by 5 percent of the property taxes paid on the homeowner's principal residence.[14]
- **Assessment limits** cap or restrict the growth in the value of a home that is subject to taxation (i.e., the assessed value), with the assessed value resetting to market value when the home is sold. Assessment limits are especially useful for homeowners in areas with rapidly appreciating land values. For example, homeowners in the District of Columbia can qualify for a 10 percent assessment cap, which means the assessed value of their homesteads cannot increase more than 10 percent a year. Seniors are eligible for a 5 percent assessment cap,

[10] In addition to property tax relief programs for homesteads, many states have adopted property tax relief programs for other uses of real property, such as agricultural, timberland, wildlife conservation, and open space preservation. While this chapter focuses on barriers that heirs' property owners face in accessing property tax relief programs for homesteads, they may also face barriers in accessing these other forms of tax relief. This is an area where further research is needed.

[11] For a comprehensive overview of property tax relief programs offered in each of the fifty states and the District of Columbia, see the interactive website created by the Lincoln Institute of Land Policy and the George Washington Institute of Public Policy, *Significant Features of the Property Tax*, https://www.lincolninst.edu/research-data/data-toolkits/significant-features-property-tax/access-property-tax-database/residential-property-tax-relief-programs.

[12] Adam H. Langley, *How Do States Spell Relief?* Lincoln Inst. of Land Pol'y, https://www.lincolninst.edu/publications/articles/how-do-states-spell-relief.

[13] S.C. Code Ann. § 12-37-290 (2019); *Homestead Exemption*, S.C. Dep't of Revenue, https://dor.sc.gov/lgs/homestead-exemption.

[14] Ill. Admin. Code tit. 86, § 100.2180 (2020); *Publication 108: Property Tax Credit*, Ill. Dep't of Revenue (Jan. 2020), https://www2.illinois.gov/rev/research/publications/pubs/Documents/pub-108.pdf.

which means the assessed value of their homestead cannot increase more than 5 percent a year.[15]

- **Tax freeze** laws cap a homeowner's property taxes when certain conditions are met. For example, in Texas, school district taxes are capped for residents' homestead once they turn sixty-five, as long as they have a senior homestead exemption in place.[16] The school district's property taxes assessed on the homestead do not increase even if the tax bill would otherwise rise due to inflation or other factors, unless improvements beyond normal repairs and maintenance are made to the property. The tax freeze also applies to homesteads owned by persons with a qualifying disability.
- **Property circuit breakers** are a variation of tax freeze and tax credit laws that target lower-income, and sometimes moderate-income, homeowners. Eligible homeowners are entitled to a reduction or refund of all or a portion of their property taxes when their tax bill exceeds a certain percentage of the homeowner's income. Circuit breaker programs have been adopted in at least eighteen states and the District of Columbia.[17] For example, lower-income homeowners in Maryland are eligible to have their property taxes capped according to a state formula, with the lowest caps for the lowest-income households.[18]
- **Tax rate** laws apply a different statutory tax rate (also referred to as the "millage rate" in some jurisdictions[19]) to residential properties as compared to nonresidential properties (e.g., commercial, industrial, agricultural). For example, the 2020 residential tax rate in Los Alamos County, New Mexico, was 24.532 mils, and the nonresidential tax rate was 28.590.[20]
- **Assessment ratio** laws apply the property tax rate to a percentage of the property's appraised value, rather than the full appraised value. The level of the assessment ratio depends on the type of property that is being taxed, with several states applying a lower assessment ratio to an owner's primary residence compared to other types of residential property.[21] For example, in Alabama, the state's property tax rate is applied to 10 percent of the value of a homeowner's primary residence, compared to 20 percent of the value of other residential properties, as well as commercial properties,[22] which results in a property tax bill that is at least two times higher for this latter group of properties (the difference is even higher once homestead tax exemptions are applied).

---

[15] D.C. Code Ann. §§ 47-863 to -864 (West 2019); *Real Property Tax Relief and Tax Credits*, D.C. Off. of Tax and Revenue, https://otr.cfo.dc.gov/page/real-property-tax-relief-and-tax-credits.

[16] Tex. Tax Code Ann. § 11.26 (West 2020).

[17] Aidan Davis, *Property Tax Circuit Breakers in 2018*, Inst. of Tax'n and Econ. Pol'y 2 (Sept. 17, 2018), https://itep.org/property-tax-circuit-breakers-in-2018/.

[18] Md. Code Ann., Tax-Prop. § 9-105 (West 2020).

[19] The millage rate is the amount of tax due for every $1,000 of a property's assessed value and is expressed in tenths of a penny. One mil is $0.001. A millage rate of 20 is equivalent to 2 percent, or $20 in taxes for every $1,000 of a property's assessed value.

[20] *Assessor FAQs*, Los Alamos Cnty., https://www.losalamosnm.us/government/elected_officials/assessor/assessor_f_a_qs.

[21] Rute Pinho, *State Tax Treatment of Homestead and Non-Homestead Residential Property*, Conn. Gen. Assembly (2015), https://www.cga.ct.gov/2015/rpt/2015-R-0288.htm (Alabama, Mississippi, South Carolina, and Utah apply a lower assessment ratio for homestead property compared to non-homestead property).

[22] Ala. Const. art. XI, § 217; *Property Tax Assessment*, Ala. Dep't of Revenue, https://revenue.alabama.gov/property-tax/property-tax-assessment.

In addition to reducing homeowners' tax bills, states and cities provide a range of additional programs that protect homeowners from property tax foreclosure of their homestead when they cannot afford their property tax bills. For example, at least twenty-seven states and the District of Columbia offer some type of property tax deferral program that give certain classes of homeowners the right to defer their taxes with interest until they die or otherwise no longer reside in their homestead, effectively protecting homeowners from property tax foreclosure if they are unable to pay their taxes.[23] These states include Texas (homeowners with a senior or disability homestead exemption),[24] California (homeowners who are low-income seniors, blind, or disabled and have at least 40 percent equity in the home),[25] and South Dakota (longer-term single-family homeowners who are low-income seniors).[26]

A related protection is offered in New York City, which exempts from the city's annual tax lien sale all qualified homeowners who are low-income seniors or persons with disabilities and behind on their property taxes.[27] Avoiding the tax lien sale protects a homeowner from higher fees and interest and, ultimately, from a property tax lien foreclosure.

A number of states and local jurisdictions also give eligible homeowners the right to enter into payment plans, with a longer period of time to catch up on back taxes before penalties and interest accrue.[28] In Philadelphia, eligible homeowners can qualify for an Owner-Occupied Real Estate Tax Payment Agreement, which allows them to make payments on back taxes, with lower-income homeowners eligible for a waiver of penalties and interest.[29] States such as Michigan also offer grant and loan programs to assist lower-income homeowners with their property taxes to avoid foreclosure.[30]

B. Promoting Housing Stability

Although there is much variation across the United States, property tax relief programs can potentially reduce an individual homeowner's property tax bill by thousands of dollars per year, depending on where the homeowner resides. Among all homeowners in the United States, local and state property tax exemption and credit programs alone delivered an estimated $16.2 billion in annual property tax savings in 2012.[31]

---

[23] *See Residential Property Tax Relief Programs*, Lincoln Inst. of Land Pol'y & Geo. Wash. Inst. of Pub. Pol'y, https://www.lincolninst.edu/research-data/data-toolkits/significant-features-property-tax/access-property-tax-database/residential-property-tax-relief-programs.

[24] Tex. Tax Code Ann. § 33.06 (West 2020).

[25] Cal. Rev. & Tax Code § 20800-20825 (West 2020).

[26] S.D. Codified Laws § 43-31-31 to § 43-31-41 (2020).

[27] New York City, N.Y., Admin. Code § 11-319; *Lien Sales*, NYC Dep't of Fin., https://www1.nyc.gov/site/finance/taxes/property-lien-sales.page.

[28] Jenna DeAngelo, *Property Tax Delinquency in the United* States 5 (Lincoln Inst. of Land Pol'y, Working Paper WP20JD1, 2020), https://www.lincolninst.edu/sites/default/files/pubfiles/deangelo_wp20jd1.pdf ("What may start out as a very small delinquent property tax bill can quickly balloon to an unmanageable amount because of interest and fees.").

[29] *Set up an Owner-Occupied Real Estate Tax Payment Agreement (OOPA)*, City of Phila., https://www.phila.gov/services/payments-assistance-taxes/get-real-estate-tax-relief/owner-occupied-real-estate-tax-payment-agreement.

[30] *Help for Homeowners*, Mich. State Hous. Dev. Auth., https://www.michigan.gov/mshda/0,4641,7-141--370865--,00.html.

[31] *Tax Savings from Property Tax Exemptions and Credits in 2012*, Lincoln Inst. of Land Pol'y & Geo. Wash. Inst. of Pub. Pol'y, https://www.lincolninst.edu/research-data/data-toolkits/significant-features-property-tax/access-property-tax

In Boston, the city's residential tax exemption on homesteads results in average annual property tax savings of $1,962 per homestead.[32] In Houston, the tax bill for a homeowner who has a senior homestead exemption on a home appraised at $100,000 can be as little as zero, with annual tax savings of more than $2,330. Seniors residing in more valuable homes in Houston save even more in property taxes with a homestead exemption. In Charleston, South Carolina, the annual property tax savings for a home valued at $220,578 with a senior homestead exemption was $2,316 in 2016—a savings of 71 percent.[33]

By alleviating tax burdens, property tax relief programs can increase the housing stability of homeowners, especially those who are financially insecure.[34] A recent study of older homeowners with a reverse mortgage, for example, found that the owners with a senior citizen homestead exemption were almost 60 percent less likely to default on their property taxes than the owners without the exemption.[35] The senior citizens' participation in a general homestead exemption program was associated with a 25 percent decrease in property tax default, while participation in a senior citizen assessment freeze was associated with a 43 percent decrease.[36] Other research has found a strong correlation between a homeowner's property tax burden and property tax default rates, as well as mortgage default rates.[37]

Circuit breaker programs in particular, if structured appropriately, can lower a homeowner's risk of property tax default by providing targeted relief to the most vulnerable homeowners and tying the level of tax relief to the homeowner's income. Circuit breaker and other property tax relief programs play an especially critical role in protecting lower-income, long-time homeowners from rapidly rising property taxes in gentrifying neighborhoods, which have historically been home to communities of color.[38] Without property tax relief, these homeowners are more likely to default on their property taxes and lose their homes.[39]

-database/residential-property-tax-relief-programs (click on "For estimates of tax savings under each exemption and credit program offered in 2012," then "All Programs" tab).

[32] Martin J. Walsh & Ronald W. Rakow, *Residential Exemption Fiscal Year 2017*, City of Bos. (2017), https://www.cityofboston.gov/images_documents/2017_ResExempt1&2Q_tcm3-53613.pdf (2016 estimate).

[33] Silda Nikaj & Joshua J. Miller, *HECM and Property Tax Relief for Seniors*, 19 Cityscape: A J. of Pol'y Dev. & Res. 29, 43 (2017). The tax savings for Charleston take into account the assessment ratio applied to owner-occupied residences as well as the senior citizen exemption, which exempts the first $50,000 in home value from taxation. *Id.*

[34] *See generally* DeAngelo, *supra* note 28, at 4 ("The inability to pay is likely the most prevalent reason property owners become delinquent on their taxes—about half of American households are financially insecure and have practically no savings to cover an unexpected expense.").

[35] Joshua J. Miller, Silda Nikaj, & Jin Man Lee, *Reverse Mortgages and Senior Property Tax Relief*, 44 J. Housing Econ. 26, 31 (2019) (research examining seniors with a reverse mortgage and property tax relief in three states: Michigan, Ohio, and Massachusetts).

[36] *Id.*

[37] *See, e.g.*, James Alm, Timothy R. Hodge, Gary Sands, & Mark Skidmore, *Detroit Property Tax Delinquency: Social Contract in Crisis*, 14 Pub. Fin. and Mgmt. 280 (2014) (finding that properties with higher statutory tax rates or assessment ratios have higher delinquency rates); Stephanie Moulton, Donald R. Haurin, & Wei Shi, *An Analysis of Default Risk in the Home Equity Conversion Mortgage (HECM) Program*, 90 J. Urb. Econ. 17, 26 (2015) (finding that a $1,000 increase in the property tax amount is associated with a 6.6 percent to 7.8 percent increase in the probability of default in reverse mortgages held by senior homeowners).

[38] *See* Lei Ding & Jackelyn Hwang, *Effects of Gentrification on Homeowners: Evidence from a Natural Experiment* (Fed. Res. Bank of Phila., Working Paper No. 16, 2020) (finding that gentrification increases homeowners' risk of property tax delinquency in Philadelphia and that the city's property tax relief programs for long-time homeowners in these neighborhoods helped mitigate the risk of delinquencies and displacement).

[39] *Id.*

In Austin, the homeowners with the highest levels of property tax delinquencies are those living in gentrifying neighborhoods that have historically been home to high concentrations of Black and Latino homeowners.[40] The impact of rising property taxes on elderly homeowners living in these neighborhoods is usually buffered, however, by the myriad property tax reduction programs and other protections in Texas for homeowners who are senior citizens.

As an illustration, a homeowner who is eighty-five and lives in the rapidly gentrifying Guadalupe neighborhood of Austin in a home that was valued at $100,000 in 2000 and is now worth $500,000 (a common scenario in this neighborhood) would owe approximately $4,000 a year in property taxes with a senior homestead exemption—versus $11,000 without the exemption. Under state law, the senior homeowner would also be eligible to defer all or a portion of their property taxes until the owner moves out of the home. Without these property tax relief protections, a low-income homeowner would be much more vulnerable to losing their home.

III. PROPERTY TAX RELIEF BARRIERS FOR HEIRS' PROPERTY HOMEOWNERS

Heirs' property homeowners face a number of legal and institutional barriers to accessing state and local property tax relief programs on their homesteads, exposing them to higher taxes and exacerbating their housing instability. To better understand these barriers, I led a study in 2020–2021 that examined how property tax relief protections in twenty-three states are applied to heirs' property homeowners, focusing primarily on states' homestead exemption and homestead credit programs.[41] Our study identified three common sets of legal and institutional barriers that restrict heirs' access to these programs on their homesteads. These barriers are examined here.

A. Clear Title Requirements

To qualify for a homestead exemption or other property tax relief program, many states and local taxing jurisdictions require homeowners to have a deed or other form of legal titling instrument that is recorded in the real property records in their name. Homeowners who have purchased their home can easily satisfy this requirement because a deed is at the heart of a home purchase transaction, with the deed typically recorded by the attorney or other professional who oversees the closing on the home.

In contrast, a recorded title requirement is a high bar for many people who have inherited their home, particularly for those with limited financial means.[42] While the exact procedures vary across states individuals who have inherited their home from someone other than a spouse, regardless of whether there is a will, typically must follow a set of lengthy, complex, and often costly legal procedures in probate court to obtain a deed. Heirs often are unaware of these procedures or the

---

[40] Heather Way et al, *Uprooted: Residential Displacement in Austin's Gentrifying Neighborhoods and What Can Be Done About It* app. 5, p. 200 (2018), available at https://sites.utexas.edu/gentrificationproject/..austin-uprooted-report-maps/.

[41] A summary of the states and laws we examined can be found in annex A at the end of this chapter.

[42] *See, e.g.*, Andrew L. Howlett, *Homestead Deduction: Pitfalls and Reforms*, WASH. LAW., Mar. 2014, at 34, 37–38 (describing the barriers that heirs face in obtaining record title in Washington, D.C., leading to the heir's loss of the district's homestead deduction and "thousands of dollars in additional tax liability").

importance of following them as a condition of preserving the property tax reductions on the home they have inherited from their parents or other relatives.[43] The lack of access to affordable legal representation also contributes to heirs lacking recorded title to their property. For homesteads that have been inherited across multiple generations via intestacy—an especially common practice among African American families[44]—obtaining a recorded title as an heirs' property owner is even more complicated and expensive.

Moreover, even if an heir can obtain a deed, lengthy probate procedures often cause the heir to lose any preexisting exemptions on the home in the process of waiting for the probate and titling process to be completed. The increase in property taxes during this lag time can create severe financial repercussions for low-income heirs.[45]

Of the twenty-three states in our study, only three states—Indiana, Mississippi, and Texas—have adopted statutory criteria that explicitly allow heirs to qualify for the state's property tax relief programs even if they are not listed as the grantee on a deed or another recorded legal instrument for the property. Most of the other twenty states in our study, along with the District of Columbia, explicitly require a homeowner to have a deed or another legally recorded title instrument in the homeowner's name, with one state also allowing for an heir to present a will that has not been probated or that has otherwise not gone through an administration in probate court. The other states lack clear standards regarding how heirs' property owners qualify for the state's property tax reduction programs, leading to a patchwork of local eligibility criteria and barriers for heirs who lack clear title. A full listing of the states in our study, and a summary of their eligibility criteria for heirs is included in Annex A at the end of this chapter.

As an example, to qualify for Florida's general homestead exemption, which can result in annual property tax savings as high as $1,000 to $1,500 for a homestead with an appraised value of at least $75,000, depending on the local tax rate,[46] state law requires that a homeowner's "deed or instrument shall be recorded in the official records of the county in which the property is located."[47] Homeowners who apply for the state's 100 percent homestead exemption for low-income seniors must

[43] *See, e.g.*, *id.* at 34, 37 (describing how many small estates in Washington, D.C. are administered by the decedent's family members, who may not know the process for obtaining or filing a deed, that the heirs are eligible for a homestead exemption if they live on the property, or that a form is required to obtain the exemption). *See also* Peter M. Ward, Heather K. Way, & Lucille Wood, *The Contract for Deed Prevalence Project* 22–27, (2012), https://www.tdhca.state.tx.us/housing-center/docs/CFD-Prevalence-Project.pdf (a study of primarily Latino homeowners in informal subdivisions in Texas, finding a widespread lack of wills and discussing how the homeowners' informal understandings about who will inherit their homestead often conflicted with intestacy laws).

[44] *See* Thomas W. Mitchell, *Historic Partition Law Reform: A Game Changer for Heirs' Property Owners*, HEIRS' PROPERTY AND LAND FRACTIONATION: FOSTERING STABLE OWNERSHIP TO PREVENT LOSS AND ABANDONMENT (Cassandra Johnson Gaither et al. eds.) (discussing racial differences in patterns of estate planning and will making).

[45] *See, e.g.*, Howlett, *supra* note 42, at 34, 37–38.

[46] Counties, municipalities, and school districts in Florida are each allowed to levy property taxes of up to 10 mils, which, cumulatively, is equivalent to a tax rate of 30 mils, or 3 percent. The total 2020 millage rate for taxpayers who reside in the City of Miami was 21.3464 mils (2.13464 percent), while in Orlando it was as high as 19.7298 mils (1.97298 percent), depending on the applicable taxing jurisdictions.

[47] FLA. STAT. ANN. § 196.031(1)(a) (West 2020). Calls to local tax assessor offices also confirmed that when an heirs' property owner applies for a homestead exemption, there must be a deed, will, or documentation from a probate court proving ownership. *See, e.g.*, Telephone Interview with Alex Luca, Staff Att'y, Pinellas County Prop. Appraiser's Off. (Jan. 21, 2021) (confirming that an heir needs a recorded instrument in the public record to access a homestead exemption).

also meet these stringent proof-of-ownership requirements.[48] Similarly, Georgia state law requires a "deed reflecting the actual ownership of the property for which the applicant seeks to receive a homestead exemption [to] be recorded in the deed records of the county prior to the filing of the application for the homestead exemption."[49] When a home passes to the heirs, any homestead exemptions that were on the homestead are removed until a new deed is filed, which can saddle the heirs with a large increase in property taxes.[50]

Alabama's homestead exemption law does not provide clear proof of ownership requirements for heirs, and so the local tax assessor offices apply ad hoc standards. For example, the Bibb County Tax Assessor requires heirs without a deed to go through probate court to obtain legal documentation of ownership.[51] In contrast, the Tuscaloosa County Tax Assessor's office is significantly more flexible, allowing an heirs' property homeowner to certify his or her ownership interest via an affidavit in the assessment paperwork,[52] although this information does not appear on the tax assessor's website.[53]

B. Co-Owner Restrictions

Even when heirs' property homeowners can meet the proof of ownership requirements to qualify for a property tax reduction, additional statutory barriers thwart their attempts to access property tax relief if they share ownership with other cotenants. Overall, thirteen of the twenty-three states in our study limit an heirs' property homeowner's access to one or more property tax reduction programs as a result of the homeowner's co-ownership interest. Annex A includes a summary of the policies we reviewed in all twenty-three states. These exclusionary policies can result in heirs' property owners paying hundreds or even thousands more dollars in property taxes annually than residents with a 100 percent ownership interest in their homes.

One way in which several states limit heir's access in this regard is by requiring all co-owners to meet the property tax relief program's eligibility requirements, instead of just the co-owner or co-owners who reside in the home. For instance, in North Carolina, a low-income homeowner is ineligible for the state's circuit breaker program for seniors and persons with disabilities unless every co-owner (not counting spouses) qualifies for the program, *even if* the applicant is the sole occupant

48 Fla. Stat. Ann. § 196.075(7) (West 2020).

49 Ga. Code Ann. §48-5-40(3)(M) (2010). *See also*, Fulton Cnty, Fulton County 2021 Homestead Exemption Guide 2 (2021), https://fultonassessor.org/wp-content/uploads/sites/16/2021/05/2021-Fulton-County-Homestead-Exemption-Guide-05-07-21.pdf [https://perma.cc/SD32-9P7X]. ("The person applying for the homestead exemption must be listed on the deed.); *Homestead Exemption*, Muscogee Cnty. Bd. of Tax Assessors, https://www.columbusga.gov/TaxAssessors/exemptions.htm (last visited Jan. 23, 2021) (stating a homestead exemption applicant must "[b]ring a copy of the recorded warranty deed, proof of occupancy and proof of Georgia Residency."); *Homestead Exemption*, Forsyth Cnty Bd. of Tax Assessors, https://www.forsythco.com/Departments-Offices/Board-of-Assessors/Homestead-Exemption (last visited Jan. 23, 2021) ("To legally change ownership into your name a new deed must be recorded in Forsyth County records."); *Homestead Exemptions*, Paulding Cnty Bd. of Assessors, https://www.paulding.gov/89/Homestead-Exemptions (last visited Jan. 23, 2021) ("In order to qualify for a homestead exemption, the applicant's name must appear on the deed to the property . . .").

50 E-mail from Frank Alexander, Professor of Law, Emeritus, Emory Law, to author (Sept. 9, 2020) (on file with author).

51 Telephone interview with Theresa, Bibb County Courthouse (Jan. 21, 2021) (confirming than an heir without record title needs to have an attorney draft a deed to prove ownership to qualify for the homestead exemption).

52 E-mail from Leigh Ann Fair, Tax Assessor, Tuscaloosa Cnty Tax Assessor Office, to author (Jan. 6, 2021) (on file with author).

53 *Assessor Department*, Tuscaloosa Cnty Tax Assessor, https://www.tuscco.com/government/departments/tax-assessor/assessor-department/ (last visited Jan. 23, 2021) ("Typically a new deed will be needed for adding or removing names on a property. Depending on the situation other legal documents may be allowed.").

of the home and pays all the property taxes.[54] As applied to heirs, the result is that an heir applying for the circuit breaker program is ineligible for a property tax deferral unless all the other heirs also meet the program's income limits ($47,250 for 2021), are at least sixty-five or disabled, and have occupied the property as their permanent residence for at least the past five years.

Similarly, in New York, to qualify for a senior citizen homeowners' exemption—which, upon adoption by a municipality, reduces a qualifying low-income homeowner's assessed value by up to 50 percent—all the co-owners must occupy the property as their primary residence except in cases of divorce, legal separation, or abandonment. All of the co-owners must also be sixty-five or older unless they are a sibling or spouse. In addition, the co-owners' combined income cannot exceed the eligibility cap.[55]

States also restrict heirs' access to property tax reduction programs by reducing the amount of a homestead exemption or other tax reduction that a cotenant can receive based on the heir's co-ownership interest in the property. For instance, Kentucky offers a homestead exemption of $39,300 for seniors and persons with disabilities. When an heirs' property homeowner in Kentucky who is a senior citizen or person with a qualifying disability obtains a homestead exemption, the exemption is limited to the lower of $39,300 or the assessed value of the heir's co-ownership interest in the property.[56] As a result, an occupying heir with a 20 percent cotenancy interest in a home assessed at $90,000 is eligible for a homestead exemption of only $18,000 (20 percent of $90,000).

In Louisiana, property tax rates are applied to a home's assessed value minus the state's homestead exemption of $7,500, which is equivalent to a reduction of $75,000 from the home's appraised market value, since residences in the state are assessed at 10 percent of their appraised market value. The homestead exemption fully exempts about 40 percent of homeowners in the state from parish and school taxes.[57] For heirs and other co-owners, however, the exemption is based on the pro rata ownership interest of the owners who occupy the homestead. If the co-owners who occupy the homestead have only a 25 percent interest in the property, their exemption is limited to $1,875, which is equivalent to a reduction of $18,750 off the home's appraised market value.[58] In addition, the state's property tax assessment cap for senior citizens' homesteads is applied only to the occupying co-owners' ownership interest.[59] The remainder of the property is ineligible for the cap.

A related restriction exists in the District of Columbia, where, to qualify for the District's tax relief program for income-eligible senior citizens and persons with disabilities (which reduces a homeowner's property tax bill by 50 percent), the eligible applicants must have at least a 50 percent ownership interest in their homestead.[60] An otherwise-qualified heir with a 49 percent ownership interest in his or her primary residence is completely ineligible for the tax credit.

---

[54] N.C. Gen. Stat. Ann. § 105-277.1B(e) (West 2021).

[55] N.Y. Real Prop. Tax Law § 467 (McKinney 2021); *Senior Citizen Homeowners' Exemption (SCHE)*, N.Y.C. Dep't of Fin., https://www1.nyc.gov/site/finance/benefits/landlords-sche.page (last visited Jan. 23, 2021).

[56] Ky. Rev. Stat. Ann. § 132.810(2)(f) (West 2021).

[57] Daniel Teles, *Louisiana*, State-by-State Property Tax at a Glance, Significant Features of the Property Tax, Feb. 2018, https://www.lincolninst.edu/sites/default/files/la_feb_2018.pdf.

[58] La. Admin. Code tit. 61, pt. V, § 101F.1.d.

[59] La. Att'y. Gen. Op. No. 07-0004 (La.A.G.), 2007 WL 1697039.

[60] D.C. Code Ann. § 47-863(a)(1A)(A)(iii) (West 2021); Instructions for Form ASD-100, Homestead Deduction and Senior Citizen/Disabled Property Tax Relief Application, D.C., https://otr.cfo.dc.gov/publication/otr-fp-100-homestead-deduction-senior-citizen-and-disabled-property-tax-relief-application-1.

A final way in which state and local laws restrict heirs from accessing property tax reduction programs exists in Mississippi, where an heir with a co-ownership interest obtained through intestacy can obtain a 100 percent exemption instead of a partial exemption, but only if all the heirs (whether occupying or not) sign an affidavit authorizing the filing of one homestead exemption.[61] This requirement can impose an especially high barrier for heirs who have inherited their property across multiple generations and are thus less likely to know the names of all the cotenants, much less how to contact them.

C. Application Barriers

Heirs also face barriers navigating the application processes for obtaining a homestead exemption. Homestead exemptions and many other property tax relief programs typically require a homeowner to affirmatively apply for the program. Homeowners who purchase their homes often receive assistance with completing the application form at the closing and with the submission of the form by their closing agent.[62] In contrast, when someone inherits their home, they are far less likely to receive guidance on how to qualify for these tax savings.

Even homeowners who are eligible for various property tax relief protections—especially those who are lower-income, Black, or Latino—often do not access these protections due to the lack of awareness about the protections and complex application requirements. One study found that 40 percent of older homeowners with a home equity conversion mortgage loan did not participate in a senior citizen homestead program they were otherwise qualified for, with Black and Hispanic homeowners less likely overall than white homeowners to have an exemption.[63] Another study found that only 11.9 percent of eligible homeowners in Detroit applied for the state's Homeowners Property Tax Assistance Program, in part because of the program's complex application requirements.[64] Heirs without record title face additional application barriers in jurisdictions that allow for alternative documentation of ownership but do not provide easily accessible guidance on the types of documentation the heir can submit with the application to qualify for the tax relief program.

D. Impacts on Black and Latino Homeowners

Research using property tax data from Texas's largest counties underscores the disparate impacts that exclusionary homestead exemption policies have on Black and Latino homeowners. The State of Texas and local taxing jurisdictions provide significant property tax relief to qualifying homesteads, especially those owned by senior citizens. In particular, homeowners sixty-five or older with a senior

---

[61] 35 Miss. Code R. § 6-03-06-103.01 (LexisNexis 2021). The affidavit that must be submitted is contained in Form 72-049, available at https://www.dor.ms.gov/Forms/72049%20Election%20Form.doc.

[62] Howlett, *supra* note 42, at 34, 38, https://www.dcbar.org/getmedia/6b3931e5-4969-4dcc-87cd-a7de75b09df0/Washington-LawyerMarch2014.pdf.

[63] Miller, Nikaj, & Lee, *supra* note 35 at 26, 29, 32.

[64] Alexa Eisenberg et al., *Preventing Owner-Occupied Property Tax Foreclosures in Detroit: Improving Access to the Poverty Tax Reduction* 2 (Poverty Solutions, University of Michigan Research Report) Dec. 2018, https://poverty.umich.edu/files/2018/12/PovertySolutions-PoveryTaxExemption-PolicyReport-r2.pdf.

homestead exemption receive large deductions off their appraised value, as well as a 100 percent tax cap on school district property taxes and, in some jurisdictions, a 100 percent tax cap on city and county property taxes. A Texas law that went fully into effect in 2020, which I drafted with my law students at The University of Texas School of Law, provides heirs' property homeowners with full access to these tax relief programs, but for heirs to qualify they must first file additional paperwork with their county appraisal district.[65] Thousands of heirs have not yet filed this paperwork and remain without a homestead exemption or only a partial exemption in Texas.

From 2019 to 2021, I led a team that analyzed local appraisal district data from Harris, Bexar, Dallas, Travis, and Tarrant Counties to identify the location of more than 10,000 inherited properties with single-family homes that are likely owner-occupied and either have no homestead exemption or have a partial exemption—using only those records where the property tax bill is sent to the home address.[66] In all five counties, these properties, where they could be identified, are highly concentrated in communities of color.

In Dallas County, for example, of the county's 4,698 heirs' properties we identified and estimated to be owner-occupied, 3,577 properties have no homestead exemption and approximately 300 properties have a partial exemption. As shown in figure 8.1, available at http://ambar.org/heirs-property-supplement, these properties are concentrated in the urban core of Dallas in older communities of color. And in Tarrant County, where Fort Worth is located, of the county's 1,736 heirs' properties we identified and estimated to be owner-occupied, 1,463 have no homestead exemption. These properties are similarly concentrated in older communities of color. See figure 8.2, also available at http://ambar.org/heirs-property-supplement.

Our team also examined the financial impacts of excluding heirs' property homeowners from the full benefits of the homestead exemption in Texas and how the state's exclusionary policies have saddled heirs' property homeowners in Black and Latino communities with higher property tax burdens, further hampering their housing security. Some examples of these impacts are provided here.

One of the neighborhoods in Dallas we examined is the Cedar Crest neighborhood—a majority-Black neighborhood and one of the few neighborhoods where Black families could purchase homes in Dallas in the 1950s and 1960s.[67] The neighborhood also has one of the city's highest concentrations of heirs' property homesteads lacking a 100 percent homestead exemption. The neighborhood

---

[65] S. B. 1943, 86th Leg., Reg. Sess. (Tex. 2019); *see also* Entrepreneurship and Community Development Clinic, The University of Texas School of Law, *Inherited Homesteads and Increased Access to the Texas Homestead Exemption Under Senate Bill* 1943, 5 (2020), https://law.utexas.edu/wp-content/uploads/sites/11/2020/08/2020-ECDC-HomesteadAppraisal-Districts.pdf.

[66] In identifying heirs' properties that are likely owner-occupied, we assumed that all of the properties in our dataset with a partial homestead exemption are owner-occupied, since a home does not qualify for a partial or full homestead exemption in Texas unless it is the applicant's primary residence. In contrast, an heirs' property without a homestead exemption is not necessarily owner-occupied—it could be vacant or a rental property. To better target only those heirs' properties that are owner-occupied, we excluded from our dataset those properties where the tax bill is sent to a different property address. For instance, with single-family rental properties, the tax bill is typically sent to the landlord's mailing address and not the rental property address. Nonetheless, our methodology in this initial round of research likely captured at least some heirs' properties that are vacant. Additional, more in-depth research is needed to determine more precisely how many of the heirs' properties without a homestead exemption in our totals are owner-occupied. Future opportunities for research also include quantifying the impacts of exclusionary homestead exemption policies on Black and Latino heirs in states other than Texas.

[67] *See* Olivia Mars & Maggie Kelleher, *Cedar Crest Neighborhood Has Been Home to Generations of Local Leaders in Dallas*, Dallas Morning News (Feb. 28, 2021), https://www.dallasnews.com/news/2021/02/28/cedar-crest-neighborhood-has-been-home-to-generations-of-local-black-leaders-in-dallas/.

has been gentrifying, with rapidly rising land values, resulting in mounting property tax burdens and additional financial strain on heirs' property homeowners.

Among the heirs' property homeowners with a partial homestead exemption in Cedar Crest is a senior citizen who holds a 15 percent cotenancy interest in her homestead, which has nearly doubled in market value since 2010.[68] Because of her 15 percent cotenancy interest, when this homeowner qualified for a senior homestead exemption on her home several years ago, the exemption was limited to 15 percent. With the partial exemption, the 2020 property tax bill on her homestead was $2,117, whereas, with a 100 percent senior homestead exemption, the property tax bill would have been $11. Lacking a 100 percent exemption and the large property tax savings that come with the full exemption, the heir and her relatives who co-own the property have fallen behind on paying property taxes. As of 2021, four years of property tax debt on the homestead, together with interest and penalties, had grown to $7,913. With the ongoing gentrification pressures in the area, the property tax assessments will continue to grow unless the heir obtains a 100 percent senior homestead exemption and the senior property tax cap that comes with the exemption.

As another example, in Bexar County (where San Antonio is located), we honed in on the tax savings that senior citizens with inherited homesteads and a cotenancy interest lose as a result of having a partial homestead exemption. These homeowners are highly concentrated in low-income communities of color in and near the urban core of San Antonio. See figure 8.3, available at http://ambar.org/heirs-property-supplement. In 2020, these homeowners' property tax bills were, on average, $1,157 higher than they would have been with a 100 percent exemption.[69] Many of these heirs' property homeowners reside in gentrifying neighborhoods with rapidly rising property values where, without access to the full benefits that come with Texas' senior homestead exemption, they will be saddled with escalating property tax burdens in the coming years.

Example of property tax impacts on an heirs' property homeowner in San Antonio	
Location: Tobin Hill neighborhood (gentrifying, predominantly Hispanic/Latino neighborhood near downtown)	
Appraised value of homestead (2020)	$150,580
Homeowner's cotenancy interest	22%
Actual 2020 property tax bill	$3,450
2020 property tax bill if property had a 100 percent homestead exemption	$704
Lost annual property tax savings	$2,746

[68] Based on the appraised values listed in the Dallas Central Appraisal District's records for the property for 2010 and 2020.

[69] Based on a random sampling of likely heirs' property homeowners with a partial homestead exemption in Bexar County, using 2020 appraisal data provided by the Bexar County Appraisal District and online records from the Bexar County Tax Assessor Office. Heirs' property ownership was estimated by including only those homes with an affidavit of heirship, will, death certificate, or similar documentation in the appraisal district records indicating the property was inherited.

IV. RECOMMENDED REFORMS

To increase heirs' access to property tax relief programs for homesteads, state and local policy reforms should focus on three core areas: (1) creating clear and accessible proof of ownership requirements for heirs who lack a recorded title instrument; (2) allowing heirs to access 100 percent of the property tax savings available to other homeowners by eliminating requirements that penalize owners with a cotenancy interest; and (3) increasing heirs' awareness of property tax relief programs and how to qualify for them. Although no state has fully removed the barriers that heirs face in accessing these important tax relief programs, several states have adopted reforms that significantly improve heirs' access.

A. Clear and Accessible Proof of Ownership Requirements

State and local property tax laws should provide clear and accessible standards for how homeowners can qualify for property tax relief on their principal residence when they have inherited their home and lack a recorded title instrument. To maximize access for heirs, reforms should include eliminating any requirements for heirs to have a deed or other recorded legal instrument in the heir's name for purposes of qualifying for a property tax break.

Ideally, taxing entities would accept a simple affidavit as proof of ownership for those who lack a recorded title instrument. The affidavit should be incorporated in the application form for the property tax relief program, or a template affidavit should otherwise be readily accessible via a website link in the application form.

The affidavit approach was adopted by the Texas Legislature as part of the comprehensive set of legislative reforms I helped draft in 2019 to expand heirs' access to the state's homestead exemption and other property tax relief programs for homeowners.[70] As a result of these reforms, Texas law now allows an heir to submit an affidavit to establish proof of ownership for purposes of qualifying for a homestead exemption when an heir is not specifically identified as the owner on a deed or other recorded instrument.[71] The application requirements for heirs are clearly spelled out in the instructions to the exemption application.[72]

Along with the affidavit, an heir without record title must provide a copy of the prior owner's death certificate and most recent utility bill in the heir's name and, if available, a citation of any available court records relating to the applicant's ownership interest.[73] The new Texas law explicitly prohibits county tax appraisers, which administer the exemptions, from requiring recorded title.[74] If there is more than one heir residing on the homestead property as their principal residence, these other heirs must provide an affidavit authorizing the submission of the application. This requirement

---

[70] S.B. 1943, 86th Leg., Reg. Sess. (Tex. 2019).

[71] Tex. Tax Code Ann. § 11.43(o) (West 2021). The affidavit is incorporated in a supplement to the state's homestead exemption application form, which is available via the Texas Comptroller's website. Tex. Comptroller of Pub. Accounts, Form 50-114-A, Residence Homestead Exemption Affidavits, https://comptroller.texas.gov/forms/50-114-a.pdf

[72] Tex. Comptroller of Pub. Accounts, Form 50-114, Residence Homestead Exemption, https://comptroller.texas.gov/forms/50-114.pdf.

[73] *Id.*

[74] Tex. Tax Code Ann. § 11.43(o-1) (West 2021).

was included to avoid issues that could arise if more than one heir were to file a homestead exemption application for the same homestead, since only one general homestead exemption and only one senior or disability exemption can be issued per homestead. Heirs who do not reside on the property do not have to authorize the application.

Similar to Texas, to qualify for a homestead exemption in Mississippi, state law allows for an heir to prove ownership through an affidavit, citation of a court record, or "such other evidence as may be required by the [Tax] [C]ommission."[75] The state's Department of Revenue has promulgated a simple one-page affidavit of heirship for heirs to complete in order to qualify for an exemption.[76]

An alternative, although less inclusive, approach to combat proof of ownership barriers is to provide heirs with an interim or conditional homestead exemption while the heirs go through the often lengthy and complex probate court process for obtaining a recorded title. However, this approach would only help heirs who have the resources to go through the court process.

To this end, the City of Philadelphia allows for heirs who lack clear title to qualify for a conditional homestead exemption for three years. If a deed with the heir's name is not recorded within three years, the exemption is revoked—although not retroactively, only for future tax years. The application requirements for a conditional homestead exemption are fairly easy for an heir to meet: An heir must submit two forms of identification or proof of address, choosing from a list of acceptable documents, which includes a voter registration card, a utility bill, and a government-issued ID.[77] The city also supports a "Tangled Title Fund," which is operated by a local legal aid organization, to assist homeowners in securing recorded title.[78]

B. Full Access to Property Tax Savings

To further improve heirs' access to property tax relief programs for homesteads, state and local legal reforms should focus on removing the barriers discussed in section III that restrict an heir from obtaining full access to property tax savings otherwise available to a homeowner but for the heir's cotenancy interest. First, this means reforming laws, such as those in Louisiana, Kentucky, Florida, Oklahoma, and South Carolina, that lower the amount of the exemption that the heirs and other cotenants can access when the ownership interest of the occupying cotenants is less than 100 percent. The heirs should be able to access 100 percent of the homestead exemption despite their fractional ownership interest. For instance, under the example in section III for Kentucky, an elderly homeowner in Kentucky with a 20 percent cotenancy heirship interest in their homestead should be able

[75] Miss. Code Ann. § 27-33-17(f) (West 2013).

[76] Miss. Dep't of Revenue, Exemptions & Pub. Utils. Bureau, Form 72-048: Affidavit of heirship (Nov. 2011). In our research, it was unclear the extent to which the Mississippi statute was being followed at the local level and whether heirs were able to easily access the information and forms they needed to qualify for a homestead exemption. Neither the affidavit nor information about the affidavit was available on any of the county tax assessor websites we reviewed.

[77] *Property, Lots & Housing*, City of Phila. Off. of Prop. Assessment, https://www.phila.gov/services/property-lots-housing/property-taxes/get-real-estate-tax-relief/get-the-homestead-exemption/ (last updated Jan. 6, 2021).

[78] *Tangled Title Fund*, Phila. VIP, https://www.phillyvip.org/tangled-title-fund/ (last accessed Jan. 23, 2021).

to access the state's full $39,300 homestead exemption rather than the pro rata exemption of $18,000 provided for under current law for a home assessed at $90,000.[79]

Relatedly, this means reforming the Homestead Deduction and Senior Citizen/Disabled Property Tax Relief program in Washington, D.C., which requires an occupying heir who is a senior citizen or has a disability to have at least a 50 percent ownership interest in the property in order to qualify for the program.[80] An occupying heir should be able to access 100 percent of the property tax savings offered to homeowners, regardless of the heir's co-ownership interest.

Second, removing these barriers means reforming laws, such as those in North Carolina, California, and New York, that require every heir—even those heirs not residing on the homestead—to meet the property tax saving program's eligibility criteria. Only the heir applying for the property tax savings program should have to meet the program's age, disability, and permanent residency requirement. And any income limits for the program should apply only to the household members living in the homestead. The income of heirs residing elsewhere should not be considered.

Third, reforms should allow heirs who reside on the property to qualify for 100 percent of a homestead exemption and other property tax relief programs without having to obtain the written permission of the nonoccupant heirs. As noted in section III, among the states that allow an occupying heir to claim a 100 percent exemption, Mississippi bars an heir from obtaining a full homestead exemption unless all the heirs, including nonoccupant heirs, sign off on the exemption. This requirement is particularly problematic for an heir whose homestead has passed down via intestacy across multiple generations, which means there could be dozens or even hundreds of heirs that have to be first identified and then located in order to secure their written authorization.

A final consideration when drafting reforms is to make sure that the non-occupant heirs are still allowed to claim a homestead exemption on a residence they own and occupy as their primary residence. In Texas, for example, state law limits a person from receiving more than one residence homestead exemption in the same year.[81] To avoid the risk of the nonoccupant heirs being denied a homestead exemption on their primary residences under this law—because of their co-ownership interest in an inherited property receiving a homestead exemption—the Texas legislation we drafted clarifies that the heirs' property owner who qualifies a parcel of heirs' property as the person's residence homestead is considered the sole recipient of the homestead exemption for purposes of the nonoccupant heirs qualifying for an exemption on their separate homesteads.[82]

A number of states already have laws on the books that provide heirs, as well as nonheir cotenants, with full access to one or more programs providing property tax savings on homesteads,

---

[79] As described in section III, if an heirs' property homeowner in Kentucky who is a senior citizen or person with a qualifying disability obtains a homestead exemption, the exemption is limited to the lower of $39,300 or the assessed value of the heir's co-ownership interest in the property. Ky. Rev. Stat. Ann. § 132.810(2)(f) (West 2021). As a result, an occupying heir with a 20 percent cotenancy interest in a home assessed at $90,000 is eligible for a homestead exemption of only $18,000 (20 percent of $90,000).

[80] D.C. Code Ann. § 47-863(a)(1A)(A)(iii) (West 2021); Form ASD-100, Homestead Deduction and Senior Citizen/Disabled Property Tax Relief Application, D.C., https://otr.cfo.dc.gov/publication/otr-fp-100-homestead-deduction-senior-citizen-and-disabled-property-tax-relief-application-1.

[81] Tex. Tax Code Ann. § 11.13(h) (West 2021).

[82] S.B. 1943, 86th Leg., Reg. Sess. (Tex. 2019) (Section 3, amending Section 11.13 of the Texas Tax Code).

regardless of the homeowner's cotenancy interest.[83] These states include Alabama (homestead exemption and assessment ratio),[84] Arkansas (homestead credit),[85] Georgia (homestead exemption),[86] Maine (homestead exemption),[87] Maryland (homestead credit),[88] Michigan (homestead exemption),[89] Missouri (homestead credit),[90] and Ohio (homestead exemption).[91] See annex A for a summary of state access policies from our study. The 2019 legislative reforms in Texas, discussed earlier, also provide heirs with full access to the residence homestead exemption and related property tax savings for homesteads. However, unlike these other states, cotenants in Texas who are not heirs are ineligible for a 100 percent homestead exemption. Furthermore, under the reforms, heirs with a Texas homestead exemption awarded prior to 2020 must submit additional paperwork to qualify for full access to the homestead exemption. [92]

C. Improved Awareness of Property Tax Savings Programs for Homesteads

A final set of reforms should focus on improving heirs' property homeowners' awareness of property tax savings programs for homesteads and how heirs can qualify for them. States, cities, foundations, universities, and other institutions can increase heirs' awareness and thus participation in these programs by supporting targeted outreach and community education in older communities of color that likely contain heirs' property. In some jurisdictions, local tax exemption data can be utilized to help target likely owner-occupied heirs' property that does not have a homestead exemption or has only a partial exemption. Taxing entities can also help improve heirs' access to property tax relief programs by including clear instructions for heirs about the programs on the taxing entities' websites and in their property tax relief application forms.

Finally, it is critical that taxing entities' frontline staff are educated about any laws that help heirs qualify for property tax savings on their homesteads. Almost a year after the enactment of legal reforms in Texas allowing heirs to qualify for a homestead exemption with an unrecorded affidavit, more than 76 percent of the local appraisal districts (which administer homestead exemptions)

---

[83] In most of these states, heirs are still barred from accessing these tax savings when they lack record title to their homestead. See annex A for a list of these states from our study.

[84] E-mail from Leigh Ann Fair, Chief Tax Assessor, Tuscaloosa County (Jan. 6, 2021) (on file with author).

[85] Telephone Interview with Elizabeth Dussex, Assessor, Pulaski County Assessor's Office (Jan 21, 2021).

[86] GA. CODE ANN. § 48-5-40(3)(H) (West 2020).

[87] E-mail from Christopher Huff, City Tax Assessor, City of Portland, Maine, to Ruthie Goldstein (June 9, 2020) (on file with author).

[88] E-mail from Homestead Tax Credit Div., Md. Dep't of Assessments & Tax'n, to Ruthie Goldstein (Aug. 28, 2020) (on file with author).

[89] E-mail from Christopher Mida, Prop. Servs. Div., Mich. Dep't of Treasury, to Ruthie Goldstein (June 22, 2020) (on file with author).

[90] E-mail from Mary Kirkweg, Revenue Processing Technician II, Income Tax Correspondence Sec., Mo. Dept. of Revenue, to Ruthie Goldstein (June 25, 2020) (on file with author).

[91] E-mail from Matthew T. Hollis, Div. Counsel, Div. of Tax Equalization, Ohio Dep't of Tax'n, to Ruthie Goldstein (June 12,2020) (on file with author); OHIO DEP'T OF TAX'N, BULL. 23: HOMESTEAD EXEMPTION FOR THE AGED, DISABLED, AND SURVIVING SPOUSE 18 (2010), https://www.tax.ohio.gov/portals/0/government/bulletin23_homestead_revised_10-2010.pdf.

[92] For a summary of the 2019 Texas statutory amendments, *see* Entrepreneurship and Community Development Clinic, *supra* note 65. Since cotenants in Texas are each responsible for 100 percent of the tax liability on their real property, providing a 100 percent homestead exemption on a homestead also benefits the nonoccupant heirs.

that were contacted in a survey I led with law students said they require heirs to have a deed or other recorded title instrument to qualify for a homestead exemption. In our study of other state homestead exemption policies, we also talked to many frontline staff with taxing entities who were unaware of the different types of proof of ownership documentation an heirs' property owner could provide under state law beyond a deed, if any, to qualify for a homestead exemption.[93] Ongoing education of taxing entities' staff will help remove their lack of awareness and misconceptions.

V. CONCLUSION

In the United States, Black and Latino family wealth is a staggering 13 percent and 19 percent, respectively, of white family wealth.[94] Property tax relief programs—by completely or partially excluding homeowners who reside on heirs' property—contribute to this persistent racial and ethnic wealth gap. Eligibility barriers such as recorded title requirements and laws that bar cotenants from accessing a full homestead exemption disparately impact Black and Latino homeowners, saddling them with excessive property tax burdens and further hampering their housing stability. Through fairly simple legal reforms, coupled with community education and better training of taxing entities' staff, state and local governments can eliminate these discriminatory policies, thereby lowering the property tax burdens and improving the housing security for potentially hundreds of thousands of Black and Latino homeowners residing on heirs' property across the country.

---

[93] For example, the Clark County Tax Assessor office in Indiana told us that a homeowner needs to have a deed in their name to qualify for the homestead exemption and assessment cap, whereas Indiana law allows for the filing of an affidavit. In contrast, the Decatur County Tax Assessor's office in Indiana was not sure of the titling requirements for heirs but said a notarized affidavit might be okay.

[94] Neil Bhutta, et al., *Disparities in Wealth by Race and Ethnicity in the 2019 Survey of Consumer Finances,* FEDS Notes (Sept. 28, 2020), https://www.federalreserve.gov/econres/notes/feds-notes/disparities-in-wealth-by-race-and-ethnicity-in-the-2019-survey-of-consumer-finances-20200928.htm.

Annex 8A

Survey of State Property Tax Relief Laws and Their Exclusionary Impacts on Heirs' Property Owners (23 States and the District of Columbia)

State	Proof of Ownership Requirements for Heirs[1]	Access Level by Cotenants[2]
Alabama	Homestead exemptions and 10% assessment ratio: Varying requirements at local level for types of proof accepted for heirs' property; several counties require a deed or other legal instrument conveying the property to the applicant.[3]	A cotenant qualifies for 100% of the state's homestead exemptions and the state's 10% assessment ratio.[4]

[1] This column summarizes what type of documentation is required for an heir, other than a spouse, to establish proof of ownership in order to qualify for a state's property tax relief programs for homesteads, with a focus on ownership interests transferred via the state's intestacy laws without a legal paper trail. The particular property tax relief programs we examined for this purpose are indicated here.

[2] This column summarizes the extent to which, under state laws and the policies of local taxing entities, a homeowner with a cotenancy interest in their primary residence is completely or partially barred from qualifying for the same level of property tax relief for homesteads available to homeowners without a fractionated ownership interest. The particular property tax relief programs we examined for this purpose are indicated here. The summaries here assume that only one of the cotenants occupies the homestead as their primary residence, with the other cotenants residing elsewhere.

[3] *See, e.g.*, Telephone interview with Theresa, Bibb County Courthouse (Jan. 21, 2021) (reporting that an heir without record title needs to see an attorney to draw up a deed to qualify for the homestead exemption); *Homestead Exemption Information*, Madison County Ala. (Aug. 2018), https://www.madisoncountyal.gov/departments/tax-assessor/homestead-exemptions (stating that a deed is required for the homestead exemption).

[4] E-mail from Leigh Ann Fair, chief tax assessor, Tuscaloosa County (Jan. 6, 2021) (on file with author).

State	Proof of Ownership Requirements for Heirs	Access Level by Cotenants
Arkansas	Homestead tax credit and assessment caps: Varying requirements at local level for types of proof accepted when heirs' property; several counties require a deed or other legal instrument establishing applicant's ownership.[5]	A cotenant qualifies for 100% of the state's homestead tax credit.[6]
California	Homestead exemptions and property tax deferral: Applicant must be listed on the deed to the property.[7]	A cotenant qualifies for the state's property tax deferral program only if all record title owners qualify for the deferral, not including spouses, domestic partners, and "direct-line relatives."[8]
District of Columbia	Homestead exemptions, property tax deferral, assessment cap, and tax credit: Applicant must be listed on the deed to the property.[9]	To qualify for the District's Homestead Deduction and Senior Citizen/Disabled Property Tax Relief program, a cotenant must have at least a 50% ownership interest in the property.[10] A cotenant with less than a 50% interest is disqualified from the program, while cotenants with a 50% or greater interest receive full access to the program.
Florida	Homestead exemptions and assessment cap: State law requires a deed or other recorded legal instrument conveying the property to the applicant.[11]	A cotenant qualifies for a partial homestead exemption.[12] The state's Save Our Homes assessment cap is apportioned based on the cotenant's ownership percentage.[13]

[5] *See, e.g.*, Telephone interview with Elizabeth Dussex, assessor, Pulaski County Assessor's Off. (Jan. 21, 2021) (reporting that an heir must have a legal transactional document in the heir's name, typically a deed or purchase agreement, to prove ownership in order to access the homestead credit or cap on assessed value); Telephone interview with Robin, Jefferson County Assessor's Off. (Jan. 21, 2021) (reporting that an heir must have a deed to qualify for the homestead credit).

[6] Telephone interview with Elizabeth Dussex, Assessor, Pulaski County Assessor's Office (Jan 21, 2021).

[7] Betty T. Yee, *Property Tax Postponement Application and Instructions for Senior, Blind, or Disabled Citizens*, CAL. ST. CONTROLLER'S OFF., https://sco.ca.gov/Files-ARD-Tax-Info/ptp_ApplicationPackage.pdf (stating that a deed is required for the deferral). *See also* telephone interview with Maria Karrillo, intermediate clerk, L.A. County Assessor's Off. (Jan. 21, 2021) (reporting that a deed is required for the homeowner's exemption).

[8] *Id.* ("Direct-line relatives" are defined to include children, parents, and grandchildren; cousins are not included).

[9] D.C. CODE ANN. § 47-802(5)(A) (West 2020) (defining owner, for purposes of qualifying for various property tax reductions as "[a]n owner of record of real property"); e-mail from Steven Skowron, Homestead Unit, Office of Tax and Revenue, District of Columbia, to Ruthie Goldstein (June 17, 2020) (on file with author) ("[T]o be eligible for the homestead benefit you must be a deeded owner . . .").

[10] D.C. CODE § 47-863(a)(1A)(iii)(I) (West 2021); FORM ASD-100, HOMESTEAD DEDUCTION AND SENIOR CITIZEN/DISABLED PROPERTY TAX RELIEF APPLICATION, DISTRICT OF COLUMBIA, https://otr.cfo.dc.gov/publication/otr-fp-100-homestead-deduction-senior-citizen-and-disabled-property-tax-relief-application-1.

[11] FLA. STAT. § 196.031(1)(a) (West 2020) ("Before such [homestead] exemption may be granted, the deed or instrument shall be recorded in the official records of the county in which the property is located. The property appraiser may request the applicant to provide additional ownership documents to establish title."). *See also* telephone interview with Alex Luca, staff attorney, Pinellas County Property Appraiser's Office (Jan 21, 2021) (reporting that an applicant needs a recorded legal instrument in the applicant's name to qualify for a homestead exemption).

[12] FLA. ADMIN. CODE ANN. R. 12D-7.012(6)(a) (2020).

[13] Telephone interview with Alex Luca, staff attorney, Pinellas County Property Appraiser's Office (Jan 21, 2021).

State	Proof of Ownership Requirements for Heirs	Access Level by Cotenants
Georgia	Homestead exemptions: State law requires the applicant to be listed on the deed.[14]	A cotenant qualifies for 100% of the state's homestead exemption programs.[15]
Idaho	Homestead exemption and tax deferral: Varying requirements at local level for types of proof accepted when heirs' property; several counties require a deed conveying the property to the applicant.[16]	The state's property tax credit and homestead exemption programs are applied in proportion to the cotenant's ownership interest.[17]
Indiana	Homestead exemptions and assessment cap: Heirs can qualify under state law by filing an affidavit of heirship with the county tax auditor and recording the affidavit in the real property records.[18] However, at least one county tax assessor office requires a deed conveying the property to the applicant.[19]	A cotenant qualifies for the full homestead exemption for low-income seniors only if the combined income of all the cotenants falls below the income cap. If one or more of the cotenants is younger than 65, then the exemption is applied in proportion to the qualifying cotenants' ownership interest.[20]
Kentucky	Homestead exemption: State law does not require recorded title,[21] but the local tax assessor offices contacted require a deed conveying the property to the applicant.[22]	The homestead exemption for seniors and persons with disabilities is capped for cotenants by the amount of the cotenant's assessed value interest in the property.[23]

[14] Ga. Code Ann. § 48-5-40(3)(M) (West 2020); Fulton Cnty, Fulton County 2021 Homestead Exemption Guide 2 (2021), https://fultonassessor.org/wp-content/uploads/sites/16/2021/05/2021-Fulton-County-Homestead-Exemption-Guide-05-07-21.pdf [https://perma.cc/SD32-9P7X] ("The person applying for the homestead exemption must be listed on the deed."). *See also* telephone interview with Sheryl, Homestead Exemption Div., Fulton County Bd. Assessors (Jan. 21, 2021) (reporting that "[t]he only proof of ownership in Georgia is a deed.").

[15] Ga. Code Ann. § 48-5-40(3)(H) (West 2020).

[16] *See, e.g.*, telephone interview with Lisa Abraham, Canyon County Assessor's Off. (Jan. 21, 2021) (reporting that an heir must have a deed to qualify for the homeowner's exemption or deferral); telephone interview with Lacy Stanger, Bonneville County Assessor's Off. (Jan. 21, 2021) (stating that an heir must have a deed to qualify for the homeowner's exemption).

[17] Idaho Code § 63-701(7) (2020). Idaho Code § 63-602G(2)(d), § 63-701(7) (2020).

[18] Ind. Code § 6-1.1-5-7 (2020).

[19] *See, e.g.*, telephone interview with Laura, Clark County Assessor Off. (Jan. 21, 2021) (reporting that an heir's name needs to be on the deed to qualify for the homestead exemption and assessment cap).

[20] Ind. Code §§ 6-1.1-12-9(a)(2), (h) (2020).

[21] Ky. Rev. Stat. Ann. § 132.810(2)(f) (West 2021).

[22] *See, e.g.*, telephone interview with Scott Bruce, deputy, field specialist, Grant County Property Value Administration (PVA; Jan. 21, 2021) (reporting that an heir must have a deed to qualify for the homestead exemption; there is no alternative way to qualify); telephone interview with Ronisha, Property Taxes, Jefferson County Tax Off. (Jan. 21, 2021) (reporting that an heir must have a deed to prove ownership for the homestead exemption). *See also The Homestead Exemption for Persons 65 Years of Age and Over*, Davies Cnty Ky. PVA, https://daviesskypva.org/exemptions.html ("The applicant for thise [sic] exemption must be the recorded owner of the property as of January 1st . . .").

[23] Ky. Rev. Stat. Ann. § 132.810(3)(f) (West 2020).

State	Proof of Ownership Requirements for Heirs	Access Level by Cotenants
Louisiana	Homestead exemptions: Varying requirements at local level for types of proof accepted for heirs' property, with several parish tax assessors requiring a deed or other recorded legal instrument establishing applicant's ownership.[24]	A cotenant qualifies for a partial homestead exemption in proportion to the cotenant's ownership interest.[25] The state's assessment freeze for low-income homeowners who are seniors or disabled is applied only to the cotenant's pro rata ownership interest.[26]
Maine	Homestead exemptions and credits: Varying requirements at local level for types of proof accepted for heirs' property; a deed in applicant's name is typically required, although some jurisdictions accept probate documents.[27]	A cotenant qualifies for 100% of the state's homestead exemptions.[28]
Maryland	Homestead credit and assessment cap: The state requires a deed or other recorded legal instrument conveying the property to the applicant.[29]	A cotenant qualifies for 100% of the state's homestead credit.[30]
Michigan	Homestead exemptions: The state requires the applicant's name on a recorded deed, will or trust, or probate court papers.[31]	A cotenant qualifies for 100% of the state's homestead exemptions and the Property Tax Fairness Credit for low-income homeowners.[32]

[24] *See, e.g.*, telephone interview with Leanna, deputy assessor, Lafayette Parish Assessor's Office (Jan. 21, 2021) (reporting that a legal document recorded in the clerk of court's office is required, but it does not have to be a deed); telephone interview with Rose Armant, serv. rep., Orleans Par. Assessor's Off. (Jan. 21, 2021) (reporting an unfamiliarity with the proof of ownership requirements for a homestead when there is not a deed or will). *See also Homestead Exemption*, JEFFERSON PAR. LA., https://www.jpassessor.com/resources/homestead-exemption (homestead exemption applicant should bring a "recorded copy" of the applicant's act of sale for the property).

[25] LA. ADMIN. CODE tit. 61, Pt V, § 101 (2020); La. Const. art. VII, § 20.

[26] 97 La. Att'y Gen. Op. No. 07-0004. (May 16, 2007).

[27] *See, e.g.*, e-mail from Christopher Huff, city tax assessor, City of Portland, Maine, to Ruthie Goldstein (June 9, 2020) (on file with author) ("A deed or trust document is what we would require for proof of ownership. We would accept a probate document if it made clear the real estate being conveyed per wishes of a will or estate."); telephone interview with Adriana, deed and recording specialist, City of Lewiston Assessor's Dep't (Jan. 21, 2021) (reporting that an heir must go through the probate process to be eligible for the homestead exemption).

[28] E-mail from Christopher Huff, city tax assessor, City of Portland, Maine, to Ruthie Goldstein (June 9, 2020) (on file with author).

[29] E-mail from Homestead Tax Credit Div., Md. Dep't Assessments & Tax'n, to Ruthie Goldstein (Aug. 28, 2020) (on file with author) ("In Maryland we go by the land records so if there is no deed to reflect that person's name then they have no legal interest in the home. If there is a will that leaves the home to someone upon the death of the owner that person just has to have the deed updated to reflect their name.").

[30] *Id.*

[31] E-mail from Christopher Mida, Prop. Servs. Div., Mich. Dep't Treasury, to Ruthie Goldstein (June 22, 2020) (on file with author).

[32] *Id.*

State	Proof of Ownership Requirements for Heirs	Access Level by Cotenants
Mississippi	Homestead exemption: The state allows for heirs to file an affidavit[33] and has promulgated a form affidavit for this purpose.[34] Several local tax assessor websites state that a deed is required or fail to mention the affidavit option for heirs.[35]	A cotenant qualifies for 100% of the state's homestead exemption as long as the cotenancy interest was inherited and all the other cotenants sign an affidavit authoring the cotenant to apply for an exemption on the entire homestead.[36]
Missouri	Property tax credit: As a general rule, the state requires a deed or other legal instrument conveying the property to the applicant, although on a case-by-case basis an applicant may be able to qualify with other documentation.[37]	A cotenant can access 100% of the state's property tax credit for homesteads as long as the cotenant pays 100% of the taxes. The credit is prorated based on the percentage of the taxes that the cotenant pays.[38]
New Mexico	Homestead exemptions: Varying requirements at the local level for types of proof accepted for heirs' property; several county assessor offices require a deed or other recorded legal instrument conveying the property to the applicant.[39]	A cotenant can access 100% of the Head of Household exemption.[40]
New York	Homestead exemptions: The state and local taxing jurisdictions require that the applicant's name be listed on a recorded deed, mortgage, or other legal instrument conveying title to the applicant.[41]	To qualify for the local-option Senior Citizen Homeowners' Exemption, (1) all cotenants must occupy the property as their primary residence, (2) all the cotenants other than the siblings and a

[33] Miss. Code Ann. § 27-33-17(f) (West 2013).

[34] Miss. Dep't of Revenue, Exemptions & Pub. Utils. Bureau, Form 72-048: Affidavit of heirship (Nov. 2011).

[35] *See, e.g., Homestead Exemption*, Harrison Cnty Tax Assessors, http://co.harrison.ms.us/elected/taxassessor/homestead.asp (last visited Jan. 23, 2021) (an applicant applying for a homestead exemption must have a "[r]ecorded Warranty Deed to property or other recorded document proving ownership to the property"); *How Do I?: File for Homestead Exemption*, Lafayette Cnty, https://lafayettems.com/how-do-i/how-do-i-file-for-homestead-exemption/ (last visited Jan. 23, 2021) (when filing for a homestead exemption, applicants must provide a "[c]opy of the warranty deed").

[36] Miss. Code Ann. § 27-33-17 (West 2013).

[37] Telephone interview with Kevin Bateman, revenue processing technician II, Mo. Dept. of Revenue (Feb. 4, 2021). *See also* Mo. Tax Credit Programs, https://www.showmeboone.com/assessor/tax-relief/ (last visited July 23, 2021) ("[The] County records should demonstrate that the Applicant [for the Missouri Property Tax Credit] is the owner of the homestead.").

[38] E-mail from Mary Kirkweg, revenue processing technician II, Income Tax Correspondence Sec., Mo. Dept. of Revenue, to Ruthie Goldstein (June 25, 2020) (on file with author).

[39] Telephone interview with Clyde Ward, chief of staff, Bernalillo County Assessor's Off. (Jan. 22, 2021) (reporting that an heir applying for a homestead exemption cannot qualify unless the deed shows that the property was legally conveyed to the applicant).

[40] *Id.*

[41] *See, e.g., Senior Citizens Exemption*, N.Y. State Dep't of Tax'n & Fin., https://www.tax.ny.gov/pit/property/exemption/seniorexempt.htm (last visited Jan. 28, 2021) (an applicant for the senior citizen exemption "can prove ownership by submitting a certified copy of the deed, mortgage, or other instrument by which you became owner of the property"); City of Rochester Bureau of Assessment, Senior Citizen's Property Tax Exemption Questions & Answers (2016), http://www.cityofrochester.gov/WorkArea/DownloadAsset.aspx?id=8589965745 (to qualify for the senior citizen exemption, "[y]ou may be required to prove ownership by submitting a recorded copy of the deed, mortgage or other instrument by which you became the owner of the property."). With advocacy, an exemption can sometimes be obtained with alternative proof of ownership. E-mail from K. Scott Kohanowski, Director, Homeowner Stability and LGBT Advocacy Projects, City Bar Justice Center, to Heather Way (Dec. 9, 2020) (on file with author).

State	Proof of Ownership Requirements for Heirs	Access Level by Cotenants
		spouse must be 65 or older, and (3) the combined income of all the cotenants cannot exceed the eligibility cap.[42]
North Carolina	Homestead exemption and property tax deferral programs: Varying requirements at local level for types of proof accepted when heirs' property. Generally, the applicant's name must appear on the deed or other legal instrument conveying title to the applicant.[43]	To qualify for the state's circuit breaker property tax deferral program for low-income seniors and persons with disabilities, each cotenant must meet the program's income limits ($47,250 for 2021), be 65 or older or disabled, and have occupied the property as their permanent residence for at least the past five years.[44] The state's senior and disabled homestead exemptions are capped by the cotenant's proportionate share of the property's valuation.[45]
Ohio	Homestead exemption: Varying requirements at local level for types of proof accepted when heirs' property. A deed in the applicant's name is typically required, but a local taxing office may allow alternative supporting documents.[46]	A cotenant can access 100% of the state's homestead exemptions and other homestead property tax relief programs.[47]
Oklahoma	Homestead exemption and tax freeze: State law requires that the applicant be listed on a deed or other recorded legal instrument.[48]	The state's general, disabled, and senior homestead exemptions are applied in proportion to the cotenant's ownership interest.[49]

[42] N.Y. Real Prop. Tax Law § 467 (McKinney 2021); *Senior Citizen Homeowners' Exemption (SCHE)*, N.Y.C. Dep't of Fin., https://www1.nyc.gov/site/finance/benefits/landlords-sche.page (last visited Jan. 23, 2021).

[43] Telephone interview with Nick Adams, tax agent, Wake County Dept. of Tax Admin. (Jan. 21, 2021) (reporting that an heir needs a deed, certified will, or probate court documents showing transfer of title to heir); *Elderly / Exemptions*, Mecklenburg Cnty Assessor's Off., https://www.meckn c.gov/AssessorsOffice/Pages/Tax-Exclusions-Deferrals.aspx (last visited Jan. 28, 2021) ("The applicant's name must be on the deed or title to the residence.").

[44] N.C. Gen. Stat. Ann. § 105-277.1B (West 2021).

[45] N.C. Gen. Stat. Ann. § 105-277.1(e) (West 2021).

[46] E-mail from Matthew T. Hollis, div. counsel, Div. of Tax Equalization, Ohio Dep't of Tax'n, to Ruthie Goldstein (June 12, 2020) (on file with author). If there is a will governing the division of the homestead, a devisee cannot qualify for a homestead exemption until the will has been probated. *See* Ohio Dep't of Tax'n, Bull. 23: Homestead Exemption for the Aged, Disabled, and Surviving Spouse 8 (2010), https://www.tax.ohio.gov/portals/0/government/bulletin23_homestead_revised_10-2010.pdf.

[47] E-mail from Matthew T. Hollis, div. counsel, Div. of Tax Equalization, Ohio Dep't of Tax'n, to Ruthie Goldstein (June 12,2020) (on file with author); Ohio Dep't of Tax'n, Bull. 23, Homestead Exemption for the Aged, Disabled, and Surviving Spouse 18 (2010), https://www.tax.ohio.gov/portals/0/government/bulletin23_homestead_revised_10-2010.pdf.

[48] Okla. Stat. Ann. tit. 68, §§ 2888, 2892 (West 2021). *See also* Oklahoma Cnty Assessor, Homestead Exemption Filing Instructions (2021), https://assessor.oklahomacounty.org/DocumentCenter/View/100/2020-Homestead-Exemption-Form-With-Instructions-OTC-Form-921-PDF?bidId= (stating that the applicant's [o]wnership of the property must be executed on or before January 1st and recorded in the office of the County Clerk before February 1st in order to receive homestead exemption for the current year."

[49] Telephone interview with Liz Medrano, taxpayer services representative, Tulsa County Assessor's Office (Jan 22, 2021).

State	Proof of Ownership Requirements for Heirs	Access Level by Cotenants
Pennsylvania	Property tax rebate and local homestead exemptions: Applicant's name must be listed on a deed or other recorded legal instrument.[50] Philadelphia provides a conditional homestead exemption for heirs with tangled title; a deed must be provided within three years or the exemption is revoked for future tax years.[51]	For the state's property tax rebate program for low-income seniors and persons with disabilities, a cotenant's rebate is limited by the percentage of the cotenant's ownership interest.[52] In Philadelphia, a cotenant is ineligible for a homestead exemption if any of the other cotenants have claimed a homestead exemption on another residence.[53]
South Carolina	Homestead exemption, 4% assessment ratio, and school tax credit: Applicant's name must be listed on the deed or other recorded legal instrument.[54]	The state's senior and disabled homestead exemptions are limited to the percentage of the cotenant's ownership interest.[55] For the state's 4% assessment ratio, state law is unclear, with most counties applying the lower assessment ratio only to the cotenant's interest.[56] County tax offices vary in how they apply the school operating tax exemption to cotenants, with at least some counties applying the exemption in proportion to the cotenant's ownership interest in the property.[57]

[50] *See, e.g.*, PA. DEP'T OF REVENUE, FORM PA-1000 BOOKLET 05-20, PA. PROP. TAX OR RENT REBATE PROGRAM 2020, at 3, https://www.revenue.pa.gov/FormsandPublications/FormsforIndividuals/PTRR/Documents/2020_pa-1000_inst.pdf (applicant's ownership interest must be "evidenced by a contract of sale, deed, trust, or life estate"); e-mail from Off. of Tax Assessment, Dauphin County, Pa., to Ruthie Goldstein (June 10, 2020) (on file with author) (to qualify for a homestead exemption in Dauphin County, an applicant must have a deed recorded in their name.).

[51] *Property, Lots & Housing*, CITY OF PHILA. OFF. OF PROP. ASSESSMENT, https://www.phila.gov/services/property-lots-housing/property-taxes/get-real-estate-tax-relief/get-the-homestead-exemption/ (last updated Jan. 6, 2021).

[52] PA. DEP'T OF REVENUE, FORM PA-1000 SCHEDULE F/G 05-20, MULTIPLE OWNER OR LESSOR PRORATIONS/INCOME ANNUALIZATION.

[53] HOMESTEAD APPLICATION, CITY OF PHILA., https://www.phila.gov/media/20201209110344/Homestead-Exemption-application-2022-form.pdf; e-mail from Sandi Ramos, administrator of Tax Credit and Assistance Programs, City of Philadelphia (Feb. 11, 2021).

[54] *See, e.g.*, *Legal Residence*, SPARTANBURG CNTY ASSESSOR'S OFF., https://www.spartanburgcounty.org/205/Legal-Residence (last visited Jan. 28, 2021) (stating that "[t]he owner must have title (deed or will) or bond for title recorded in the Register of Deeds Office or have an equity interest (Contract for Sale)"); *Guide to Real Property and Assessment*, HORRY CNTY ASSESSOR'S OFF., https://www.horrycounty.org/Departments/Assessor/Guide-To-Assessment (last visited Jan. 28, 2021) ("The owner must have title (deed or will) or have an equity interest (contract or purchase) and the property must be occupied by the owner as his legal residence.").

[55] S.C. CODE ANN. § 12-37-250(J) (2012).

[56] S.C. CODE ANN. § 12-43-220-(c)(8)(ii) (2015); telephone interview with Amelia Rupple, supervisor, Government Services, South Carolina Dept. of Rev., (Mar. 8, 2021).

[57] Telephone interview with Amelia Rupple, supervisor, Government Services, South Carolina Dept. of Rev., Mar. 8, 2021).

State	Proof of Ownership Requirements for Heirs	Access Level by Cotenants
Texas	Homestead exemption, tax freeze, and deferral: A state law adopted in 2019 allows heirs to provide a simple affidavit, death certificate for the prior owner, and a utility bill in applicant's name; local taxing entities are barred from requiring a recorded titling instrument.[58]	A cotenant can access 100% of the state's homestead exemptions, tax freeze, tax deferral, and other tax savings if the cotenant files an updated application with the local tax appraiser designating the property as heirs' property.[59] To qualify for 100% of the savings, an heir must receive permission of all the other heirs occupying the property as their primary residence.[60]
Virginia	Homestead exemptions, tax freezes, and deferrals (local option): In cases where there is no will, Virginia law allows for an heir to establish ownership by recording an heirship affidavit, which the county clerk then sends to the local tax revenue commissioner.[61] Varying requirements at local level for types of proof accepted when heirs' property.[62]	A cotenant's eligibility for local taxing entities' senior and disability exemptions and tax deferral programs varies by local taxing jurisdiction: Limits imposed on cotenants include prorating the exemption based on the cotenant's ownership interest and requiring all the cotenants to meet the programs' eligibility requirements, including occupancy of the property.[63]

[58] TEX. TAX CODE ANN. § 11.43(o) (West 2021).

[59] TEX. TAX CODE ANN. §§ 11.13(h), 11.26, 11.261, 11.41, 33.06, 33.065 (West 2021).

[60] TEX. TAX CODE ANN. §§ 11.43(0-2) (West 2021).

[61] VA. CODE ANN. § 64.2-510 (West, Westlaw through 2021 Reg. Sess.).

[62] *See, e.g.*, RICHMOND OFF. OF THE CITY ASSESSOR, EXEMPTION APPLICATION: FOR VETERANS WITH 100% SERVICE -CONNECTED DISABILITY OR CERTAIN SURVIVING SPOUSES (Revised Apr. 14, 2015), https://www.rva.gov/sites/default /files/2019-02/form_DisabledVeteranExemptionApplication.pdf (requiring an applicant for the disabled veteran exemption to certify that their home is legally titled in their name); e-mail from Justin Nejad, manager, Tax Relief Section, Dep't of Tax Admin., Fairfax County, to Ruthie Goldstein (June 22, 2020) (on file with author) (reporting that an heir must "be able prove that they are the owner with the county court before being considered" for property tax relief).

[63] *See, e.g.*, TAX RELIEF PROGRAM, CITY OF PORTSMOUTH, VA, https://www.portsmouthva.gov/215/Tax-Relief-Program ("If the applicant is a co-owner, the exemption is prorated.") (last visited Jan. 23, 2021); 2019 FAIRFAX CNTY TAX RELIEF APPLICATION FOR SENIORS AND PEOPLE WITH DISABILITIES, FAIRFAX COUNTY, VA, https://www.fairfaxcounty.gov/taxes /sites/taxes/files/assets/documents/pdf/2019-tax-relief-application.pdf (stating that the amount of the homestead exemption for seniors and people with disabilities "shall be in proportion to the applicant's ownership interest in the property") (last visited Jan. 23, 2021); REAL ESTATE TAX RELIEF PROGRAM CITY OF ARLINGTON, VA, https://topics.arlingtonva.us/realestate /taxes-payments/real-estate-tax-relief/ (stating that to qualify for property tax relief, "all owners who have title to the property must reside in the property").

Afterword

THE UNIFORM PARTITION OF HEIRS PROPERTY ACT AND THE PATH FORWARD

It is a privilege and honor for the American Bar Association Section of State & Local Government Law to collaborate with Professor Thomas Mitchell and the authors of this book. We are grateful to Professor Mitchell for his dedication, inspiration, scholarship, and advocacy that has brought the Uniform Partition of Heirs Property Act (UPHPA) to fruition, to twenty enactments so far, and to this point in the national consciousness, and for the role he continues to play.

The UPHPA, in addition to being far more successful than almost anyone predicted it would be, in recent years has been incredibly generative of additional legal reforms and policy proposals at the state and federal levels. It also has improved national awareness about property issues that have long plagued disadvantaged communities of color and economically disadvantaged communities more generally. This awareness has developed largely due to almost 150 media articles or documentary news programs about heirs' property that were inspired by or referenced the UPHPA, including major, nationally prominent media outlets such as *The Atlanta Journal-Constitution, Mother Jones, The Nation, The New York Times, The New Yorker Magazine,* NPR, NY1 television station in New York City, ProPublica, Vice, and *The Washington Post*. In most of them, Professor Mitchell has been interviewed, almost always as the national expert on heirs' property.

The MacArthur Foundation named Professor Mitchell a MacArthur Fellow (popularly known as the MacArthur Genius Grant) for 2020 in recognition of the substantial impact his overall professional work has had in assisting disadvantaged farmers and property owners, farmers and owners who are disproportionately African American and other people of color. In 2021, he was awarded the Howard University Alumni Award for Distinguished Postgraduate Achievement, an award that Thurgood Marshall, VicePresident Kamala Harris, Zora Neal Hurston, and the civil rights icon James Farmer, Jr., among many other Howard luminaries, also have received. Further, this year, *The Journal of Black Innovation* honored Professor Mitchell as one of the 50 Most Important African-Americans in Infrastructure because protecting property rights for communities of color helps ensure a more just infrastructure system.

As Professor Mitchell has pointed out in numerous articles and this book, the UPHPA is not a silver bullet to solve all the various manifestations of heirs' property problems within the African American community and other socioeconomically disadvantaged communities in the United States, nor does it provide redress for those who have lost everything, including their property, homes, livelihood, heritage, and even lives. What we can and must do is work to bolster property rights protections for those who still have property rights and to help people and communities derive greater benefits from whatever property rights they may have, while also exploring remedies for those whose property rights have been unjustly extinguished.

We hope this book will prove to be a valuable resource for heirs' property owners and that it will provide a path forward for individuals and families and communities. We also hope the book can be drawn upon as a helpful resource by those who sponsor much-needed community legal education workshops and other legal programs for disadvantaged heirs' property owners, who often have very poor and inaccurate information about the laws impacting their ownership.

In a broader sense, for lawyers and government officials and leaders reading this book, the path forward is not linear, but we have a role to play. Although the UPHPA has been enacted in nineteen states and the United States Virgin Islands and likely will become the majority law governing partition of heirs' property parcels within just a few years, laws on the books are not self-executing. It is necessary to educate those who carry them out, starting with the existence and then the terms of the laws. As described in several chapters, long-cherished court procedures, such as standards for partition, die hard. So do administrative actions concerning title to property, even when the law has changed. Some federal policies have changed, notably the 2021 update to the Federal Emergency Management Agency's Individual Assistance Program and Policy Guide, but this is very recent.

As ABA President Reginald Turner has pointed out in the Foreword, heirs' property first came to the attention of the ABA as a result of the 2001 Associated Press articles entitled "Torn from the Land." This award-winning three-part series, written by Todd Lewan and Dolores Barclay, chronicled African American land loss, and the concluding article in the series focused on predatory partition actions. To seek ways to address the heirs' property problems the Associated Press article brought to light, the Section of Real Property, Trust and Estate Law (RPTE) formed the Property Preservation Task Force in 2002, with David Dietrich, one of the chapter authors, and later the RPTE section chair, as co-chair.

David Dietrich invited Professor Mitchell, the lead editor of this book, to join the Property Preservation Task Force and contribute his substantial expertise. In 2006, the Property Preservation Task Force submitted a proposal to the Uniform Law Commission (ULC), requesting the ULC to establish a drafting committee to develop a model state statute (a "uniform act" in the ULC's lexicon) to address partition law abuse. The ULC accepted the proposal in early 2007 and formed a drafting committee soon thereafter. The ULC appointed Professor Mitchell to serve as the reporter (the person vested with principal authority for drafting a uniform act) for the ULC's drafting committee for the UPHPA, making him just the second African American ever to serve as a reporter for a uniform act since the ULC was established in 1892. The ULC promulgated the UPHPA in 2010 and the ABA approved it for consideration by the states in 2011.

Twenty years later, the ABA Section of State & Local Government Law is committed to continuing heirs' property education and outreach, including working with young lawyers and law students, judges and court personnel, and heirs' property owners themselves, as well as the organizations that serve them. The Section's broad reach in state, regional, local, and tribal government law gives us a strong platform. Cultural changes, which underlie legal changes, are even more difficult to implement. Doing so is essential and we must reach out and talk with one another, especially with those who do not share our background or espouse our point of view, to further diversity, equity, and inclusion in our lives and our legal institutions. Because heirs' property issues are so crosscutting in terms of the race and ethnicity of heirs' property owners and the location of heirs' property in many rural and urban communities alike, the UPHPA is an important vehicle on the path forward.

Steven F. Stapleton,
Chair, ABA Section of State & Local Government Law

Erica Levine Powers,
Immediate Past Chair,
ABA Section of State & Local Government Law

Appendix A
Uniform Partition of Heirs Property Act

Drafted by the

NATIONAL CONFERENCE OF COMMISSIONERS
ON UNIFORM STATE LAWS

and by it

APPROVED AND RECOMMENDED FOR ENACTMENT
IN ALL THE STATES

at its

ANNUAL CONFERENCE
MEETING IN ITS ONE-HUNDRED-AND-NINETEENTHYEAR
IN CHICAGO, ILLINOIS
JULY 9-16, 2010

WITH PREFATORY NOTE AND COMMENTS

October 19, 2010

ABOUT ULC

The **Uniform Law Commission** (ULC), also known as National Conference of Commissioners on Uniform State Laws (NCCUSL), now in its 119th year, provides states with non-partisan, well-conceived and well-drafted legislation that brings clarity and stability to critical areas of state statutory law.

ULC members must be lawyers, qualified to practice law. They are practicing lawyers, judges, legislators and legislative staff and law professors, who have been appointed by state governments as well as the District of Columbia, Puerto Rico, and the U.S. Virgin Islands to research, draft and promote enactment of uniform state laws in areas of state law where uniformity is desirable and practical.

- ULC strengthens the federal system by providing rules and procedures that are consistent from state to state but that also reflect the diverse experience of the states.
- ULC statutes are representative of state experience, because the organization is made up of representatives from each state, appointed by state government.
- ULC keeps state law up-to-date by addressing important and timely legal issues.
- ULC's efforts reduce the need for individuals and businesses to deal with different laws as they move and do business in different states.
- ULC's work facilitates economic development and provides a legal platform for foreign entities to deal with U.S. citizens and businesses.
- Uniform Law Commissioners donate thousands of hours of their time and legal and drafting expertise every year as a public service, and receive no salary or compensation for their work.
- ULC's deliberative and uniquely open drafting process draws on the expertise of commissioners, but also utilizes input from legal experts, and advisors and observers representing the views of other legal organizations or interests that will be subject to the proposed laws.
- ULC is a state-supported organization that represents true value for the states, providing services that most states could not otherwise afford or duplicate.

DRAFTING COMMITTEE ON A UNIFORM PARTITION OF HEIRS PROPERTY ACT

The Committee appointed by and representing the National Conference of Commissioners on Uniform State Laws in drafting this Act consists of the following individuals:

ROBERT L. MCCURLEY, P.O. Box 861425, Tuscaloosa, AL 35486, *Chair*

WILLIAM R. BREETZ, Connecticut Urban Legal Initiative, University of Connecticut School of Law, Knight Hall, Room 202, 35 Elizabeth St., Hartford, CT 06105

GEORGE H. BUXTON, 31 E. Tennessee Ave., Oak Ridge, TN 37830

ELLEN DYKE, 2125 Cabots Point Dr., Reston, VA 20191

LANI L EWART, 1099 Alakea St., Suite 1800, Honolulu, HI 96813

PETER F. LANGROCK, P.O. Drawer 351, Middlebury, VT 05753-0351

CARL H. LISMAN, 84 Pine St., P.O. Box 728, Burlington, VT 05402

MARIAN P. OPALA, Supreme Court of Oklahoma, State Capitol, Room 238, 2300 N. Lincoln Blvd., Oklahoma City, OK 73105

RODNEY W. SATTERWHITE, Midland County Courthouse, 441 1st District Court, 500 N. Loraine St., Suite 901, Midland, TX 79701

NATHANIEL STERLING, 4180 Oak Hill Ave., Palo Alto, CA 94306

M. GAY TAYLOR-JONES, 18 N. Foxhill Rd., North Salt Lake, UT 84054

THOMAS W. MITCHELL, University of Wisconsin Law School, 975 Bascom Mall, Madison, WI 53706, *Reporter*

EX OFFICIO

ROBERT A. STEIN, University of Minnesota Law School, 229 19th Ave. S., Minneapolis, MN 55455, *President*

BARRY C. HAWKINS, 300 Atlantic St., Stamford, CT 06901, *Division Chair*

AMERICAN BAR ASSOCIATION ADVISOR

PHYLISS CRAIG-TAYLOR, Charlotte School of Law, 2145 Suttle Ave., Charlotte, NC 28204, *ABA Advisor*

STEVEN J. EAGLE, George Mason University School of Law, 3301 Fairfax Dr., Arlington, VA 22201-4426, *ABA Section Advisor*

EXECUTIVE DIRECTOR

John A. Sebert, 111 N. Wabash Ave., Suite 1010, Chicago, IL60602, *Executive Director*

Copies of this Act may be obtained from:
NATIONAL CONFERENCE OF COMMISSIONERS
ON UNIFORM STATE LAWS
111 N. Wabash Ave., Suite 1010
Chicago, Illinois 60602
312/450-6600
www.nccusl.org

UNIFORM PARTITION OF HEIRS PROPERTY ACT

TABLE OF CONTENTS

UNIFORM PARTITION OF HEIRS PROPERTY ACT

PREFATORY NOTE

Introduction and Summary

The Uniform Partition of Heirs Property Act is an act of limited scope which addresses a widespread, well-documented problem faced by many low to middle-income families across the country who have been dispossessed of their real property and much of their real property-related wealth over the past several decades as a result of court-ordered partition sales of tenancy-in-common properties. The highly unstable ownership these families experience stands in sharp contrast to the secure property rights wealthier families typically enjoy. Further, the loss of real property-related wealth these low to middle-income families have experienced has been particularly devastating to these families given the fact that real property constitutes by far the single greatest asset that these property owners typically own, unlike the much more diversified asset portfolios that wealthier families normally possess. In addition, the Act may be very helpful to a surprising number of wealthier families who own tenancy-in-common property under the default rules and who also experience great problems with this ownership form.

The law has made the tenancy in common, a common ownership structure under which two or more cotenants own undivided interests in particular property, the default ownership structure for two or more family members who inherit real property. In addition, the law presumes that two or more people who acquire undivided interests in real property by conveyance or devise take ownership to the property as tenants in common and not as joint tenants unless the intention to create a joint tenancy is very clear. But certain key features of tenancy-in-common ownership under the default rules create serious problems for those who seek to maintain ownership of their property for themselves and their relatives, or at least the wealth represented by such real estate holdings.

- Any tenant in common may sell his or her interest or convey it by gift during his or her lifetime without the consent of his or her fellow cotenants, making it easy for non-family members – including real estate speculators in a number of instances – to acquire interests in family real property. At a tenant in common's death, his or her interest in the tenancy in common property may be transferred under a will, or if the will is not probated in time or if there is no will, under the laws of intestacy.
- A significant feature of tenancy-in-common ownership – a feature that this Act does not disturb – is the universal right of any cotenant to file a lawsuit petitioning a court to partition the property, even if that cotenant only recently acquired its interest in property that the other cotenants had owned within their family for a long time and even if that interest is very small (e.g., a five percent or even smaller interest).
- In resolving a partition action, the two principal remedies that a court may order are partition in kind of the property into separate subparcels, with each subparcel proportionate in value to each cotenant's fractional interest or partition by sale, in which case the property is forcibly sold in its entirety with the proceeds of the sale distributed among the cotenants, again in proportion to their relative interests in the property. In the overwhelming majority of states, statutes governing partition mandate that partition in kind is the much preferred remedy because a forced sale of a person's property has always been viewed as an extraordinary remedy which undermines fundamental property rights.

- Despite the overwhelming statutory preference for partition in kind, courts in a large number of states typically resolve partition actions by ordering partition by sale which usually results in forcing property owners off their land without their consent. This occurs even in cases in which the property could easily have been divided in kind or an overwhelming majority of the cotenants had opposed partition by sale or even in some cases when the only remedy any cotenant petitioned the court to order was partition in kind and not partition by sale.
- A de facto preference for a partition by sale in many states has arisen in part because courts often only consider the theoretical beneficial economic effect of ordering a partition by sale as opposed to a partition in kind. The many courts that utilize this approach do not place much value on upholding basic property rights and do not take account of the noneconomic value which many owners place upon their property. These noneconomic values can be substantial as families often value their family real property for its ancestral and even historical significance or its capacity to provide shelter that in some cases may prevent homelessness.
- Further, courts typically order the property sold at an auction utilizing forced sale procedures that are notorious for yielding sales prices well below market value. A sale under these forced sale conditions normally harms the tenants in common economically by depriving them of the market value of their property but gives the buyer an unjustified windfall because the buyer acquires the property at a significant discount from its market value and often for fire sale prices. The forced sale conditions under which partition sales occur virtually guarantee that wealth will not be maximized for the tenants in common even though judges frequently order partition sales because they claim that a partition sale will be wealth maximizing for the cotenants.
- To make matters worse, in many states cotenants who unsuccessfully resist a request for a court-ordered partition by sale are then required to pay a portion of the attorney's fees and costs incurred by the cotenant who petitioned the court for a partition by sale, forcing them in effect to pay for the deprivation of their property rights and their resulting loss of wealth. These fees and costs are in addition to the attorney's fees they must pay the attorney they hired in their unsuccessful effort to resist the sale and maintain ownership of their property.
- Given these rules and practices which many courts utilize in partition actions, it is often the case that an unscrupulous real estate speculator purchases a very small interest in family-owned tenancy-in-common property with the sole purpose of seeking a court-ordered partition by sale. Often such a speculator submits the winning bid in the subsequent auction sale of the property even though the winning bid represents just a fraction of the property's market value.

For these reasons, estate planners and real estate lawyers believe that tenancy-in-common ownership under the default rules represents one of the most unstable forms of real property ownership. To address the dangers of this form of ownership, these professionals routinely advise their wealthy and legally savvy clients to enter into privately negotiated tenancy-in-common agreements with their fellow cotenants or work with their other cotenants to reorganize their ownership under a different ownership structure altogether such as a limited liability company.[1] However, a substantial percentage of tenancy-in-common property owners are not able to afford the services of these professionals or are not aware of the legal benefits of hiring such professionals because they do not understand the inherent risks of owning property under the default rules of the tenancy in common.

Accordingly, this Act seeks to remedy the serious problems many of those who own family real property have faced in keeping their property and their wealth as a result of the application of the default rules governing tenancy-in-common property by providing a further set of coherent, default rules reforming the worst substantive and procedural abuses that have arisen in connection with the partition of tenancy-in-common property. Specifically, this Act imports certain core property preservation and wealth protection mechanisms already commonly used by wealthy and legally sophisticated family real property owners as well as protections legislatures and courts in other countries now afford cotenants in partition actions as a result of modern reforms, and establishes those mechanisms as the default rules for the partition of real property owned by families under a tenancy in common. On the other hand, this Act does not seek to make wholesale changes to the law of partition. For example, this Act does not apply to any real property which is the subject of a written tenancy-in-common agreement which contains a provision governing the partition of the property (all such agreements typically contain such a provision) or which is owned under any other form of ownership (*e.g.*, a joint tenancy, a limited liability company, a partnership, a limited partnership, a trust or a corporation) other than the tenancy in common.

Tenancy-In-Common Property Owners of Modest Means Are Particularly At Risk

There is a subset of tenancy-in-common property owners who are particularly vulnerable to losing their property and significant wealth as a result of court-ordered partition sales. Scholars and practitioners who have worked with poor and minority property owners have observed that a particularly high percentage of these owners tend to own their real property under the default rules governing tenancy-in-common ownership and not under a private agreement among the cotenants governing the ownership of the property. This phenomenon is explained in large part by the fact that many low to middle-income property owners transfer their real property by intestate succession instead of by will, which is consistent with studies that have documented low will-making rates among Americans of more modest economic means.

The more that property is transferred from one generation to the next by intestate succession, the more likely it is for an increasingly large number of people to acquire an interest in the property, resulting in increasingly unstable ownership given that each cotenant possesses an unfettered right to request a partition by sale of the entire property irrespective of the wishes of the other cotenants. Given the prevalence of this pattern of property transfer, real property transferred from one generation to the next and held in a tenancy in common is referred to colloquially in many communities from those in the Southeast to those in Appalachia to those in Indian Country as "heirs property" or "heirs' property." Families who own tenancy-in-common property within these communities refer to their family real property holdings as heirs property whether some or all of the members of these

---

[1] *See* Thomas W. Mitchell, Stephen Malpezzi, & Richard K. Green, *Forced Sale Risk: Class, Race, and The "Double Discount,"* 37 Fla. St. U. L. Rev. 589, 616 (2010).

families acquired their interests by intestate succession, by will, or by gift. Consistent with the widespread usage of the term within these communities, this Act utilizes the term "heirs property" and defines it under Section 2 consistent with how many communities throughout the country understand the term; therefore, the definition of heirs property is not limited to property in which one or more cotenants acquire their interests by intestacy as usage of the term "heirs" may suggest in some technical sense.

Many if not most of these heirs property owners have little or no understanding of the legal rules governing partition of tenancy-in-common property as studies have revealed, due to the fact that many of the rules are counterintuitive. For example, many of these owners believe that their property ownership is secure because they pay property taxes, they live on the land, and they make productive use of the land. They also believe that their property may only be sold against their will if a majority or more of their cotenants agree, which gives some of these families with a large number of members with an interest in the property false confidence that their ownership is extremely secure.

These families think it is inconceivable that one cotenant with a very small ownership interest can force a sale against the wishes of all other cotenants. Unfortunately, the first time that many of these owners are informed about the actual legal rules governing partition is after a partition action has been filed, and often after critical, early court rulings have been made against them. In contrast, there have been many well-documented cases in which an outside speculator who acquired a very small interest in a parcel of heirs property that had been owned by a family for decades has been able to convince a court soon after the speculator acquired its interest to order a partition by sale of the property despite the fact that the family opposed the request for a partition by sale and despite the family's longstanding ownership. In short, the law of partition often functions to give those cotenants who petition a court to force a sale upon their fellow cotenants an eminent domain-like power of condemnation. Unlike eminent domain, however, under a partition by sale, those who end up losing ownership of their property at the conclusion of the forced sale are not entitled to be paid fair market value compensation or any minimum level of compensation for that matter for having their property rights extinguished.

Partition Sales and Other Heirs Property Problems in Certain Select Communities

African-Americans have experienced tremendous land loss over the course of the past century. For example, although African-Americans acquired between sixteen and nineteen million acres of agricultural land between the end of the Civil War and 1920, African-Americans retain ownership of approximately just seven million acres of agricultural land today. Scholars and advocates who have analyzed patterns of landownership within the African-American community agree that partition sales of heirs property have been one of the leading causes of involuntary land loss within the African-American community. A considerable body of legal scholarship has highlighted the fact that partition sales have been a leading cause of African-American land loss.[2] Many newspapers have

[2] *See, e.g.*, The Emergency Land Fund, Inc., The Impact of Heir Property on Black Rural Land Tenure in the Southeastern Region of the United States (1980). *See also* Phyliss Craig-Taylor, *Through a Colored Looking Glass: A View of Judicial Partition, Family Land Loss, and Rule Setting*, 78 Wash U. L.Q. 737 (2000); Chris Kelley, *Stemming the Loss of Black Owned Farmland Through Partition Action: A Partial Solution*, 1985 Ark. L. Notes 35; Harold A. McDougall, *Black Landowners Beware: A Proposal for Statutory Reform*, 9 N.Y.U. Rev. L. & Soc. Change 127 (1979-1980); Thomas W. Mitchell,

published articles documenting the manner in which particular African-American families have lost land that had been in their families for generations after an outsider acquired a small interest from a family member and then in short order was able to convince a court to order the property sold at a partition sale. The Associated Press's 2001 award-winning series on African-American land loss, *Torn from the Land*, brought national attention to the manner in which partition sales have stripped African-American families of large amounts of land and wealth.[3]

As a result of this legal scholarship and media attention, several years ago the American Bar Association's Section on Real Property, Trust and Estate Law established its Property Preservation Task Force. Along with the public interest and civil rights law firms and the community development and community-based organizations that have been working on heirs property issues for decades, the A.B.A.'s task force has been working to decrease the incidence of forced sales of heirs property that has so negatively impacted African-American and other poor and minority property owners.[4] Nevertheless, the organizations that have been working tirelessly with families who wish to maintain their heirs property holdings or at least the wealth associated with such real estate holdings will continue to face nearly insurmountable obstacles in providing meaningful assistance to significant numbers of those with heirs property problems until the default rules governing the partition of tenancy-in-common ownership are reformed to make the law of partition more just and more sensible.

Although the issue of the substantial loss of African-American land due to partition sales has received more national attention than the land loss in other communities resulting from partition sales, it is important to recognize that forced partition sales have negatively impacted other communities as well, especially other low-income and low-wealth communities. For example, Mexican-Americans lost hundreds of thousands of acres of land in New Mexico and other states after a significant amount of their community-owned property was improperly classified as tenancy-in-common property and was then ordered sold under partition sales in the aftermath of the Mexican-American War. In most instances, the land was sold for a price that was far below the market value of the land.[5] This occurred in part because, like heirs property owners today, the members of the community who had rights to the land prior to the partition sales were not able to bid effectively at the partition sale auctions because they were land rich but cash poor.[6]

Property owners in other communities have been negatively impacted as well. For example, in parts of Appalachia, heirs property has been hypothesized to be correlated with, and a cause of, the

---

From *Reconstruction to Deconstruction: Undermining Black Landownership, Political Independence, and Community Through Partition Sales of Tenancies in Common*, 95 Nw. U. L. Rev. 505 (2001); Faith Rivers, *Inequity in Equity: The Tragedy of Tenancy in Common for Heirs' Property Owners Facing Partition in Equity*, 17 Temp. Pol. & Civ. Rts. L. Rev. 1, 58 (2007).

[3] *See, e.g.*, Todd Lewan & Dolores Barclay, *Quirk in Law Strips Blacks of Land*, Tennessean, Dec. 11, 2001, at 8A.

[4] To date, the Property Preservation Task Force has made available to the public some materials that can be helpful to those who want to stabilize their ownership of tenancy-in-common property. These materials include a sample tenancy-in-common agreement and a document addressing some of the ways in which limited liability companies can be used to prevent land loss. *See Section of Real Property, Trust and Estate Law: Property Preservation Task Force*, American Bar Association, http://www.abanet.org/dch/committee.cfm?com=RP018700 (last modified May 11, 2010).

[5] William deBuys, Enchantment and exploitation: The Life and Hard Times of a New Mexico Mountain Range 178, 180, 184, 190 (1985).

[6] David Benavides & Ryan Golten, *Righting the Record: A Response to the GAO's 2004 Report Treaty of Guadalupe Hidalgo: Findings and Possible Options Regarding Longstanding Land Grant Claims in New Mexico*, 48 Nat. Resources J. 857, 886 (2008).

persistence of poverty.[7] Case studies suggest that heirs property owners in Appalachia are often concerned that one of their fellow cotenants might sell his or her interest to a wealthy buyer who will request a court to order the property partitioned by sale and then will purchase the property at the auction.[8] Some American Indians also have had their family property sold against their will at partition sales.

Heirs property ownership has presented vexing problems to property owners in cities such as New Orleans. In New Orleans, many poor property owners were not able to draw upon governmental programs such as the "Road Home" program administered by the Department of Housing and Urban Development which were established in the wake of Hurricane Katrina to provide financial assistance to property owners who had been harmed. A significant percentage of these poor property owners owned heirs property, which created merchantable title problems which needed to be resolved before the property owners could qualify for the governmental programs. These problems typically could not be resolved without hiring attorneys whom most of these property owners could not afford in contrast to the surprisingly large number of wealthy heirs property owners who were brought to light in the aftermath of Katrina who were able to hire attorneys to resolve their title problems. As in rural areas, partition sales have also resulted in the deprivation of property rights and the loss of wealth in urban areas undergoing gentrification.

As the post-Katrina New Orleans experience demonstrates, a surprising number of property owners who are not poor or minority also experience significant problems with heirs property ownership. In Maine, for example, heirs property is commonly referred to as "heir-locked property." Those who own such property in Maine experience many of the same problems that those who own heirs property elsewhere experience, including problems with unstable ownership. This has occurred in part because many properties that were not considered economically valuable in Maine fifty or sixty years ago increasingly lie in the path of development and because the ownership of many of these properties has become more fragmented with the passage of time as many interests in such property have been transferred by intestacy. Those who own heirs property in Maine also are often unable to manage their property in a rational way because some passive or uncooperative cotenants either do not contribute their share of the expenses needed to maintain ownership of the property or refuse to give their needed consent to plans that their more active fellow cotenants formulate to improve the management, stability, and utilization of the property. As is the case all across the country, many of those who own heirs property in Maine who are committed to maintaining ownership of the property within their families find themselves locked into a dysfunctional common ownership arrangement because there are no legal mechanisms to consolidate title to such property among family members who have been active and responsible owners.

Tenants in Common Often Lose Significant Wealth as a Result of Partition Sales

Those who own tenancy-in-common property under the default rules are not only at risk of losing their real property at a forced partition sale, but also are in danger of losing a significant portion of their wealth. In many states, a court will order a partition by sale under an "economics-only" test in which the court considers the hypothetical fair market value of the property in its entirety as

---

[7] B. James Deaton, *Intestate Succession and Heir Property: Implications for Future Research on the Persistence of Poverty in Central Appalachia*, 41 J. of Econ. Issues 927 (2007).

[8] B. James Deaton, Jamie Baxter, & Carolyn S. Bratt, *Examining the Consequences and Character of "Heir Property,"* 68 Ecological Econ. 2344, 2350 (2009).

compared to the fair market value of the subparcels that would result from a partition in kind. If the court finds that the fair market value of the property as a whole is greater than the aggregated fair market value of the subparcels, the court will order a partition by sale. Under this approach, the tenants in common theoretically should receive an economic benefit from the partition by sale.

In fact, most tenants in common are economically harmed when a court orders a partition by sale. First, the courts usually order the property sold at auctions in which the property is sold utilizing the procedures used for forced sales such as a sale under execution. These forced sales are notorious for selling property well below its fair market value which is ironic because judges often order the partition sale in the first instance because they claim that the cotenants will receive an economic benefit based upon an assumption that the sale will yield a fair market value price. When auction sales are challenged for yielding low sales prices, courts rarely overturn such sales as most courts utilize a "shock the conscience" standard to evaluate the sale. Under this standard, sales have been confirmed even though the property sold for twenty percent or less of its market value even though the court ordered a partition sale in the first instance because it indicated that a partition sale would likely provide the cotenants with an economic benefit.

Next, a number of fees and costs must first be paid to others before the remaining proceeds of a sale are distributed to the tenants in common. These fees often include costs incurred in selling the property including the fees of court-appointed commissioners or referees (often five percent or more of the sales price), surveyor fees, and attorney's fees which usually constitute ten percent of the sales price in the many states that permit such an attorney's fee award in a partition action. At the time a court orders a partition by sale under an economics-only test, these fees and costs are not taken into account although they can in fact be quite substantial and undermine any hypothetical economic benefit a cotenant would receive from a partition sale.

Poorer families who own heirs property are particularly at risk of having their property sold for a low sales price at partition sales. This phenomenon can be explained by the fact that these heirs property owners are not able to bid competitively at the partition sale auction because they are unable to secure any financing to make an effective bid and because they are cash poor. Banks and other lending institutions will not accept a partial interest in tenancy-in-common property as collateral to secure a loan and most of these heirs property owners cannot otherwise obtain financing because they often have few other assets to offer as collateral to secure a loan. Given that partition sales in general often attract few bidders, an auction of heirs property in which family members of limited economic means are unable to make any competitive bids is likely to yield a particularly low sales price as the winning bidder often needs only to submit a lowball bid in order to acquire the property as few if any other competitive bids are typically made in such cases.

Partition sales that result in an involuntary loss of property rights and in the loss of wealth may be very harmful, and even devastating to one or more of the cotenants and their relatives, depending on the facts of the particular case. The purpose of this Act is to ameliorate, to the extent feasible, the adverse consequences of a partition action when there are some cotenants who wish, for various reasons, to retain possession of some or all of the land, and other cotenants who would like the property to be sold. At the same time, the Act recognizes the legitimate rights of each cotenant to secure his, her, or its relative share of the current market value of the property and to seek to consolidate ownership of the property. Overall, the Act seeks to improve the law of partition with respect to cases involving family-owned tenancy-in-common property by ensuring that each cotenant in a partition action is treated in a fair and equitable manner.

UNIFORM PARTITION OF HEIRS PROPERTY ACT

SECTION 1. SHORT TITLE. This [act] may be cited as the Uniform Partition of Heirs Property Act.

Legislative Note: *Consider including this Act as a part of the state's existing partition statute.*

SECTION 2. DEFINITIONS.

In this [act]:

(1) "Ascendant" means an individual who precedes another individual in lineage, in the direct line of ascent from the other individual.
(2) "Collateral" means an individual who is related to another individual under the law of intestate succession of this state but who is not the other individual's ascendant or descendant.
(3) "Descendant" means an individual who follows another individual in lineage, in the direct line of descent from the other individual.
(4) "Determination of value" means a court order determining the fair market value of heirs property under Section 6 or 10 or adopting the valuation of the property agreed to by all cotenants.
(5) "Heirs property" means real property held in tenancy in common which satisfies all of the following requirements as of the filing of a partition action:
  (A) there is no agreement in a record binding all the cotenants which governs the partition of the property;
  (B) one or more of the cotenants acquired title from a relative, whether living or deceased; and
  (C) Any of the following applies:
    (i) 20 percent or more of the interests are held by cotenants who are relatives;
    (ii) 20 percent or more of the interests are held by an individual who acquired title from a relative, whether living or deceased; or
    (iii) 20 percent or more of the cotenants are relatives.
(6) "Partition by sale" means a court-ordered sale of the entire heirs property, whether by auction, sealed bids, or open-market sale conducted under Section 10.
(7) "Partition in kind" means the division of heirs property into physically distinct and separately titled parcels.
(8) "Record" means information that is inscribed on a tangible medium or that is stored in an electronic or other medium and is retrievable in perceivable form.
(9) "Relative" means an ascendant, descendant, or collateral or an individual otherwise related to another individual by blood, marriage, adoption, or law of this state other than this [act].

SECTION 3. APPLICABILITY; RELATION TO OTHER LAW.

(a) This [act] applies to partition actions filed on or after [the effective date of this [act]].
(b) In an action to partition real property under [insert reference to general partition statute] the court shall determine whether the property is heirs property. If the court determines that the property is heirs property, the property must be partitioned under this [act] unless all of the cotenants otherwise agree in a record.
(c) This [act] supplements [insert reference to general partition statute] and, if an action is governed by this [act], replaces provisions of [insert reference to general partition statute] that are inconsistent with this [act].

SECTION 4. SERVICE; NOTICE BY POSTING.

(a) This [act] does not limit or affect the method by which service of a [complaint] in a partition action may be made.
(b) If the plaintiff in a partition action seeks [an order of] notice by publication and the court determines that the property may be heirs property, the plaintiff, not later than 10 days after the court's determination, shall post [and maintain while the action is pending] a conspicuous sign on the property that is the subject of the action. The sign must state that the action has commenced and identify the name and address of the court and the common designation by which the property is known. The court may require the plaintiff to publish on the sign the name of the plaintiff and the known defendants.

SECTION 5. [COMMISSIONERS].

If the court appoints [commissioners] pursuant to [insert reference to general partition statute], each [commissioner], in addition to the requirements and disqualifications applicable to [commissioners] in [insert reference to general partition statute], must be disinterested and impartial and not a party to or a participant in the action.

Legislative Note: *Nearly every state uses the term "commissioner." However, there are some exceptions. For example, California uses the term "referee" and Georgia uses the term "partitioner."*

SECTION 6. DETERMINATION OF VALUE.

(a) Except as otherwise provided in subsections (b) and (c), if the court determines that the property that is the subject of a partition action is heirs property, the court shall determine the fair market value of the property by ordering an appraisal pursuant to subsection (d).
(b) If all cotenants have agreed to the value of the property or to another method of valuation, the court shall adopt that value or the value produced by the agreed method of valuation.

(c) If the court determines that the evidentiary value of an appraisal is outweighed by the cost of the appraisal, the court, after an evidentiary hearing, shall determine the fair market value of the property and send notice to the parties of the value.
(d) If the court orders an appraisal, the court shall appoint a disinterested real estate appraiser licensed in this state to determine the fair market value of the property assuming sole ownership of the fee simple estate. On completion of the appraisal, the appraiser shall file a sworn or verified appraisal with the court.
(e) If an appraisal is conducted pursuant to subsection (d), not later than 10 days after the appraisal is filed, the court shall send notice to each party with a known address, stating:
 (1) the appraised fair market value of the property;
 (2) that the appraisal is available at the clerk's office; and
 (3) that a party may file with the court an objection to the appraisal not later than 30 days after the notice is sent, stating the grounds for the objection.
(f) If an appraisal is filed with the court pursuant to subsection (d), the court shall conduct a hearing to determine the fair market value of the property not sooner than 30 days after a copy of the notice of the appraisal is sent to each party under subsection (e), whether or not an objection to the appraisal is filed under subsection (e)(3). In addition to the court-ordered appraisal, the court may consider any other evidence of value offered by a party.
(g) After a hearing under subsection (f), but before considering the merits of the partition action, the court shall determine the fair market value of the property and send notice to the parties of the value.

SECTION 7. COTENANT BUYOUT.

(a) If any cotenant requested partition by sale, after the determination of value under Section 6, the court shall send notice to the parties that any cotenant except a cotenant that requested partition by sale may buy all the interests of the cotenants that requested partition by sale.
(b) Not later than 45 days after the notice is sent under subsection (a), any cotenant except a cotenant that requested partition by sale may give notice to the court that it elects to buy all the interests of the cotenants that requested partition by sale.
(c) The purchase price for each of the interests of a cotenant that requested partition by sale is the value of the entire parcel determined under Section 6 multiplied by the cotenant's fractional ownership of the entire parcel.
(d) After expiration of the period in subsection (b), the following rules apply:
 (1) If only one cotenant elects to buy all the interests of the cotenants that requested partition by sale, the court shall notify all the parties of that fact.
 (2) If more than one cotenant elects to buy all the interests of the cotenants that requested partition by sale, the court shall allocate the right to buy those interests among the electing cotenants based on each electing cotenant's existing fractional ownership of the entire parcel divided by the total existing fractional ownership of all cotenants electing to buy and send notice to all the parties of that fact and of the price to be paid by each electing cotenant.
 (3) If no cotenant elects to buy all the interests of the cotenants that requested partition by sale, the court shall send notice to all the parties of that fact and resolve the partition action under Section 8(a) and (b).

(e) If the court sends notice to the parties under subsection (d)(1) or (2), the court shall set a date, not sooner than 60 days after the date the notice was sent, by which electing cotenants must pay their apportioned price into the court. After this date, the following rules apply:
   (1) If all electing cotenants timely pay their apportioned price into court, the court shall issue an order reallocating all the interests of the cotenants and disburse the amounts held by the court to the persons entitled to them.
   (2) If no electing cotenant timely pays its apportioned price, the court shall resolve the partition action under Section 8(a) and (b) as if the interests of the cotenants that requested partition by sale were not purchased.
   (3) If one or more but not all of the electing cotenants fail to pay their apportioned price on time, the court [, on motion,] shall give notice to the electing cotenants that paid their apportioned price of the interest remaining and the price for all that interest.

(f) Not later than 20 days after the court gives notice pursuant to subsection (e)(3), any cotenant that paid may elect to purchase all of the remaining interest by paying the entire price into the court. After the 20-day period, the following rules apply:
   (1) If only one cotenant pays the entire price for the remaining interest, the court shall issue an order reallocating the remaining interest to that cotenant. The court shall issue promptly an order reallocating the interests of all of the cotenants and disburse the amounts held by it to the persons entitled to them.
   (2) If no cotenant pays the entire price for the remaining interest, the court shall resolve the partition action under Section 8(a) and (b) as if the interests of the cotenants that requested partition by sale were not purchased.
   (3) If more than one cotenant pays the entire price for the remaining interest, the court shall reapportion the remaining interest among those paying cotenants, based on each paying cotenant's original fractional ownership of the entire parcel divided by the total original fractional ownership of all cotenants that paid the entire price for the remaining interest. The court shall issue promptly an order reallocating all of the cotenants' interests, disburse the amounts held by it to the persons entitled to them, and promptly refund any excess payment held by the court.

(g) Not later than 45 days after the court sends notice to the parties pursuant to subsection (a), any cotenant entitled to buy an interest under this section may request the court to authorize the sale as part of the pending action of the interests of cotenants named as defendants and served with the complaint but that did not appear in the action.

(h) If the court receives a timely request under subsection (g), the court, after hearing, may deny the request or authorize the requested additional sale on such terms as the court determines are fair and reasonable, subject to the following limitations:
   (1) a sale authorized under this subsection may occur only after the purchase prices for all interests subject to sale under subsections (a) through (f) have been paid into court and those interests have been reallocated among the cotenants as provided in those subsections; and
   (2) the purchase price for the interest of a nonappearing cotenant is based on the court's determination of value under Section 6.

SECTION 8. PARTITION ALTERNATIVES.

(a) If all the interests of all cotenants that requested partition by sale are not purchased by other cotenants pursuant to Section 7, or if after conclusion of the buyout under Section 7, a cotenant remains that has requested partition in kind, the court shall order partition in kind unless the court, after consideration of the factors listed in Section 9, finds that partition in kind will result in [great] [manifest] prejudice to the cotenants as a group. In considering whether to order partition in kind, the court shall approve a request by two or more parties to have their individual interests aggregated.

(b) If the court does not order partition in kind under subsection (a), the court shall order partition by sale pursuant to Section 10 or, if no cotenant requested partition by sale, the court shall dismiss the action.

(c) If the court orders partition in kind pursuant to subsection (a), the court may require that one or more cotenants pay one or more other cotenants amounts so that the payments, taken together with the value of the in-kind distributions to the cotenants, will make the partition in kind just and proportionate in value to the fractional interests held.

(d) If the court orders partition in kind, the court shall allocate to the cotenants that are unknown, unlocatable, or the subject of a default [entry][judgment], if their interests were not bought out pursuant to Section 7, a part of the property representing the combined interests of these cotenants as determined by the court [and this part of the property shall remain undivided].

Legislative Note: *In the overwhelming majority of states that have a strong statutory preference for a partition in kind as opposed to a partition by sale, most state courts within these states apply a statutory "great prejudice" or "manifest prejudice" standard in deciding whether it is appropriate in a given case to order a partition by sale instead of a partition in kind. Under this Act, there is also a strong preference for a partition in kind. In Section 8(a), select either the "great prejudice" or "manifest prejudice" standard.*

SECTION 9. CONSIDERATIONS FOR PARTITION IN KIND.

(a) In determining under Section 8(a) whether partition in kind would result in [great][manifest] prejudice to the cotenants as a group, the court shall consider the following:

  (1) whether the heirs property practicably can be divided among the cotenants;

  (2) whether partition in kind would apportion the property in such a way that the aggregate fair market value of the parcels resulting from the division would be materially less than the value of the property if it were sold as a whole, taking into account the condition under which a court-ordered sale likely would occur;

  (3) evidence of the collective duration of ownership or possession of the property by a cotenant and one or more predecessors in title or predecessors in possession to the cotenant who are or were relatives of the cotenant or each other;

(4) a cotenant's sentimental attachment to the property, including any attachment arising because the property has ancestral or other unique or special value to the cotenant;
(5) the lawful use being made of the property by a cotenant and the degree to which the cotenant would be harmed if the cotenant could not continue the same use of the property;
(6) the degree to which the cotenants have contributed their pro rata share of the property taxes, insurance, and other expenses associated with maintaining ownership of the property or have contributed to the physical improvement, maintenance, or upkeep of the property; and
(7) any other relevant factor.

(b) The court may not consider any one factor in subsection (a) to be dispositive without weighing the totality of all relevant factors and circumstances.

SECTION 10. OPEN-MARKET SALE, SEALED BIDS, OR AUCTION.

(a) If the court orders a sale of heirs property, the sale must be an open-market sale unless the court finds that a sale by sealed bids or an auction would be more economically advantageous and in the best interest of the cotenants as a group.

(b) If the court orders an open-market sale and the parties, not later than 10 days after the entry of the order, agree on a real estate broker licensed in this state to offer the property for sale, the court shall appoint the broker and establish a reasonable commission. If the parties do not agree on a broker, the court shall appoint a disinterested real estate broker licensed in this state to offer the property for sale and shall establish a reasonable commission. The broker shall offer the property for sale in a commercially reasonable manner at a price no lower than the determination of value and on the terms and conditions established by the court.

(c) If the broker appointed under subsection (b) obtains within a reasonable time an offer to purchase the property for at least the determination of value:
(1) the broker shall comply with the reporting requirements in Section 11; and
(2) the sale may be completed in accordance with state law other than this [act].

(d) If the broker appointed under subsection (b) does not obtain within a reasonable time an offer to purchase the property for at least the determination of value, the court, after hearing, may:
(1) approve the highest outstanding offer, if any;
(2) redetermine the value of the property and order that the property continue to be offered for an additional time; or
(3) order that the property be sold by sealed bids or at an auction.

(e) If the court orders a sale by sealed bids or an auction, the court shall set terms and conditions of the sale. If the court orders an auction, the auction must be conducted under [insert reference to general partition statute or, if there is none, insert reference to foreclosure sale].

(f) If a purchaser is entitled to a share of the proceeds of the sale, the purchaser is entitled to a credit against the price in an amount equal to the purchaser's share of the proceeds.

SECTION 11. REPORT OF OPEN-MARKET SALE.

(a) Unless required to do so within a shorter time by [insert reference to general partition statute], a broker appointed under Section 10(b) to offer heirs property for open-market sale shall file a report with the court not later than seven days after receiving an offer to purchase the property for at least the value determined under Section 6 or 10.

(b) The report required by subsection (a) must contain the following information:
(1) a description of the property to be sold to each buyer;
(2) the name of each buyer;
(3) the proposed purchase price;
(4) the terms and conditions of the proposed sale, including the terms of any owner financing;
(5) the amounts to be paid to lienholders;
(6) a statement of contractual or other arrangements or conditions of the broker's commission; and
(7) other material facts relevant to the sale.

SECTION 12. UNIFORMITY OF APPLICATION AND CONSTRUCTION.

In applying and construing this uniform act, consideration must be given to the need to promote uniformity of the law with respect to its subject matter among states that enact it.

SECTION 13. RELATION TO ELECTRONIC SIGNATURES IN GLOBAL AND NATIONAL COMMERCE ACT.

This [act] modifies, limits, and supersedes the Electronic Signatures in Global and National Commerce Act, 15 U.S.C. Section 7001 et seq., but does not modify, limit, or supersede Section 101(c) of that act, 15 U.S.C. Section 7001(c), or authorize electronic delivery of any of the notices described in Section 103(b) of that act, 15 U.S.C. Section 7003(b).

SECTION 14. EFFECTIVE DATE.

This [act] takes effect . . . .

Appendix B

Map of Jurisdictions Where the Uniform Partition of Heirs Property Act Has Been Adopted

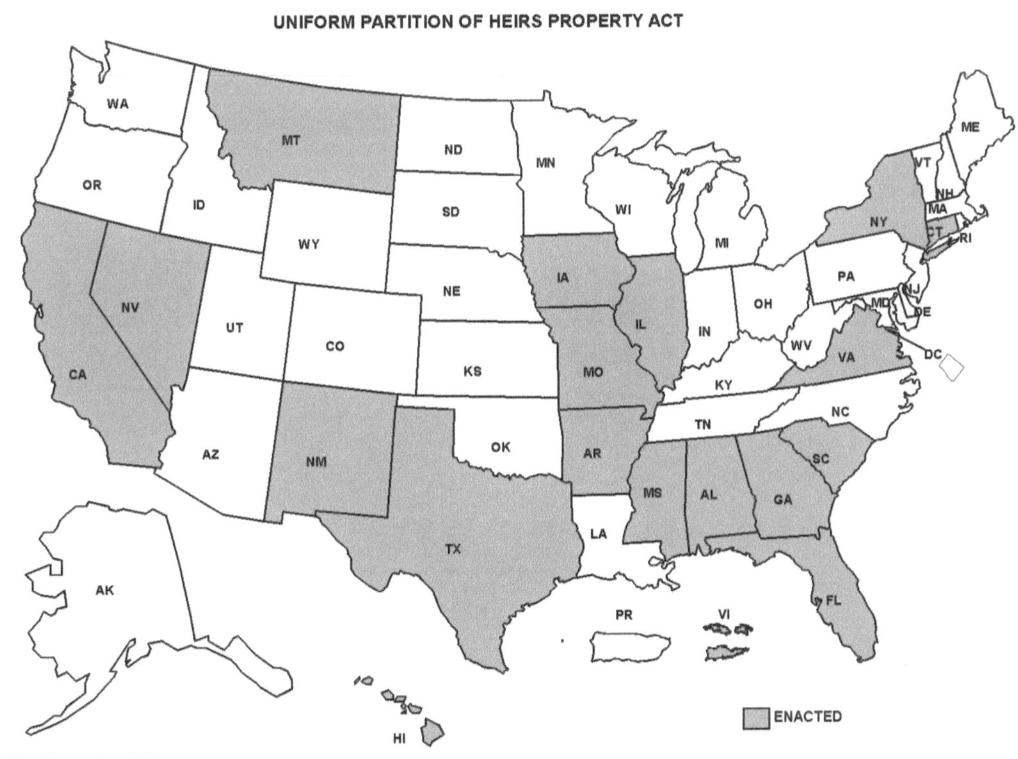

Index

N